Faith and Belief

Wilfred Cantwell Smith

PRINCETON UNIVERSITY PRESS
PRINCETON, NEW JERSEY

Published by Princeton University Press, Princeton, New Jersey
In the United Kingdom: Princeton University Press,
Guildford, Surrey

Library of Congress Cataloging in Publication Data will be
found on the last printed page of this book

Publication of this book has been aided by a grant from
The Paul Mellon Fund of Princeton University Press
This book has been composed in Linotype Granjon

Clothbound editions of Princeton University Press books
are printed on acid-free paper, and binding materials are
chosen for strength and durability.

Printed in the United States of America by Princeton
University Press, Princeton, New Jersey

CONTENTS

PREFACE

WHAT has faith to do with believing this or that? What has faith to do with being human?

In the past, it seems evident, the religious communities of the world have believed differently, from each other and from what we in the modern world believe. Only recently, however, has the matter of believing received central attention, in religious or indeed in human life (a subtle and surprising discovery, but important). Classically, the emphasis was on faith, rather: a different matter. How different, wherein, why, and with what implications, it is the business of this study to lay bare. Considered in global perspective, it becomes evident that in the matter of faith, diversity has been less stark than with belief, and of quite another order.

There is a good deal of evidence, from all over the world and from a long sequence of centuries, that faith has generally been regarded as almost the most important of all human qualities. Also, in the twentieth century the remoteness of faith is for many disquieting. The "crisis of faith" in our day is not simply a problem of belief; although the belief issue is engaged. It seemed good to investigate carefully the relation between faith and belief, across the world. The results turn out to be dramatic.

Our study is historical. Furthermore, it is comparative. It is also in a preliminary way theological, and in various senses philosophic. These four approaches are seldom combined. I call it "in some senses" philosophic, since much in present-day philosophy (in the English-speaking world) is scarcely historical and not at all comparative, so that a study that is primarily these may hardly be admitted—nor one that is concerned with ultimate as well as with "technical" questions. Yet this work is directly concerned with the clarification of concepts and the careful analysis of the usage of words, in the modern fashion. Theology is more historically conscious; yet it also is normally not comparative (instead, we have had on earth "Christian theology", "Islamic theology", and the like as disparate enterprises). Nonetheless, theologians have become aware of the comparative question, and I am therefore hopeful that the judgements here presented will be recognized as serious: as impinging and worth assessing, whatever the assessment may turn out to be. The foundation of the presentation here is, however, historical; on the historical validity of the theses its force finally rests.

My conviction is that if the work be historically valid, as I trust, then theology and also philosophy will find the innovative positions relevant, and perhaps compelling—and one may hope, helpful. History, as well as or even more than science, proffers knowledge. With that knowledge both theology and philosophy cannot in the end but reckon; and because of history's fundamentally human quality, cannot in the end but profit from reckoning. Our human condition to-day is precarious and perplexing. We do well to face it armed with the world-wide and centuries-long awareness that modern historical consciousness makes available.

One way of considering this study is to see it as an answer—however inadequate and partial—to a question highly important, and relatively new: namely, what can our present awareness of the world history of religion and comparative culture contribute to our understanding of man; and particularly, of faith. One part of the answer is that historical understanding enables us, and indeed forces us, to distinguish between faith and religious belief. We can no longer condemn our neighbours or deprecate their faith on the grounds that they have believed differently from us. Nor can we condemn ourselves, or rule out faith for us, on the grounds that we do not, should not, believe what our forebears did. Beliefs have changed, and will go on changing; but that, it emerges, is not and has hardly ever been the point at issue. Various beliefs may have conduced to faith, but they have not constituted it. Also *vice versa*: beliefs have at times remained relatively constant, while faith has varied. Two persons may have believed much the same thing, but the faith of one been strong and good, been beautiful, warm, humble, loving, joyous, while the faith of the other may have been minor, inept, awry. Beliefs may have conduced to faith, but they have not guaranteed it.

And recently, for many persons, and not without reason, inherited religious beliefs have proven an obstacle to faith.

A discrimination between the two matters turns out to be but a first step on a long and venturesome journey. A reconceptualizing of faith becomes implicated, continuous with yet beyond the positions of traditional Christian theology, traditional Islamic, traditional Hindu, and other —subsuming and transcending. A reconceptualizing of believing is involved also, in a drastically new awareness of the historical specificity and limitations of that seemingly innocent concept, and then of all human ratiocination. To think clearly and to live faithfully, in the new world in which we begin to find ourselves, means a radical revising of our inherited religious—and also secular—categories. And yet, strikingly, the bold new positions propounded, in their novel generic pluralism, although at odds with certain recent particularist thought, turn out to be strangely closer to the several classical positions than those recent particularisms are.

Man is entering a new phase in his and her self-consciousness, planetary, pluralist, and historical; and human society, a new phase of global conflict or community. The ideas for our new life together must themselves be new. This present work is offered as an intellectual's contribution to new thinking about man and his and her spiritual—human—living. The new thinking is radically new, yet is based upon, and continuous with, the past: the variegated classical heritage.

Faith is a comprehensively human, even more than human, quality; yet it has ever evinced an intellectual component, and this work attempts to think about it afresh, and to invite others to do so.

Wilfred Cantwell Smith
Dalhousie and Harvard Universities

ACKNOWLEDGEMENTS

THIS work has occupied my time and thought and effort over much of the past twelve years. Although some of my regular academic duties and involvements naturally distracted me from it, some contributed to it, at least indirectly. I am much indebted to Dalhousie University, for providing me for five years with an admirable situation in which I was able to devote much of my time directly to this book and its supplement (*Belief and History*, recently published), and with the stimulus to do so. Also, of course, my colleagues and students and the facilities of Harvard have contributed greatly. The work may in significant part be interpreted as a product of The Center for the Study of World Religions there. To other institutions also I am indebted: several have unwittingly helped by, for instance, inviting me in the course of this period to give lectures that constituted the occasions for developing one or another of the various ideas finally culminating in synthesis here. The Canada Council, further, eight years ago awarded me a fellowship for a sabbatical in Toronto, devoted largely to the first draft of one chapter in this work; and it has lately made more minor grants to help with library searching, xeroxing, and the like. The material on which Chapter 2 was based was first set forth more than a decade ago in the Charles Strong Lectureship in the Australian universities, and was published in the Melbourne journal *Milla wa-Milla*; I am grateful to the editor for permission to reprint here this revised version. Similarly the Islamics chapter (and part also of Chapter 6) make use of material that I had the opportunity in 1974 to submit to a largely Muslim audience as the Iqbal Memorial Lectures of that year at the University of the Punjab, which were then published in the Pakistan journal *Al-Hikmat*; again I am happy to acknowledge my thanks. Not only other scholars, and various thoughtful religious friends, Christian, Muslim, Hindu, Jewish, and a few Buddhist, but also my children, now all adult, and above all my wife, have in conversation and in more or less exact criticism contributed to my formulating my understanding.

A NOTE ON STYLE

FURTHER expression of thanks is due to Princeton University Press for many matters, including its deep respect for an author's integrity, extending to a generous acquiescence in what may seem idiosyncracies of mine in certain areas of style. An equally generous indulgence from readers is requested. My Canadian (sc. British) spellings and forms have been accepted. Also, certain classical usages are preserved, such as the abbreviations "voll.", "edd." and the like as the plurals of "vol.", "ed." (cf. "pp." for "pages"); comparably, I am among the minority who have not abandoned a judicious use of the subjunctive in English. Since my basic thesis is radical, it seems appropriate for me not to surrender such traditionalisms and conservatisms as are also sincere. (The drastically innovative conclusions, theologically and philosophically, to which my work has led turn out to be in some ways more in keeping with our past heritage than currently received positions.) Similarly, I have followed what seem to me more strictly rational patterns in the order of multiple punctuation at the close of a quotation, or with regard to reference superscripts, and in a few other such details, rather than conventional usage—once again the point being that I am arguing that we must be willing to abandon established and comfortable ways if intellectual rigour requires; and I feel it appropriate that this mood be applied in typography as well as in metaphysics.

Faith and Belief

Chapter 1

INTRODUCTION

WHAT is to become of our concept "faith", in modern awareness? We are moving into a position where it will be possible for us to forge for ourselves a quite new understanding. The present study is proffered in the conviction that it is important that we begin to attempt this; and in the further conviction that a major corner can be turned by seeing the issue in historical and comparative perspective.

Our quest is to understand faith as a characteristic quality or potentiality of human life: that propensity of man that across the centuries and across the world has given rise to and has been nurtured by a prodigious variety of religious forms, and yet has remained elusive and personal, prior to and beyond the forms. What kind of being are we, that throughout our history we have created great systems of religious patterns and programmes, ideas and dances, images and institutions, and then have lived our life in terms of them, in ways both grotesque and sublime?

Modern intelligence has begun to have a pretty fair idea of the various systems; but the new challenge is to understand the impulse that lies behind them, and the meaning that they have had for, or have conferred upon, their participants. For some time now the academic world has devoted fruitful energy to exploring the religious traditions of Asia and now Africa as well as of the West, to reconstructing the history of the overt data of mankind's religious life. Accordingly, the observable forms through which that life has been channeled are increasingly known, in detail and in wide compass. It is one thing, however, to observe those observables, to know those overt data; and it is another to understand the faith that inspired them or is inspired by them. To live religiously is not merely to live in the presence of certain symbols, but to be involved with them or through them in a quite special way—a way that may lead far beyond the symbols, that may demand the totality of a person's response, and may affect one's relation not only to them but to everything else: to oneself, to one's neighbour, and to the stars. It is that special involvement that pleads to be elucidated.

We are concerned with meaning: not only the meaning that a person's tradition has for him or her, if they are involved, but more significantly, the meaning that life and the universe have for them, in the light of their involvement.

To illustrate, let us take an example from India. For approximately a thousand years now, much of the rich profusion of the religious phenomena of that country can be roughly divided into two great classes, which we may call respectively Islamic and Hindu. If we consider, let us say, a committed Muslim in India and note his involvement with the Islamic complex of religious symbols, we see that his relation to that complex is indeed remarkable. It is quite different from his relation to the other complex, the Hindu. To the latter he may maintain an attitude of indifference, or of hostility; of deep respect and even sensitive appreciation, or of contempt; of historical curiosity, of theological speculation, or of aloof ignorance. Of that relation he himself remains in some sense the master. To his own Islamic system, on the other hand, his relation is quite other. If he takes it seriously it in a sense may master him, though through it he may master himself and the world. It may mould his personality: because of his involvement with it he becomes a very different person from what he would otherwise be.

His relation to the Islamic data may be radically different not only from his relation to the data of another tradition, but quite different also from the relation to this Islamic complex itself even of another Muslim who is less involved, or even of himself at another period of his life. It is possible even to practise all the observances, but to do so without faith, certainly with little faith. The Islamic data themselves, in the same form, are there for an academically interested Western scholar; for a Hindu next door; for a nominal Muslim who is insensitive, insouciant, "irreligious"; and for our devout and pious Muslim who is deeply involved. It is the involvement that we are concerned to try to understand.

We may note that it is this involvement that bestows on the data their religious significance, as well as bestowing on the persons their changed lives. An unreflecting Muslim may feel that the Qur'an is a religious document because of its inherent quality (although if he is theologically sophisticated he knows that the matter is considerably more complicated and subtle than that). An outsider, however, has no option but to hold that the Qur'an becomes (and keeps becoming) a religious document because, and insofar as, some men and women direct to it, generation after generation, their capacity to become religiously involved. It is the faith of Muslims that has made the Qur'an the Word of God. It is the faith of men and women that elevates a system of symbols to the religious level. Without this human involvement, the system would remain inert.

This is one reason why I demur to using the term "religion" for a pattern of observable forms. What others may call "Christianity" or "Hinduism" or the religion of the Trobriand Islands must rather be thought of as but the Christian or Hindu or Trobriand tradition, a potential pattern for personal involvement, which becomes religious as it expresses or elicits men's faith. It is faith that generates the tradition in the first place, and that continues to be its *raison d'être*.

As we look back on now twenty-five hundred years of Buddhist history, we see it as a surging movement, mightily creative. Siddhartha Gautama did not produce the Buddhist religion, with subsequent generations of Buddhists passive recipients of a fixed and self-subsisting entity or idea. (Nor have they held that he did.) Rather, their active and activating response, their participating involvement, have themselves constructed, and kept constructing ever afresh, the on-going vitality of the dynamic enterprise. Siddhartha launched something out of which a series of ever-changing congeries of elements was educed and constructed and revised which the faith of hundreds of millions of men and women for century upon century has turned and has kept turning into a great religious force.

Faith is nourished and patterned by the tradition, is formed and in some sense sustained by it—yet faith precedes and transcends the tradition, and in turn sustains it.

K'ung-fu-tzu ("Confucius") was no doubt an unusually intelligent and wise man, and said some penetrating things. Yet the great so-called Confucian movement, which has characterized Chinese history, and which the Chinese do not call by his name, is the product of the faith of Chinese persons, who in varying degrees also for twenty-five centuries have found that through involvement with the Ju Chiao, this classical tradition, they could live lives of richness and integrity and discipline and courage and social harmony in a way that was persuasively of stable, shall we say of ultimate, significance. The point about K'ung-fu-tzu is that he provided, almost unwittingly, formulations that have lent themselves to this kind of large-scale involvement. The ability of one man to say such things is certainly interesting, certainly historically important. No less interesting, no less historically important has been the ability of hundreds of millions of men and women to become creatively involved with his sayings; or should we not say, to become creatively involved through his sayings with life, with each other, and with the world.

Faith, then, is an engagement: the involvement of the Christian with God and with Christ and with the sacraments and with the moral imperatives and with the community; the involvement of the Hindu with caste and with the law of retributive justice and the *maya*-quality of this mundane world and with the vision of a final liberation; the involvement of the Buddhist with the image of the Buddha and with the moral law and with an institutionalized monastic order and with the dream of a further shore beyond this sea of sorrow; the involvement of the primitive animist with the world perceived in poetic, if bizarre, vitality and responsiveness.

Since it is an *engagement*, to know faith authentically is to become oneself involved, to know it in personal committed fashion in one or another of its varied forms. And the historian notes that most persons in most countries at most times have in fact so known it, little or much. Since palaeolithic times, by far the overwhelming majority of human beings on this planet have been men and women of faith. Can we know it, however, in another sense: in intellectual apprehension? Can we understand it? Alongside, or over against, a practical and particular involvement, can we discern it theoretically and generically? Now that it can survey the panorama of mankind's religious history, the intellect is challenged to understand what it is that we and our neighbours have been doing all these centuries in our diverse involvements, as we have lived each in his or her faith; and what it is that is happening now, to us and to our societies, if or insofar as we are losing faith, are living or are perhaps to live without it. The pursuit of such understanding is an exciting venture.

This is *fides quaerens intellectum*[1], faith in pursuit of self-understanding, in the new and rich and enriching sense of *fides humana*, the faith, the involvement, the final truth of humankind. It is the search for conceptual clarification of man's relation to transcendence.

"Faith", then, I propose, shall signify that human quality that has been expressed in, has been elicited, nurtured, and shaped by, the religious traditions of the world. This leaves faith unspecified, while designating its locus. We do not yet say what it is, but indicate where we are to look in order to find out. Thus an inquiry becomes possible, historical and empirical. That it can also be rewarding will, we believe, become evident in the course of the investigation.

Yet however significant this particular problem—whether for understanding world history or for understanding ourselves in our modern predicaments—a query could nonetheless be raised as to whether it be legitimate to use, in this new and wider sense, the term "faith". This word has had in the Western tradition a venerable and specific Christian connotation. What has been at stake in that concept, and what is now at stake in the new inquiry before us, are both far too serious for any touch of glibness. A linking of the two should not be surreptitious, or irresponsible. It will become apparent as we proceed, however, that there is in fact continuity of the new conceptions that emerge, however seemingly novel, with classical positions, both Christian and other. Since the study is historical, such continuity is not incidental, even though both the changed orientation and the widened range ensure also innovation, reformulation, enrichment (not of faith, but of our idea of faith). Our search for a new understanding, along the historical and comparative lines here proposed, is important and worthwhile in itself but will prove doubly rewarding if the answers to the new question are seen to illuminate and to subsume the old.

Faith, the historian reports, is the fundamental religious category; even, the fundamental human category. The theologian—Christian, Islamic, or other—may hardly dissent[2]. What is nowadays possible, however, and nowadays imperative, is to attempt a generic understanding. Earlier attempts to elucidate faith have regularly been made in the particular instance of one's own tradition. Christian thinkers have theorized about the Christian form of faith[3], Muslims about the Islamic. (Even most debunkers have been concerned to attack or to explain away some particular form of faith with which alone they were familiar and from which they were seeking liberation or transcendence.) Relatively little careful study has been done as yet, in universities or in seminaries, on the faith of other men, or on human faith generically.

Moreover, the sense of faith as relating to the timeless has tended to distract some, especially theologians, from a concern with its historical aspect. The sense of its involvement with certain creeds, practices, institutions, has tended to divert some, especially descriptive observers, from its personalism. Both insiders and outsiders have thus often focused on something other than faith itself.

In the case of one's own system, faith has been almost always of course envisaged, but also defined, in relation to its explicit and particular "object"[4], indicating then not what faith itself is, but where it is directed: faith is faith in God, in the Dharma, in God and the Qur'an, in Christ, or the like[5]. We shall return to explore some implications of this in our next chapter.

Academic "open" enquiry, also, even when not particularist, has tended to be object-oriented, though in an empirical sense, rather than concerned with the relation of persons to that object. A prodigious effort over the past century, for instance, has gone into a critical study of the Bible and how it was put together; relatively little study has been made of the role of the Bible, once it had become a scripture, in the consciousness and the lives of men and women over the centuries since, to whose faith alone it owes its significance[6]. The modern upsurging study calling itself Phenomenology of Religion, which is certainly generic enough, is also object-oriented in that it has addressed itself to religious phenomena but hardly to the persons who relate themselves to some or other among these and thereby make them religious.

Our new endeavour is to see and to interpret, rather, the human side of these involvements[7]. It would hold that the distinctly religious has lain not in those observable things with which men and women have been concerned in their variegated religious life so much as in that life itself: in the interaction with these things of those persons, and indeed in their interaction, in relation to these, with their environment at large.

No interpretation of faith in general is liable to be persuasive that is not solidly grounded in a wrestling with faith in particular. Yet also *vice versa*: one may readily argue that even Christian conceptualizations of faith for the Christian case, and Muslim for the Islamic, will halt a little until they are illumined by being set now within the wider context. Buddhist understanding of Buddhist involvement, in the past and in the future, with Buddhist symbols will both contribute to and learn from elucidation of the comparable problematic for other traditions. Collaboration, further, between the *engagé* participant and the open observer will surely prove fruitful.

No interpretation of faith is liable to be persuasive that is insensitive to the mundane elements and even to the aberrations and pathology of religious involvement. Yet here too the contrary also holds: none can be cogent that does not take seriously the historically manifest capacity of persons and groups through their faith to attain their greatest heights, and indeed to transcend both themselves and their environment, to transcend the mundane, to become most authentically human.

In averring that faith is personal, one hopes that one need not stress that "personal" does not necessarily mean "individual". The counterpart to individual is social; the counterpart to personal is impersonal. A society may in varying degrees be personal or impersonal. An individual becomes a person only in community—although also one may become less a person if falsely submerged in the group. To be a person is, in fact, to be involved in the individual/social polarity. To recognize that the locus of faith is persons is to note that faith touches the corporate and the private. It has much to do with both the gregarious and the lonely aspects of human life.

An exposition of what faith has been, in this and that instance, this and that community, this and that century, will constitute, of course, a vast undertaking. Over the past century much effort has gone into uncovering and studying the traditions of mankind, and this will continue. Over the coming century it will be supplemented by equally elaborate studies of faith. "The history of religion has at times been mistaken for the history of its symbols; but this is superficial. . . . The true history of religion, not yet written, is the history of the depth or shallowness, richness or poverty, genuineness or insincerity, splendid wisdom or inane folly, with which men and women and their societies have responded to such symbols as were around them"[8], and of their capacity to generate new symbols or to neglect old ones. Such a history of religion will include a history of faith; indeed, it will be constituted in significant part by a history of faith and of its absence, and its weaknesses, aberrations and perversions.

What, then, is faith? Until its history is written, preliminary attempts to theorize about it generically must be constructed tentatively, on the basis of such knowledge as is available and in critical relation to what has been said about it in particular cases. As one contribution to this important task it would be helpful to have collections setting forth in careful sensitivity what the various communities have traditionally, through representative participants over the centuries, affirmed their own faith to be[9]. As another small contribution to the total task this present study is proffered. It has two objectives. The first is simply but eagerly to plead the significance of the problem: calling attention to the nature and to the centrality of the issues involved, and urging on others the value of pursuing them. No answers that I may proffer can be nearly so important as my insistence that the question itself is major. The second objective is to take an interim step towards elucidating the nature of man's faith by exploring one particular question within the whole: namely, the relation between faith and belief.

It will emerge in the course of our inquiry that a clarifying of this relation is now more possible, and is more crucial, than has heretofore been imagined. One discovers, and the discovery can prove unexpectedly illuminating, how disparate faith and belief are, and have classically been seen to be, despite recent tendencies to converge them. (These tendencies also will be investigated.) Indeed, it becomes evident that the recent Western confusion between them is itself an aberration; it underlies much of the contemporary disarray. In any case, as we shall in due course see, it arose historically and its rise can be traced. Its rather devastating consequences also begin to be descried.

It would over-simplify but perhaps not altogether distort our thesis to say that the most important next step towards an understanding of faith, whether other peoples' or one's own—what faith has been in world history, and what it shall be to-morrow—is the recognizing that, and how, faith is not belief. (We shall even discover, almost incredibly, that *credo* has come to be mistranslated "I believe".) This over-simplification, however, requires elucidating, and arguments will take us rather far afield in both time and space, to let us move beyond the misapprehensions of our recent and narrow past.

In an earlier study[10] we found that faith is not the religion, and not the cumulative tradition. If the present investigation were to be seen simply as making the comparable negative point that, further, faith is not belief, even so a *neti, neti* progression of this sort (*via negativa*) could itself prove useful. A fuller aspiration, however, is to make a contribution towards a new planetary self-consciousness about faith by attending to one question within the larger complex: namely, the relation for all of us between faith and belief, both positive and negative: what that relation has been, and may be.

We begin by looking very briefly in our next chapter at faith in the early Buddhist instance, where it is most conspicuously separated from a belief in God or the gods. We turn next to the Islamic, where faith is embedded—some would say inextricably, but we shall find, instructively—in a system of belief that is exceptionally firm and clear. The following chapter, turning to India, deals with a particular Hindu concept not of faith as a quality so much as of "the act of faith", to borrow a Roman Catholic phrase. Finally we look at Christian developments, devoting one chapter to the Church's term *credo* and another to the history of the English word "believe", which turns out to have changed its meaning over the centuries drastically, and again instructively. Our conclusion reflects on faith, in its manifest diversity of forms, as an evidently universal human quality, and on the issue of conceptualization.

In the remainder of this present chapter, we continue to lay a foundation for the more detailed discussion that follows by considering the faith/belief relationship in a general comparativist perspective. We shall even glance for a brief moment at the philosophic and scientific instances of the matter. The particular re-interpretations that then follow in an understanding of Buddhist, Islamic, Hindu, and Christian concepts are made possible by seeing each in the context of a comparative vision. (Yet once thus opened up, the re-interpretations are made cogent by seeing internal historical considerations in each case, I shall contend; and of course in turn only an awareness of each position in its integrity generates the comparative vision.)

Before we move on, then, to our specific elucidations, let us first in a general way consider how a comparativist viewing of the matter sees the faith/belief issue. The starting-point is clear: that in Western, especially Christian, and especially modern development there has been a tendency to use the two terms interchangeably, as though belief and faith were the same thing. When one considers the matter on a more global scale, however, it quickly becomes apparent that they are not.

Two considerations stand out, as one views the situation globally. First is the obvious point that in the world-wide range of mankind's history, religious beliefs have of course differed radically, whereas religious faith would appear to have been, not constant certainly, yet more approximative to constancy. It is not the presupposition nor the conclusion of the present thesis that faith is everywhere the same. We do not yet know enough about it, for one thing. What we do know would suggest that there have been several types of faith within the arena of a single system of belief—for instance, the Islamic[11]; and according to, for instance, Hindu belief there is supposed to be more than one type of valid faith, for the different types of person in any community, and even to some extent for the different stages of one person's lifetime[12]. A case may certainly be made, and must be reckoned with, that even in interaction with a single tradition, within a single community, faith may vary. It is not clear that Christian faith—or more narrowly, the faith even of Roman Catholics[13], or more narrowly still, that of Baptists in the nineteenth century in the one city of London—is or was identical. Faith is too personal for that. One may go further and say that my faith, for instance, is not the same to-day as it was ten years ago, let alone not the same as my neighbour's.

Nonetheless, it does seem legitimate, after making a survey of the religious history of mankind in its manifold diversity, to report two things. One is that the variety of faith seems on the whole less than the variety of forms through which faith has been expressed. The second is that such variety of faith as is found cuts across formal religious boundaries.

To speak more concretely, many persons in modern times have found, once they have penetrated beyond the outward patterns to the quality of personal life that those patterns nourish, that there is less difference between the faith of Christians and that of Muslims and of Hindus than there is among the formulae and symbols by which that faith is visibly expressed. Secondly, they have found that the faith of a particular Christian may, once the outward wrappings are set aside, differ from the faith of a Muslim or a Hindu less than it differs from the faith of another Christian, next door or in a different denomination or a different century. Scholars have counterpart experiences in studying ancient texts.

Faith varies, yes. Yet it does not vary so much as, nor quite in accordance with, the variations of overt religious pattern.

Of course, this is exactly what one would expect if faith is what certain theologians have always said that it is: a direct encounter with God—mediated, no doubt, by the sacraments or the doctrines, or the moral obligations involved, but significant precisely because it transcends these, and enables the person to transcend them. It is also exactly what a humanist or an atheist would expect. In any case, it is what the historian finds.

On looking around the world in the light of modern religio-historical knowledge, then, while one is struck by divergences among religious beliefs, which in fact turn out on scrutiny to be greater than one would have imagined, one is also struck by similarities of religious faith, which also turn out to be greater than one might have supposed.

Faith is deeper, richer, more personal. It is engendered and sustained by a religious tradition, in some cases and to some degree by its doctrines; but it is a quality of the person, not of the system. It is an orientation of the personality, to oneself, to one's neighbour, to the universe; a total response; a way of seeing whatever one sees and of handling whatever one handles; a capacity to live at a more than mundane level; to see, to feel, to act in terms of, a transcendent dimension.

Belief, on the other hand, is the holding of certain ideas. Some might see it as the intellect's translation (even reduction?) of transcendence into ostensible terms; the conceptualizing in a certain way of the vision that, metaphorically, one has seen; at a less spontaneous level, that one hopes to see (the experience that one has had, or hopes to have; the transformation, liberation, realization . . .). To believe religiously—truly to believe—it has often been held, especially by recent Christians, is to believe with faith; in this and in other ways, the matter has become unduly intricate, as we shall be carefully noting. At this point we shall not elaborate the varying notions of "belief", although we shall return in later chapters to explore them; for the moment, we simply emphasize that we use the term strictly for an activity of the mind. (It is possible, therefore, to believe without faith.)

Faith, then, is a quality of human living. At its best it has taken the form of serenity and courage and loyalty and service: a quiet confidence and joy which enable one to feel at home in the universe, and to find meaning in the world and in one's own life, a meaning that is profound and ultimate, and is stable no matter what may happen to oneself at the level of immediate event. Men and women of this kind of faith face catastrophe and confusion, affluence and sorrow, unperturbed; face opportunity with conviction and drive; and face others with a cheerful charity.

The historian who personally is, for instance, a Christian, and owes the occasion for much of whatever faith he or she may have to the Church, is presumably happy to observe as an historian that faith in this sense of the word has been found also in the Jewish and Islamic and Hindu and Buddhist and other communities (and among humanists), throughout the centuries and throughout the world. Similarly skeptic historians, humanist or other, for whom such a quality in their own case or that of their friends is explicitly not linked to any religious pattern, are presumably entranced to discern that in most cases in human history it has been explicitly so linked; and are presumably fascinated to endeavour to understand this.

The opposite of faith in this sense is nihilism: a bleak inability to find either the world around one, or one's own life, significant; an absence of mutuality, in that one cannot respond either to the universe or to one's neighbour knowing that one will be responded to; an almost total dependence upon immediate events coupled with a sense that immediate events cannot really or for long be depended upon; a sense of lostness. The current terms for this are alienation, loss of identity, uncommittedness.

At another extreme from faith in this warmly humane, open sense adumbrated here, and also from its opposite, nihilism, stands the mean, cramping faith of blind and fanatical particularism. This aberration too cuts across distinctions of belief, for it too is found in all communities. Beliefs may differ; but narrow faith, like broad faith, wherever it be found can be remarkably constant.

A second point about belief and faith strikes a comparativist student of the world's religious history, and is salient for our concerns. It is that the two, though different, have often been related; further, that the relation between them has itself varied, from place to place and from century to century. Especially, one notices that belief and faith have been linked by Western Christians more closely, more deliberately, more emphatically, than by any other group. In a later chapter, and more elaborately in another study[14], we discover that even by Christians this link has not always been made out to be so tight or so unobtrusive as is sometimes thought. First, however, we must remind ourselves that the Church has established for itself in this matter a quite special place.

One of the first points that an observer of the world's religious systems must learn is that they are not all variations on a theme; they do not give differing answers to the same questions; they do not operate in a common mode. Before this lesson was learned, Westerners used to go around asking about new religious communities, "What do they believe?"—as though this were a basic, or at least a legitimate, question. (We shall discover, however, that it was ambiguous, and owed what legitimacy it might have had to that ambiguity.) Since they themselves believed something, religiously, they presumed that others would too. But not so. It is not only belief that varies from group to group, but also the role of belief in religious life.

In the Christian case, the role of belief has been quite major, at times decisive. Doctrine has been a central expression of faith, has seemed often a criterion of it; the community has divided over differences in belief, and has set forth belief as a formal qualification of membership. No other religious community on earth has done these things to the same degree; and some have not done them at all.

For the Christian Church, theology has been a conspicuously important matter. There are many religious groups, however, that have not had theologies at all. (Shinto may be cited as one example. Traditionally it was not customary for practitioners or priests of this "way" to construct formal theories about what they were doing, or for intellectuals among them to seek to order their exuberant myths into rational coherence[15].) Many religious groups have not developed systematic theologies. (These are exemplified by, for example, the magnificently impressive religious life of ancient Egypt, through which that civilization sustained itself in sumptuous elegance for two thousand years[16]—and also by the Christian Church in its early history[17].) Some religious groups have had systematic theologies but have regarded them as peripheral or worse. (The Islamic community, for example, developed classically a scholastic school of considerable finesse and depth, but distrusted the whole enterprise. One of the greatest of Muslim religious leaders, spokesman for what a Westerner's impulse would be to call Islamic orthodoxy until remembering that "orthodoxy" is itself a theological concept, put the attitude a whit stridently when he averred that theology is a work of the devil; faithful Muslims should steer clear of it[18].) In Hebrew there is no word for "theology". The Jews have seldom, in the course of their long history, had to attend to the matter of whether their faith prescribes belief; on the few occasions when the question has been raised, their answer has as often as not been a vigorous "no". (These occasions have been chiefly two: following the participation in the mediaeval Arabic-speaking world by some of their thinkers in the Aristotelian-based scholastic movement, first Islamic then also Jewish and later Christian; and then again following the participation of their Western-European thinkers in the eighteenth-century Enlightenment[19].) Even the Hindu tradition, which has developed the intellectualist way of faith as elaborately and as centrally as has the Christian, if not in some ways even more so, so that Hindu philosophy of religion is perhaps the most impressive in the world, yet has conceived the relation between faith and belief in ways that are instructively and provocatively different from those either of the Christian Church or of the Western philosophic tradition.

All this can sound strange to ears accustomed to hearing of belief and faith as synonymous or at least intertwined. The historical fact is that faith is expressed in a great variety of ways, and that in the Christian case one of the primary and basic expressions has been conceptually, in propositional doctrine; but in other traditions it has been expressed primarily and basically in other forms[20]. What theology is to the Christian Church, a ritual dance may be to an African tribe: a central formulation of the human involvement with final verity[21]. For some time now it has been recognized that the counterpart concept to orthodoxy, the traditional Christian term, should for the Jewish and Islamic cases be rather "orthopraxy". For in those two cases, the fundamental form of expression of faith has been not doctrine but law—*torah* and *sharīʿah*. In modern English, under Christian influence, the word "creed" has come to be used in non-technical parlance for a religion altogether, as in such a phrase as "without distinction of nationality, colour, or creed"; the modern Hebrew word for "a religion", on the other hand, in a different but comparable evolution, is *dath*, originally "law". There are many groups for which ritual is felt to be primary[22], for whom a ritualist rather than an intellectualist expression is fundamental. Even within the Christian community there are certain sub-groups for which the ratio of importance of ritual to doctrine is greater, for instance for Anglicans/Episcopalians, than it is for other sub-groups, for instance Presbyterians. Similarly, within the Roman Catholic Church a more intellectualist and a more moralist emphasis are illustrated respectively by the Dominican and the Franciscan Orders. Whatever the variety of emphasis, however, virtually all Christians, except perhaps Quakers, are expected to evince their faith in the realm of ideas; whereas in other parts of the world it may not have occurred to the religious that as evidence of his or her faith a person should believe something.

The relation between faith and belief, then, varies. The issues, even as regards the unusual Christian case, should not be confused with the traditional Western question as to the relation between faith and reason. On this latter, neighbouring, problem much ink has flowed; we do not take it up here, except to make one new point by touching on one particularly germane aspect. My own thesis, advanced on other occasions[23], is that the problem, arising in a special historico-geographic context, is more truly seen from a perspective of comparative world religious history, in terms of two traditions, as a primarily historical rather than philosophical problem: as a relation then not between reason and faith but between faith in reason and faith in God, and Christ. That a Chinese may belong to two or three religions at once, as the outsider has ineptly put it, or more accurately, may have faith through more than one tradition, may be personally involved in or through them, has here its counterpart in that the Westerner has (and should have) two involvements, in the tradition from Greece and in the tradition from Palestine.

As remarked, I do not wish to pursue this here, fascinating though it be (we shall touch on it once again in our concluding chapter), beyond evoking the serviceable point that for the Western world's Greek philosophic tradition alone there is an important and potentially illuminating instance of our basic problem, the relation between belief and faith. It is not only as regards the Christian him- or herself that this issue arises, as we have been discussing; and not only as regards the Christian in his or her relation to the philosopher, as we will refrain from discussing; but also as regards philosophers in their relation to and involvement with the philosophic tradition in which they participate and to which, to the spirit of which, they give their loyalty.

It is not what a philosopher believes that makes him or her a philosopher but rather his or her faith, the faith out of which the beliefs, the particular "philosophy", are born and by which they are sustained. We cannot formulate that faith, any more than one can formulate any religious faith, since as in the other instances it precedes and transcends and pervades and eludes all its formulations. Some might wish perhaps to make a pass at it, by suggesting, for instance, that his or her faith has traditionally been a commitment that the life of the mind is worthwhile and reliable, that the universe is (at least in part) intelligible or at least that the striving to render it intelligible is valid or obligatory or rewarding or humanly proper—or, more etymologically, by suggesting that his or her faith is a love of wisdom. The relation between the belief of individual philosophers (which is their philosophies) and the faith of all philosophers (of which their philosophies are the expressions, varied and un-co-ordinated and always inadequate) constitutes a tricky but potentially fruitful question.

The significance of the question is enhanced because although that faith seems unfortunately to be somewhat petering out in our day, there arises a comparable question as to the faith of scientists. I mean their faith in science, in the spirit of science: in science not as an objective actuality in disparate parts, but as an elusive and integral dynamic of which the outward expressions at any given moment, although worthy, are always and in principle inadequate and to be superseded—a dynamic that is both demanding and rewarding, in which they delight to be involved, and in which their involvement gives meaning to their work and even in some degree to their life. This faith undergirds and informs and elicits and transcends their work. Their beliefs (the concrete parts of the specific sciences of the day) come and go; but their faith, with all its ultimate ineffability, persists. As long as it persists, the scientific tradition will creatively flourish; what would be the meaning and contour of a dying of that faith it is hard to say, although obviously it could die[24].

Let us return, however, to our more immediate instance, of belief and faith in the more familiarly religious movements, and especially the Christian. We have discriminated between belief and faith, and have argued that belief is one among many of the overt expressions of faith. Every great religious movement has had many expressions. We can observe that, of these, one or a few tend at times to be singled out for special emphasis and centrality—probably never to the exclusion of all others, although it can happen that the others come to be interpreted then in terms of that central one. These may then be seen less as immediate expressions of the fundamental faith than as secondary expressions of the primary expression. Thus in some communities dance and music are a straightforward and unmediated expression of religious faith, whereas in the Christian case some people would see the singing of a hymn, or Handel's composing of the *Messiah* or one's listening to it, as a musical expression of a theological position. This can also work the other way around. The two prime forms of Jewish religious faith are membership in the community and obedience to divine imperatives, so that theology then becomes the attempt to give intellectual expression to these two more primary realities. In both the Jewish and the Islamic instances, moreover, it is hardly an exaggeration to say that monotheism, which by a Christian is liable to be thought of as primarily a doctrine, is felt rather as primarily a moral command: that one must worship only God, and serve Him alone. The oneness of God is less a metaphysical description than an ethical injunction. The mood is imperative, not indicative.

Given such an analysis, it becomes not too difficult to see the historical relation between faith and its specific forms in active operation. We have used the term "expression", and in justification of this usage can argue that each item in a given religious tradition—a statue of the Buddha, a Shinto shrine, an African dance pattern, a Hindu law code, a Christian doctrine, or whatever—has come into existence as the overt, tangible expression of someone's faith. Yet the term "expression" is inadequate, and in danger even of being misleading. For once the form has been set up, and especially once it is preserved by becoming incorporated into the on-going tradition, where it may serve for decades or even for millennia, it functions not only to express the faith of its formulator and then that of subsequent generations, but more importantly to induce and to nurture the latter, and to give shape to it. The reason why Westerners abroad at first mistook for the religion itself the external pattern, the observable complex of rites and practices and ideas and institutions, was that these were the locus of involvement, these served in each case to engender and to sustain the transcendent, unobservable faith of the participants. It is only on more careful inquiry, more sensitive understanding, that one comes to an awareness of the constant two-way traffic that is going on here: the dynamic interplay of worshipper and symbol, wherein what was originally an expression of an earlier generation's faith becomes an elicitor and focus of this generation's, and at best but a passive expression of it. Great men contribute to a tradition new forms which express their personal faith; but that faith has itself in its turn been stimulated by earlier forms, so that all religious men, great and small, derive from (or we may better say, through) the forms of a tradition the faith by which they live their daily lives.

I could not have dreamed up the cathedral at Coventry or Benjamin Britten's "Rejoice in the Lamb" cantata or Augustine's or Wesley's doctrinal systems; to concoct these, men were needed of greater faith and greater creativity than I. But by my worshipping in the one and listening to the other and pondering the third, my capacity to live in the world Christianly is made possible, is kept alive, is enriched. The Sunday morning service at my local church is not my faith; at times it may not even be an accurate expression of my faith. Its form is the erstwhile expression of other men's faith, yet by my participating in it week by week and by other such involvement my own faith as a child was evoked and as an adult is nourished.

Further, if I sing a hymn or observe a liturgy or repeat a creed mechanically, nothing happens; but if I do it as an expression of faith, however weak, it becomes in turn an evocator of faith both for me, since my own faith is therefore enlarged, and for my neighbour or for my children. The forms of any tradition function as occasions for faith not in themselves, but insofar as persons are actively involved with them. The temples of ancient Egypt once served to inspire and to crystallize the faith of men and women, though now they are but tourist attractions. The ideas of the Manichees once served as channels of faith for millions; now they are but the subject of doctoral dissertations in history.

Theology, then, for the Christian has, in comparative perspective, played in the Church a role such as that played in Islamic history by the *sharīʿah*, the Muslim systematized and ritualized moral law, or by Persian mystical poetry. Any given theological statement or doctrine or system arises first of all as the expression in verbal or conceptual form of someone's religious faith. Assuming that it is sincere, it is first personal and indeed individual; insofar, however, as it is accepted, either formally by the Church or in modern times informally by many Christians, it expresses the personal faith of many men and women. It serves, however, not only as an expression of faith for one person or group or generation, but then as an avenue to faith for another. Like a statue or a ritual or a poem or a corporate life, a belief introduces the believer to something beyond itself. Its significance is transcendent, is in terms of the life of those involved in it; its potential meaning lies in the realm of a person's relation to her- or himself, to his or her fellows, and to the world. It induces faith; it nurtures it; it gives it shape and force and depth and richness.

Beliefs have the very special quality, among faith's many expressions, of being subject also to the imperious pressure to be true. In their case a double demand arises: that they be symbolically true and straightforwardly true. Similarly, artistic expressions ideally should be aesthetically beautiful as well as symbolically true, moral expressions should be ethically right as well as symbolically true, and so on. By "symbolically true", we mean that life lived in terms of them should be true: true in relation to the mundane environment in which it is lived, and truly human, in the highest, final, cosmic sense. (This role may differ from person to person; something may be more true symbolically for one person than for another.) The faith that any symbol expresses or elicits ought to be true faith. A belief, in addition, insofar as it is propositionally structured, is expected also to be cast in the form of true statements.

Or—inasmuch as truth about the universe in all its mystery is not easy to come by; and true faith in personal life is a lofty goal—perhaps we may say, more charitably, that of a religious belief as conceptual symbol one may appropriately ask how it approximates to truth, at either level (or both).

Before we raise issues of that magnitude, however, we must explore more solidly the relation between belief and faith historically.

Chapter 2

THE BUDDHIST INSTANCE: FAITH AS ATHEIST?

SOMEONE has remarked[1] that the only true atheist is he who loves no one and whom no one loves; who does not care for truth, sees no beauty, strives for no justice; who knows no courage and no joy, finds no meaning, and has lost all hope.

The aphorism is clearly a theist's formulation. It could be rendered more neutrally, less metaphysically, for our purposes more definitionally, in terms rather of faith. It could serve as a suggestive or poetic characterization of the absence of this human quality. In this sense perhaps no human being is, ever has been, utterly without faith, although some have in despondency come at times close to that bleakness. And by the same token no one has total faith, although some are gifted with its warmth in generous measure. For all of us, the question would be of how much, and of what kind, rather than a facile yes-or-no.

Manifestly there is a major difference between faith, when thought of in some such personalist and qualitative terms as these, and belief, as a set of ideas or propositions. There is a major difference even between faith in God, conceived in some such fashion, and belief in God. Yet both the difference between the two, and the relation between them, stand in need of clarification—as, even for someone who might otherwise like the aphorism, and perhaps especially for him or her, does the elaboration "faith in God". It is evident that the person who formulated the remark in the terms here first cited himself believed in God (hence his word "atheist"), while proceeding to affirm that belief in God is, in fact, not the basic issue. Both parts of this may be elucidated by our looking beyond the boundaries of Christendom.

In the West, the fundamental religious question was for a time[2] widely held to be the question of whether one believed in God or not. More recently, the newer query to be canvassed has been, rather, what belief in God means, as a theoretical proposition. We are urging that one may now more rewardingly, and perhaps more truly, ask, What does it mean to have faith in God? And, whether as a subordinate part of that or *vice versa*, What does it mean to have religious faith?

To attempt an answer is a large venture: monumental in proportions and formidable in profundity and subtlety—in both of its parts, historical and existential. What has it meant to men and women, over the centuries and across the world, in the West, Asia, and Africa, to have faith—at times, faith explicitly in God? And, what shall it mean to us now, to-day, and as we enter our strange and man-made to-morrows, to have, or not to have, such faith?

We begin our exploration by turning first to the early Buddhist movement.

Any substantial inquiry into early Buddhist faith, or even into early Buddhist concepts of faith, would be a large undertaking, beyond the scope of this present investigation[3]. For our more limited concern, however, as to the relation between faith and belief, and especially the relation among faith, faith in God, and belief in God, even an outline sketch of this movement can prove instructive. It may serve as an illuminating starting-point for our wider task.

For the early Buddhist movement was atheist: not in the sense of our opening aphorism, certainly, but in the more usual sense that it dispensed with the idea of divinity. As a movement it had beliefs, and took them very seriously, but they were explicitly not theocentric. (In our next chapter, we shall consider the Islamic case, which on this particular matter offers a stark contrast.)

The movement gathering around the figure of the Buddha was a movement not only of ideas. In addition to his teachings, it was inspired by, oriented towards, symbolized in representations of, his total personality and character. His silences played a role, as well as his words; his smile, his compassion, his serenity, his courage as well as the articulated statement of his message. One may be sure that subsequent developments would have been quite different if the man who propounded these ideas had not had, in addition to them, also such qualities as, for instance, personal integrity by which there was a close convergence between the life that he lived and the thoughts that he enunciated. His faith, and not only his beliefs, have affected the history of the world.

As regards the community that emerged, its mutual loyalty and cohesion were evoked by him, and were sustained by its never-failing memory of him, as a person; in turn, its memory of him and indeed its very preservation of his teaching were sustained and enlivened by that community's mutual loyalty and cohesion, its group spirit, its members' ability to find nurture and encouragement in and through each other. They themselves emphasized this multi-dimensionality, in their joyous proclamations of The Three Jewels (the Buddha, the Dharma, the Samgha). They found themselves involved, ultimately concerned with, found their lives finally validated through, a pattern of teachings, certainly, but also the person and the example of him who had made these available and compelling, and the corporate life in and by which both of these—the teachings, and the personal example—were available and compelling and delightful now.

There was more going on here than a process of abstract ideas, therefore. Indeed the community itself differed and in due course divided—not acrimoniously—on the question of the relative importance of what he was and what he said. In the imagination and religious commitment of some of his followers, his cosmic function took precedence over his precepts. For many, the truth that he saw was expressed in his life and example at least as significantly as in his pronouncements.

The role of belief, then, of ideas, in early Buddhist developments is a complex question. Nonetheless, it is one into which we shall not here go further, since whatever other factors may have been at work, beliefs were indeed one factor, and for our purposes the fact is instructive that these beliefs were in atheistic form. We shall simplify our inquiry by deliberately choosing that group among his followers that has traditionally been regarded as the earliest and most conservative, and that in any case most firmly gave weight to what the Buddha taught: namely, the School of Elders (Theravadins). We shall focus similarly on those writings in which presently they enshrined what they had preserved of his teachings, the Pali Canon. These, more than the communities that later developed into the Mahayana with metaphysically exuberant scriptures, were both systematic and austere in their beliefs.

Because this belief system has been seen as atheistic—although not for any other reason—Westerners have sometimes questioned whether the movement that it served ought to be called religious. We shall come in a moment to give somewhat closer attention to how far and in what ways the epithet "atheist" is here indeed warranted. First, however, it must be urged that whether the movement be called atheist or not, it is certainly to be recognized as religious. It undoubtedly played a religious role in the lives of those men and women who espoused it. It undoubtedly was an alternative to other movements, other ideas, other loyalties, other organizations, that are plainly religious. It inspired and disciplined; it won response and evoked devotion; it proffered ideals and transformed character; it generated cultural totalities extending over great areas and enduring over long centuries and replete with social institutions, conceptual systems of metaphysical ultimates, and qualities of personal character, which both those within and outside observers have recognized as the counterparts to those that are called religious in every other cultural whole. If this was atheism, it was a religious atheism.

The question that ensues, however, turns out to be more problematic than at first appears. Given that it was religious, was it also atheist?

This can be considered in relation both to belief and to faith. Even at the former level, let alone the latter, there is room for interpretation.

The reasons for the atheist verdict are fairly straightforward. The Buddha deliberately or by implication dethroned the Hindu gods, both from their final place in the universe and from their final role in the destiny of humankind[4].

Having dethroned those gods, however, which most religious movements have done of the gods of rival movements, did the Buddhist replace them with new gods of his own?

The answer is "no", so far as any concept of a personal God is concerned. The Buddha himself, and the early Buddhist movement, were non-theist, certainly, to use a Western term. The theistic, however, is of course not the only interpretation of divinity, even in the West. Did the new movement put forth, and did those whom it inspired and activated and delighted, accept, some new divinity to replace the old? Did they form and teach some new concept of God?

To this also the answer "no" has been given, especially at the turn of the present century. More recently, this answer has been qualified by scholars and observers who have argued that the concept "Nirvana" as the Buddhists developed and emphasized it is, if looked at closely, not the negative notion that was once supposed but something gloriously real, some sort of counterpart to the Western concept "God"; or at the least, that it played a role significantly comparable to that played by the concept "God".

Jews, Muslims, Hindus, for that matter Presbyterians and Methodists, all have something different to say about God, yet all are admitted as talking about Him. One must not deny Buddhists the right to say something different about God, also. Yet that they were saying something different has not deterred these interpreters from arguing that it is still God about Whom or Which these early Buddhists were talking. And the reasons that they adduce are not unimpressive. As one scholar has summarized it: "we are told that Nirvana is permanent, stable, imperishable, immovable, ageless, deathless, unborn, and unbecome, that it is power, bliss and happiness, the secure refuge, the shelter, and the place of unassailable safety; that it is the real Truth and the supreme Reality; that it is the *Good*, the supreme goal and the one and only consummation of our life, the eternal, hidden and incomprehensible Peace"[5]. A considerable number of other modern Western scholars have adopted this interpretation[6], and one might almost regard the point as now virtually established. Nirvana was apprehended by the Buddha and his early followers as having qualities of the divine, if by "divine" one understands what theists in the West intend by this term.

A more recently proposed parallelism, at the level of ideas and beliefs, is that between the Buddhist concept "Dharma" (Pali, *dhamma*)[7] and the Western concept of God. In addition to perceiving some overlap between "Nirvana" and the notion of God, one may recognize further that the Dharma idea is also, and perhaps even more, akin. That it constitutes another counterpart to the Western conception, in significant ways functionally comparable and metaphysically convergent, will appear as we proceed.

It may be mentioned in passing that, curiously, Westerners have on the whole been much more fascinated by Nirvana than by Dharma. They have given it much more emphasis and attention; it has been popularized much more widely in Western thought. It is not quite clear why this is so; Buddhists themselves give the impression of being rather restless at this, tending, perhaps inchoately, to be disquieted at all the Western fuss about the Nirvana notion. This is partly, no doubt, because what is a sacred mystery to them seems perhaps in danger of being pried into and even bandied about by Westerners, certainly irreverently handled. The outsider seems presumptuously to plunge at once towards the goal, theoretically, without piously giving heed first to the inescapably prior question of how to reach it. Besides this there is the point that for most Buddhists the dominant and central concept of the Buddha's teaching has probably been felt to be Dharma. It is to this, we suggest, that the outsider should give prime attention if he wishes to come to grips with the early Buddhist position. It too can be understood by theists if they realize that for a Buddhist it has had qualities that they themselves characterize as divine.

Of course, just as some Westerners may, in either case, resist a proposed convergence on the grounds that it seems to "read too much into" the Buddhist notion, so some Buddhists resist it for exactly the opposite reason: namely, that the comparison belittles the Buddhist term, and reads too much out of it[8]. As understanding of each other's position grows, such disagreement may find itself dissolved historically: the number of intellectuals on both sides who come to accept such correlation will probably increase, and in any case this will be a practical test of the proposal's validity. A further dynamic aspect of the matter is that this newer assessment in the West of concepts such as Nirvana and Dharma is at the same time an historical innovation or development in the West's interpretation of its conception of God. Theistic understanding of divine activity on earth becomes enlarged as it contemplates Buddhist history in deepening awareness. Buddhists, similarly, as their appreciation of world history grows, enhance their understanding not only of human affairs in new range and variety, but also of human response to cosmic truth.

In any case, our primary concern here is not to establish that certain ideas in the Buddhist scheme are ideas of transcendence (though a case for this can be made, and it would then follow for some that these Buddhists believed in God). Our concern, rather, is to attempt to show that these ideas, this scheme, in fact introduced men and women to transcendence, not in theory but in practice; that through these symbols they were enabled to be existentially aware of and to live in terms of this added dimension; that, whatever their beliefs, they in fact lived lives of faith.

We turn, then, to faith. Our argument has to do with the faith of which these beliefs of early Buddhists were an expression and for which in turn they came to constitute a ground.

So far as the teachings of the Buddha are concerned: with regard to human life his first point, proffered as an empirical observation and strongly emphasized, was that that life is *dukkha.* This is usually translated "suffering", which up to a point is valid though I personally also like to translate it as meaning that all life is awry; in any case, we cannot here elaborate that immensely interesting matter. So far as the universe is concerned, his first point, again strongly emphasized and reiterated and carried through more radically than perhaps by any other system of thought until the twentieth century, was that the empirical universe is an unmitigated flux. Things come and go; events emerge, cause other events to emerge, and then vanish; elements coalesce for a moment into patterns, which disintegrate again and are replaced by others; the whole sorry tale is one of ceaseless, and ultimately meaningless, happenstance. In this ocean of events, nothing is stable, nothing is of permanent significance. He did not deny that in the flux there could be fleeting moments of pleasure; but these were balanced by many moments of pain, and undercut by their own fleetingness—so that a wise man could find nothing in the flux to which to attach himself with commitment, or hope, or to which to give a serious loyalty.

Now no one in the twentieth century, with our inundating awareness of process and instability, of the ephemeral quality of mountain ranges and of social institutions, of ideas and ideals, the historical transformations of galaxies and of religious systems—no one of us need be reminded that the Buddha here had quite a point. In other ages, perhaps, the Buddha may have seemed too pessimistic in his assessment of the observable mundane universe as a drifting chaos—but hardly to-day. Aristotle rejected an endless chain of cause-and-effect out of hand, as inconceivable; many moderns accept it out of hand, as inescapable. So far as the empirical universe is concerned, one can feel that the Buddha was right. The great religious question has always been, however, is there something more? Is there anything beyond the ocean of phenomena that come and go?

The Buddha affirmed with vigour that within the ocean, nothing persists. Hence his alleged atheism. Even the gods, he said, rise and fall. The ocean is fluid, through and through.

He did, however, affirm that there is a "further shore". This phrase echoes through his teachings. He was adamant in refusing to describe it in words, or to encourage his followers to speculate as to what it might look like when they got there. His teaching was concerned not to elucidate the nature of that "further shore", but to delineate how to attain it, to invite people aboard the raft that he saw, and preached, would carry one to it. His seeing that it would carry one across constituted his Vision, his Enlightenment, his Buddhahood. The name of that Other Shore is Nirvana. The recognition in relatively recent Western studies of its transcendent quality, and its ultimacy in the Buddhist scheme of things, has led to the recent suggestion that we were hasty, and perhaps simply wrong, in calling his position atheist, or even world-denying.

No modern logical positivist or linguistic analyst has outdone the Buddha in insisting that human language is incapable of dealing with metaphysical reality, that our terms and categories and conceptual capacities are just inadequate for handling the Transcendent. Nonetheless, unlike most of them, he was sure that it was there—partly through his mystical experience or personal holistic insight, partly for other reasons. He knew that it was there—as other people could find out for themselves, he affirmed, by living morally.

Though Nirvana was a distant reality, indescribable, not profitable of discussion, yet the Buddha saw and preached another absolute reality immediately available to every man. This is the moral law. The Buddha taught that in the universal flux, one thing is firm. In the chaos of events, one pattern is permanent. In the ebb and flow of human life, one form is absolute, is supreme, is reliable, is effective for salvation. Ideas come and go; religious institutions rise and fall; the gods themselves have their histories; men's and women's goals are frustrated, and anyway are themselves historical; all human strivings, whether to construct something on earth, or through piety or asceticism to try to escape from or to dominate earthly ambitions, are doomed sooner or later to pass away. Yet through it all one thing is certain, stable, firm, enduring—and is always immediately to hand. That is Dharma: the truth about right living.

Both the Buddha and his followers were resolute in asserting that

Siddhartha Gautama did not dream up his views on Dharma. It would puncture the whole Buddhist system of thought like a noisy balloon to suppose that the Dharma is simply his ideas, his teachings, something that he constructed. He did not concoct this; he discovered it. The teachings of the Buddha began in the sixth century B.C.; but the Dharma did not begin then, it has always been. When a modern Buddhist writes of "The Buddha's Ancient Path"[9], he does not mean that it is a mere twenty-five hundred years old. It was already an ancient path when Gautama discovered it. "Even so, brethren", he himself said, "have I seen an ancient Path, an ancient Road, trodden by Buddhas of a bygone age . . . the which having followed, I understand life, and its coming to be and its passing away. And thus understanding, I have declared the same"[10]. The Pali term here is *Puranamagga*; and it re-echoes in the texts.

The Dharma that he taught does not owe its validity or authority to the fact that he was a wise and great man; on the contrary, he became a wise and great man because he awoke to its pre-existent truth. He became a Buddha by discovering what if one were to speak in Greek terms one could only call the pre-existent logos.

All else is evanescent. But the Saddharma, the True Law, is eternal.

It is a question whether it would be legitimate to affirm that the Dharma has always existed. Just now we choose to say rather that it has always been. The situation is closely parallel to that of the Christian theologian who finds it controversial whether "exist" is the right word for God, being tempted to reject it for seeming to imply that He is one existent among others; that various things exist, we know, and we are answering a question as to whether also God does—whereas rather we must say that God *is*; or even further, that He is the ground of being: it is He through whom whatever does exist exists, and through whom whatever is has been[11].

The Buddhists distinguished between the *paramartha saddharma*, the True Law in its supreme or final form, and the *samvrti saddharma*, meaning that Law in its objectified or empirical version, the Law as taught. The latter is subject to history; and Buddhist writers expressed opinions on its vicissitudes, on what was to be expected for it after five hundred or a thousand years. The former, on the other hand, the transcendent version, is independent of its being transmitted to men by the Buddhas at all. The nature of the transitory flux, as well as the scheme of liberation taught by the Buddha, is an independent truth, an objective reality. As the scriptures put it, "Whether the sages appear or not, the legitimacy of the law remains stable"[12]. It is the higher version of the Law, of course, that it is legitimate to consider, as suggested above, as analogous to a pre-existent logos, though both are adumbrated in a remark such as this by a careful scholar: "the function and hall-mark of a Buddha was not to devise, or create a new Dhamma, but to rediscover, recreate and revive that ancient norm"[13].

One of the points that has been most urged by Western students is that the Buddha taught that man must save himself; that there is no outside power that can come to his rescue. The Mahayana stream stemming from him and his teachings, the religious movement constructed round his memory and the inspiration of his life and thought that developed perhaps later and carried his message and "good news" to China and Japan, has often been contrasted with the allegedly earlier Buddhist movement precisely on this point. For the Mahayana schools preached a divine agency in the cosmos that would come to the help of individual men and women, to save us. In contrast, the early Buddhist movement is presented as rejecting all such notions.

Now it is true that the Buddha took a rather Pelagian attitude to the moral life. He firmly believed, and taught, that each man could and must make his own decision as to whether he would live morally; and having made it, he must himself implement that decision. For the historical Buddha, there is no vicarious morality. Nonetheless, there is at least this sense in which it is false to say that he believed, or taught, that man could save himself. There is in the universe, he proclaimed, an ultimately real, a final truth in accordance with which if a man lives he will be saved. If the universe consisted only in the flux of *samsara*, only in the coming-and-going of evanescent phenomena with the epiphenomena of our transient lives, if there were no eternal Dharma, then man could not possibly save himself. If there were only flux, man would be lost; and nothing that we could do would salvage us. It is living according to Dharma, the pre-existing law, that saves.

The decision so to live is man's own; but the fact that living so brings salvation is prior to man, independent of man. And the confidence that it will work, that it is worth pursuing: this is based on a confidence in the very structure of the universe. That we live in the kind of universe where such a truth obtains, firm, reliable, and permanent, is the "good news" that the Buddha preached, and that his movement carried half across the world.

If the universe were not as he apprehended it and taught it to be (as it was disclosed to him as being), then man would be without recourse. This is implied throughout his teachings; and so far as that other realm is concerned to which the path leads, there is an explicit text affirming it: "There is, O monks, an unborn, not become, not made, not constructed. Had there not been that unborn . . . " (etc.), "no way could be discerned here of transcending that which is born, become, made, constructed. But inasmuch as there is an unborn . . . " (etc.), "so a transcending is recognized . . . "[14].

It has sometimes been said that early Buddhist preaching is pessimistic. This is simply wrong: it is a gospel, good news, a joyous proclamation of a discovery of a truth without which life is bleak, is suffering, but with which there is not merely serenity but triumph. It is indeed fortunate for man that he has been born into a universe where evanescence is not the last word. Because there is Dharma, he can be saved.

To be a Pelagian, even conservative Christians might concede, is hardly the same as to be an atheist.

It is not even quite true that this saving Truth, in all its firm and cosmic stability, saves indifferently, dispassionately, just by being there. Certainly the Buddha himself, having striven through to a recognition of that eternal truth, and thus having achieved his own salvation, was not content to leave it at that. The one great temptation portrayed in the Pali Scriptures is that where the Buddha, once having attained his Enlightenment, was faced with the challenge to keep it to himself, to live on quietly and withdrawn, in the serenity of his own achievement. It was pointed out to him by Mara, the Evil One, that other men are obtuse and distracted, that they would not understand his teaching, nor follow it if they did—why should he not simply enjoy the bliss to which his own struggles had finally brought him? The Buddha rejected this, and spent the next forty-five years of his life walking up and down the length and breadth of much of India proclaiming to all mankind the vision that he had seen, the avenue to the release from sorrow and bondage that he had discovered, and knowledge of which he wished to share with a suffering humanity. Nor was his decision adventitious: part of the truth that he had found was precisely that to live for others is the way to live one's own life well. "As with her life a mother cares for her own, her only child, so in your hearts and minds let there be boundless love for all beings great and small"[15], the Scriptures present him as saying. The infinite compassion that he preached has to be taken seriously, after all—for it is part of the central Truth, the only enduring truth, of the universe.

Accordingly, it is not only the Buddha as a person who is concerned that other men too should find the beatitude that he had found. The birth of the Buddha, the occasion of his Enlightenment, and his death are presented in the Scriptures as events accompanied by cosmic manifestations—signs and wonders and portents as indications that the whole universe was astir in the process of the Dharma's being made known to mankind. The early Buddhist movement may not have believed in personal gods; but it certainly held that there were cosmic reverberations to the life and teaching of the Buddha.

Haeckel has reputedly remarked[16] that the fundamental question about the universe is, "Is it friendly?" The Buddhist hardly says "no".

And even Nirvana itself, the Absolute, it is once hinted, if not subordinate to, yet is itself validated by, the moral law: "it could not be said: 'There is not Nirvana.' Why is this? Because the practice of Dhamma is not barren"[17]. A Westerner is reminded of Kant's argument that morality validates immortality: God makes morality possible, morality makes God necessary[18]. "The practice of Dhamma is not barren". In other words, the Moral Law is absolute not only in its demands, but in its rewards.

In historical terms our argument can be summed up in this way. The Buddha was born into a world of Indian culture where the fundamental notions were those of God and the gods, an ultimate transcendent Reality which could not be mundanely known, an elaborate system of religious observance, a caste system, and a striving to transcend the ordinary workaday world by ascetic austerity, by spiritual insight, and in other ways. Within the total ideological complex was a concept of *dharma*, designating propriety or custom or obligation. Each caste had its own *dharma*, its own pattern of religio-social behaviour. It was important to observe *dharma*, the moral law, so long as one were operating at the level of mundane living; but the truly major endeavour, in both the religious and the intellectual worlds, was to transcend that level, to attain a numinous Reality ("Brahman") beyond it. What the Buddha did was to reverse the order of these levels. For him, Brahman and the Gods, while not negated, became part of this world; while *dharma* was elevated to finality, to absolute transcendence.

In the early Buddhist scriptures, one sees the Buddha launching a radical revolution in the ideological and social complex of the India of his day by propounding a basically simple yet profound and fundamental thesis. Essentially one hears him as saying that in the last analysis it does not really matter what theology a man espouses, what ritual observances he performs, what caste he belongs to, what intellectual or mystical or ascetic feats he may rise to. All this is beside the point: interesting for the historical record, but of no final significance. There is only one thing that really matters—but it does matter, cosmically. It is, whether one lives a truly good life. All else is vanity, or worse. This, however, is not vanity: this is the one eternal principle in a universe otherwise chaotic. Castes and creeds, fame and fortune, institutions, success, personal achievement, even interpersonal relations are, no less than failure and loss, doomed to be unsatisfying to man in a universe whose one and only stable law is that of righteous living. Yet just as everything else can be depended upon to pass away, to let us down, so this can be depended upon always to hold[19], and always to save us—in fact, to carry us across the raging sea of evanescent phenomena and interim event to the indescribable bliss of ultimate serenity.

In theoretical terms, this is a metaphysics of morality: that the only final truth is goodness, that a human life well lived reflects, exemplifies, transcendent reality. The point is not to transcend the world, but to live well within it. If you do live well within it, you will find that you have transcended it.

Act on faith in this, he said in effect, and you shall be saved. Man has been made restless till he finds rest in this law. "The sky will fall, and the moon and the stars . . . but what the wise have said will never prove false"[20].

What is the content of the moral law as the Buddha preached it, is formally not at issue here; though in fact what he taught has won the admiration not only of hundreds of millions of Asians who have responded creatively to his impact, but also of countless outside the Buddhist movement, and perhaps specially Christians, who often see Buddhist moral teaching as the most attractive and ideal of any major tradition outside the Church. This is hardly negligible. Yet the point that we must make here is not only of substance but of form: that he taught human morality not as part of, and subordinate to, the historical flux but as cosmically derived, and cosmically justified. The moral law is absolute; and human life lived in accord with it is thereby delivered from the relativity in which all else consists, to participate in transcendence.

We come now to the crux of our argument. What I wish to submit is not that early Buddhists believed this to be true (although they did), but that they found it to be true. It is on this that the whole matter finally turns (both historically, for them, and theoretically, for us). Through the Buddha's character and personality and impact, through the movement that he launched and the teaching that he formulated, men and women were enabled to recognize, yes, but more important, to discover, that transcendence is not another world, afar off; it is this world lived in truly, compassionately. They heard the teaching, and they appropriated it, and passed it on to their children, and to their neighbours half across the world, in joy—because it worked. Not fully in every case, of course: not everyone went the whole way, to attain Nirvana. Maybe none did. Yet the movement has persisted for twenty-five hundred years because those who have accepted it as an ideal have found for twenty-five hundred years that there is then a quality in their lives that gives them confidence that yes, the world is like that.

We said at the beginning that the early Buddhist movement was religious; and to establish the point remarked that it played a role in their lives parallel to that played by admittedly religious patterns in others. We can now move beyond that second-hand argument to the direct, immediate situation internal to the Buddhist community. The movement is religious because through it men and women's lives were lived in what the Western world has traditionally called the presence of God. Through their systems of beliefs, they were enabled to live lives of faith. They tasted transcendence; and accordingly their lives were touched by compassion and courage and serenity and ultimate significance.

By shifting the question from whether the Buddha and his followers believed in God (to which the answer is evidently "no") to whether they had faith in God, we hope to have demonstrated that for some in the latter case the answer can or must be "yes". At least, one's answer will be "yes" if one means by God, at least in part, that quality of or reality in the universe in which he and they did have faith.

It could readily be argued that these days those Westerners who use the term "God"—whether to affirm or to deny—would do well to include, or can hardly escape including, this quality or reality in their meaning for that term. A time, surely, has come when they must incorporate these Buddhist insights into what they do or do not believe. The primarily pertinent point, however, is not at this level, which even in speaking about faith is still concerned with belief. Both the historical datum, and the ultimate significance, are faith. Belief is its attempted, but manifestly not universally agreeable, interpretation.

The Buddha certainly had faith: a religious faith mighty, contagious, creative; one that has powerfully affected the shape of human history and the personal lives of men and women for now twenty-five centuries. It is a fact that he had that faith. Whether we should go on or not to call it faith in God, depends directly on what we think of the universe, *not on what he thought of it.*

Chapter 3

THE ISLAMIC INSTANCE: FAITH AS THEOCENTRIC

Beliefs, in the Buddhist instance, have served along with other matters to express and to inculcate faith. In the Islamic case, to which we next turn, beliefs of a dramatically different sort have played in relation to Muslim faith a role comparable and yet different: one that will repay investigation. If Buddhist belief has been atheist, the Muslim system would seem to have made belief in God spectacularly central. On it, an observer might be tempted to report, surely no other community on earth has put so much weight. If, then, we can elucidate here the relation to faith of belief—in this instance explicitly, emphatically, belief in God—we shall have taken a second sizeable step towards our goal. If we are to recognize faith rather than belief as the fundamental religious category, are to discern that it has been wrong to suppose of late that believing is what religious people centrally do, then we must take very seriously the Qur'an, and Islamic monotheism.

It turns out that these are, indeed, greatly illuminating for our problem. Here too our distinction holds, and indeed is firmly if subtly corroborated. This proves to be so, on close inquiry, even within the classical Islamic conceptual scheme itself. Belief is not there considered as of ultimate significance; faith, on the other hand, is.

In the Islamic tradition, as in the Christian, faith has been a central category of thought. (The Arabic term is *iman*.) It is presented, indeed, as man's most decisive quality. The Day of Judgement, to use that mighty metaphor, is envisaged primarily as a determining of who has had it and who not. Heaven and Hell are felt to be not too stupendous characterizations of the cosmic significance for man of the question involved. Muslims take their stand with those across the world who perceive faith as the ultimate human issue.

Believing, however, in relation to faith, the Islamic instance also illustrates, is more subtle than at first appears. Belief is here closely linked with faith; almost, it would seem, fused with it—and yet it turns out that believing is not a religious category in this powerfully conceptualist system. It is the purpose of this present chapter to inquire into the absence of belief, as a concept, in the Islamic world-view. Specifically, we shall observe that a notion of believing, as a religious category, is not to be found in the Qur'an. It will prove instructive to explore how this is so: how it relates, on the one hand, to the concept of faith, explicitly and emphatically there set forth, and on the other hand, to the general patterning of ideas in that scripture, to its dramatic verbalization of what might nowadays be called the Qur'anic "belief-system". Here is a "belief-system" that does not believe in believing.

There is an awkwardness here, in that to deal with this issue we must first attend to the notion "belief" itself. Faith, infidelity, and various other Islamic concepts we shall explicate in terms of what the Qur'an says about them, and of subsequent Muslim commentary and thought. Such empirical procedure is feasible, appropriate, and obviously important. Since the Qur'an has no word for "belief" in the modern sense, we cannot in its case do the same, although we shall look closely at terms there that others have on occasion so rendered. Manifestly, to argue that a particular idea does *not* occur in the Qur'an requires a preliminary and independent delineation of that idea, in a fashion that runs the danger of being arbitrary or superficial. The difficulty is compounded in that several differing concepts have been verbalized by the English words "belief", "believe"; one of our general tasks is to help to clarify this.

In a later chapter below, and more fully in a separate volume[1], we explore an historical development, even transformation, in the uses of these English terms. There was a time, we shall see, when they did serve as verbal counters for the concept "faith". (Hence, in part, the recent confusion.) Yet that was long ago, and although there are some Western Christians who still use "believe" at least partly in this older sense, they are a dwindling group. And even they are ambivalent. Here, our concern is not with the classical conception of what was called believing but with the modern. In fact, much of the point of this present Islamic inquiry lies in the fact that we may advance our general understanding by specifically becoming aware of a contrast between two things: the modern concept of belief, on the one hand, and the outlook presented in the Qur'an, on the other.

On the former, we shall be brief. We wish neither to anticipate the historical discussion of our later chapter or separate volume, nor to attempt a sophisticated theoretical discussion of belief in its modern sense in relation to knowledge (in which relation its modern sense has primarily situated it). This would take us far too far afield. The relation between religious belief and knowledge has become a central issue for much modern thought; but our concern is other, since we find believing to be not a prime religious category. All that is requisite here is to remind ourselves, almost casually, of present-day ordinary-language usage. This will over-simplify, but illumine.

Although in our day certain persons and groups, especially in certain situations, consciously or unconsciously add other connotations (and may prize them), yet there is, I suggest, a dominant modern meaning of "believing", common to virtually all uses; an inescapable minimum, which we can quickly isolate, and on which I feel that many can probably quickly agree, at least for the interim. This minimal conceptual component, then, we shall apply to the Qur'an. From finding that it does not fit we may learn something already instructive in itself and in due course contributory as we later return to develop further and to refine more carefully our understanding of belief in generic relation to faith. Readers who feel that our presentation of belief at this stage is manifestly preliminary only, and even leaves out much, will perhaps find that later elaborations in subsequent chapters[2] serve to redeem the interim inadequacies.

Modern "believing", we have suggested, is placed in relation to, contradistinction from, knowing. Let us consider this briefly, for everyday usage. For the man in the street, may we not say that knowledge involves two things: (a) certitude, and (b) correctness, in what one knows. To use quite unsophisticated terms, in ordinary parlance one knows whatever one knows when there is a close positive relation of one's ideas both to inner conviction and to objective truth. At this same level of casual yet prevalent usage, unphilosophic and unanalytic yet by the same token both widely and deeply held, there is the common-sense notion of believing. This is similar to knowing in that it is thought of as conceptualist, as in the realm of ideas in one's mind (even, of propositions). It differs from knowing in that it involves one or other of again two things, and perhaps both: (a) lack of certitude; (b) open neutrality as to the correctness or otherwise of what is believed.

Thus one may say that so-and-so knows that Bern is the capital of Switzerland. Alternatively, one may say that someone else believes that Geneva is the capital of Switzerland. Belief need not be that negative, however: one may also say that a third person believes that Bern is the capital. In this case we may know that he is right, yet by our phrasing the point that he believes it, we communicate the notion that he himself is not sure. His opinion happens to be correct, yet it is not knowledge because he himself holds it with a certain tentativeness. Alternatively, he might be quite sure, but such wording could indicate that *we* are uncertain: it is the speaker who is tentative. On the other hand, the view of our second man, who is under the impression that Geneva is the capital, is also not knowledge, no matter how strongly he may hold it. The intensity of his own assurance may rise however high, but it will not turn his belief into knowledge so long as his view is mistaken (or in a different case, even *might* be mistaken). Similarly in his neighbour's case: the actual accuracy of his position may be total, yet this will not turn his belief into what we may call knowledge so long as either he himself, or we, harbour misgivings.

In ordinary parlance then, "believing" is the concept by which we convey the fact that a view is held, ideationally, without a final decision as to its validity—explicitly without that decision.

Small wonder that believing in this sense has become the standard characterization for religious positions, in the modern world. For when we turn from ordinary (secular) usage to the specifically religious domain, the situation is nowadays not strikingly different.

It is in this sense that it is regularly said that Muslims believe that the Qur'an is the word of God, and Christians, that Christ is; and both are presumed to recognize that this is so.

On the one hand, so far as inner conviction is concerned, this notion of believing may for some correlate smoothly with the lack of confidence that in our day characterizes a large, and growing, number of believers. They believe something, perhaps hesitantly, or perhaps deliberately, even to the point of being willing to stake their life upon it; yet in either case, they are not quite sure. Not quietly sure, with that unruffled awareness of intellectual perspicuity. Or again, believers may recognize that however confident they themselves may feel, those to whom they speak may disagree. The word leaves open for others the position that it describes: to say "I believe" does not claim that others must concur. (It may invite; but, unlike "I know", it does not foreclose. It is not universalizing or fully socializing.) Secondly, and in line with this last, there is the question, in addition to inner conviction, of external, objective validity, of some kind of recognizable factual correctness of the positions held. The very notion of believing makes room nicely, and indeed necessarily, for the wide variety of religious views with which moderns are inescapably familiar (as well as for the prevalence and forcefulness of a further modern view, that all or most religious beliefs are conceptually wrong).

Both the believer and the non-believer have come to recognize that any position that they may or may not hold is one among many. Jews believe *x*, Muslims believe *y*, Christians believe *z*. Even among Christians, Seventh Day Adventists believe one thing, Roman Catholics another, Presbyterians still another. And all of them know that this is the case.

Before we go on, then, to re-ponder in relation to the Qur'an the current assumption about believing as a finally adequate religious category, let us first stress a recognition of its apparent appropriateness to the modern scene. An emphasis on this point might be regarded, in fact, almost as part of the argument. Having acknowledged that what modern persons in the modern world do religiously has "of course" come to be interpreted in terms of believing, I do not then go on to suggest that "nonetheless" at other times and places things have been different. My thesis comes closer to being rather that insofar as believing has become an apparently appropriate category for the modern world it is *therefore* not proper elsewhere. Its seeming modern aptness is correlated with its not having been a classical religious category.

Our first point, then, is a simple one: namely, that "believing" has come to be the straightforward and almost innocent interpretation of what religious people do in the modern world when they take a given position. For they are seen, rather naturally, as taking it as some sort of ideational venture; and, as one possible venture among others. Some believe one thing, others another. Neither they nor the rest of us are quite sure that they are right (nor doubters, perhaps, any more, even that they are wrong); even though many be confident that even so, the venture is well worth taking.

Both the participant and the observer seem able to agree that in taking the stance, they are doing something to which "believe" happily applies. Where one cannot know, let's believe, say some; where one cannot know, let's not believe, say others; where no one knows, many believe, say several. What do they believe, has become a standard question about other religious people; what do we, or what shall I, believe, a standard question about oneself.

At least, this was the case at an unsophisticated level until fairly recently. On more careful scrutiny, it turns out that the concept has even in modern times been serviceable at a critical level only with reservations. The popular notion, though understandable as rough-and-ready conceptualization, has had to be interpreted, sometimes uneasily, by more reflective thinkers. Both the philosopher, in attempting to analyse, and the theologian, in attempting to formulate, statements of what is believed, and what is involved in believing it, and also the anthropologist, in attempting to describe and to interpret the believing of primitive tribes[3], have found themselves having to operate with more refined notions of belief than the man-in-the-street has been content to employ. And as we have suggested, religious persons' current usage is often complicated by their incorporating, often unwittingly, earlier and drastically different implications, residual from more classical times.

We shall be taking note of these refinements in our later chapter. In the meantime, when we speak here of believing, we intend believing in the modern prevalent sense of that term, as signifying that an opinion is held about which the person who holds it, or the society that gives or receives information about his or her holding it, or both, leave theoretically unresolved the question of its objective intellectual validity.

Believing so conceived has become, it would seem, the religious category *par excellence* of the modern world. Outsiders have held that religious people do believe, and insiders that they ought to believe, certain things. We turn to our matter at hand, to show that such an idea is altogether foreign to the Qur'an; that a category of believing, in any current meaning of the term, is alien to that scripture. This will constitute one stage in our general argument that believing has been religiously misconceived: that as a dominant religious category it is inept, illegitimate, and even for the modern world has become unserviceable[4]. For the moment, our thesis is more limited, and for it the evidence more complete. The thesis is simple: that in the Qur'an the concept "believe" (as a religious activity) does not occur. Further: that it does not occur for very good reason. I have developed elsewhere the unexpected thesis that it does not occur in the Bible[5]; and we shall be presently be exploring that also it is not to be found in classical and mediaeval Christian thought[6]. That religious people are expected to believe something is a modern aberration.

Now the facts are that any English translation of the Qur'an that one may pick up, whether by Muslim or by Westerner, is replete with the words "belief", "believing", "believer", "non-believer", and the like, and that these are pivotal. Yet I am suggesting that to render in this way any term in the Qur'an, or in the classical Islamic world-view based upon it, is a serious mistranslation. My thesis, then, could seem rather absurdly bold. It is not quite so radical as this might make it appear, however; for these translations, or mistranslations, the reasons are various, although in some respects fairly straightforward. Given the history of the English word, which as we shall see has been changing its meaning, given also the influence of Biblical language, given the religiously plural condition of the modern English-speaking world, and so on, it is not difficult to see why a notion of believing has got into the renderings, even if the contention be valid that we now put forward. Qur'an translations into English illustrate, and participate in, the recent Western confusions that it is our aspiration in this study to move beyond.

A question of concepts is or involves a question of terms. This, if not constantly the case, is true at least for literary texts, especially for scriptures, and pre-eminently for so verbal a revelation as the Islamic. We shall have, therefore, to note certain Arabic terms, though the aim will be to keep the presentation as little technical as is feasible.

To show that a religious concept "believe" does not occur in the Qur'an, then, we begin by calling attention to the fact that words for "knowing" are frequent and emphatic[7]. The notion of knowledge is re-iterated and vivid. Indeed, in the official (erstwhile Royal) Egyptian edition of the Qur'an text, now standard, one or other of the two chief terms for knowing occurs on the average more than once per page[8].

Secondly, the standard word for "believing" in later Islamic theology[9] does not occur in the Qur'an.

Thirdly, of the terms that do occur in the Qur'an and that have been translated as "believe", two stand out, and constitute the crux of our inquiry. They are drastically different from each other; the fact that nonetheless in relatively modern times both have regularly been translated—again, we would say, mistranslated—into English as "believing" illuminates our whole matter. One means, "to have faith". They are, first, *amana* (with *iman*, "faith", as its verbal noun[10]); and second, *zanna*, in modern Arabic "to think", "to opine", to hold an opinion.

Without any question, the fundamental concept in the Qur'an, overwhelmingly vivid, is that of God, presented as Creator, Sovereign, and Judge; powerful, demanding, succouring, majestic; laying upon mankind inescapable imperatives and offering us inexhaustible rewards. The fundamental category on the manword side is that of faith: the positive recognition and acceptance of the divine summons, the committing of oneself to the demands, and thus being led to the ultimate succour. The term for faith, *iman*, is itself a verbal noun, and it is of some significance that the more strictly verbal forms predominate; so that it is more just to speak not of faith, simply, but rather of the act of faith. Faith is something that people do more than it is something that people "have"; although one may also say that it pertains to something that people are, or become.

The Qur'an presents, in reverberatingly engaging fashion, a dramatic challenge wherein God's terror and mercy, simultaneously, are proclaimed to mankind, whereby we are offered the option of accepting or rejecting His self-disclosure of the terms on which He, as Creator and Ruler of the world and of us, has set our lives. "What the Qur'an presents is a great drama of decision: God has spoken His command, and men thereupon are divided, or, rather, divide themselves, into two groups—those who accept and those who spurn; those who obey, and those who rebel"[11]. This is the way the universe was originally set up, and man's life within it: that this is so is now made known, with resonant clarity and force; and men and women, now that they have this knowledge, must act accordingly.

There are two or three terms used for the act of rejecting the invitation. Of these the most strident is *k-f-r*, from which the word usually translated "infidel" is derived, with its radically pejorative sense of "spurner". Even in modern Arabic, let alone mediaeval, classical, and

Qur'anic, and in Persian, Urdu, and Turkish, this word never comes to mean simply not to believe. (It would be foolish to translate with any form of this root the notion that so-and-so does not believe that an undiagnosed fever in a given case is malaria, or that it will rain to-morrow.) It implies ingratitude, and designates the blatant declining of what is proffered. Indeed, there are verses that explicitly indicate that the mind recognizes or accepts but the will repudiates. Two clear examples: "And when there comes to them what they know, they reject it" (2:89)[12]; and (with an alternative verb), "They rejected them [the signs of God] although they knew very well in their hearts that they were true" (27:14)[13]. These various verbs, moreover, are regularly found embellished with adverbs indicating that man's rejection of God's bounty and authority is out of haughtiness, arrogance, stubborn wilfulness[14]. It is a choice, actively made.

To speak at a mundane level, one might be tempted to say that the whole matter was to Muhammad himself so vivid, so overwhelmingly convincing, so startlingly clear, so divinely authentic, that it never really crossed his mind that one would not *believe* it. How could anyone not believe God? "Infidelity" (*kufr*, from this same root), the heinous sin, the incomprehensibly stupid and perverse obduracy, is not unbelief but "refusal": it is a spitting in God's face when He speaks out of His infinite authority and vast compassion. It is man's dramatic negative response to this spectacular divine initiative.

The positive response, over against this, equally dynamic, is called "faith" (*iman*). The "infidel", the ingrate *kafir*, is he who says "no" to God; and "the man of faith" (*mu'min*) is he who accepts, who says "yes". As the theologians subsequently explain, *iman*, faith, is self-commitment[15]. It means, and is said to mean, almost precisely, *s'engager*[16].

Another interpretation is that just as the word "amen" in English[17], from this same Semitic root via Hebrew, is used at the end of a congregational prayer or worship service as an act whereby the members of the congregation participate, in their turn, in what the leader has done or said, accepting it then for themselves or incorporating themselves into his act, saying "yes" to it, so the *mu'min*, the man of faith, the yes-sayer, the amen-sayer, is he who volunteers, who says "I, too!". By it, he identifies himself with the communal, and cosmic, activity. *Iman*, the act of faith, names the positive response to the divine and dramatic challenge.

We should not overstress the component of the will in the act of faith. For Muslim writers have differed on this point; and the analysis is subtle[18]. Some affirmed, for example, that faith is a free gift from God, hardly under man's voluntary control: the ability to respond to the divine initiative and summons is itself at that divine initiative[19]. Again, the element of intellectual recognition should not be excluded. Some of the early schools affirmed that faith is knowledge, awareness[20], although this position did not gain much currency[21]. (No doubt it is important to recognize the truth. Yet the Qur'an affirms that such apprehension is not enough—as when it refers to those who recognize the truth intellectually as clearly as they recognize their own children[22], and yet still do not respond with faith.) Even at this level, the concept is to be rendered not by "belief" but rather by "recognition" or the like: we shall be returning to this important issue in our later chapters.

Meanwhile, the Qur'an provides another example from which its orientation may be illustrated quite sharply. Let us consider the concept usually translated "polytheist". The Arabic term is *mushrik*. This designates what would be rendered in modern-day terminology as a man who—if one must use the term—"believes" in many gods. Now in a sense the Arabic term does indeed mean polytheist, but with a difference that, though at first it may seem subtle, is in fact radical, and of crucial import for our entire discussion. The word is formed from a root (*sh-r-k*) meaning "to associate", which in technical Islamic vocabulary provides also the concept (*shirk*: again basically a verbal noun) that is translated "polytheism" but that means, more literally, associating other beings with God—which in the Islamic scheme is explicitly the unforgivable sin. It means, one soon enough realizes on reflection, treating as divine what is in fact not so. God is seen as being one, alone; He only is to be worshipped. This overwhelming affirmation is, of course, fundamental to the Qur'an's whole presentation; so that to associate any second being with Him is stupid, wicked, and wrong.

The person, accordingly, characterized as *mushrik* is not the man who simply believes in many gods; rather, if one is to use the term "believe" at all, it is the man who *perversely* believes in many gods. Or, more precisely, one may note that at this level the Arabic means, more or less literally, "to believe in more gods than there are"; better, "to hold to more gods than there are". Built into the term as a term, and into the concept as a concept, is the fallacy of what it names. It is, therefore, a vehement pejorative. The inherently derogatory quality is not merely connotation, but denotation.

Therefore, one could not use this term of oneself. No man could call himself an "associator" (*mushrik*)—except that penitent Muslim who was repudiating his former sin and blindness, or later that mystic Muslim who confessed in tears imperfection in his sincerity, pleading that his intellectual recognition of God's oneness was not matched in full purity by a total singleness of heart in his devotion. Otherwise the phrase "I am a *mushrik*" is at the intellectual level a logical self-contradiction, since if one actually did believe that there are more gods than one, then this term would not describe that belief. It describes and analyses such a position from the point of view of those who reject it. It is a monotheist concept for a polytheist.

Indeed, once again a notion of "believe" is not quite appropriate anyway, since in a sense Muhammad or any convinced Muslim did not doubt that the idols of the pagans existed, but simply affirmed that they were not gods, were merely sticks and stones. It was not their existence that was in question, but the absurdity of worshipping them, of treating them as if they were divine. (The Qur'an proffers belief in *jinn*s ["genii"], and Islamic culture has believed in them; but neither would countenance faith [*iman*] in them, which would constitute a sin.) At still another level, to-day: the man who worships money, or devotes himself to the advancement of his own career, or panders to self-gratification, is an "associator" (*mushrik*) not in the sense that he recognizes the existence of these distractions—we all know that they exist—but in that he is associating them with God in, a modern might phrase it, his scheme of values, is consecrating his life in part to them rather than consecrating it solely to the only reality that is worthwhile, worshipful, worthy our pursuit: namely, God.

The atheist, the monotheist, the polytheist, then, to use the modern neutralist terms, form a series that in the Qur'an and in classical Islamic consciousness is seen, and felt, and designated, as all within the monotheistic framework. All three are conceptualized from the point of view of the truth: *al-Haqq*. Accordingly, the series is set forth as, respectively, the "infidel" (*kafir*), the cantankerous ingrate who rejects; the "man of faith" (*mu'min*), that blessed one who, by divine grace, recognizes the situation as it is and loyally commits himself to acting accordingly; and the "associator" (*mushrik*), who distorts the situation by elevating, in his fond imagination or perverted behaviour, to the level where only God the Creator sits, some of God's creatures, treating *them* as if they too were divine.

In much the same fashion the so-called "creed" of the Muslims is not a creed at all, if by creed one means an affirmation of belief. It is, rather, explicitly a "bearing witness" (*shahadah*). The Muslim does *not* say, I believe that there is no god but God, and I believe that Muhammad is the apostle of God. Rather, he asserts: "I bear witness to" these facts. His regarding them as facts, not theories, as realities in the universe not beliefs in his mind, is, as we have elsewhere urged[23], of quite basic significance. The witness formula affirms that he is relating himself in a certain way—of recognition, obedience, service—to a situation that already, and independently, and objectively, exists. He is corroborating it, not postulating it. Monotheism, for him, is the status quo, cosmically. In the formula it is not in process of being believed but is assumed, is presupposed, and is in process only of being proclaimed.

The concept of witnessing in Islamic life is a profound one. It, indeed, is a major category. It is a religious category worthy of the name.

Further, the personal pronouncing of the witness formula is a public announcement whereby one aligns oneself with this truth not only inwardly and individually but in corporate fashion, overtly joining the community of those actively oriented to the implementation of its implications. One therein publicly assumes the privileges and responsibilities of belonging to the organized group of those dedicated (*muslimun*) to living in terms of this cosmic purpose.

Now one may protest that this is all very well, but does it not presuppose that there is, indeed, a God, that He has indeed spoken, and all the rest? The answer is that this is precisely the point: these notions are not believed, they are presupposed. Belief in them is not commended, is not set forth, as a virtue; it is taken for granted—and is not even recognized as belief.

We come here close to the crux of our inquiry. It is decisive for us to apprehend the relation between belief and presupposition, if we are to go on to seize the relation between faith and belief.

The matter is clarified by noting, as one must, and indeed by insisting, that the system of ideas is presupposed equally in *both* the "yes" *and* the "no" cases. The concepts not only of faith but of infidelity (*ḳufr* as well as *iman*) both presuppose the whole outlook. The one does not imply belief, the other lack of it. Rather, both equally imply a preceding conceptual framework within which the one designates active acceptance, the other, active rejection. (That rejection is not of the framework, but of something conceived also within it.)

We have already seen, similarly, that the concept translated "polytheism" presupposes monotheism.

The difference between believing something, and presupposing something, is crucial. The concept "belief" does not occur in the Qur'an: and it would be self-contradictory to ask that what is presupposed should be explicated.

Perhaps the following illustration will seem too homely; yet I trust, not too irreverent. The case of a Muslim may perhaps be compared, on a radically lower plane, to a driver looking for a parking place and confronted with a "No Parking" sign. In such a situation, there are various possible reactions. He may, for instance, on the one hand, simply obey the sign and go off to look elsewhere. Or, he may park anyway, thinking "Oh, well, the police are not very vigilant in these parts, and I will try my luck—maybe I will get away with it". Or, he may feel that, even if caught, he can trust the lenience or friendly indulgence of the authorities. Or, he may think that it is worth paying the fine, even if it does eventuate, so urgently does he wish to park. Or, he may simply lack the self-discipline to submit to regulations, though he have some sort of haunting sense that he ought to do so. On the other side of the matter, if he does obey the regulation, he may do so out of fear of punishment, or out of respect for the law, out of a sense of good citizenship, or whatever. Now all these reactions, whether positive or negative, all presuppose his acceptance of the validity of the sign. A new situation arises when some skeptic comes along and suggests that the sign is in fact not authentic, that it has been put up not by the police, but by some pranksters who are simply making mock of strangers.

A quite new dimension is introduced into the whole situation if our driver is now asked, or asks himself, whether he *believes* the sign. Previously he took it for granted that it was authoritative; the only problem was whether or not he should obey it. Former questions about his character, about his relation to the law, to the community, to his own self-discipline, about his being able or willing to afford a fine, and the like —all these become transformed once one makes possible for him, and especially once one makes necessary or central for him, the new question of whether he *believes* it. On the tacit assumption that the "No Parking" sign was authoritative, a whole spectrum of possible actions was involved, a whole series of questions, a whole range of significance.

Thus far we have envisaged the matter primarily in individual terms; but it is important also to recognize that, if an entire community makes that same tacit assumption, then in terms of it a whole community life becomes possible—with a full gamut of loyalty and disobedience, cohesion and dissent.

Once the prior assumption is called into question, however, the matter assumes a drastically new aspect. The issue of its authenticity raises an utterly new series of questions, and shifts the range of significance—for both the individual and the community—to quite new, quite different, ground.

We are not yet saying that whether he believes the sign's authenticity is an illegitimate question: we are merely saying that it is a different question.

All the above is illumined if we turn to the other Qur'an concept that has been translated in modern times into modern English as "believe": namely, the Arabic word *zanna*. So far as the modern world is concerned, this is pretty much what this term has, indeed, come to signify. It means to think something, to form in the imagination an idea or opinion or assessment, to adjudge, to conceive. And for immediate day-to-day matters, it leaves fairly well open the question of the validity or correctness of the conception: or is used in cases both good and bad. It occurs here and there in the Qur'an in this relatively neutral sense. It occurs also, however, and more often, in another sense, functioning more closely as a specifically religious category, and here it takes on a different and rather special meaning.

This root occurs in various forms seventy times in the Qur'an. Thus it is reasonably common—although the verbs signifying to have faith or to make the act of faith (*amana*), and to know (*'alima*), each occur more than ten times as often. We must not overstate our case: among the seventy occurrences of *zanna*, perhaps as many as twenty, certainly some fifteen, have various other connotations than the one to which we here draw attention. These include half-a-dozen or so where the usage implies a pondering, reflecting upon, entertaining in the mind, even occasionally of religious realities (falling into The Fire; the Resurrection; the encounter with the Lord), as well as a few that are ambiguous, and some casually neutral, plus three or four where the judgement being reported is clearly seen as correct[24].

In the great majority of cases, however, some forty-nine or fifty (roughly seventy percent) the term is used for persons' having an opinion about God or His doings, but one that is woefully and manifestly awry. It designates in these instances a religious belief, no doubt, but a belief of a particular kind: namely, a wrong one. Far from being neutral as to the validity of the position held, the term is used in contexts where the idea is to convey the absurdity or perversity of that view. It is the full, clear opposite of "knowledge", and designates human whimsy and foolish fancy—in a clear polarity not unlike the dichotomy that a thinker such as Calvin later sets up between God's revelation, on the one hand, and the arrant absurdities of human imagination on the other[25]. If this be religious belief, it is yet radically different from faith. Indeed, between what is designated by this concept of conjuring up fond fancies (*zanna*) and that of responding positively to God's clear summons (*amana*, faith), the contrast is stark.

We may put it more bluntly. The divergence here between belief in this sense and faith in the true sense is the difference between Hell and Heaven.

Yet the antithesis is not usually direct, or explicit. It comes out, rather, in the differing relation of each to knowledge. Faith in the Qur'an is closely correlated with knowledge: the two refer to the same matters, so that one accepts that which one knows[26]. Fanciful belief, *zanna*, on the other hand, so far as this religious level is concerned, comes into sharp collision with it. The connotations of *zanna* as a religious category are fixed in terms of its clear opposition to knowledge.

Both relationships, it may be remarked in passing, are reminiscent of and also divergent from the classical Western distinction (between Greek *doxa* and *gnosis*, or *episteme*) in which opinion is intermediary between ignorance and knowledge, if not a first step on the path to eventual knowledge[27]. In the Qur'an case, rather, knowledge comes first, and is central, being given by God; faith is the positive response to it, *zanna* is the pitiful and puny alternative to it.

In the Qur'an, then, in these half-a-hundred usages the ideas of *zanna* are roundly derided[28]. In most instances, the reference is to man's *zann* as wicked or pitiable or ridiculous—and in any case, wrong. The term is used to characterize with disdain the opinions of men that lead them astray.

This particular term, then, does not normally mean simply to believe, but to believe wrongly. Insofar as the word for the act of faith (*iman*) means "to believe" at all, it means, even those who would like to press that interpretation would have to admit, to believe rightly—to recognize. Yet even this is inadequate, as is made clear, and our general thesis further illumined, if we consider once again that matter of *jinn*, that class of spirits or genii whose activities, in the Islamic world-view, at times impinge on the affairs of human beings. Outsiders say that Muslims "believe" in them; Muslims—since they are set forth in the Qur'an—that they do and should recognize them. Yet it would not do to use here the verb *amana*. For it would be patently wrong for Muslims to give their allegiance to those *jinn*, rather than to God. Nor did the culture give its loyalty to them, put its faith in them[29].

Neither, however, could the verb *zanna* be used. If *amana* is too positive, this is too negative. It would not merely imply, but specify, that the notion was a mere human conjecture. And there is no neutral term. The fact is that the modern proposition that Muslims have believed in *jinn*, have believed that there are *jinn*, is not capable of being rendered in Qur'anic Arabic. The reason is simple: that this concept of believing is part of another, skeptical, way of looking at the world. It does not—cannot—occur in the Qur'an.

(Similarly, one cannot say in New Testament Greek that Jesus believed in devils—though the fact that in the New Testament he speaks freely about them leads a modern reader to hold that he did.)

All this is because, of course, implicit in the Qur'an, and also explicit in it, is the view that the truth is given, is clear[30], is known. If the truth is known, then men's and women's beliefs may be categorized in terms of it—whereas this is precisely, as we have seen, what the modern Western concept of believing explicitly does *not* mean. On the contrary, modern "believing" as a concept inherently implies, or even postulates, that truth, in the religious field, is not known.

The difference here is that modern "believing" is an anthropocentric concept, while the Qur'anic world-view is theocentric. It is theocentric not only as a whole, but in all its parts: the concepts with which it operates are concepts whose meaning, implication, and presupposition are saturatedly theocentric. And of course, once one reflects upon it, one realizes that this is all very natural. We said above that the whole vision was so vivid to Muhammad, and it became so vivid to his community, and presently it was so foundational for their corporate life and the civilization that they erected, that in a sense one might almost say that it never occurred to him or them that men and women would not believe it, unless somehow their hearts had been hardened and their capacities sealed by God Himself. At least, the question that it might or might not be true was hardly an intellectual issue for them. Their problem, rather, was how to orient themselves within it.

Yet even to speak of Muhammad here, or of the community, is to betray one's own anthropocentric skepticism. It is the way of speaking of the outsider who thinks of the Qur'an in relation to Muhammad, or to the Muslims. Within its own terms, however, and as it is read by Muslims, the Qur'an is the word not of Muhammad but of God. It is not their scripture, but His. And since it is God who is speaking, after all He knows what is true and what is false. It is entirely logical, and indeed natural, entirely legitimate and indeed inescapable, that when God is speaking, men's opinions are assessed and interpreted in the light of His truth. Since God knows what is right and what is wrong, the terms in which He addresses mankind leave no room for our human epistemological bewilderments. It was partly in order to salvage us from these that, in this presentation, He mercifully came to our rescue. Within this system, accordingly, what becomes significant is not men's opinions (that issue having been disposed of), but the quality of their lives.

The Qur'an view is theocentric, then, in sharp contrast to the anthropocentrism of the modern Western view. "Believing" as a religious category has become an anthropocentric concept. Small wonder, then, that it characterizes our modern age; but small wonder also that, once subordinated to it, faith seems to become problematic, and feeble.

To believe is not only different from faith; one might almost ask whether the two are not in some measure alternatives. One might find oneself toying with an aphorism that if faith, classically, presupposed belief, then belief, modernly, presupposes skepticism.

Certainly presuppositions are important. This, at least, the Qur'an may teach us; as indeed, may the whole cultural history of our race. The history of religion is ultimately the history of faith. Insofar as the intellectual or conceptual dimension is concerned, the history of religion is the history of presuppositions as much as it is of the ideas that men and women have explicitly held. It is only in terms of presuppositions that overt ideas reveal their import—or indeed, have their meaning, or have any meaning.

Accordingly, the history of religion, conceptually, is primarily the history of presuppositions—but as background for what has been going on, religiously, and not to be confounded with this latter. The task of the historian of religion is to ferret out those presuppositions, for other peoples and times, in order then to understand the foreground of their lives. (And concomitantly, then, for ourselves, as we shall presently consider.)

It is no small achievement to generate a world-view, a comprehensive ideational system, one that gives order to man's perception of the universe and within which man's destiny may be discerned and discussed. Nonetheless it is that destiny, and not that world-view, that is and always has been crucial. Historically, the Islamic Weltanschauung was an enormous accomplishment; and by the civilization built and sustained in terms of it it would be obtuse not to be impressed. Personally, on the other hand, the fundamental questions were, and are, more searching than that, more ultimate. What Muslims believed enabled those questions to be asked; but asking them in that particular articulation did not constitute their answer, did not constitute an answer. This, like the civilization itself in substance if not in form, was rather a matter of faith, that inexpressible transcendent human quality to which they gave expression, empirically in art, in ritual, in a patterned moral code, and also in ideas, all of which were formulated in terms of their comprehensive order.

In modern times the outsider may view that order as postulated, and may admire or reject it as a vast imaginative construct; but we should remember that those within were hardly conscious of believing anything[31]. This is the way that they perceived the world, and all within it: virtue, vice, a sunrise, leaves fluttering on a tree, human destiny, truth. In these terms they set forth all their perceptions and conceptions.

Two people need not converge on what actually in any given case is true or false, to agree very closely in their definition of what lying is—for instance, as the deliberate telling of falsehood with an intent to deceive. Similarly the rest of the world may have other world-views and another sense of how to express in finite terms what is finally true, and yet find not merely interesting but instructive, even quite congenial, Islamic expositions of what faith is, as these were formulated subsequently in the light of the Qur'an, following upon the construction of a social, cultural, and intellectual order built upon it.

Faith, in Islamic theology[32], was set forth as first a personal relationship to truth[33] (*tasdiq*[34]): a recognizing of it, appropriating it to one's self, and resolving to live in accord with it. Some would add as further interpretation the "verifying" of it in the sense of discovering for oneself by living it out that it is indeed true, that it becomes true in practice. The truth being in this vision primarily or largely moral, "faith" thus becomes a name for a recognition of goodness, and the recognition in theory and practice, the acknowledgement, that its injunctions apply to oneself: that *x* is right not only abstractly but right for, obligatory upon, *me*. In this connection, too, faith is making what is right and true in principle come true in practice—or at least the commitment to doing so. The mystics went on to add: the discovery in practice that truth and goodness converge, ultimately even that one's person converges with them/it/Him.

Faith was defined by the theologians, then (with the words *tasdiq bi-l-qalb*) as an appropriating to oneself inwardly of objectively valid truth, which one intellectually recognizes. Most added to the definition also an overt acknowledging of this (*taqrir bi-l-lisan*), as a public act. Whether a third element, works—the carrying out in practice of what one inwardly has undertaken to implement—is a part of faith, or rather a concomitant of it, was debated. By all, faith was interpreted as self-engagement with truth. It includes not only that interiorizing act of the heart whereby one's person finds inner integrity (mind and heart and bodily actions[35] converging to obviate hypocrisy [*nifaq*]), and outward realism (a living in accord with objective reality [*al-haqq*]). Faith includes also, and is defined in terms of, that transition from the individual to the social, whereby one transcends the loneness of one's private self, however loftily ordered, to be received into a group, in dynamic solidarity. Faith is that movement (the word is basically a verb, and even the noun is a verbal noun) of the person whereby one transcends the duplicity of a divided (*munafiq*) self, the atomism of an isolated self, and the confusion of a whimsied self of impulses and unrealism (*ahwa'*, *batil*), to participate in a community (*ummah*) that in turn participates in, is engaged in the movement towards and in accord with, the final truth and goodness of reality[36].

Infidelity is deliberate and self-destructive refusal (*kufr*) to participate in these manifest (*mubin*)[37] goods; it is the lie in the soul (*takdhib*) that says "no" to the truth and goodness that one knows.

Once one has understood the community's conceptual system—which participants were not conscious of "believing"—one may fairly readily realize both that the delineation within it of faith was indeed perceptive, even persuasive, and that the interest in belief was indeed minimal. Yet there was one area in which even in classical times a problem could and did arise, potentially serious. It involved primarily outsiders only, and one's relation to them.

A systematic ideological framework, as something not *at* which one looked, but *through* which one looked, at the world and at life, could serve well—in the Islamic and in other such instances—for ordering one's affairs, personal and social. Great cultures and empires could be and were constructed in terms of it. In terms of it the basic human questions, including, as we have urged, the fundamental religious question of faith and unfaith, could be and were intelligently interpreted and handled. Not so manageable, however, were those same fundamental questions as they involved outsiders, non-members of the system. Those within were well aware that faith was not automatic, within. They never made the mistake of identifying faith with acceptance of the conceptual system[38]. Yet some were tempted to imagine[39] that faith was non-existent without; and they then confused non-acceptance of the system (non-"belief") with non-acceptance within the system, lack of faith: thinking the former to be non-truth, non-loyalty, non-integrity, and the rest.

It is the thesis of this book that faith has been found on earth in many forms; but interpretations, intellectualizations, of faith-in-many-forms have been less widely available. Just as many Christians and other outsiders have failed to recognize and to appreciate the faith of Muslims, articulated as it has been within their Islamic theocentric system (or that of Buddhists, within their atheistic one), so those Christians and Buddhists and other outsiders have historically at times failed to have their own faith recognized and appreciated by a certain type of Muslim theorist[40].

Belief is not faith, it has been classically recognized and affirmed; but that non-belief is not unfaith has been a rare insight.

(Still more rarely has it been systematically intellectualized. The Islamic belief-system made possible a conceptualization of faith in its Islamic forms; also, as we have seen, of man's capacity for faithlessness, in Islamic forms. Except in its Sufi modes, it was markedly less successful in making possible a conceptualization of other forms of faith and unfaith.)

This issue, however, though important (indeed to the point of, at times, war, and certainly of alienation and much sorrow), has in the past tended to be literally somewhat peripheral. In modern times it has become more central as diversity becomes more diffused, with cultures living no longer even partially to themselves. The problem of interreligious understanding in our day is acute. Yet the primary question remains, as ever, that of self-understanding. The classical Islamic position has helped us, perhaps, as we move on to wrestle with faith in a modern form, and specifically as we continue our inquiry into the question of faith and belief.

Classical Islamic culture has moved historically to give way to a situation where its presuppositions can now be seen as such; and a clarifying awareness of that may help towards an understanding of both the faith and the beliefs of those who once lived in terms of them. More: it may help towards an understanding of one's own. The presuppositions of modern Western thought are equally far from absolute, but are mostly not yet articulate, not yet examined. Few who live in terms of them have moved to a point, although certainly it will in due course come, when a clarified awareness here can prove equally available, and one may hope, equally helpful[41].

For our modern task inescapably includes a major problem in relation to presuppositions, both our own and those inherited from an earlier age that are no longer ours. It will not be easy to attain sophistication in the matter of the relationship, whether direct or indirect, of presuppositions to truth. At least we can derive some help in this by reflecting on those of others, and on the processes through which in the modern world they (and we) have been going.

We spoke earlier of a contrast between modern ideas of belief and classical Islamic religious ideas. We may now move beyond that simple antithesis, by observing something of the dynamics by which the one situation has become transmuted into the other. There is a discernible movement (to be examined also in later chapters) by which presuppositions ceased to be that. What had been taken for granted was no longer granted, and its ability to be taken came into question.

One way of putting this is to say that the presuppositions, which had been unconscious, were raised to the level of consciousness. Another metaphor would be horizontal rather than vertical: what had been background to one's viewing of the world was objectivized, was moved around to the front and away from oneself to a distance and looked at as an object. Or again: what had formed the basis for the superstructure on which in each case our particular drama was mounted, was itself brought on stage for critical intellectual scrutiny—and could no longer serve as presuppositional base on which faith, and the whole pattern of religious and indeed social life, could move.

When these things happened, we unwittingly shifted our categories. (And that "unwittingly" is crucial.) We diverted our attention from the meaningful question of faith (the question of what one does, given the ideational symbol system) to the modern question of belief (which has become the question of whether to have that particular symbol system or not).

As the presuppositions of each system, one's own and others, moved in recent times into critical self-consciousness, there was a time when belief and faith seemed synonymous. This meant that many ostensibly religious men urged that it was important to say "yes" to the belief question; and many critically thinking men, that it was important to say "no" to the faith question. The confusing of the two has bedevilled modern culture—substantially before, but conspicuously since the moment when even religious persons have been finding that when it comes down to it they perhaps do not, in fact, believe the erstwhile presuppositions. Our presuppositions are no longer those of our forefathers. Fortunately, however (even if it prove painful), a synonymity can no longer be maintained.

In the new situation, some might wish to suggest that a sophisticated modern position would be to recognize the presuppositions as, classically, presuppositions, now seen to have been obtaining on earth in a variety of forms, and to recognize, modernly, the ideational systems as symbol systems—with the significant question having always been, as it is still to-day, what one does within the ideational symbol system of one's choice, or birth; what response one makes in terms of it.

It has always been significant, what system one chose; and will continue to be. Yet the central religious question has always been not that, but another. The final religious category, as the Qur'an well illustrates, is the category of faith, of response.

This much is clear: that the significant question for to-day, or at least for to-morrow, has become new. Not, for others, what do men and women believe; but rather, with what system of ideas and symbols do they choose to operate; and given it, what does each do within it, and all, corporately, through it. (Is the system one that enables the great questions to be posed, is there an inheritance of grandeur of interpretation on which to draw, does it recognize a truth beyond its own system? Do they take advantage of its strengths, criticize its weaknesses, and how do they answer its questions?) And for oneself, some might wish to speculate: not what do we, or shall we, believe; but rather, with what symbol system shall we operate; and now that we self-consciously know it to be that, so that we cannot naively either presuppose it or believe it, what does it mean to have faith in terms of a system of ideas and symbols that *qua* system is anthropogenetic, although the life lived in terms of it may be, as it was designed that it should be, theocentric. The ideas and the symbols, we now know, are all human; but what they symbolize, we may still find, is (to use, in speaking, a man-made term) divine.

Before we either settle for such a position, however, or, wrestling with its problems, aspire to a better one, we must move on to look also at Hindu and at Christian visions.

Chapter 4

A HINDU CONTRIBUTION

To THE new notion of faith that the modern world is to forge for itself, obviously India must contribute. The experience of India over the millennia, and the analytic reflection of India, have been too rich and too deep for it to be otherwise.

The new notion must, as we have said, be helpful in interpreting not merely the particular religious involvements of one's own community, in relation to the particular forms that it may have inherited and that one may oneself have accepted, or rejected, or thought to modify. The notion must be helpful in interpreting man: interpreting us in our historical variety of orientations to the world, and in our capacity to find and to fail to find in and through them self-fulfilment, transcendence, and harmony with our fellows, or to be found by these, or to delude ourselves about them. The new notion must be global enough to do justice to the multitude of diverse forms through which faith has kept appearing among humankind. This means, comprehensive enough to cope with communal variety from place to place, dynamic enough for the continuous changes from century to century, large enough to make room for personal diversity from saint to sinner, peasant to intellectual, aesthete to activist.

All this is apart from the fact that, in addition, the new understanding must also be related to what else is nowadays known, through science and analytic awareness, about the world and about ourselves within it. Our modern idea of faith must be consonant with our modern understanding of ideas in general[1].

On the former score, of human comprehensiveness, India's significance is unique. Its ability to contribute to our new understanding derives not only from Hindu experience, and interpretation of experience, in general, impressive though both these be and highly instructive. It derives also and specifically from the complexity of India's religious life and the fact that that complexity has been overt and accepted, and has been worked into interpretive theorizing. "Hinduism is to India what Comparative Religion is to the world"[2].

Specifically, more than most lands India has recognized that life is lived religiously by different persons or groups in a variety of differing forms. More than most lands it has felt that no one of these is exclusively deserving of respect, from either men or gods: that many forms are valid.

Moreover, *à propos* of our special interests here, it has explicitly noted that among these forms some but not all are intellectual, or predominantly so—and has explicitly reflected on this point. In all valid forms, on the other hand, whether intellectual or not and whatever their variety, it has observed that faith is involved.

We cannot here develop a systematic study of Hindu conceptions of faith. That is a larger task; fascinating, but for some future inquiry[3]. Indian considerations, however, are relevant and helpful even in the quite preliminary matter with which our present study is concerned, of discriminating between faith and belief; and therewith also in discerning in what direction faith is most promisingly to be looked for.

It would be possible, one may suppose, to approach the panorama of Hindu religious material with some such modern-Western question in mind as: What is the role of believing in this complex of positions? In India, how has belief been envisaged as a religious activity? Has believing been a religious category for Hindus? One would presently discover, however, that such a question is over-simplified, or inappropriate. A whole series of prior discriminations is in order, whose effect is finally to discredit this orientation.

If we begin with the current Western notion of "believing" as a neutral concept designating the holding of an opinion ("believing that . . . "), we may observe that of course Sanskrit has terms for this common human activity[4] but may note that this notion seems to play only a quite minor part in Hindu religious consideration. The terms are not usually pejorative[5], like the Qur'an term *zanna*, yet are casual, are relatively feeble. The anthropogenetic forming of opinions, at this level, seems to have interested Hindu writers but little. It has not been regarded as carrying much religious significance.

No doubt, notions of intellectual apprehension, of the mind's awareness, as among the avenues that lead man to salvation or to reality, have been highly important for Hindus, to put it mildly. To see the universe as it truly is, many have insisted, is a central, even a saving, virtue. Questions other than believing, however, are here at stake. One might speak rather of knowing. Yet even this is gross. With this facet of religious life, even beyond the level of "believing", there come into play at least two distinct levels of human knowledge or awareness. As the higher, there is the supreme knowledge (designated usually by the word *jnana*)[6]. This is not a "knowing that . . . ", but an immediate knowing of: a direct knowledge of Reality with a large capital R, a transcendental knowledge of ultimate truth (Brahman). Such knowledge should not be said to lead to salvation so much as to constitute salvation. It not merely transcends but negates the lower truths of discursive reasoning and propositional knowledge. In this monist, ecstatic knowing, knower and known are fused (rather, are no longer falsely separated)[7], to say nothing of there being left far behind the subject-predicate analysis of our piecemeal objective knowledge of disparate parts of the workaday world.

This supreme kind of "knowledge" is a far cry from "belief", and perhaps no one has ever thought of translating it so.

Secondly, below this supreme knowledge are other lesser kinds of human awareness which we may perhaps still call knowledge although in a different, less exalted sense. At issue here is quite another order of human engagement. The object of this lesser knowledge may be a truth that can be formulated in a proposition, although it is the truth rather than the proposition that one significantly knows. Here we have in mind what is expressed by quite an array of verbs used in the literature, the meanings of which diverge among themselves significantly but which may for our present purposes be grouped together here, since they have this in common: that a foreigner, not himself subscribing to the positions being reported, may be tempted to translate them all as affirming that Hindus "believe" this or that. And indeed such a translation can seem on the surface to make good sense, since the texts are themselves evidence that the Hindus concerned do in fact so believe. Yet more subtly considered this turns out to be a mistranslation, since the verbs used imply the validity of what is being reported, which "believe" precisely does not. The usual terms found in crucial passages are more exactly "to apprehend", "to perceive", "to recognize", and the like—especially as used in the relevant contexts. These are words and phrases that presuppose for those who use them the validity of what is being portrayed[8].

As we saw in the Qur'an instance, there is substantial difference between our conceptualizing of a person's awareness of what actually is the case, and our conceptualizing of someone's imagining that something is or may be the case. "He recognizes that A is B" expresses a different notion from "He believes that A is B". This is so, even if the two states of mind being reported in the two cases seem subjectively to resemble each other (and even if an outside observer who does not himself perceive B, and especially a post-Kantian Westerner, feels incompetent to distinguish the two stances). When a Hindu writes about one's perceiving or recognizing or apprehending something, we have misunderstood his thought if we translate him as speaking of one's believing something[9].

What from the skeptic's point of view is belief ("Hindu" belief, if the skeptic be also an outsider), from a Hindu point of view is insight. And Hindu writings convey as much. It would take us much too far afield here to develop, certainly to substantiate, a thesis that believing has not been a religious category of significance in India. Such evidence as has come to hand in the course of my exploring the separate notion of faith, has suggested this, but here I leave it at hardly more than that. Certainly a concept of belief has not dominated, has not even been salient, in Hindu thought[10].

Neither has a concept of disbelief; but this is for somewhat different, or at least additional, reasons. No one doctrine or system of doctrines being "orthodox", or even standard, a generalized conception of "disbelieving" hardly arises. Some persons have perceived the world differently from others, admittedly. In that situation, however, the general tendency has been to ask how one perceives truth, or how much, rather than whether. A negative position then is not so naturally generated. It has hardly been clear in India what an unbeliever would not believe[11].

Most of the conceptual terms in this realm, then, are, unlike the modern Western notion of believing, positive rather than neutral, and unlike that of disbelieving, fractional rather than negative.

This is not unrelated to the point that India on the whole has been critical rather than skeptical. It has scrutinized relentlessly, questioned boldly, analysed meticulously, debated trenchantly; yet there has been a general predisposition in favour of the validity of religious positions, in all their variety, a certain tendency to hold that each position, especially if maintained by an intelligent person of disciplined sincerity, is to be presumed to be valid until it has been shown otherwise, rather than *vice versa*[12].

Such sympathy has tended to be productive of insight into the nature or quality of an unusually wide range of diverse types of religious life.

Before leaving this sector of our inquiry and moving on to a consideration rather of faith, we must note as a somewhat transitional matter a significant pair of concepts that has seemed to have to do with belief, or with faith, or both. This is the pair *astikya/nastikya.*

The Sanskrit word *asti* (Greek *esti*, Latin and French *est*, German *ist*, etc.) means "is" or "it is" or "there is". A contrasting counterpart arises when the negative *na-* is compounded with this, to give *nasti* (French *n'est, Latin n[on] est,* etc.): "it is not". The terms *astika* and *nastika* were developed from these as adjectives and adjectival nouns to characterize persons or orientations that took respectively a positive or a negative attitude religiously ("is-y", "isn't-y", would be comparable forms; or *ist-ig, nicht-ist-ig*; etc.). Substantially, though not formally, one might think of "yes-men" and "no-men" respectively. "Believer" and "non-believer" have naturally suggested themselves as corresponding Western concepts, and it is evident that the analogy is pertinent, even though as we shall see it is not close. The abstract terms *astikya* and *nastikya*, designating affirmation and negation respectively, became religious technical terms. Some Westerners have been tempted to translate *nastikya* as "atheism", which is perhaps understandable although wrong. More plausible and less obviously inadequate has been a rendering of the positive term by "belief" or "faith".

Some sort of sociological motivation might perhaps be urged for an apparent functional equivalence, as it were, between "atheist" and *nastika*, since the *nastika* person has been looked upon in Indian society in somewhat the same way as was an atheist classically in Western society: as the renegade who stood out against the central traditions and primary values of the culture. It might be understood as specifying the one who repudiates. Yet it is unquestionably inaccurate to call him an atheist, for what he repudiates is not a belief in the gods. India has not only known devout atheists but has accepted them, and has explicitly enumerated atheistic religious positions as within the Hindu complex, even integrally so; they are among the "orthodox" alternatives proffered. And in general the *astika/nastika* division is hardly in terms of what one believes[13]. The Mimamsa school, for example, hears the Vedic Word as fully authoritative (this is sometimes proffered as the decisive criterion for *astikya*: we shall return to this) but apprehends it as an imperative, not an indicative; as communicating not propositional truth, not a state of affairs, but an injunction to be obeyed. The authority, therefore, is moral, ritual, practical, rather than doctrinal. Belief, if not quite optional, is mundane, and radically subordinate to practical obedience[14]. The Samkhya school, on the other hand, while it takes ontology with high seriousness, and is equally in "the establishment", has, as is well known, a carefully-wrought atheistic position conceptually[15].

A Muslim, on the other hand, is outside the pale for Hindus, is *nastika*, despite his intense theism, because he is not reverential to the Hindu heritage, not subservient to it. Here we begin to see the crux of the *astikya/nastikya* polarity. It is not what a man believes, nor what he practices, that makes him a Hindu or an outsider. Rather, it is his attitude to the inherited tradition. *Astika*, indeed, might almost be translated "Hindu", for which concept otherwise neither Sanskrit nor, until recently, the Indian vernaculars have had a term[16].

Moreover, it is well known that the Hindu complex is indeed complex, is variegated inherently and on set principle; variety not merely exists and not merely is accepted but is postulated. Human religious life not only is, but rightly is, diverse[17]. Inapplicable in this Hindu complex is the Christian term "orthodox" (which has been proposed by some to render *astika*), positing as it does ideally an ideological norm; and similarly inapplicable is "orthoprax", coined for, for instance, Muslims and Jews, with its positing of ideally a given moral or practical or procedural norm. The Hindu locates the criterion of whether a person is or is not within the system not in any ideal norm, but in personal attitude. (One may wonder whether in the realm of our concerns, the most significant and in the end most contributory characteristic of the Hindu may not turn out to be this personalizing of the decisive locus of religious life.)

It is an attitude, in the first instance or overtly, to a cumulative and undefined tradition[18]. What one ought to make of the tradition is not priorly given. (It is recognized that different men and women have made differing things of it, of this or that part of it.) What a person makes of it is up to him or her. Decisive, however, is whether that person feels that it is worth making something of, is worth becoming involved with.

Explicitly left undefined is what it is that one will find through the religious life, what is the significance, either potential or actual, of the tradition. This, each must discover for himself. *Astikya* is a person's decision or hunch that there *is* significance, that there is something there to be found, worth finding. To be a Hindu is to say "yes" to the cogency of the community's corporate and personal heritage.

At stake here is the subtle and elusive question of authority: the human capacity to look upon something as authoritative. *Astikya* and *nastikya* name a person's acceptance and rejection of . . . of what? An answer often given is: "of the authority of the *Veda*(s)". Yet that word means "knowledge"; and it refers not as an outsider might innocently suppose to certain books bearing that name[19], but rather, if one thinks in terms of books at all, then to their content, to what those books say. More exactly, to what they truly say. It refers, if one will, to truth. An *astika* is one who says "yes" to what is known.

A foreigner might go so far as to qualify this—to specify it—as: what is known in India.

Astikya is the positive response to the spiritual tradition, is the "yes"-attitude to the significance of the religious life. The *astika* agrees that there is, the *nastika* contends that there is not, validity in this religious venture; that there is, or is not, a reality, as the sages have reported, beyond appearances, a truth more ultimate than the immediate, gross, and mundane[20].

We said above that, overtly, and as a first approximation, the attitude at issue is to the Hindu tradition. More carefully, and trenchantly, we may now say that it is an attitude rather to that to which the tradition testifies, or has been testifying. For those for whom there is a transcendent quality to the universe and to man (and it is by such persons that the term has been used), *astikya* is the recognition of that quality. It is the awareness of transcendence.

Clearly we are here approaching matters of faith, and also of belief, especially if by belief one means rather presuppositions or intellectual framework than formulated doctrines. Indeed certain important Hindu writers have explicitly affirmed that faith (*sraddha*, the term to which we will turn in a moment, for more careful investigation) is *astikya-buddhi*: the orientation, one might say, of yes-ness.

This interpretation is found especially in the most rationalistic or intellectualist of the classical Hindu schools, that of Vedanta, although it is not their only rendering, as we shall see. It also then appears occasionally in Vedic exegesis, being offered a few times by the major commentator, Sayana[21]. We may take as illustrative of this position the great Sankara. This powerful mediaeval thinker regularly in his commentaries when he meets the above term for faith sets it forth as *astikya-buddhi*[22]. Let us consider for a moment, then, what is being asserted in this equation.

Astikya, as we have seen, is the affirmative religious attitude, the positive rather than negative stance on moral and spiritual matters, the "yes" response to the meaning of the cultural tradition of India. *Buddhi*, the second term of this compound, has lent itself, however inadequately, to being associated by certain modern exponents with believing, since it has to do with the mind[23]: with intelligence, understanding, reason. Less reifyingly, *buddhi* is awareness, perception, discernment. It comes closer, consequently, to knowing than to neutral believing, since it designates apprehension by the mind, not fabrication by the fancy. The root meaning of the word is "to be awake": accordingly, to be conscious, to appreciate what is going on, to be alert to one's environment. (The most illustrious form of this root is one that has imposed itself also in languages outside India: its past participle, *buddha*, he who is awake. The Buddha is "the enlightened one", the man who has waked up to the realities of the universe while the rest of us were sleeping.)

Astikya-buddhi, then, is awakeness to transcendence.

To hold that faith is this is to aver that faith is the apperception that there is indeed something in what saints and seers have been saying over the ages: the recognition[24] that yes, the transcendent dimension of the world and of our lives is indeed there.

In a more homely way, one might suggest that this term is characterizing faith as *the ability to see the point* of a religious tradition.

(i) Sraddha

Let us turn, then, to the subject rather than the predicate of this avowal: the concept for faith itself, *sraddha*. The remainder of our discussion will endeavour to elucidate this notion. That faith is *astikya-buddhi*, awakeness to transcendence, is but one among many things that Hindus have had to say about it. And apart from the several characterizations that they have proffered, several of which will, as we shall see, prove helpful to us and illuminating, there are further the more numerous occasions on which it has not been explained but been taken as self-evident. This fact is in itself significant; and such occasions are potentially serviceable if we can sensitively discern contexts and implications. What men and women have taken without explication is, as always, of prime importance.

For, apart from all questions of understanding, awareness, knowledge, and indeed prior to all questions whatsoever as to a particular form or content or goal or method of the religious life, Hindus have rather consistently spoken in terms of another element in man's involvement: a prior element, decisive, underlying all else. This is *sraddha*; this is faith[25].

Traditionally, no Hindu seems ever to have devoted a treatise specifically to this[26]—although there is a hymn to *sraddha* in the Rg-Veda[27]. Yet the word is extremely widespread in virtually all subsequent Indian religious literature. There is no question but that *sraddha* has been seen as important, in every phase of Hindu life, even as crucial, and often as explicitly the starting point. Yet it has also seemed obvious, more or less to be taken for granted[28].

In the overwhelming majority of cases the term *sraddha* has been consistently and naturally translated in modern times as "faith"[29]. Scrupulous and sensitive scholars, however, have from time to time expressed reservations about this rendering, on the grounds that the one term has not precisely meant in Sanskrit what the other has conveyed in modern Western life[30]. Both points, of course, are well taken. The concepts are similar, but have not been identical. As usual, both similarities and divergencies are instructive. The former in particular, it will presently appear, can prove significant especially for mankind's present-day concerns.

We will attempt here to elucidate the term's meaning in its own right, as authentically as is feasible, and then will call it an Indian concept of faith; suggesting that this is part, at least, of what Hindus have conceived faith to be, which may then be compared—fruitfully—with what others have discerned. We use the word "faith" for it on the grounds that although in the past, as one would expect, it has not covered in India quite the same range of notions as has "faith" in English, especially in the light of the recent uncertainties of this latter term (for one thing, *sraddha* is manifestly not "belief"), yet in the future its meaning will be tributary to what the term "faith" is now going to mean as, globally, we broaden and deepen (and sharpen) our corporate understanding in this realm. For those whose task is, as ours here, to understand faith as a general human quality, and not merely as it has until now been conceptualized in

Western or Christian thought, then the concept *sraddha* becomes not only pertinent but integral[31].

First, then, faith, *sraddha*, has been postulated as requisite by each of the major Hindu sects: Vaisnava, Saiva, Sakta[32]. Furthermore, it has been held as prerequisite in every one of the various ways of salvation: the way of knowledge, the way of works, the way of devotion, and the way of Yoga[33]. Historically, also, it has been regarded as foundational from the earliest times until the present. Indeed, it seems first of all to have been set forth as related to ritual performance of cult, and then to have been developed subsequently as a quality with which a person undertakes any or all of the whole range of forms of the religious life: the liturgical, but also the intellectual, the devotional, the mystical, or whatever. It classically almost constitutes the differentiating characteristic that qualifies any human activity as religious[34].

What does the term signify? In one sense, the answer is altogether simple and straightforward. It means, almost without equivocation, to set one's heart on. It is a compound of two words, *srad* (or *srat*), heart, and *dha*, to put[35]. Indeed, in the Rg-Veda the two parts usually occur separately[36], but even there they are occasionally combined[37], and later are regularly so[38]. The combination develops a use in secular writing, where it means to put one's heart on something mundane: to long for, to desire something, and also to put one's heart on a person in the sense of trusting him, regarding him as trustworthy, credible, or worthy of much respect[39].

It is primarily the religious usage that interests us, however, and that has in fact predominated in Sanskrit. *Sraddha* became, as we have said, an exceedingly widespread notion, used in all sorts of diverse religious contexts. That on which one puts or might put one's heart, in the gamut of India's complex religious life, has been varied. Yet the religious man has been characterized (might we not say, "of course"?) by the fact that he has put his heart on *something* within it. The term *sraddha* is open, in the sense that it does not itself specify or even suggest what it is on which one puts one's heart. The concept as a concept has no particular object, or type of object.

This has led some students to argue that *sraddha* in Indian thought has been lavishly complex. They then analyse its "many meanings" into a series of types, speaking of ritual *sraddha*, intellectual *sraddha*, moral *sraddha*, and so on, and elaborating each[40]. This betrays the strong modern-Western impulse to understand faith not as such but primarily or solely in terms of its "objects"[41]. One may, on the contrary (and, it would seem, more felicitously), infer from the very diversity of its many involvements rather the inherent simplicity of the concept itself. It does not designate a relationship to anything[42]. The relationships that men and women have to the many objects of religious concern are notoriously varied; this term indicates rather the attitude or initial act whereby they enter into one or another relation. *Sraddha* is not itself a bilateral concept, though it refers to what generates relationships. It has to do with man's capacity to become involved: the tendency or quality inherent within each human person to move outside him- or herself and to become engaged[43].

Indeed, the concept *sraddha*, one might argue, comes in some ways remarkably close to that of "involvement", as we have used this in our opening chapter above.

Hindu religious literature is largely an exploration of or comment on the various relationships that men have had or may have with transcendence; *sraddha* not being one of them, it has not been much investigated. Indian thinkers observed that man must do something, whether in initiative or response, for such relationships to obtain, and named that doing of something, *sraddha*; but they were interested in the relationships, and took somewhat for granted man's capacity to enter them. It is our modern world with its loss of faith that has become entranced with the question of the very first step in the religious life, which turns out not to be so easy to take as was once supposed.

Once it has been affirmed that *sraddha* means "placing one's heart on", there is in a sense nothing more to be said. Whatever the nuances and subtleties, the overtones and complications, the specifications of particular contexts and the diversities of various schools, it remains the case that this interpretation seems to fit every occurrence; to illuminate it; and to tie them all together[44]. The religious life, whatever its form, begins, India has said, with faith; and faith, in its turn, is one's finding within that life (one's being found by) something to which one gives one's heart. To what one should give one's heart, and what happens once one has given it in this or that direction, form the subject-matter of much of India's religious literature, and are not our concern here. But whatever the venture, and whatever the prize, the first step, whether in initiative or response, is a setting of one's heart.

This rendering of *sraddha* has the advantage of, as we have said, leaving unspecified the object of faith. (In this respect, it is in some ways like Tillich's "ultimate concern"[45].) It has the further considerable advantage of being, after all, a metaphor—one that happens to be serviceable as such also in English. Accordingly, although in a way no more need be said, yet at another level we may perhaps do well to explore the matter by amplifying a little what has been at issue.

The significance of the concept becomes clearest, perhaps, in various instances of negative usage. It was repeatedly averred in India that something done without faith is religiously worthless. Such a sentiment is paralleled, of course, in other religious communities throughout the world[46]. What is meant by this in the Hindu case, however, is nicely brought out by rendering: "one's heart is not in it". We may take as representative of numerous passages one resonant verse of the Bhagavad Gita, which asserts that any sacrificial oblation, any donation, that may be offered, any austerity that may be practised, any deed that may be performed, is regarded as vacuous *if one's heart is not in it*[47].

There is no point in going through a ritual mechanically. There is no merit in an ascetic or a moral deed done insincerely. There is no virtue in believing a doctrine, if one believes inertly, with one's mind only and not also with one's heart. The religious life, in whichever of its diverse forms or facets, fails from the start, indeed is not religious life at all, if a person takes it up but without putting his heart into what he is doing[48].

We shall return to the point that this truth pertains not to "religious" life only; it touches the truth of all human affairs. Man is excluded from the reality of whatever he may do, if his heart be not engaged.

More positively, various commentators emphasize the notion of focusing one's attention on, giving consideration to, taking an interest in, having respect for—and indeed doing so to a very marked degree[49]. To have faith is then to take something with extraordinary seriousness. The man of faith is a man who cares[50]. To be without faith is—pitiably—not to care. In other passages, the idea of concentrating solely on one matter, without distraction, is brought to the fore[51].

Sankara also, whom we have otherwise already seen as regularly giving the more intellectualist interpretation of *astikya-buddhi*, at times brings forth rather this aspect of "paying close heed". In one of his commentaries, he contrasts *sraddha* with the mind's becoming bogged down in externals, arguing that the subtle truth of things is difficult of apprehension for many persons unless their natural tendency to be distracted be offset by a "putting of the heart", a concentrated application of attention. When a point is difficult to grasp—he says—one must be intent, or one will miss it. If, on the other hand, one concentrates, insight is attained. Otherwise, the kind of situation arises alluded to in such scripture passages as "My mind was elsewhere"[52]. *Sraddha*, then, contrasts with a mind that is wandering[53].

In a similar vein, lack of faith (*asraddha*) is by other writers equated with diffuseness and irresolution[54].

The opposite of faith is thus not disbelief so much as either indifference, or a scattering of concern[55]: absence of faith is "ego-diffusion".

Another facet of setting one's heart on something or someone, a facet emphasized by some, is desire[56]; and another, confidence or trust[57]. Both these have been important[58].

More striking, however, for our purposes, are two further facets. One is a certain delight, as it were, in that with which one is involved. Thus, *sraddha* is contrasted with murmuring, complaining. One might accept a given teaching, an obligation, a rite, or whatever, but grudgingly, wishing it were otherwise. To accept it with *sraddha*, on the other hand, is to put one's heart in it in the sense of doing so without sulking; indeed, of being pleased that it is so[59].

The other facet, closely related, is that of accepting something for its own sake, not with an ulterior motive. To believe, to do, to choose anything because of what one may get out of it, is not faith. This is the famous Hindu thesis of detachment, of disinterestedness in the "fruits" of one's behaviour. *Sraddha* is putting one's heart on something (someone) in the sense of esteeming it (him, her) (recognizing its value) not instrumentally but intrinsically, absolutely[60].

In our typically modern-Western way we have here been speaking of faith as if it were something that a person may "have". And indeed one can make it an object thus of conceptual thought, and Indians have occasionally done so, in passing. Yet in fact in ordinary usage Sanskrit regularly employs it adverbially or adjectivally[61]. That is, it is rather a *quality* of man's life. Faith pertains to *the way in which* one does things. This helps to explain, also, how it is that *sraddha* is found in all the diverse "paths" of Hindu spirituality and practice. It is not an item in each system[62] so much as a way in which any system is to be practised—wholeheartedly. Or, if that demands too much, then at least "heartedly".

Sraddha, then, denotes a way of doing things, in the religious life: the way a ritualist performs a rite, the way a moralist carries out an obligation or a set of injunctions, the way one listens to the Gita, the way an intellectualist relates his mind and himself to the truth, the way a *bhakti*-devotee worships, and so on. The last of these may detain us a moment, for it might seem that the placing of the heart that is *sraddha* is particularly closely linked with that devotional adoration that is *bhakti*, or even is identical with it. Indeed it has so seemed to some Hindus, classically[63], and to some modern students[64]. Others, however, have insisted that the two must be seen as distinct[65].

Viewed within a wider context, *bhakti* as theistic adoration or even as the life of the devotee in the Lord is either something done, to be done, lived, "with faith", or in faith[66]; or, it is one form of faith.

Sankara on occasion elaborates his regular equation of *sraddha* with *astikya-buddhi*, by averring that it is the latter accompanied by *bhakti*[67].

It would be attractive to translate this somewhat as follows: Faith is awakeness to transcendence accompanied by an adoring devotion to it and a permeating participation in it.

Since *sraddha* is a placing of the heart, without a specifying of "on what", one way of looking at the matter might be that of seeing men and women as inevitably concerned with something, so that the only question of moment is that "what". This position has, indeed, found expression in India and its implicit force doubtless underlies, as we have already suggested, the general fact that *sraddha* has been less specifically investigated in Hindu literature than one might expect. That literature does deal with the "what". It is only the modern world, with its loss of faith, its *anomie* of the "uncommitted"[68], that has become alert to the preliminary issue of what is involved in human beings' ability genuinely to take an interest in *something*, to give their heart at all[69]. Thus we meet the view that faith is a universal human characteristic, with the significant point about any person being the particular kind of faith that he or she has. As Radhakrishnan puts it, it is the striving (or being pushed) "towards what is better"; and he compares Plato's " 'the trend of our desires and the nature of our souls' "[70].

Such a view is formulated most notably in the penultimate chapter of the Bhagavad Gita, where the elements (*guna*) of a man's character come through as corresponding elements of his *sraddha*—of where and how he puts his heart. "As a man's faith is, so is he"[71].

It is perhaps not illegitimate to be reminded of the comparable point made in a Western formulation:

> Whate'er thou lovest, man,
>   That to become thou must:
> God, if thou lovest God,
>   Dust if thou lovest dust[72].

In India some such view of *sraddha* in its indeterminateness goes along with a position that what one should strive for is the marriage of faith and truth[73]. When these two are coupled, one has arrived. (Otherwise, *sraddha* is rather the starting point of one's journey.) The elements into which the ideal position of a person may be analysed, are then these two: that he or she should be intent on *x*, and that *x* should be true. There is no point in being exposed to the truth, or the good, to reality, if one is indifferent to it, if one's heart is not in it; but similarly, one should give one's heart to the right things: that to which one gives it should, obviously, be worthy.

In fact, the universe and man were created in such a way that faith is the intrinsically appropriate human orientation towards what is true and right and real, its absence or opposite (*asraddha*, unfaith, disinterest) being apportioned similarly as the proper human attitude to what is false and awry. The Creator, "observing two forms, differentiated them as Truth and Wrong; He then established faithlessness (or: lack of interest) for Wrong, faith for Truth"[74].

One particular placing of the heart, not much developed in Indian analysis but important in passing to Hindus and important centrally to Western religious man, is on myths, on the tales that are told. *Sraddha kathayam* is "faith in the stories"[75], not in the sense of believing them so much as in that of taking them seriously. Menotti's *Amahl and the Night Visitors*[76] is a modern "legend", not even a myth: a minor legend on a major matter, Christmas. Let us hope that no one will believe it; or at least, that no one will deem it important to believe it. Yet of two persons who hear this opera, the one who is moved spiritually, and whose understanding, reverence, compassion are stirred is distinguishable from another who sees and feels no truth in it, who hears it without his heart being engaged.

To see the point of a parable, to be gripped by the purport of a myth, to appropriate to oneself in existential commitment the moral of a tale, even to rejoice in the singing of praises—these[77] are acts of faith. To believe in a tale of the gods, in the modern sterilized sense of the word "believe", may be no more than gullibility or intellectual error. To have faith in a myth, on the other hand, is to take it to heart, to recognize its human implications and to accept them as implicating oneself.

Commenting on Shakespeare's play *Macbeth*, the literary critic Northrop Frye has remarked[78] that if one wishes to know the history of eleventh-century Scotland, one should look elsewhere for information, but if one wishes to know what it is like to gain a kingdom and to lose one's soul, then one should read this drama. In modern English the word "true" has tended to become used in such a way that a given portrayal of eleventh-century Scottish history may be adjudged as, and dubbed, more or less true, but decreasingly in such a way as to allow us to assay and to verbalize a portrayal of human character—for instance, artistically —in terms of its truth and falsity. This is so, even though the latter portrayal may, manifestly, be more true or less, may come close to or fall-far short of the truth; and it is presumably no less important that our understanding of the one matter be accurate than that our understanding of the other be.

Further, however true Shakespeare's portrayal, it is possible to read his play and to fail to see the point. It is possible, also, to see the point and to fail to be moved by it: to come away from the drama and still to be ambitious. Either of these would be to read it without *sraddha*.

May one hope that the term "faith" in English will develop in such a way—that English-speaking persons' discernment of what faith is, and has been, will develop in such a way—that these will come to be called reading "without faith"? If those who disagreed with Shakespeare as to the data of Scottish history were to be said not to believe the play, or not to believe in the play, this would clearly be a quite different issue.

We close with two quotations, one from a disciple of Sankara and one from India's other great mediaeval thinker Ramanuja, to illuminate our notion in more general vein. Sankara, as we have already seen, speaks of *ṣraddha* at times as *astikya-buddhi*, the awareness that transcendence is indeed there. His disciple, in a text attributed to his teacher, amplifies this, characterizing *sraddha* as the "decisive" awareness: *that* awareness—of spiritual truths—whose particular quality it is to lead to resolve, decision, *engagement*[79]; that kind of recognition of truth that incurs an active response.

At issue here, might one not suggest, is something like that step of involvement or its lack that differentiates between the man in the Gospel "who hears these words of mine and does them" and that other man "who hears these words of mine and does not do them", so far as their inner orientation is concerned[80]: a putting of one's heart in the sense of committing oneself. Similarly, as we have seen, some Islamic theologians define faith as not simply knowledge, but that recognition of a truth that reaches the point of decision, active involvement[81].

Ramanuja, similarly, speaks of faith as presupposing a confidence about a particular religious system, that it will prove effective: given that conviction, faith is then the plunging in. *Sraddha* arises, he says, where something is attractive, is seen to be worth while: it is the move, of initiative or response, whereby one becomes involved, the act of engagement. It is the eagerness with which one responds positively to what one has recognized as calling[82]. When one knows what is worth doing[83], faith is a putting of the heart in the sense of plunging in and doing[84] it.

In closing, then, if we revert to our consideration of the relation between faith and belief, we may say that for these two thinkers that relation is one wherein faith follows upon intellectual judgement. The "leap of faith", if one were to use that Western phrase, is here the leap of the person who not merely knows but is willing, eager, to act in terms of what he or she knows. It is the leap out of the armchair into the fray. It is the leap from objective into existential knowledge.

Also, however, *vice versa*. Faith precedes as well as follows intellectual awareness. *Sraddha* is prerequisite to ascertaining truth. The desire to know, the resolve to know, a commitment to knowing, a reverence for the truth that one hopes and wills presently to attain: without these, one does not learn. The intent to pursue truth is, at least in part, faith for the intellectual[85].

For other Hindu thinkers, as we have seen, it is not linked especially with intellectual questions one way or another. Rather, it is one's taking up of the religious life seriously and genuinely—at whatever point; whatever the form of one's involvement. And not merely the religious life. If we may end on what to some may seem a secular note, faith as a putting of the heart may be seen as pertaining to all aspects of our condition, and a lack of faith as a sorry nihilism, not irreligious so much as inhuman. *Sraddha* is that putting of the heart that is commitment, concern, sincerity.

In the modern world, alas, including the West, it can no longer be taken for granted. Students who attend schools and universities but whose heart is not in their studies, who do not have faith in their own intellectual venture; teachers whose concern is with their own careers, whose heart is not in their teaching, so that, as teachers, they are then not men and women of faith; workers whose activity is aimed at their pay cheque but whose heart is not in their craft, so that the working hours of their lives are therefore lived without faith; wives who seek liberation from household work in which they can no longer put their heart; business executives whose mind and whose will but not whose heart can legitimately be in their organizations; advertising agents whose ingenuity but not whose integrity is in their job, not in a calling; audiences being entertained in ways that titillate the rest of their persons but their heart is not engaged—these constitute a society in which faith is sparse.

India's religious life has taken many forms, and has been lived and theorized about at many levels. *Sraddha* names but one step in that life; and the concept constitutes only one particular contribution that the Hindu complex may make to mankind's understanding of faith at large. That complex will provide many other contributions richer, deeper, more ultimate; but perhaps none more primary.

Chapter 5

CREDO AND THE ROMAN CATHOLIC CHURCH

In the Qur'an case above it became clear that the faith of Muslims classically would be rightly understood by God and by non-Muslim observers, as it was by Muslim theorists themselves, as something different from their belief, indeed seriously other than it, although not unrelated to it. As seen by the first two, the belief-system provided the conceptual framework in relation to which members of this community either had, or failed to have, faith. It was also in terms of and from within that framework that most classical and mediaeval Muslims articulated their own awareness of the decisive difference. In modern times, as consciousness in these realms is transmuted into self-consciousness, critical and analytic, the view of the matter set forth in our second sentence above becomes appropriate not only for God and for outside observers but nowadays, one may venture to suggest, also for modern sophisticated intellectuals among Muslims themselves[1]. Our contention is that this is an accurate statement as to what was actually going on. The ability to recognize it as accurate is presumably independent both of whether one has faith or not and of whether one is a Muslim or not. (This fact is not unrelated to the statement's potential validity; statements about faith in the past have not always had this quality.)

We turn next to the Christian case, where the belief-system has been different but otherwise the situation is formally comparable. With Hindu systems the Christian is less comparable formally, whereas as regards the specific notion of *sraddha* there is a certain substantial comparability. (Indeed, that notion may be correlated with both Islamic and Christian commitments. It has often turned out that it is Hindu visions that enable Christian and Islamic positions to be simultaneously grasped[2].) On the Christian instance light is thrown from one side by the Hindu exposition, from another by the Islamic.

In our next chapter, we will consider the concept "believing", in the English language, which beginning as a general matter became for a time to some degree a significantly Protestant matter (the dominant majority of English-speaking religious persons having been Protestant), and recently also a secular one, although certainly not solely so by any means. In this present chapter we look at earlier, and for recent centuries somewhat more Catholic, orientations, focusing primarily on classical expositions, particularly on the concept *credo* and on some modern

Roman Catholic thought on faith. An inquiry into usage in the Bible, both Old Testament and particularly New, where a concept "faith" was innovatingly and decisively developed, would be important for completeness of our study, but it is set aside for separate publication[3] (except for a couple of passing remarks below, at the end of this present chapter). Obviously, I do not pretend to proffer an essay, however brief, on Christian interpretation of faith, a vastly elaborate topic, nor even any adequate inquiry into its changing relation to belief over the centuries and among differing groups. All that we can hope for, and all that I intend, is by choosing certain illustrative instances from the wide-ranging array to suggest that the two matters have been linked in ways less unambiguous than is widely supposed.

It would be easy to select from the total development particular positions setting forth non-intellectualist dimensions of Christian faith. These have been many, and illustrative. To cite a Thomas à Kempis or a St. John of the Cross, however, or a Christian whose faith was expressed primarily in art or music or social activism, would illuminate the matter only peripherally, leaving the central issues unresolved. It would be altogether too easy to show that the faith of such Christians was understood and was expressed primarily in ways other than doctrinal. Rather, we attend to the first introduction of credal forms in the Church, which was in liturgy, and to saliently intellectualist and official expositions, on the grounds that here if anywhere the matter of faith's relation to belief will be clarified. Accordingly, I choose for our investigation the following four moments, plus a codicil: early Christian baptism (and specifically, St. Cyril of Jerusalem, ca. 315-386 A.D.); St. Thomas Aquinas (1225-1274); Vatican I (1869-1870); *Le Dictionnaire de théologie catholique* (1899-1950) and *The Twentieth Century Encyclopedia of Catholicism* (1958-1971); plus a miscellany of classical observations.

We turn first to St. Cyril.

(i) Baptism

Dramatic, decisive, transforming: these are the characteristics of early Christian baptism. We may call the act a "ceremony" or "rite", but we do so in danger of seriously under-representing what was then involved, so sanitized in present-day usage have such terms become. For moderns usually understand formal liturgical actions in a constraining fashion, as events pigeon-holed within a larger scheme of their lives, as items subordinate to a general order, social and personal. Not so, Christian baptism in the early centuries. It represented rather the deliberate replacing of one general order with another, drastically and excitingly different.

The earliest full description of baptismal procedures that has come down to us is from the middle of the fourth century and from Jerusalem. Certain lectures are available which were given there (in Greek) to those preparing for this act, and just after their completing it. The lectures are traditionally attributed to St. Cyril of Jerusalem, although they may have been revised into or even written in their present form by his successor as bishop in that city, John[4]. The lectures make vivid reading. One may remember that the era of persecution of the Church had been left not very far behind: within the memory of the older generation of the time, to take the step of overtly and formally becoming a Christian had meant to accept the risk of torture or violent death. Immediate issues, and not only eternal, were at stake.

A change in earthly life was involved: if not leading to the fateful end of martyrdom, in any case signifying a radical switch in day-to-day behaviour. A change, also, in one's metaphysical status was implied, which began not after death so much as with baptism itself, and with it a new orientation of one's thinking, one's vision, one's loyalties. Monumental matters were therefore at issue—as becomes clear as one reads the pages of Cyril's to us almost melodramatic account.

The company of those who were to be baptized gathered on Easter eve (they had spent Lent in meditative and instructional preparation), just outside the Jerusalem church, and stood first facing west. They all stretched out their hands and ceremonially took leave of the world of confusion, oppression, and evil on which a few moments later they would both literally and figuratively turn their backs. The west, the direction of sunset (and, from Jerusalem, of Egypt), represented darkness, death, and sin. They were reminded of the liberation of the children of Israel from the tyranny there of the wicked Pharaoh who had held them cruelly enslaved—and who, along with his armies, pursuing them when they escaped, perished by going down into the waters of the Red Sea, in which he and his hosts were overwhelmed and drowned, while the Israelites came up unscathed on the other side, freed, to march in triumph towards their promised land in the east. This prefigured the going down into the waters of the baptismal tank, which this group was about to do; in these waters the old tyranny of this-worldly enslavement would perish while they themselves would come out on the other side free men, to enter a new world of light and joy. Moses had been sent by God to lead the ancient company, as symbol of Christ coming from God to lead the present one.

The baptizands ("those to be baptized") formally pronounced a formula of rejection ("renunciation") of Satan and all his works, parallel to the subsequent acceptance of, or ranging of oneself on the side of, Christ and His. The symmetrical pair of Greek words[5] designates cutting oneself off from the one and then aligning oneself with the other. Satan here is explicitly the mean and crafty usurper who rules a world of insidious wickedness and fatuous superficial show: a world of individual moral weakness and dissolute behaviour on which the baptizand has undertaken and will be enabled, now, to turn his back, and a world of social decadence—more or less that of the then degenerating Roman Empire—that he has come to reject. (This rejection some might be inclined to compare to the rejection in the late twentieth century by many a youth of "the system" of his elders that he sees around him, as corrupt and corrupting: something from which he radically turns with disdain and with relief. The comparison is not inept; unlike his later counterpart, however, the fourth-century Christian-to-be was turning from the old order to a new that was given, waiting to receive him: divinely ordered, historically settled, and clearly structured, at the levels of moral pattern, of theory, and of institutional organization.)

Having then pronounced the formula by which they abandoned their old life, the company next turned round, each baptizand turning his back on the old order to face east, towards light and the source of light, towards the erstwhile paradise of Eden, man's original and true home from which his actual condition has alienated him. Entering the sanctuary, each then doffed his clothes, as symbol again of leaving utterly behind his former life and its ways, and stood naked like Christ on the cross, whose victory over the power of worldly darkness was accomplished in this humility; the unashamed nakedness is emblematic also of man's pristine innocence. Each was then led by the hand down into the sacred baptismal pool of the church ("just as Christ was carried from the cross to the tomb over there"[6]: the tomb near which the Jerusalem church was built, and which the company could actually see from where they stood). Each was immersed three times in the water, symbolizing the burial of Christ in the tomb for three days. Baptism represented dying and being born again ("that salvation water was both your grave and your mother"[7]): being crucified with Christ and sharing then in His resurrection. One emerged from the pool regenerated, a new person, having repudiated the old and partaking now from this day forward of a brand new life, with new power, new grace, a new role, a new cosmic status. In Christ's suffering and death, it was affirmed, the new Christian's participation is symbolic only; but in His salvation, it is actual.

Central to the action was the crucial question-and-answer rite accompanying the three immersions. The group had been told, during the theoretical explication that preceded the ceremony—and indeed re-iterated stress had been laid on the point—that the observance of the procedures in itself was of no consequence if the participant's heart were not in it. This was explicitly not a magic performance: instances were cited of men who had been baptized with false intention or impure resolve, for whom then the outward symbols remained but outward symbols, while they themselves remained unchanged[8]. The crux was authenticity of purpose: a man's genuine intent to move from the old life to the new, his determination to turn from "the world" to Christ.

Accordingly, the central moment in the ceremony, the plunging into the water, involved each participant's expressing verbally and publicly his personal dedication to the purpose of the act. Each was asked if he committed himself to God the Father, and it was on his answering in the affirmative that he was immersed. He was then asked whether he committed himself to Jesus Christ; and again he committed himself by saying verbally that yes, he took on this commitment, deliberately and in full seriousness, whereupon he was again immersed. Similarly a third time, with the Holy Spirit.

On rising then from the water, the new Christians were anointed with olive oil, as was Christ with the Spirit after *His* baptism. One might say that thus they were literally "christened"; it was in fact said that they "became christs"[9]. ("Christ" means "anointed one": this part of the ceremony was called *chrisma* or anointing, from the same root.) From this point they were called Christian, participating in Christ and through Him able to vanquish the enemy and indeed to do all things. They all donned new white garments, symbolizing the new pure persons that they had become. They were indeed told that they should now go "in white all your days. I am not at all saying that the ordinary clothes that you will wear must always be white, but that you must be clad in truly white and shining spiritual garments"[10]. They then partook of the eucharist, taking Christ into themselves and thus becoming participants in the divine nature, ready now throughout their lives (and through all eternity) to move "from glory unto glory"[11].

Although St. Cyril's presentation of baptism, as here summarized, is more elaborate than other early writers', the scene that he describes would appear to be fairly typical. Each thinker has his own nuance, each century its special emphasis, each area and school its particular orientation[12]. Yet there seems little question but that by and large, for the early Church and for those who chose to join it, the act by which they did so, dramatized and sealed in this rather spectacular ceremony, was seen as an act of momentous right-about-face, the discarding of one life and the adopting of another. It marked a transition of decisive consequence, by which was transformed the inner and outer life of the person concerned, both historically and cosmically.

"Baptism involved becoming Christ's man", as the careful scholar Nock says, speaking of an earlier period when it was more simply "in the name of Christ"[13]. From the first it had been a question of opting for this new, radically new, enterprise in human living, in time and in eternity—opting for it, and undertaking it. It designated a "decision for Christ", and meant becoming incorporated into a new kind of history, one that various modern scholars like to call "salvation history"[14]; meant opting out of a stream of history that was going nowhere, to plunge into and to be caught up in this surging movement.

Military metaphors were common[15]. To be baptized was to join the new salvation army, with its discipline, its perils, its commitments, its fellowship, and its pursuance of ultimate victory. The oath that Roman army recruits took on being received into the armed forces, an oath wherein they pledged their personal fidelity to the emperor, was termed *sacramentum*. The Latin-speaking sector of the Church took over this word to characterize baptism, and other ritual acts, as Tertullian, for instance, amply illustrates[16]. In other wording, also, the notion of a solemn contract is evidenced: a contract entered into between the baptizands and God[17].

The analogy with a wedding was frequent[18]: with the commitment (the central "I do"), the joy, the start of a new life.

The points that in all this I would stress are three. They are all closely linked. The first, obvious enough, is the self-transformational character of the action. The initiate was taking on a new life, with baptism as the implicating sign of his or her becoming involved in it. Thus one was taking an existentially decisive step: one of utter self-commitment. In this act, one was engaging himself. The words were performative.

Secondly, we may note a certain polarity in the matter giving rise to a double possibility of view-point. Through baptism, as we have said, the person was leaving a world of atomistic disorder for a new and divine world of liberating service to God: one was oneself choosing the latter, and also was being welcomed into it. From one point of view, accordingly, the emphasis was on this decision, on one's dedication of one's own person to the new venture. From the other side, the magnificent availability of the new order could be stressed, the readiness of God to receive one. The momentous decision—it was starkly that—could be sensed as something that in the one case one strikingly made, and that in the other one was astonishingly enabled to make.

St. Cyril's exposition of baptism, we have said, is on the whole typical. So far as this one facet goes, however, his attention tends to be oriented towards the existentialist move of the actor. The presentation—in which abound words like "will", "purpose", "resolve", "intent"[19]—is so much fuller than earlier writers' that comparisons cannot readily be set up; but later the development can be discerned of a tendency to stress what was happening *to* the baptizand, as well as, or within, his or her acting. So vivid and emphatic in the fourth century were the notions of deliberate choice, of the will, and of firm resolve, that a question was presently canvassed—most notably in the following century between Augustine and Pelagius—as to the respective roles of the human person and of God in the transaction between the two. In the transmuting relation between such persons and God or Christ, which their baptism sealed, Christians could be thought of as choosing to engage themselves, or as recognizing their engagement. The counterpart to—or the possibility of—their move was the free gift on God's part to them. In either case, however, engagement it was. Whether they had the power to make the commitment themselves, or could make it only if that power were given them, the fact remains that the act was primarily an act of commitment, and continued to be seen as such.

In a wedding, one of the parties may be envisaged in terms of his choosing the other, and choosing the new life of marriage with that other, and of the commitments that are therein being undertaken (especially with that central rite, his pronouncing of the "I do"). Or, he may be envisaged, or envisage himself, in terms rather of the other's being willing to accept him, of his being received into the new life. There is thus both deliberate action, and joyous reception. (Paradoxically, the more total and sincere his choice, the more vividly will he be aware of the other side of this polarity.)

An active and a passive involvement were similarly to be seen in the act of becoming a Christian.

One might think this analogy a trifle carefree; but St. Cyril also uses it[20].

On the active-passive matter, our author recognizes God's initiative: He calls the individual baptizand, and the baptizand responds[21]. We give ourselves to Him; He, seeing our resolution, in turn gives us the change of heart that saves[22]. Our resolve must, of course, be sincere: nothing occurs if a man's lips affirm his willing (*sic*), but his heart does not[23]. God even can turn the faithless into a faithful person, however, if he but give his heart[24].

This "putting of the heart" leads to our third point. When the Western Church (well before St. Cyril's day) came to render the baptismal service from Greek into Latin, the verbalization that it chose to express the performatory utterance of commitment at the centre of the baptismal rite was, interestingly for our purposes, the Latin cognate for *sraddha.* Latin and Sanskrit are both Indo-European languages and share many roots in common, even though pronunciation and spelling have in many cases diverged sufficiently that it may take an etymologist to discern them. In this case, whether by co-incidence or out of an inherited fundamental religious vocabulary, the Latin version of our Hindu term was used, and continues to this day. The "I do" by which the baptizands affirmed and effected the consecration of themselves to God, to Christ, and to the Spirit, the giving of themselves in full sincerity and in formal commitment, is, more aptly, "I set my heart". The term selected was the Latin for this phrase: namely, *credo*.

This word, it seems, is a compound from *cor*, *cordis*, "heart" (as in English "cordial", "accord", "concord", and the like; compare also, from the closely parallel Greek cognate *ḳardia*, the English derivatives "cardiac", "electrocardiogram", etc.)[25], plus **do*, "put, place, set", also "give"[26]. The first meaning of the compound in classical Latin had been and its primary meaning continued to be "to entrust, to commit, to trust something to someone", and of money, "to lend". (This commercial usage survives in the English term "credit". To give financial credit to someone is not a derived meaning from giving credence to him, but rather *vice versa. Credere eo* meant not to trust him to the point of believing him worth advancing funds, so much as to trust him by actually advancing the funds, taking the practical step of committing one's goods.) A secondary meaning in secular usage was "to trust in", "to rely upon", "to place confidence in". There had also developed a derivative usage wherein *credo* meant "to believe" (usually a person); but that was tertiary. To believe a proposition was quaternary and relatively rare.

There would seem little question but that as a crucial term used at a crucial moment in a crucial liturgical act of personal engagement—namely, Christian baptism—*credo* came close to its root meaning of "I set my heart on", "I give my heart to" ("I hereby give my heart to Christ"; "I herein give my heart to God the Father"; . . .); or, more generally: "I hereby commit myself" ("to . . . "), "I pledge allegiance".

The obviousness of this can be somewhat obscured for those who come to it with their minds saturated with interpretations derived from usages a thousand years and more later. We shall turn to these presently. Modern scholarship is virtually unanimous, however, in recognizing that what we call "creeds" were used first liturgically, and only later doctrinally[27]. And there seems no doubt but that *credo* as a Latin term was used by the Church first in the ceremony of self-dedication that is baptism, and only a good deal later in the realm of theoretical issues. The whole tone of discussions about baptism in Latin is like St. Cyril's in Greek, where the concern is about a passing from a life of sinfulness to a life of purity, from darkness to illumination, from the mundane to the divine, from an involvement in one order to a committed involvement in another. It is not at all a question of moving from non-belief to belief[28].

Contrary to modern impressions, the classical creeds of the Church include no propositional statements[29].

We are not, of course, suggesting that the early Christian movement did not believe anything, nor that what early Christians believed was or is unimportant. Such a suggestion would seem[30] ludicrous. What needs affirming is that the Church did not use (or, very rarely used) the particular word *credo* to denote such believing[31]. This is not what the term meant[32]. And it is in our day[33] a misunderstanding to read and a mistranslation to render their documents as if it had been. Believing[34] is not what in those centuries Baptism[35] and the Creeds[36] were about.

In the course of the ceremony there was no inquiry of the baptizands as to whether they believed anything. Just as they were not asked whether they believed in a devil, before being asked solemnly and ceremonially to repudiate him, so they were not asked whether they believed in God or Christ or the Church before being asked solemnly and ceremonially to pledge their allegiance.

While this was the situation for at least three centuries, and in principle for very much longer, yet presently in this matter there was, as in all matters there always is, transition. The historical development seems to have been somewhat as follows. Formulae characterizing in words what later centuries came to call the "object"[37] of faith gradually evolved, as verbal delineations of that to which (Him to Whom) the Christian pledged allegiance, took on commitment. As this happened, men who had ideas about these matters—theoretical interpretations of that "object of faith"—endeavoured to have their ideas incorporated in the official formulae, or endeavoured to have ideas implicit in other formulae to which they took exception, modified. Given the liturgical affirmations and their central place in the life and worship of the Church, intellectual controversies gravitated towards them. This eventually brought about a situation where the focus of attention was shifted from the operative verb *credo* (which had originally been decisive, the rest of the statement being at first simple in the extreme, and for long being taken largely for granted in the Church) to, rather, the predicate of that verb.

The question began by being: "Do you commit yourself to this, or do you not?" Later it was transformed into the quite different question: "Do you commit yourself to this, or to that?"—or, effectively, "Is it this, or is it that, to which we all commit ourselves?" Commitment, at first, was simply to Christ (especially among converting Jews); and presently (among Greeks) to God as Trinity. Gradually—but very slowly—attention was diverted to defining with some precision how best to state to what. At first, and liturgically, God and Christ were taken as given, and the great issue was commitment. Much later, and theologically, commitment was taken as given, and the great issue was God and Christ.

How to formulate in words the object of commitment became eventually a prime controversial intellectual question. This was so especially[38] after the Church eventually became established, so that baptism and worship—expressions of becoming and being Christian—were now no longer choices differentiating a new life, so much as standard community practices. The moral question as to whether some of us should opt to become involved, gave way to the theoretical question as to what it is in which all of us are involved. A situation thus arose where some people could almost seem to forget that that self-involvement is what the word signified; and could begin to treat the term itself casually as if it were no more than a preamble to a theoretical delineation, designating a relationship to one or another of various possible intellectualizations.

On inquiry, however, as we shall now observe, it turns out that this process has occurred much less thoroughly, and much more recently, than might be supposed. (For example, the phrase "baptismal vows" is still in use[39]. Much is gained if one re-examines the history of *credo* bearing in mind at least lightly the illuminating fact that it is, after all, first cousin of *sraddha,* and fundamentally means to put one's heart on; bearing in mind quite firmly the notions of commitment, of *s'engager*, of self-involvement, the pledging of allegiance; and having always near the forefront of one's vision that central act of baptism depicted so compellingly by St. Cyril of Jerusalem. To turn from all else in indifference if not disdain, becoming dead to that old life of darkness, and to plunge into the venture of beginning a quite new life, rising to live it in purity and joy and the freedom of a new allegiance: this dramatic decision, this decisive transformation, this transforming drama, is, basically, *credo.*

(ii) St. Thomas Aquinas

In accord with a subtly formative and strikingly persistent propensity of Indo-European thought patterns towards the triadic[40], a threefold division of our human psyche or its modes has tended to dominate Western culture over much of its course. Since the advent into that culture of the Christian movement, the division has tended to be into intellect, will, and in recent centuries, feeling[41]—although such division can be and has been criticized. Into no action or state of man does any one of the three not enter, as a more or less integral component. Given that heritage, however, and the persisting tendency to operate within it, one may perhaps classify human doings as falling under one or another of the three primarily, as having no doubt all three facets but with one uppermost. If we use some such conceptual framework, we may observe that historically Christian understanding of faith has seemed to go through certain main phases.

Credo began in Christian usage as a term to designate an act of self-commitment, in which the will is predominant—whether under a person's own option or divinely salvaged from its own incapacity to choose the true and the right over distorting pseudo-self-interest. Even at the close of the early period, St. Augustine, who championed the notion of faith as a divine gift, not available to man's own choice except through grace, was on occasion quite explicit that it is a matter of will[42]. With him and with other early Christian thinkers the mind, of course, is not unengaged, even though its role be less prominent or be felt less decisively.

Later, *credo* came to be regarded by some as denominating rather a somewhat differently understood act—perhaps a somewhat different act, perhaps rather the same act differently perceived: an act in which the mind plays a predominant role. In this development manifestly St. Thomas Aquinas is a figure of prime importance. Probably no one in Christian history, and almost no one in human history, perhaps, has done so much to integrate the life of the mind and the life of faith. He was by no means unaware of or unconcerned with a role of the will in the act of faith[43]; yet he himself was primarily[44] an intellectual. One might perhaps aphorize that *credo* for the early Church was an act of the will, in which the mind was implicitly involved; for St. Thomas it is an act of the mind, in which the will is explicitly involved.

This over-simplifies, of course. We leave aside feeling, an issue delicate and complicated enough but not of explicitly major importance for our particular purposes until the late eighteenth century. Between will and intellect the interrelation within the act of faith are in Thomist thought subtle; we leave aside that complex question too, except insofar as it impinges on the interrelation that we do wish to canvass: that between belief and faith. That too is subtle, but has been examined less, if at all. It is a question on which it would be important to have a study by a competent Thomist scholar; failing that, we may perhaps proffer some preliminary observations, partly in the hopes of eliciting such a study. Our purpose is not to delineate what the relation is in Thomas's vision between the two, but simply to suggest that the question is significant: that there is such a relation, that for him faith and belief are not the same.

It is obvious enough that the two are not the same in the piety of a St. Bernard of Clairvaux, for whom in the cosmos and in a person's relation to God the function of the human mind is relatively minor[45];

nor are they the same in the piety of a devout village grandmother. It is true also for a scholastic theologian like St. Bonaventura, Thomas's colleague and critic, for whom there is indeed a journey of the mind to (into?) God[46], but it is a decidedly spiritual ascent culminating in a "mystical ravishment"[47]. St. Thomas, on the other hand, is the religious intellectual *par excellence*, whose commanding achievement lay precisely in the realm of intellectualizing the Christian Church's awareness: the man who, one might say, did more than anyone else to give expression to faith—his own, and in due course it became apparent also that of many millions of others—in conceptual structures, as belief. (A very large number of persons in later centuries who might not agree with his particular pattern of belief has yet been profoundly influenced by the fact of his accomplishment in this direction, his having demonstrated the possibilities, and the force, of this form of expression for faith.) He was a man of profound and contagious faith, and of powerful and spectacularly successful belief. Further, his intellectual integrity was such that these were held together triumphantly[48].

Even for a St. Thomas, nonetheless, it would be a misunderstanding to confuse the two.

The relation between faith and belief in his conceptual scheme has been but little elucidated in the past perhaps because of three major considerations complicating it. One is the very fact of his being so pre-eminently an intellectual. He was a member of that group in the Western tradition for whom man's personal fulfilment and highest relation to the universe and to ultimate reality are through the mind. Knowing—knowing the truth; knowing God—is supreme. In it final human beatitude will consist. Meanwhile, here on earth his own life was dedicated to understanding and to helping persons to understand. Not only faith, therefore, but all human matters, from love to wilfulness (and indeed ultimately all matters, including the reality of objects in the material universe[49]), receive from his pen an intellectualistic interpretation[50]. This was his supreme achievement; other orientations were left for other men and women. He had faith in God, but he also was like Aristotle in having faith in the human intellect—a faith that, even if relatively inarticulate and at this level un-self-conscious, was profound, and decisive.

Secondly: his views on faith, like all thinkers' views on all matters, are of course implicated with his total system of ideas, are expressed in terms of what we might call his own beliefs, are set forth within the parameters of his particular conceptual framework. This framework we, looking back, misunderstand either if we view it simply from the outside—whereas his mind operated *within* it—or if we forget that, however profound and brilliant, it was indeed particular, one among others. His system of ideas constituted a language that was not his faith, but in which he said what he had to say about faith (or for that matter, about infidelity). Our task is to translate out of that language into our own (which also we misunderstand if we forget that it too is particular). His expressed interpretation of faith is his view of faith explicated in terms of his view of the world.

So also his interpretation of belief.

Some of what seemed to him obvious, not being so to us, we may perhaps dub his belief; but we misunderstand him if we fail to realize that for him it was not a conscious belief but an unconscious presupposition, or a platitude, or the recognition of a logically inescapable truth.

Thirdly: the relation between faith and belief in his thought has been obscured, not to say obfuscated, by a tendency to translate, not indeed his word for faith (*fides*) as "belief", but his word for the initiatory "act of faith", *credo*, by the verb "believe". In what follows, we shall endeavour, if not to rectify this error, at least to make clear that it sorely needs rectifying. (He has other terms for what he regarded as belief, believing.)

Of these three matters, we turn first to the question of his faith as an intellectual.

Significant here is not merely his giving a theorizing interpretation to faith, as to all matters. Certainly this is major; yet the question is a good deal further involved. He took an intellectualist view of faith, but also he took what one may call a faith view of intellect. Knowledge (in conceptual terms) is for man finally possible (the human intellect truly apprehends reality), and is of final value intrinsically (not just instrumentally): these are positions that not everyone shares. And even if they believe these things, some may not orient their lives in accord with them. The intellectual, however, is one who holds these, and indeed tends to take them for granted, and feels them: holds them theoretically, but also practically as an emotionally powerful driving force in his or her life. For intellectuals as a class, one may suggest, faith is an attitude to truth, and specifically to truth as conceptualizable, and more specifically still, to transcendent truth—not yet discovered[51], not yet known. What characterizes them as intellectuals is not the relation of their mind to a particular truth but the attitude of their person to truth as such. It is not their knowing that A is B but their determination to know what A is, what B is, what X is; and (this too is important) their delight to know. Love of truth that is known may make one a fanatic; but love of truth not yet apprehended is what makes one an intellectual. Required is a good mind able—also, happy—to recognize truth when it sees it, but also the will to pursue it when it does not. Thus for intellectuals as such the role of the mind may be defined in terms of a subtle involvement both with the will[52] and with transcendence.

Certainly St. Thomas was an intellectual in this sense; and his understanding of faith included an understanding of it in this sense. He was well aware that truth transcends our present grasp; but also that man is so constituted as to be aware of this very fact, to perceive dimly (yet in a sense, to know) that there is more to truth than we have yet perceived: to know of it what we know and to be aware of and attracted by what of it we do not know[53].

For him, as we shall be returning to note, the "object" of faith is ultimate truth (*prima veritas*).

He was, however, not merely an intellectual, but a religious intellectual, for whom truth and goodness are ultimately identical; so that the love of truth, and our giving our allegiance to it (*credere*), converge with love generally (*caritas*), which informs them. Faith is not merely a dedication to the truth but an applauding (*assensio*) of it, and an acting in terms of it; it is lifeless if the will that is involved in the pursuit of truth be not also a will to good[54]. As an intellectual in the Greek tradition, as we have said, he held that man's highest relation to the universe and to ultimate reality is through the mind. Yet for him the whole person should accompany the mind in the involvement.

For a distinction—with momentous consequences—is made between *fides formata* and *fides informis*: faith with and without love. The latter for Thomas is not a virtue[55]. Apart from the larger question as to goodwill in general—love of neighbour, and love of the good as such—and its relation to faith, there is involved here also a particular question of a love of truth[56], and its place in that human relation to or attitude to truth that is faith. One might perhaps aver that to recognize transcendent truth as true without also willing it is *fides informis*, formless faith, and is not a virtue. Are there not echoes here perhaps of the Sanskrit *anasuya*[57]?—as also perhaps in his use, following Augustine, of *assensio* as the mind's agreement[58] to what is true being true (and to what is real being real[59]): agreeing, and approving. One is hardly a true intellectual if one's recognizing a truth is reluctant, begrudging—if one arrives at an understanding of how things are but does not accept the truth, wishing it were otherwise. Giving one's own desires or whims priority over the truth that one apprehends may not infringe the intellect, but it does distort the person. The intellect's inert recognition or acceptance of truth, even its giving its allegiance to truth, is still faith, but of an unvirtuous sort, imperfect and unformed; it is insufficient for salvation.

For Thomas, then, faith is a commitment to the truth—of the mind, and significantly of the whole soul. We turn next to our second consideration: his explicating of his position on this as on all points within his total conceptual scheme.

What he himself proximately considered to be true coloured, of course, his formulations to a certain extent, as is always the case; but that is secondary for our present purposes. Many studies of his concept of faith have been distracted by this. From what he himself said about faith it is quite apparent that for him any view that he (or anyone else) might happen to hold that was not correct ought to be discounted[60]. Faith, he held, is a relation to truth as such, not to belief or opinion and only incidentally, even, to any particular formulation even of truth (as we shall note in a moment). The role of explicit belief[61] in his articulated view of faith is altogether subsidiary or minor and even at times negative.

He did not identify his system of ideas with faith, nor specify agreement with it as constituting faith. Nor, within that total system, did he define the element of faith as the holding of certain ideas. On the latter point we shall touch presently, in considering the meaning of *credo*. On the former: even at his most intellectualistic, at the height of his rationalism, he would view those who might disagree with his articulations, whether in whole or in part, as being perhaps intellectually wrong[62], but not faithless. (This is quite apart from the famous instance towards the end of his life when, in more mystical mood, he is reputed to have said that all his theorizings were as straw[63] compared to one moment's direct love of God.)

Some of his views, of course, he felt not as "his views" but as expositions of manifest truth; as we have remarked. This introduces, no doubt, a complication into our efforts to-day to understand him; but for a modern cultural historian it is a quite standard one, to be taken in stride. Knowing faith only in its Christian forms, he was not a comparativist of faith, except in ways that we shall be considering presently. And he was not a comparativist of world-views at all. (Most religious positions throughout history have been set forth so; and most secular positions still are.) They would be insensitive students to-day who allowed themselves to be precluded by these particularities from penetrating to an understanding of what, *within* his conceptual framework, he is saying. The only form of faith of which Thomas was aware, that he recognized as faith, was deeply implicated with the only set of ideas and propositions that he would regard not as beliefs but as universal truths, as straightforward descriptions of how things in fact are. Of course, therefore, he interpreted the one in terms of the other. *But he did not equate the one with the other.*

He was aware that various ideas and propositions are presupposed in the Church's analytic interpretation of what faith is; and accordingly he characterizes these as faith's "preamble". We can discern others of which he was unaware. Both what in his eyes were assured universal truths constituting the preamble to faith, and what he took for granted as axiomatic, we might call certain beliefs constituting a Christian preamble to faith, although we would have to qualify that further by characterizing those beliefs as Christian preamble at a certain period in historical development. In any case, what could nowadays be called his beliefs certainly then coloured his theoretical interpretation of faith; but equally certainly, neither did he nor should we identify nor confuse the two.

This brings us to our third consideration, his use of Latin terms. I suggest that he is misrepresented if *credo* as he uses the word be translated as "believe" understood in the predominant current sense of that English term. Whether *credo* in any given passage should be rendered by "believe" depends, of course, on what "believe" means; this is the topic for our next chapter. There are, no doubt, some moderns who still attach to "believe" in isolated (religious) contexts a meaning coloured, if not formed, by the meaning of *credo* for such thinkers as St. Thomas; but there are others who, rather, are in danger of attaching to *credo* a meaning coloured, if not formed, by the meaning of "believe" in general modern parlance. This, I submit, quite distorts his vision of the world.

No doubt, as we have observed, faith for him involves the relation of a person, and specifically a person's mind, with truth, who for him and for the mediaevals generally is God. It involves, accordingly, a certain sort of knowledge, as we shall presently be noting. Its relation to knowledge and to reason have often been canvassed; its relation to belief less so, partly because that relation was much more tenuous. The starting point for any discussion of this last relation must be a recognition that for "belief" and "believing" in the standard modern sense of those terms and especially as applying to the believing of propositions, the Latin words are the noun *opinio* and the verb *opinari*. What most present-day persons understand by the question of believing or not believing, in the religious and the secular realm (we anticipate here a little our next chapter's discussion), would be accurately rendered by these words.

Abelard had posited, rather, another set of terms: *aestimatio* (also *existimatio*), with the verb *aestimare*. By doing so, he was understood by many of his contemporaries as meaning what most to-day would mean by "belief". He was, accordingly, roundly denounced, for seeming to say that faith is simply belief. To his contemporaries this was shocking. It was as if a person's having faith were simply his believing, were something therefore that each could feel and speak about as it might strike him; and as if Christian life were a function uncertainly of the inconclusive and diverse beliefs of those who practised it[64].

St. Thomas, and the Schoolmen generally, held quite firmly that the act of faith (*credo*) is different from, is more than, believing in this sense. For them, *credo* is the pledging of allegiance, the committing of oneself —through one's mind—loyally to truth; although for him and the other scholastics it goes beyond the earlier centuries' accepting for oneself, towards signifying now a recognizing and accepting. Faith (*fides*) is such loyalty. It involves also an awareness of truth, though it is of a truth that transcends one's present grasp. A person who knew truth but were not loyal to it, or one loyal only to such truth as he or she had already apprehended but with no openness or commitment beyond it, no reaching out in pursuit of yet fuller truth, would in Thomas's eyes not have faith, in his language would not be said to have *fides*; the act called *credere* would not be ascribed to him.

In rejecting belief as equivalent to faith, he was aware that some confused the two notions. He explicitly distinguishes his own, Christian, use of the term *fides* from Aristotle's[65] (*fides* in the Latin translations[66]; originally, *pistis*): this latter is persuasion, conviction, very strong belief[67]. He also speaks of this as *fides communiter accepta* (or, . . . *sumpta*)[68], which some might translate as "believing as it is ordinarily understood". Faith is not that, he is at pains to affirm.

Having prepared the ground, then, with these preliminary considerations, we turn to explore the situation that emerges in the light of them. Our thesis would affirm flatly that for St. Thomas, believing in the modern meaning of that word is *not* to have faith. How, then, are the two related?

So far as the intellectualistic or cognitive dimension is concerned, he saw faith, as we have remarked, as closer to knowing. Explicitly he sets it up as within a series along with belief and a certain type of knowledge, standing somewhere between these two[69]. That belief, faith, and this sort of knowing form a series in that order was a view not shared by all thinkers in the mediaeval Church, of course. None had a good word to say for belief; but some would rank faith, as did the Muslims[70], as more than, higher than, knowing—for instance, St. Bonaventura[71].

For St. Thomas, there is nothing higher than knowing; and the ultimate end of man is to know God. Faith for him is a kind of knowing; but it is a kind less than perfect[72]. It differs for him from the sort of knowing that he calls *scientia* by not being immediate or discursively demonstrated; but it is a knowing of another sort, one that he calls *cognitio*[73], also *notitia*[74]. One might perhaps say in modern French that it is not *savoir* but *connaître*? More confidently, in modern English as most persons use the terms, one could affirm that *scientia* for Thomas designated knowing and understanding—even, knowing and wholly understanding. Faith for him is knowing a truth without yet a total understanding of it: it is an apprehending that is not yet a comprehending. (Over against this, for many moderns knowledge has become often so impersonal[75] a concept as to descend to the level of "information". Faith is a kind of knowing well above that level. Hence my use, in endeavouring to render Thomas's position, of the terms "knowing" rather than knowledge, of "apprehending"; and my pointing to its being a full or final understanding that alone is lacking.)

Most today would certainly call knowledge what alone he was willing to call faith, in that it is necessarily and by definition characterized by both correctness of object and certainty of subject. If the object of a position not be true, or if the person who holds it not be certain, then for St. Thomas it is not faith. *Fides* is the name for something no less sure, no less certain, than *scientia*: neither objectively nor subjectively. Insofar as a notion of "belief" involves neutrality in these two respects, or indeed in either one of them—which for him is *opinio*[76]—faith is definitely not that.

So far as propositional beliefs are concerned, we may consider four cases.

First, if the object of a belief be false, then it is not faith[77].

Second, if the subject be hesitant, dubious, tentative, then he or she has belief, not faith[78].

Even when a judgement rises to the level of firm conviction, yet such a heightened belief, however "vehement"[79], is still not faith[80].

Finally, even if the object of propositional belief be in its turn raised from neutrality to certainty, there is still a gap. He carefully discriminated among *credere Deo, credere Deum*, and *credere in Deum*[81], as three facets of one's relating oneself in faith to God. More revealing for our purposes are his relatively little attended remarks, made more or less in passing, on a fourth phrase, *credere Deum esse*[82], which one might wish to translate perhaps "believing in God"[83] in the modern sense of believing that He exists. For one thing, it is not unimportant that his discussion is rather incidental. For another, such a translation is not quite legitimate. For Thomas, that God exists is not an article of faith[84], and certainly not an article of belief[85]. For him, the phrase does not mean "to believe that God exists". Rather, it signifies at a minimum "to recognize that God exists". Nonetheless even this is not faith: for all rational men, he affirms, recognize intellectually God's existence, including persons without faith[86]—although these latter's recognition is conceptually inadequate.

Faith, for St. Thomas, is a virtue[87, 88]; and while in his system there are intellectual virtues, faith is not one of them[89].

(We shall return to this point about the intellectual recognition of God's existence towards the end of this chapter, with reference to a New Testament passage.)

Rather, for him it is a quality of personal life. "Faith", he says, "is that tendency of the human spirit by which our living in the realm of absolutes is launched. It is the capacity of the intellect to recognize the genuineness of the transcendent"[90].

Nevertheless, there are for St. Thomas propositions—there is propositional truth—in the man-God relationship that is faith. Crucial to the whole matter, however, is that these are on the human side of that relationship. On the other side is simply God Himself. Thomas, so far as the "object" of faith is concerned, is quite clear that it is not a proposition, but *veritas prima*: ultimate Truth & Reality; God[91].

In faith we apprehend God[92]. Not fully. Not as He is in Himself[93]. Not as we shall apprehend Him in the beatitude to which finally we are called, when we shall *see* Him (an important concept for St. Thomas[94]) in His fullness. Yet we do apprehend Him.

Propositions are a means to an end[95]. Propositions are human constructs that serve as a means to lead us to the end which is God. Ultimate Truth & Reality, or truth as such, the formal object of faith, and in a way even its material object, is simple; the human mind is so constituted as not to be able to grasp that (or indeed any) reality in its simple form, and has to work with complex truths, propositions, that represent it to us[96]. Yet although our mind has to make do with these complex elaborations, it is not faith if it is not to God that we are directed[97].

This is clarified if we consider his position on heresy. Here, a stance is taken that is quite similar to the Islamic view, that faith is the personal orientation of acceptance, infidelity that of deliberate rejection, of what is clearly known to be right[98]. At issue is not whether this or that be right, but rather one's response to manifest rightness. A heretic, St. Thomas makes clear, is one who rejects an article of the faith—just one, even—perversely or stubbornly (*pertinaciter*)[99]: otherwise, he is not a heretic but merely in error (*non haereticus, sed solum errans*[100]). Such persons, even though accepting all other articles, do not have faith[101]. What they have in regard to those other articles is, he says, merely belief[102]. Faith, thus, is a total attitude, one and indivisible. Furthermore, over against this case, a man who is not wilful may be in error on a given article, but is not a heretic[103].

Thus it appears that of these two persons, the one has faith, although not right belief; whereas the other, who is sound on many articles, has, in relation to them, right belief but not faith.

For him, then, faith and belief are not the same thing. Nonetheless, for him if for anyone they are intertwined; and finally to unravel the close tie between them in his understanding we turn to his position on the point where a comparativist is most fully engaged: the decisive question of diversity of beliefs among persons of faith. On this issue, Thomas's position is entrancing.

—If, that is, one may say that he has a position on this issue. He sets forth a position, no doubt; but it is on *this* issue, some might hold, only by inference, and bold analogy. He does indeed speak of a unity of faith underlying a diversity of belief; yet our awareness of this matter is so radically more elaborate than his, that many today would quickly say that it is by no means the same problem. The twentieth century is not the same as the thirteenth, certainly; Thomas was simply not aware of, and not interested in, a possible difference between Shintoists and Buddhists[104], or a possible similarity between Muslims and Taoists[105]. Of Jews, and more remotely of Muslims, the two groups just within the horizon of his consciousness (but not within his understanding), he was like most Christians of the time, and many since, not aware that they had faith. He was aware of faith in only one series of forms, the Christian (which he called "universal": *fides catholica*[106]).

Yet for this very reason, there is no simple answer to a query as to whether he was thinking and speaking about Christian faith, or about faith. He thought that he was speaking of faith, generically; and this is important. Inevitably his horizon was so limited—by to-day's standards—that in fact he spoke of what a modern is tempted to call (and has some reason to call) Christian faith. Yet one must recognize the limitations of our seeing of the matter that way. In fact what one has in Thomas, we may suggest, is for a modern reader neither a view of faith as such, nor a view of Christian faith as such. Rather, his was a Christian view of faith.

Moreover, and this too is crucially important, it is a thirteenth-century-Christian view of faith. A modern counterpart would be a twentieth-century-Christian's view of faith, generically. Anything else would not stand in continuity with Thomas[107].

It is misleading to perceive his position as a position on Christian faith[108]; for to-day "Christian" inevitably means (among other things) Christian as distinct from Hindu, Buddhist, or whatever (and as distinct from humanist or secular or scientific)[109]. And Thomas did not, could not, have a position on that. What is more: such, he did not wish to have. His Christian view of faith was so implicated within Christian orientations that a modern may have some difficulty in separating out the Christian from the generic. Thomas himself saw no difference between these two. More positively, he firmly held that there is no difference: that they are not two, they are one. Faith is generic, he affirmed[110].

We to-day cannot help but see a difference between the two. Having seen it, we misrepresent him if we imagine that his position is about faith on the Christian side of this polarity (on the specific, as distinct from the generic, side of what has now become this polarity).

Although his mind and heart looked out on a much less broad array of faith than do ours, nonetheless it would be false to suppose either that he saw no diversity, or that he was unsympathetic to such as he saw. On matters of this sort that did come within the range of his comprehension and his concern, he had penetrating things to say.

To the question, whether for Thomas men differing in belief may nonetheless have an underlying unity of faith, there are two possible answers. One is that he never really considered the question. The other, technically more accurate, is that insofar as he did consider it, his answer is "yes". In fact, that answer is clear, strong, deep. Faith is one, despite the diversity of its many human forms[111].

Within the limitations of his awareness, he recognized that beliefs differ, while emphasizing with some force that faith is nonetheless always and everywhere the same. Thus in this he goes beyond our own more cautious position put forward in our opening chapter above[112]. He recognizes a problem in the articulation of faith in articles, and then in the formulation of those articles into "symbols" (creeds, statements of belief). His justification of these is, basically, that they have the authority of the Church (though he goes on to defend them rationally)[113]. The differences among creeds constitutes a problem; but he solves this by affirming that they differ only that "in one some things are implicit that in others are more fully explicit"[114]. With that many moderns would be quite happy; though they would be tempted to apply it around the world.

Thomas even goes so far as to acknowledge that the beliefs of some men of sound faith may be so determined by their historical situation as in the literal sense to be, if we may put it bluntly, false. What he says in effect is that the formulations of their faith are human and as it were accidental, historically conditioned, while the faith itself, mediated by them remains divine[115]. What more could a modern comparativist ask? What more could a modern Christian ask, pondering the divergence between his forefathers' conceptualizations and his own? Thomas comes in fact very close to saying that the implicit substance of faith is in every case God Himself, while the explicit articulation of it in conceptualized patterns is mundane. Again, what more could a comparativist, or a modern, ask? He does not go so far as would some moderns, to say that all authentic creeds contain the truth—the ultimate truth, and that is God Himself—implicitly, none explicitly. Yet he does say some explosive things.

Thus in his own way, even if not in ours, he emerges as a comparativist of sorts after all. Over against the position above mentioned, of someone who might urge his non-involvement in this problem, we might suggest that he did recognize and deal with it in a diachronic though not a synchronic fashion. He was not aware, as moderns vividly are, of a diversity of faith across the world, in space: communities of persons who share a planet in polymorphic fidelities. He did, however, perceive change in time across the centuries, within that faith of whose transcendent reference he was very much aware: faith in what a modern might call the historical series of its Christian forms, and also Old Testament ones (Christianly interpreted—mediaevally-Christianly), if only those. And he was certainly intelligent enough, honest enough, and large-hearted enough, to acknowledge such change and to seek for it a rational interpretation that would do it justice (and do justice severally to each of its forms).

Admittedly, we to-day are inclined to chuckle over the drastically restricted scope of the problem for him, compared to ours. From a twentieth-century vantage point the parameters within which he sets up the issue are charming in their simplicity and innocence. Some will find it fascinating, some a whit ludicrous or even pitiful, that he was in a position where the chief illustration to occur to him of diversity of belief through which faith finds expression is this: on the one hand Israel, whose apprehension of divine grace and salvation took the form of saying that Christ "will be born" (*nasciturus est*[116]), over against later-in-time Christians, on the other hand, for whom it takes the form ". . . has been born" (*natus est*). Is it not delightful to picture to oneself living in a world where that is the sharpest divergence that one can think of, among formulations of faith? Yet the principle is the same as ours: the expressing of faith in formulae that are time-bound and culture-specific.

He even then goes further to discuss what one might call erroneous beliefs. His example is the situation of persons taught in the old dispensation and living after the coming of Christ but before the Gospel had been preached to them. For such men, their awareness of God and His salvific act would be expressed in a formula that would, strictly, be inaccurate: for they would use the future tense of a by then past fact. They, says Thomas, would have faith in its Old Testament form, articulating a part of it in the phrase *nasciturus est*. This is the case where he says that the belief is human and fallible, but the substance is true[117].

His own beliefs were those of a thirteenth-century Christian. His understanding of faith, on the other hand, though articulated within the framework of those beliefs, was universal.

The starting point and foundation of Thomas's view of faith is that its object is primal truth and ultimate reality[118], is God; immediately so of its formal object, finally also of its material object. Meanwhile various other material objects that come into play and are not themselves God do not for him constitute objects of *faith* except insofar as they are oriented to God, and through them persons are oriented to God[119]. A modern wording might be that in Thomas's vision faith is man's relation to transcendent reality, and the mundane objects through which faith is expressed, whatever they be, including, he says, ritual and ceremony, the sacraments, scripture[120], but also explicitly[121] including propositions, belief, and other intellectual constructs, have to do with faith insofar, and only insofar, as they serve as activating symbols or effective channels of that reality.

(iii) Vatican I

To ultimate truth and reality man owes not only his existence but his allegiance. Truth, reality, goodness are objectively given. They are independent of and prior to man, and to his awareness of them; they are greater than he. Human reason, the human spirit, thus does not create truth or other values but discovers them as pre-existing. Since this is so, man's task is one of pursuing what is in some sense already "there"; loyally subordinating both one's mind and one's will to truth and reality (to transcendent value) insofar as these disclose themselves (or, are disclosed, are uncovered; insofar as they make themselves discernible to us). Such "loyalty" is the foundation of man's wholeness; it is the gate to his ultimate, final well-being.

The universal Christian Church proclaims this loyalty to be a quality that is not automatic, inhering in the empirical order of things, but one that is, rather, a special gift or virtue with which man is endowed in such a way that by it we recognize and commit ourselves to the validity of what is disclosed. We do this with the assistance of the very goals that we are enabled to pursue. The ability to recognize truth, reality, and goodness and loyally to pursue them, to subordinate ourselves to them, is not a function of the intrinsic nature of things as rationally apprehended by observation. It is a function rather of a moral authority that pertains to ultimate Truth and Reality themselves—which by the Church are called "God"—from which they are disclosed to us (or, as He discloses them to us). He is (they are) incapable, of course, of being "wrong" themselves or wrong for us: either of being misled or of misleading. For, as the New Testament puts it, this loyalty—or, as Christians call it, faith—is the realizing of what things are worth hoping for (or, to use the technical term, man's hypostasizing of them); it is the case in favour of the transcendent.

Two annotations would seem to follow from all this.

First: Any suggestion, then, is repudiated outright that the human spirit is so autonomous that loyalty to a pre-existing Truth or Reality greater than man cannot reasonably be exacted from him.

Second: Similarly, any suggestion is repudiated that would suggest that faith is like belief: that the sort of final loyalty of which we are speaking is no different from ordinary knowledge about the universe or about metaphysical or ethical matters, and that accordingly for such ultimate (cosmic) loyalty it is not requisite that such truth and values as have been uncovered should by us be recognized and committedly pursued because of the authority of the cosmic source from which they have been made known. Christians call this source God; and say that the authority for us of whatever truth we see is the authority of God who enables us to see it and whose truth it is.

The above is (the above five paragraphs are) a paraphrase in modern terms of a statement on faith (*De Fide*) of the first Vatican Council, 1870, with its two anathemata. The original reads:

> *Cum homo a Deo tamquam creatore et Domino suo totus dependeat et ratio creata increatae Veritati penitus subiecta sit, plenum revelanti Deo intellectus et voluntatis obsequium fide praestare tenemur. Hanc vero fidem, quae "humanae salutis initium est", Ecclesia catholica profitetur, virtutem esse supernaturalem, qua, Dei aspirante et adiuvante gratia, ab eo revelata vera esse credimus, non propter intrinsecam rerum veritatem naturali rationis lumine perspectam, sed propter auctoritatem ipsius Dei revelantis, qui nec falli nec fallere potest. "Est enim fides, testante Apostolo, sperandarum substantia rerum, argumentum non apparentium".*
>
> *Can. 1.—Si quis dixerit, rationem humanam ita independentem esse, ut fides ei a Deo imperari non possit: anathema sit.*
>
> *Can. 2—Si quis dixerit, fidem divinam a naturali de Deo et rebus moralibus scientia non distingui, ac propterea ad fidem divinam non requiri, ut revelata veritas propter auctoritatem Dei revelantis credatur: an. s.*[122]

A modern annotation on this nineteenth-century exposition might be the following.

Why should we pursue, or even trust, what we see to be true? Why should we commit ourselves to what we recognize to be good? How do we acknowledge that values are indeed valuable; that what is intrinsically valuable is valuable for me, personally? To such questions, this document contends, there are no purely rational or empirical answers. Given human freedom and given the kind of mind that man has, truth, reality, goodness are not naturally compelling. The ability to recognize them as genuine, authoritative, and engaging, and to dedicate ourselves to their pursuit, to subordinate ourselves loyally to them, is by Christians called "faith". And Christians have a good deal to say about this as a gift from God, given to man by God historically in dramatic ways.

It is important to note, and indeed to emphasize, the derivative role of the interpretation of faith in this scheme. Faith is envisaged not as the acceptance of the scheme, not as the adoption of the conceptual framework as such, but as one item within it. It is an item that, as set forth, is understandable (let alone significant) only if the scheme has been priorly acknowledged. What is called faith within this over-all delineation of the human condition is not constituted by, and does not even include as part of itself, a seeing of the world in these comprehensive terms. Rather, quite explicitly, it is said that, given this analysis of the human condition as a prior orientation, then the relation of man so conceived to the universe so understood includes a quality that may be termed faith. If, the document is virtually saying, it is the case that there is a transcendent truth prior to the empirical world, prior to man, prior to man's awareness both of what is and of what ought to be, so that man, though free to do as one likes, will in fact flourish in any ultimate sense only if one align oneself with this truth-reality—if this is the case, then one's so aligning oneself, one's decision so to do and one's capacity so to do, are a gift.

That is, within this scheme these matters are not derived from the way mundane things are, but are related rather to the way that transcendent truth is. Man is free to do as he or she likes; and there is nothing in the nature of the empirical world, or of man, that requires one to commit oneself to the transcendent reality from which, according to this view, both are derived. It is reasonable, in this interpretation of the universe, for man to choose a transcendence-oriented destiny for him- or herself; yet it is not strictly unreasonable not to do so. Commitment ("faith") is not rationally inescapable. If one does so choose, it is because the final truth beyond the natural world and beyond oneself is somehow inherently attractive, cogent, and somehow helps one to rise above oneself and above one's empirical environment to go out in pursuit of that higher reality. It is not merely that once one dedicates oneself (*credit*, to use the Latin term) to ultimate reality one finds oneself transformed into something more than a purely natural phenomenon, something better than an empirical organism reacting to its environment. Rather, the very ability so to dedicate oneself, the human capacity to commit oneself to what is better than, greater than, truer than, either oneself or the empirically given: this itself involves a transformation. The ability even to start to live, to decide to live, in terms other than of oneself and the immediately given, comes to man from outside oneself.

It is clear, then, that the entire discussion is—and candidly admits to being—postulated on the view that the situation of the world is as this analysis holds it to be. If the universe is like this—and the authors of this statement felt quite sure that it was—then man's role within it involves or may involve something that they call commitment, faith. If it were not the case that the world is like that, what happens to faith? These men never addressed themselves to that question. For they did not, probably could not, imagine that things were not like that. *Since* things are so-and-so . . . , they began, in so many words (*Cum . . . sit*), therefore, they went on, one's giving of oneself to transcendence is itself a "gift" from transcendence.

What faith might be interpreted as being, in a world differently conceived, it is up to others to spell out. For a modern Muslim, or Buddhist, for example, or a modern post-Christian, the significant question is not whether one agree with the ideas and doctrines that constitute a language within which the characterization of faith is explicated here, or in Thomas six centuries earlier, or in the Qur'an a further six, so much as whether one understand them. More searching, more consequential for one's daily living and one's eternal destiny, certainly, but also more germane to one's understanding of what faith has historically been seen to be, than whether one regards the preambles as "true", is whether one judges the position established in terms of those preambles, to be valid (and, in a not merely intellectual sense, cogent[123]).

(iv) The twentieth century

The Vatican document at which we have looked illustrates a traditional relation between faith and belief but does so still with a certain degree of innocence, which in the twentieth century to a considerable extent gave way rather to ambiguity and confusion. We may observe that transition by glancing first at a restatement of inherited positions, before we move on to note one or two more recent trends.

The innocence is lost, the ambiguity manifested, in that what is ostensibly the re-affirmation in modern times of a traditional Thomist position turns out to have become unwittingly and subtly yet substantially different just because the environment in which it was proffered, the intellectual climate in which it had now to take its place, had meanwhile grossly changed. A thirteenth-century understanding had been transformed into a twentieth-century belief. The explication of a personal relation to God, set forth with logically consummate artistry and ease, gave way to an apologetics of an intellectual and even moral relation to doctrine, set forth with logically strained ingenuity and nervous insistence.

The decades following Vatican I were times of considerable turmoil within the life of the Church, and of considerable controversy between the Church and the culture surrounding it. Since the presuppositions of what was said on the varying sides differed, it is not always easy to reconstruct, and at the time for many it was not possible to discern, where the actual differences lay, what the points at issue actually were. (The problem was certainly much more widespread than merely in Church statements.) Certainly Church pronouncements evinced an ambiguity between a defence of belief which they still refused to equate with faith and yet floundered in failing to distinguish from it[124]. (One sorry byproduct was that the Church as an institution began, it would almost seem, to use its members' personal faith to uphold its own ideological position—rather than *vice versa*.)

Proponents believed the doctrines in some cases in the problematic sense, as in the Vatican pronouncement, still of presupposing their validity, but also now in many cases in a new sense of postulating that validity or defending it. Or, they virtually affirmed that, although not themselves faith, those doctrines are inescapably prerequisite to it, morally as well as logically. Believing is the price that one must pay, in order to have faith, they seemed to be averring. (Protestants also had by this period found themselves victims of that same distortion.)

The ambiguity of which we speak is illustrated in that the expositions can hardly be understood unless seen simultaneously in two contrasting ways. From one point of view, one might say that it did not seriously occur to the spokesmen that the teachings might be otherwise than literally true. (Moreover, from this it followed for them that alternative views must be false.) That is: it did not strike them that, rather than universal truths, straightforward and accurate descriptions of how things in fact are, these propositions, in a fashion with which we have now become familiar, were, indeed, beliefs. The situation appears then as in some ways quite comparable still to the Qur'an case earlier noted, and that of St. Thomas: their minds operated within a particular intellectual framework, through which they viewed the world and at which from the outside they were hardly in a position critically to look. Historically, however, they were moving into an era when not faith but the intellectual framework was becoming the problematic object of discussion. From this point of view, therefore, their situation was deeply different from that of classical Islam or of the mediaeval Christian scholastics—different both externally and internally, even though they did not much realize this (nor, did their critics).

Their faith being articulated in terms of their (or, their predecessors') belief, they felt that to abandon the belief would involve abandoning faith—which, complicatedly, for themselves might perhaps have been so, but they were unable to see that this was not necessarily the case for those who differed from them—and indeed, that it might be faith itself that would impel some to differ. Theology, from being the honest human endeavour to conceptualize the faith that one has, had moved to becoming rather the almost amoral prior condition of being allowed to have it.

The Church believed, for instance, that there is a God; that He created the world; that He revealed Himself in history in ways of which that Church has preserved the record; and the like. And indeed, these beliefs were part of the dogma (the teachings) of the Church, explicitly and emphatically. Equally explicitly, however, these beliefs *are not faith*, as that Church continued to set it forth.

In fact, around the turn of the century the Church roundly condemned, under the heading of "fideism", the position of those who held that these beliefs should be accepted on faith. In a formal Church presentation, a theologian of then considerable authority gets quite cross with such persons in a major exposition that appeared in 1920. These beliefs, he held, are perspicuous; and any reasonable man must accept them rationally[125]. He defends with vigour the notion that God's existence and nature and the fact of revelation are self-evident[126]—in a way that sounds, one must confess, naive to us (to us who are not Roman Catholics? to us who live half a century and more later?). Yet one fails to understand what was going on if one misses either the sincerity or the foundationality of that rationalist conviction on his part.

In fact, it proves rewarding to consider this particular statement with some attention. It illustrates the developments that we have been noting, and in a fairly official way. It is a major contribution of a major thinker made on a major occasion: the article FOI in the weighty *Dictionnaire de théologie catholique* (Paris, 1899-1950, in fifteen volumes[127]). The article (by S. Harent) is marred, many a modern reader would say, by its polemical tone and the datedness of the controversies in which it ardently engages; but it is hardly the less illuminating for that. It has, in fact, the more cogency for us in that it was written precisely to uphold an intellectualist interpretation of faith over against, among other things, a nineteenth-century tendency that had been developing to speculate whether faith is not primarily an affection, a matter largely of the third and most recent of the West's trichotomy, feeling.

At first reading one might in fact be tempted to conclude that the article's chief thesis is that faith is an activity of the intellect. On more careful scrutiny, however, it presently becomes clear that nonetheless, even for this position, faith is still not belief. (Once again, that ambiguity. Insofar as he is writing for a modern audience, the author argues that a person of faith must believe what the Church does. Insofar as he sets forth what the Church believes on this issue, he then makes it evident that it has taught and teaches that faith is in fact not a question of belief.) This is so in various ways, and also in this: that what the statement is speaking of is inherently generic. Faith, in this exposition, is a human relation to God. It has been made universally available to mankind through Christ and is found therefore normally only in the Church (and the Roman Catholic Church at that). The author still writes, therefore, not primarily of *foi chrétienne*[128] (Christian faith, let alone Christian belief), and not even of right and wrong belief or faith, of true or heretical belief or faith—but simply of *foi*: of faith absolutely.

What other people have is, for this stance, not faith. It is not even distorted or inadequate or mistaken or unsalvific faith. It is, at this level, nothing at all; or better, more substantially, it is "infidelity". (This term, in English and in French, still carries with it an implication of rejection: no mere lack of belief, and hardly even a mere lack of faith, but a lack of faithfulness, a wilful lack of loyalty.) The fact reverberates more loudly, and illuminates more clearly, than is generally noted, that a substantial thinker at this significant moment could write on *foi* at great length (the article is the size of a several-hundred-page book) and, in effect, in the course of it say *nothing at all* about the position, or the beliefs, of other communities.

It is altogether obvious that Jews, Hindus, Muslims, Buddhists, and others all do have belief. Indeed, they all have religious belief. These do not figure in his article for a quite simple reason: that the article is not about religious believing. It is hardly even about Christian believing, except insofar as it deals with right and wrong beliefs, of Christians, about faith. The author is much exercised about, and deals at length with, what he considers the wrong beliefs that various Christians (chiefly Protestants but also some Catholics, especially modernists) have expressed on this subject. Faith, he makes quite clear, is something about which Christians' beliefs differ, about which it is important to have right beliefs, and easy to have wrong ones. Nonetheless, he says quite explicitly[129] that it does not matter if ordinary Christians—the masses, simple peasants, children, and the like—do not have a right understanding of their faith.

Their ideas on the matter (we might say, their beliefs) hardly count, so long as they have faith. It would, according to him, be tendentious or pedantic to insist that the intellectual theories of such persons be sound. What is distressing, in his view, is for intellectual leaders to harbour and to propagate wrong ideas about faith. Intellectuals—people whose business it is to conceptualize ("believe"), both for themselves and for society—should conceptualize (believe) accurately. To formulate and to hold correct beliefs, he would say as would we, is the duty of intellectuals as intellectuals (it is the task of a book such as this); while the duty of Christians as Christians is other, is the more important matter of having faith.

His article, then, is about faith, not about religious belief. He says in it that *foi* is *croyance*[130]. Yet the ambiguity of which we have spoken is evinced in that he is the author also of the article CROYANCE in the same encyclopaedia[131], and under that heading he does, indeed, consider other *croyances* than Christian ones. He deals there with false beliefs, with philosophic beliefs, and the like. It is true that his intellectual horizon is, by to-day's standards, woefully limited, practically to the Western world. (One must of course not "blame" him for this, considering the 1920 date; but neither must one under-estimate how deeply this fact must colour his interpretation of an issue such as the relation between faith and believing.) Yet within those limitations he is of course altogether aware that men's beliefs/*croyances*[132] are wide-ranging, they may be true or false, and so on. Faith, on the other hand, is for him not the sort of thing of which there is more than one kind, not the sort of thing that can be false. (For him, it is God-given: how then could it be false? *Nec falli potest nec fallere.*)

The result of all this is that any reader who did not happen to share Professor Harent's particular mind-set would not find it easy to dig through to what it is that he is presenting faith as being. A Buddhist, for instance, or a Jew, a Muslim or a Western humanist, even a Christian near the end rather than the beginning of the twentieth century, would manage only with excessive difficulty to discover from this presentation what Christian faith is like; how it differs from other forms of faith, if it does; even why it is interesting or worthwhile, and why it has been historically major. This is a pity, since if one does succeed in penetrating his conceptual framework, it turns out that, however dated or circumscribed or inflexible his language, he speaks of something indeed rich, profound, and of ultimate importance. That such readers might be interested in such questions never occurred to him.

To-day, therefore, the significance of his statement is almost wholly historical. It represents a spirited defence, at the beginning of a pluralist age, of one particular intellectual position which in his eyes was not faith and yet within which alone, among many now emerging, for him faith could be either found or understood. Earlier writers (such as the St. Thomas whom ostensibly he followed) had not felt that faith itself was threatened by honest disagreements as to its intellectualization; nor were they familiar with radical and powerful alternatives. Subsequently, writers would not again feel Harent's vacillation between conviction that his intellectual position was right and apprehension that if not, then his and indeed everyone's spiritual position was hopeless.

Finally we turn to more recent developments. Had our aspiration been to follow the evolution of Roman Catholic interpretations of faith for the modern period, a much more elaborate inquiry would, of course, be required than is here appropriate or attempted. For our limited concern, however, the faith/belief relation, it will be sufficiently suggestive if we note this matter with regard to one major tendency: a movement away from scholastically intellectualist, objectivistic and towards more personalist and experientialist (and richer, fuller, more transcendentalist, and in my view truer) interpretations of faith. This has constituted a widespread and growing development. As representative of this general trend we might consider any of a number of thinkers: among the forerunners, for instance the French lay philosopher Maurice Blondel[133], or more recently the prolific and influential German theologian Karl Rahner[134], or the winning and deeply sensitive French writer Jean Mouroux[135], or others[136]. Instead, we may for formal reasons once again take as illustrative a presentation set forth in a more or less official Church exposition: the 150-volume *Twentieth Century Encyclopedia of Catholicism* (1958-1971) of which one volume is entitled *What is Faith?* "Faith is an engagement" and "Faith is an encounter" are the titles of two of the chapters[137]. The presentation includes sentences such as the following: "Faith is an encounter with the living God; it means letting God in"[138]; "The encounter between God and each person is a mystery which cannot be put into any category"[139]; faith is "like love, . . . something alive"[140]. Another of the descriptions is: "Faith is laying oneself open to dissatisfaction and to desire. Faith is readiness to set out on the journey, to go further and further. Faith is the search for God . . ."[141].

Nonetheless, at another place the statement not only speaks of, but insists upon, faith's "intellectual content"[142]. It does not explain that phrase, difficult in itself[143], nor elucidate how or in what sense, if faith is a living encounter between two persons, divine and human, propositions are "the content" of that encounter. It simply affirms that "belief . . . is the content" of faith[144]—a belief which is provided "infallibly" by "the teaching Church"[145]. It calls faith and belief "inseparable"[146], over against what it dubs the Lutheran, and generally the Protestant, separation of faith from belief, with the latter being "a human formulation, something inadequate, contingent and perpetually reformable"[147]. One gets the impression, however, that this interpretation itself in fact separates the two in almost the same fashion, the difference being that for it belief is not a human formulation and inadequate, but a divine formulation and infallible. There is an ambiguity here: in giving as an example of the truth that we do not perceive by reason, "the presence of Jesus Christ in the Eucharist"[147a], there is some ambivalence as to whether faith is perceiving that presence, or believing the proposition that it is there. And over against the vocabulary of encounter, *engagement*, and mystery, the text at one point speaks of God's having revealed (not Himself, but) a truth "about" God and religion[148].

There is a revealing discussion developed from a considering of the famous verse in the Book of Hebrews at which we too shall be glancing briefly in our next section: "Without faith it is impossible to please him. To go to God it is necessary to believe that he exists"[149]. The discussion elaborates and emphasizes faith's involving "believing" that God exists, but inasmuch as the assumption is, clearly, quite firm that God is indeed there, this in fact means "knowing" or "recognizing" that God exists. Indeed on the next page surreptitiously there is a shift from believing to knowing, as one reads: "Faith is the search for God in the knowledge that he exists"[150]. Apart from the unconscious shift in language, this last statement is itself illuminating, is even perhaps finally representative of the Church's position on our whole problem.

This text does not say, or imply, that faith is belief; and in this important sentence it does not say that faith is knowledge. On the contrary, it says that it is the search, presupposing the knowledge. This is, formally, precisely in line with the Qur'an, and with St. Thomas. Faith in the Islamic, the Christian, and in other instances (also in the Buddhist instance, but in that case not with the concept God) has been interpreted throughout the centuries with an ideational substratum; but as here, this conceptualized part is in each case preamble or presupposition, it is not faith itself. More accurately, we might say that for all these interpreters faith involves, includes, an awareness; but the propositional verbalization of that awareness appears on scrutiny as not intrinsic.

In less formal presentations, the renewed emphasis on the personalist and transcendent quality of faith has tended in several instances to resolve the faith/belief issue in one or other of two ways[151]. Both tendencies are shared with recent Protestant thought on the matter, and we postpone consideration of them to our next chapter. One is the thesis that faith is explicitly "more than" belief but includes it: that is, intellectual belief (usually meaning, beliefs in the modern sense in relation to inherited doctrines) is requisite but is "not enough", and faith "goes beyond it", faith is "belief plus". The other tendency, perhaps growing, is anti-intellectualist. In this, faith is seen as something other than believing, and indeed as other than thinking and other than knowing. Ideas are not involved. This leads to faith as a quality not of the whole person but of parts, those parts other than the mind: for instance, to return to the Western triad, the will (and the pragmatic realm generally; for example, in social activism), and especially the feelings.

Some readers might perhaps be tempted to misunderstand my own argument as of this sort, or as if a case were being made for envisaging faith as purely subjective. On the contrary! My thesis is rather that, insofar as faith is a human involvement with a transcendent reality—which Christian thinkers like others certainly have affirmed, and do well to continue to emphasize; insofar as, if one were to use these two terms, it constitutes a subject-object relationship; then belief is on the subjective side of that relation. It is for this reason that a Christian may find it misleading—not to say, blasphemous—to idolize that belief: that is, to mistake it for the "object", or for the reality to which one is related (or even for part of that). A belief is far too historical and transient a phenomenon, too vulnerable, too *mundane*, to be confused with the object of faith. Nonetheless, a "faith" unconcerned with truth would be discontinuous, to put it mildly, with past history—not least, Christian history —as well as disruptive of human integrity. On both scores it would not deserve the name. We shall return to these mighty problems in our final chapter.

At the moment, we are not arguing the thesis, generically, that faith is not belief (in the modern sense). Rather, we have simply been clarifying the observable point that, when considered carefully, Christian writers have not, in fact, contended that it was.

(v) Varia

Finally, we close by turning to a few disconnected, and it may seem almost random phrases and passages that are illuminated when seen in the light of our general considerations—and that in turn then illumine further the question that concerns us.

First, in the New Testament. I mostly leave aside here the Biblical area; the investigating of especially New Testament concepts of faith from the new point of view is a highly rewarding task, undertaken in our companion volume[152]. There, we consider such facts as that in many instances—far more instances than are usually remarked—the concept "faith" in the Gospels and even the Epistles has no object. That is, it designates a certain quality of human life (". . . shall he find faith on earth?"[153]; "O ye of little faith!"[154]; ". . . now abideth faith, hope, charity"[155]), rather than specifies a relationship to something external, as later came to be assumed. We reflect there also on the several instances where the object (if indeed that be the right word) is personal: God, or Christ. Here I do wish, however, to consider briefly[156] one of the rare instances where the object of the verb is a proposition, since this class of usage has become of increasing importance in subsequent Christian history, and especially in recent times with the vigorous attempt still to push hard a distinction between "believing in" and "believing that". The passage is the noteworthy instance in the Epistle of James (James 2:19) where the object of faith is the clause[157] "that God is one", and there follows the remark[158] translated in the King James version as "the devils also believe, and tremble". This translation may have been accurate in 1611, but is a misrendering in the 1970's (on which more in our next chapter). This is the sole instance in the Bible where the word otherwise designating the new Christian conception of faith is used to denote a theoretical awareness without a positive response to that awareness.

Now it is certainly the case that this passage, however exceptional, has been influential for the intellectualist interpretation of faith, eventually as belief. Yet there is one crucial consideration that usually gets overlooked: namely, that the writer himself was in no doubt whatsoever, and expected his readers to be in none, that God is indeed there, and is indeed one. Monotheism is his presupposition, in the Qur'an sense. Therefore, in our contention, the accurate way to express in our day, in English, what he was saying in his day, in Greek, would be: ". . . to recognize that God is one. The devils also recognize, and tremble". For with us, the concept "to believe" explicitly leaves open the validity or otherwise of that to which it refers, as we have remarked. Our word to describe the intellectual awareness of what is in fact the case, and is known to be so, is rather: "to recognize".

Other words for this are "to acknowledge" and "to realize". Given the ambivalence, in modern English, of "realize" (which can mean to actualize, to make real, or can mean to recognize theoretically the actuality of), one might suggest—for those for whom the concept "God" is meaningful—that a component of faith is the realization of God in one's life. St. James may then be rendered as saying somewhat punningly that to have faith is to realize God's oneness; but since the devils also realize this, to their dismay, therefore faith without works is dead. This is pretty much how the passage was read during the Middle Ages, and indeed has throughout been read by the Church.

Second, we take note of a handful of post-Biblical passages of which new translations are here propounded serving perhaps to illustrate our orientation. These, having been chosen *ad hoc*, are presented not to prove a point but to illuminate it, showing how much more meaning and depth emerge when faith, rather than belief, is recognized as under discussion.

We begin by being deliberately incidental. A 1536 tombstone inscription in Chichester Cathedral reads *Operibus Credite* as the motto on the coat-of-arms of Robert, bishop of that city, buried there. If one happens to come across this[159], one may recognize that it begins to make good sense if *credo* here is recognized as implying a giving of the heart: a having or showing faith, in the sense of inner activated allegiance. "Let your faith be through your deeds", it might be rendered; or, elaborating that, let your devotion to God be operative—and not simply theoretical, one might add. "Have faith, actively: don't merely believe", the maxim might almost be taken as advising.

Faith, I have been urging, is a self-commitment, a dedicating or consecrating of one's life to. Therefore, to give one's allegiance to God is to do His will. In Latin, *credere autem ei est facere ejus voluntatem.* The statement is St. Irenaeus's[160].

Again: "For a person to give his or her heart loyally to Christ is the same as loyally to observe God's commandments"—Salvian. *Fideliter hominem Christo credere, id est . . . fideliter dei mandata servare*[161].

No one devotes himself to anything, unless he first has reflected that it is worth devoting oneself to, says St. Augustine. *Nullus quippe credit aliquid, nisi prius cogitaverit esse credendum*[162].

"Understand in order that you may become committed. Become committed in order that you may understand"—St. Augustine. *Intellege ut credas, crede ut intellegas*[163].

To translate *credo ut intelligam*[164] as "I believe in order that I may understand" makes it seem ridiculous and offensive. On the other hand, it becomes not merely intelligible but illuminating when rendered, "I become involved, in order that I may understand"; "I dedicate myself, I give my heart, in order that my mind may truly penetrate". Any physicist, chess-player, or administrator says as much, if he is to be any good (perhaps not in Latin)[165].

A comparativist looking out over the religious history of mankind is liable to hold that faith cannot be defined; and yet he or she might be attracted to a characterizing of it as the capacity of human beings to devote themselves to transcendence. At least, there is a certain delight in coming across that very formulation in the writings of St. Augustine. "Faith", he long ago said, "is the virtue [or power] by which commitment is given to the transcendent". *Fides est virtus qua creduntur quae non videntur*[166].

In closing, may we cite in illustration of this act of commitment one more instance as dramatic, as decisive, as the baptism service with which we began—but this time in music. Let one who hears Bach's *B Minor Mass* listen to the *credo* part with the sense of *credo* as the "I do" of a deliberate giving of the heart, a committing of the self, a decision of the will. Belief, in the modern sense, sorts ill with those crescendi, that crashing of the sound. Represented here is clearly not a *theoria* but a *praxis*, when one opts for a new life fatefully, and excitedly takes on the momentous consequences. Belief is presupposed. One believes what one's culture takes for granted, or what seems reasonable, quietly, perhaps even a whit tentatively (Bach's believing, though tacit, was not tentative); but one's deliberate act of taking sides, of *s'engager*, is a decisive drama—whose movement Bach profoundly caught.

* * *

The Church's early ceremonial, St. Thomas Aquinas, Vatican I, modern Catholic theology, St. Augustine, Bach, all bear us witness that *credo* means what it says: "I place my heart". They confirm that the depths of Christian life in God, Christ's life in man, are a matter of faith, rather than of belief.

No future age, we predict, will ever again translate *credo* as "I believe". Faith is not belief; and those who wrote in Latin did not imagine that it was. For coming generations, and for many members of the present one, if they are to make sense of their past heritage and to do justice to its spokesmen, all extant translations will have to be revised so as to remove this serious misinterpretation of the key concept. For this English word does not express (any longer) what the term has meant.

A suggestion so provocative, seemingly so monumentally brash, would actually *be* brash, but also incredible, if it were to imply that translators in the past, who did render *credo* as "believing", did not understand their texts[167]. It is not their misunderstanding, however, but ours. Whether *credo* has signified "believing" depends, as we have remarked, on what "believe" has signified. We turn to that.

Chapter 6

THE ENGLISH WORD "BELIEVE"

THINGS change.

By now, most of us have become accustomed to the fact that all here on earth is in transition. The continents drift back and forth across the oceans, their mountain ranges which look so solid and firm in fact rising and falling. The Dipper did not point to a Pole Star in the northern sky for the classical Greeks as it does for us. Social institutions, although not always in such rapid flux as at present, have, we now know, constantly been transformed.

Languages, too, have histories. Words change their meanings with the centuries, some more than others. "Manufactured" used to mean "made by hand"[1]; and "villain" was once simply "rustic", originally one holding land bound to his lord's villa. The "outlandish women" who made Solomon sin[2] were merely foreigners. And so on. Most such changes are merely quaint and of passing interest; they matter little. A major shift in the meaning of the English word "believe", however, not only has, I find, occurred over the centuries, as can be demonstrated, but also has proven of massive consequence and fateful significance, as I shall argue —so deeply imbedded is the term in Western religious life and thought, and so central has it remained, until to-day.

Let us begin with etymology.

Literally, and originally, "to believe" means "to hold dear": virtually, to love. This fact—and it is a hard, brute, fact—provides the underlying force and substance of our thesis here. Let it be emphasized, and reiterated. Let it be remembered, throughout the remainder of this chapter and even, if one be allowed so to plead, throughout the remainder of each reader's life. Literally, and originally, "to believe" means "to hold dear".

This is what its German equivalent *belieben* still means today. *Die beliebteste Zigarette* in an advertisement signifies quite simply the favourite among cigarettes; the most popular cigarette; the most prized. Similarly the adjective *lieb* is "dear, beloved" (*mein lieber Freund*, "my dear friend"). *Die Liebe* is the noun "love"; and *lieben* is the verb "to love" (*Ich liebe dich*, "I love you"). *Belieben*, then, is to treat as *lieb*, to consider lovely, to like, to wish for, to choose. This root survives in English in the modern-archaic "lief", as in Tennyson's *Morte d'Arthur*: "As thou art lief and dear"[3]—that is, beloved. One finds it, too, in quaint phrases such as "I would as lief die as betray my honour".

This same root shows in Latin, as in *libet*, "it pleases"; in the Latin phrase used in English, *ad lib.* (for *ad libitum*), "as one likes, at pleasure"; and in the noun *libido*, "pleasure", projected into modern usage by the Freudians. Latin *libet* and *libido* are also found, although less commonly, in the forms *lubet* and *lubido*[4].

Modern English "lief" (dear, beloved) goes back to Old English ("Anglo-Saxon") *leof*, *liof*, of the same meaning, with which there was a cognate and more or less parallel form *lufu*, "affection, love"[5]. The latter is the form that has come down into Modern English in our word "love", noun and verb. This pair of related words, with what the linguists call different grades of vowel but the same consonants, is widespread. Forms from a reconstructed original root **leubh-* in proto-Indo-European are found widely in the Indo-European language family[6]—as far away as Sanskrit, where *lubh-*, *lubhyati*, "to desire strongly, to be lustful"[7], is the same root. This serves also in passing to make the point, as with the Latin *libet*, *libido* (or *lubet*, *lubido*), that the notion of passionate longing or attachment is also somewhere in the background. For the Teutonic languages, however, it is admittedly a matter usually of cherishing, rather.

In Old English, from *leof*, "dear, beloved", was formed the verb *geleofan*, *gelefan*, *geliefan*, "to hold dear, to love, to consider valuable or lovely"; this later reduced phonetically to *ilefen*, *ileven*, with the same meaning[8]. From the other grade came Old High German *gilouben*, again with the same meaning[9]. This last has developed into Modern German *glauben*, first "to hold dear, to regard as lovable, to attach oneself to"[10], and now "to have faith in". Along with this is the noun *der Glaube*: the act or condition of, if you will, endearing; now, "faith". In Middle English it was the lighter of the two grades that prevailed with the meaning "to hold dear, to consider lovely, to value, to love": namely, be-lēve(n). This gave the early Modern English "believe" ("to cherish"; later, "to have faith"; we shall explore its meaning presently). A verb "to belove"[11] in English has not survived beyond the nineteenth century, except in the past particple: "beloved".

The two original variants in the vowel gradation show also in modern German *sich verlieben*, "to fall in love with", and (*sich*) *verloben*, "to betroth, to engage" (to become engaged)[12]. Note also *geloben*, "to promise" (virtually the same word as *glauben* originally—which is a nice comment on this being chosen as a translation of the Church's term *credo*). *Loben*, "to praise", is closely akin[13].

The word "believe", then, began its career in early Modern English meaning "to belove", "to regard as lief", to hold dear, to cherish. The object (if any) of the verb was for many centuries primarily, and often only, a person, as with the cognate term "love". All other meanings are derived. To believe a person, or to believe "in", or "on", or for a time "to" or "of", a person, was to orient oneself towards him or her with a particular attitude or relationship, of esteem and affection, also trust—and more earnestly, of self-giving endearment. The noun "belief", whose development accompanied but later outpaced that of the verb, similarly meant literally endearment, holding as beloved, and specifically then a giving of oneself to, clinging to, committing oneself, placing—or staking—one's confidence in.

If one looks at specific usages from past centuries illustrating these developments, one must remember that we of course approach any given passage or quotation in which the words "believe" or "belief" occur, by bringing to it the connotations and clusters of meanings from our own century, our minds influenced by all the intervening evolution from the Enlightenment, the nineteenth century, and the modern world. The first hearers of the passage in question, on the other hand, of course approached it out of their own cultural inheritance, bringing to it the then *past* history of the terms, as we have just sketched this.

In other words, we tend to read, let us say, a thirteenth- or a sixteenth-century sentence in the light of the subsequent history of the words, while its contemporaries read it or heard it in the light of their preceding history. Especially when the believing is in or on or of a person, the passage may ambiguously lend itself to either interpretation. By quoting such a passage, therefore, one often cannot prove that this or that is the correct rendering. One can merely discover the possible illumination afforded by construing it in terms of its older meaning, instead of, or as well as, its newer.

Thus when we read from the mid-fifteenth century, "it is a grete merveile that ye haue so grete bileve to this man", we are inclined to think of credence being given to his statements, whereas a fifteenth-century person hearing the words would more likely think in terms of the man's being trusted and esteemed as a person, his lead being followed. And indeed on scrutiny it turns out from the context that this latter seems in fact to be what the author had in mind. The sentence is from *Merlin, or The Early History of King Arthur*[14]. No *statement* of Merlin ("this man") is adduced in the passage; and the implication is that if any verbal matter at all is at issue, it is a question rather of advice than of propositions. It seems more probable, however, without being incontrovertible, that the speaker of the sentence, who is "one of the Barons", was envious of the king's high regard for Merlin generally and his according him a major role at court and in royal policy decisions. The king's *bileve* here is his giving a place of honour: it is a question of whose counsel he heeds, in the light of whose judgement he orders his behaviour, whom he operationally esteems. The other courtiers were jealous of Merlin's being the king's favourite (his most cherished).

Again, to take a formulation two centuries later and indeed more explicitly proposition-linked: Milton in *Paradise Lost* (10:42-43) writes of man's "believing lies against his Maker". Now at first blush one could interpret this in either of two ways. It could be seen as meaning in the modern fashion his imagining those lies to be true: that is, his gullibly but in good faith regarding as accurate statements that in fact are false. Or, one may read it, in more mediaeval mood, and more in keeping with the rest of the passage, and with Milton's voluntarism generally—also, more compatibly with the moral quality of the term "lies"—as suggesting that man here is depicted as opting for lies, and taking pleasure in them, clinging to them, deliberately choosing what is clearly false: a moral act, not an intellectual error. It is difficult, admittedly, for a twentieth-century reader not to feel perhaps that this latter interpretation is far-fetched and forced, so powerfully does the recent history of the word operate on our minds. Yet a study of the context bears it out; and the more familiar one is with Milton the more readily one recognizes this second interpretation as right. This flavour is, indeed, discernible enough to any reader once the passage is read carefully in full[15].

Let us note one more instance of this sort of manifest ambiguity. When John Fisher, Bishop of Rochester, preaches in St. Paul's Cathedral on May 10, 1509, the funeral sermon[16] for Henry VII, he more or less admits that the king was more or less a sinner but hopes to prove that nonetheless he ended his life "in our lorde", and adduces in evidence four chief points, one of which (not the first) includes Henry's "byleue of god"[17]. There is no way of showing indisputably whether this means that for all his sins Henry believed that God exists, in a modern fashion, or whether, in the mediaeval fashion—it being taken for granted all round that God exists—that Henry directed to God a certain ultimate loyalty and allegiance, set his heart on Him, and put his trust and confidence there. In favour of the latter interpretation, however, is virtually the entire context. For one thing, Bishop Fisher characterizes this "byleue" as "stedfast" (not that this clinches the argument, by any means. In modern times there can be stubborn intellectual belief, against evidence; we shall return to this). There is the further point, however, that this "stedfast byleue" is not simply "of God" but "of god and of the sacramentes of the chyrche" (there is the story of the twentieth-century Oxford don who was asked if he believed in baptism, and replied: "Believe in it? Why, I have actually seen it happen!"). More telling is the surrounding material. This steadfast belief is, as I have said, one of four points that Bishop Fisher enumerates. "The fyrst is a true tournynge of his soule from this wretched worlde vnto the loue of almighty god."[18] We shall find subsequently that the notion of a turning of the soul away from one thing and towards another runs rather persistently through these early discussions, as it did in the baptism service. The question is very much of where one focuses one's attention, to what one directs one's concern, what one depreciates or values. Notice also the use of "true" here ("a true turning of the soul") in the Platonic, rather than the propositional, sense of truth, comparable to our speaking of a true note in music, a true university, a man's being true to his word—not logically true, as a statement. The second is a "fast hope & confydence" ("fast" meaning firm, stable, "stedfast", as in the next item) in prayer. The third, already mentioned, was the steadfast belief of God and of the Sacraments of the Church; and the fourth, a diligent (again, that adjective is revealing) asking of mercy. Later on in the sermon, the Bishop elaborates these points, and remarks, for instance, that the cause of his hope was "the true byleue that he had in god, in his chirche & in the sacramentes therof"[19] and speaks of his receiving these "with meruaylous deuocion"[20]. The nineteenth-century editor[21] of the sermon glosses "byleue" here as trust. However that may be, the cluster of surrounding terms—diligence, devotion, steadfastness, confidence—all make good sense along with an interpretation of *byleue* in its mediaeval connotation, of holding in high esteem, cherishing. The fact that this item comes third in the list also makes propositional belief extremely dubious.

Now I have deliberately chosen these rather ambivalent passages, which continue on for many centuries, and indeed in some sense almost until yesterday, and which are not in themselves fully convincing, in order to make the point that this ambivalence or potential ambiguity in various passages has played an important role in what would be otherwise an almost incredible situation: namely, that modern people can have failed to notice the radical difference of meaning that once underlay these terms. To misread into such writing as we have noted a twentieth-century notion of believing, although on inquiry it turns out to be wrong, nonetheless admittedly does not disrupt the sense so starkly or vividly as to make one consciously and conspicuously stumble. Let us turn now, however, to other early passages where the notion is more inescapable that believing is a deliberate adherence. In these, the idea is unquestionably of committing oneself: of ordering one's behaviour in obedience, either to an authority deliberately accepted, or to a value personally recognized and deliberately pursued. The fact that *leve* and "love", "believe" and "belove", were once varieties of the same word, as Latin *libet* and *lubet*, German *liebe* and *loube*, *belieben* and *glauben*, then becomes transparent—as does the validity of the mediaeval translation into English of the Latin *credo* as "believe" in the sense of "I hold dear, I give my heart".

Indeed, as we have noted, there is reason to suppose that this ambiguity probably continues in certain Church circles even until to-day, in a way that is superficially quite surprising[22].

The interchangeability of "believe" and "belove" is an empirical fact, historically. Here is one[23] example. *Laȝamons Brut, or Chronicle of Britain; a poetical semi-Saxon paraphrase of the Brut of Wace*[24] was edited in 1847 from two surviving manuscripts, one from "the early part of the thirteenth century"[25] and the other a little later, in Henry III's reign. The texts of the two manuscripts are quite close, but not identical. A certain King Bladud, for instance, is presented as having built a temple, perhaps at Bath, dedicated to Minerva. One of the manuscripts reads: *to hire he hefde loue* (to her he had love), while the other has, *in hire he bi-lefde*[26]. That is, here *bi-lefde* manifestly means "he held dear"—virtually, he loved. In a later passage another king is being urged to honour his pledge; to uphold an oath that he has sworn; not to hold cheap a pledge that he has given. The wording is: *bi-lef þene æð* (second manuscript, *bi-lef þane oþ*)[27]. Nobody can believe his own oath, in the modern sense; but it makes good sense, and is indeed unavoidable, to translate "believe" here as "to value highly, to hold fast to, be loyal to, keep allegiance to". The modern phrase would be "honour thine oath". Just as the king honoured Merlin, to the irritation of his rivals at court, so here a man is being asked to hold his oath in honour.

We may note in passing, also, that the English word "to honour" in such phrases means not merely to consider honourable, to hold in high esteem, at the theoretical level, but to add to this an active operational thrust. In present-day English, "to honour one's word", "to honour one's bond", "to honour one's pledge", signify not merely an attitude, mental or emotional or both, but a following through in practice. "To believe" in mediaeval English meant almost exactly what "to honour" means in these usages in modern English.

At another point in this poem the following lines occur:

> *Cnihtes ȝe beoð me leofue!*
> *ah þas tiðende me beoð laðe . . .*
> *ah ȝe ileoueð a þene wurse*[28]

(I have omitted two lines between the second and the last here.) Literally, this is: "Knights, ye be to me lief / But these tidings to me be loathe / . . . But ye ileve the worse". Note the contrast, in the first and second lines, between *lief* ("dear, beloved, cherished") and repellent, loathesome[29]; and the parallel between the first and the last line: you are dear to me, and you have held dear—have chosen, have opted for, have elected to pursue—the worse. Let us fill in now the missing spaces. The second line above is followed by the following:

eouwer ileuen beoð vnwraste[30]

—"your choices [what you cherish, your commitments, your loves; or we might say in the modern jargon, your values] are not good" (the nineteenth-century editor translated this as: "your creeds"). And this line was in turn succeeded by the following:

ȝe ne ileoueð noht an cristre[31]

—"ye do not esteem—do not love, hold dear, give high regard to—Christ" but, as the fifth line goes on then to say, "rather you opt for, gave your allegiance to, something less good". To summarize, and paraphrase, the whole:

Knights, you are lovable to me,
But what you proclaim is unlovely;
Your supreme values are bad,
You do not love Christ,
But hold beloved what is of lower value.

The only difference in manuscripts here is that the second has in the second line *bilefues* for *tiðende*, which transfers the third line to the second. This makes it a whit more pithy: "You are loved, but what you belove is loathe".

We are here dealing with partly secular, partly religious, contexts. (The double usage of *leof* in this passage is itself interesting: for the speaker's cherishing of the knights, and the knights' cherishing of Christ.) Let us turn to more strictly Christian usage. It is not clear to me whether this was indeed the primary and dominant usage of our word, for early centuries, as it would seem, or whether it is so simply in those sources that have survived.

One of the earliest recorded[32] instances in English of the word "belief" is from a homily from the late twelfth or early thirteenth century, where it is averred that Christian men should not set their hearts, we might say, on worldly goods. The phrasing is ". . . should not set their belief" on them[33]. There is no suggestion here that Christians should regard the material world as unreal, illusory, should not believe in it, in that modern sense. On the contrary, it is implied that the mundane is concrete enough, but is not worth esteeming, should not become beloved. One is certainly expected to give it intellectual recognition, but should not give it one's allegiance, nor award to it one's reliance—and thus, one's soul. The question is not, what exists: rather, what is to be one's attitude and orientation to what exists. (This is exactly as we saw in the Qur'an case.)

It is assumed here that both God and the world are recognized. At issue is, which gets one's allegiance.

Two contrasts are set up in this passage. First, one should set one's heart, one's *bileafe*, not on temporal possessions but on God alone[34]. Second, Christians, who hold not the world dear but God, are contrasted in the next sentence, in fact the next word, with *þe ȝitsere*, the covetous one, the greedy, "who sets his mind on his goods". The person who does this is said to be the devil's child[35]. Thus the opposite of "believing in God" here is not not believing; it is devoting oneself to, thinking highly of, material possessions and therefore being the child of the devil.

Now this last is illuminating, if we consider it carefully. Since the preacher says that a Christian should set his heart on God, and that the person who sets his heart on things of this world is a child of the devil, we to-day would say that that preacher believed in the devil. In our sense of the word, undoubtedly he did believe in the devil; but in his sense of the word it would be an insult and a libel to say this of him. He recognized the existence of the devil, right enough; but the whole point of his homily was that one should, partly for that very reason, "believe"—that is, *belieben*, hold dear, love, give one's heart to—God alone. If he heard us speak of believing in both God and the devil simultaneously, he would think that we were mad—schizophrenic. To him, God and the devil were obviously both there: but (or therefore) you have to choose between them for your behaviour. The question of import was, to which do you give your loyalty.

The situation here is once again like the Islamic instance at which we looked earlier. What we would call believing in God, and what we would call believing in the devil, are both presupposed, *both* in the case of a good Christian whose commitment is to the divine, *and* in that of the covetous man whose heart is set on this world. Belief in the modern sense of the term is simply not at issue. In this sermon the word *bileafe* serves to designate what we call faith, and what he in effect called loving, cherishing, holding dear.

A further refinement is instructive. When that mediaeval preacher says that the covetous or greedy man is a child of the devil, we can understand him perfectly well, and even be said to agree with him—*euen if we ourselves do not believe in a devil.* Now this is quite curious, if one reflect upon it. In this instance we readily enough, and cheerfully enough, recognize his intellectual framework, his theoretical presuppositions; and we are ready enough cheerfully to move quickly beyond them, and in a sense to dismiss them, in order to deal with the substantive point that he was making. We do not allow the fact that our conceptual system is different from his to stand in the way of our sensing and coping with his position. On the other side of these matters, on the other hand, most moderns are unwilling or unable to do as much with the mediaeval notion of positive faith. They can see that faith went beyond, and still goes beyond, belief; but they insist that nonetheless it included it, and somehow must include it.

A belief in the devil is not necessary to a recognition of greed as devilish. Yet a belief in God is thought to be required for a recognition of faith as divine.

Is that too poetic for moderns?

Another twelfth-century homily makes more or less explicit the point that the theoretical presuppositions of the theological system were indeed presuppositions underlying, as in the Islamic case, *both* faith *and* infidelity. In this case the anonymous preacher is holding forth on the Latin term *credo*. He says in the learned fashion of the day[36] that it may be understood in three ways (*credo Deo*, *Deum*, and *in Deum*). The first two of these, he explicitly says, "all heathen men do: the third, only good Christians do, and the God-fearing and men of faith"[37]. The first two, which then are common to both sides, include, he says, the recognition that God exists. What only the man of faith does is *credere in Deum*, which he renders alternately as *bileued in god* and as *to luuene ine god*[38]. This involves, he says, five things: to acknowledge God as Lord over all things, to love Him over all things, to have awe of Him over all things, to value Him over all things, to obey Him over all things. In other words, belief in our modern sense characterizes, he says, both Christians and non-Christians, both men of faith and infidels. (In our modern jargon: it was part of the world-view of the time, of the accepted presuppositional framework.) What distinguishes those with faith is what he sometimes calls *ileve*, once or twice *bileve*, and sometimes *luve*. Explicitly, what he is saying is that faith is loving God, holding God dear. To believe in God, or to believe that He exists, he says in virtually so many words, is not at all at issue. Everyone does that. Faith, on the other hand, is holding God more dear than anything else. "To hold God dear", he affirms, means, among other things, "to hold Him dearer than everything else", or, since he uses *leve* and *luve* more or less interchangeably, a more precise rendering is, "To love God is . . . to love Him over all things".

One could go on piling up the evidence for English usage in the Middle Ages, which in the end is overwhelmingly conclusive that words such as *bilefe*, *bileve*, and the like designated allegiance, commitment, the placing of one's heart, choice—and not propositional constructs[39]. In

Langland's *Vision of Piers Plowman*, for instance, there is many a passage where in quite bitter irony or blunt invective the poet denounces clerical learning as a substitute for charity (in the old sense of loving-kindness)[40]. He has little use for clerics who talk about God much, but whose love of Him (and of their fellow men) is little[41]: intellectuals, we might say, whose beliefs are fine but whose goodwill, and whose commitment to act in terms of their beliefs, are wanting. None is so readily ravished, he says, from what a modern editor reads as "right doctrine", as "these clever clerics who pore over many volumes"[42]. "Doctrine", here is an absurd rendition, I would submit, for the original *riȝte byleue*. I am sure that these many-tomed cunning intellectuals were at their best in doctrine. Their trouble was by no means that, but rather their faith: faith in the sense of the quality of their lives, and particularly their dedication to carrying out in practice what they talked about so glibly. This is what the poem is all about.

Similarly the other poet, anonymous, who not many decades later wrote a work called *Piers Plowman's Creed*[43], a tale of a seeker who goes about asking instruction in true faith, and meets with clerics who fleece him and live lives of hypocrisy, extravagance, and haughtiness, and embroider it all with refinement of theory rather than righteous living and meekness. Finally the seeker meets a humble and poorly dressed peasant, Piers Plowman (a fictitious character recently made famous by the earlier poem), who answers his request. Now it would be a ludicrous anticlimax if after all this morally oriented prelude the poem were to culminate in a plea to *believe* anything at all, in doctrinal theory. He has all this time been denouncing that sort of thing. The poem emerges as a significant work of art, however, as well as of genuine spirituality, if *leve* is recognized as German *Liebe*, English "love", or perhaps more technically German *belieben*: "give your allegiance to", "attach yourself to sincerely". That is, the climax to which the poem rises at the end must surely be recognized as a kind of crescendo on *love*. The word *leue* occurs three times at this climax, as the opening word of three successive pairs of lines:

> *"Leue Peres," quaþ y . . .*
> *"Leue broþer," quaþ he . . .*
> *Leue þou on oure Louerd God· þat all*
> *þe werlde wrouȝte . . .* [44]

It goes on a little later: ". . . And on gentyl Jesu Crist . . ."[45], and so on[46]; and ends with a disparagement of those masters of divinity who do not fully practise what they preach[47].

Now it is quite clear that the first two of these three *lief*'s mean "dear":

> "Dear Piers", quoth I.
> "Dear Brother", quoth Piers.
> "Leue thou our Lord . . . "

Obviously the third *leue* here, the verb, also means *belieben*, to hold dear, and in fact simply to love. (In this case the actual form is *leue*, not *bileve*[48], though various modern translators, with modern notions of creeds in their minds, mistranslate it as "believe"[49].) The poet avers: "This is the holy *beleue*"[50]—that is, creed not in the modern sense of statement of belief, but in our last chapter's sense of "this is where one's heart is to be put; this is the sacred reality to which one's allegiance is to be actively given".

This sort of thing is the thrust also of Wycliffe's preaching. I have unearthed many a passage in his sermons where the word *bileve* designates that dedication by which one follows through on what one affirms. Explicating Christ's saying, "By their fruits ye shall know them" (Matthew 7:16, 20), he preaches that false prophets—and, Wycliffe adds, false priests, false friars—are distinguished from true *by their fruits*: by their actions and lives, not by their words. "Men do not gather grapes of thorns, nor figs of briars", he quotes (Matthew 7:16); and he says that these false ecclesiastics, whatever their theoretical preaching, live evil lives. They evince neither the grapes of devotion—that is, of devoting themselves to what they preach—nor the figs of what he calls *bileve*, which we might translate here as dedication to, or appropriation to themselves of, the Gospel that they profess[51]. It is not sufficient, he goes on, to say "Lord, Lord", but it is requisite that one live well to the end of one's life; priests must both say well and live well, for otherwise a person shall not be saved[52]. In other words, he is saying—he is preaching a sermon on the point—that what we to-day call "belief" is in Christian matters not enough. A true Christian, he proclaims, is known by his works, by the quality of his life, that quality including what Wycliffe called *bileve* or consecration. Of course, many a modern preacher propounds the same thesis; our point here is simply that, unlike the modern case, the *word* that Wycliffe used for what we might call "faith" as here distinguished from belief, was *bileve*.

Again, attributed to Wycliffe, here is a passage where the notion is clearly one of obedience, along with what at the theoretical level would in modern terms be called, rather, disbelief. It describes a situation where one follows, and patterns one's behaviour upon, here under force, something that one's mind explicitly rejects. "They make us *beleue*", he writes, "a false law"[53]. Obviously no one can compel us to believe, in the twentieth-century sense of the word, what we deem to be a false proposition; this would be meaningless. We can by compulsion, however, be brought to serve, to act in terms of, what we regard as (believe to be) a wrong injunction.

In the same fashion Wycliffe used "belief" for "obeying" when in his translation of the New Testament into English he rendered Acts 26:19 ("I was not disobedient unto the heavenly vision"[54]) as Y *was not vnbileueful to the heuenli visioun*[55]. That is, I did not fail to act out in practice what I saw to be God's will for me. In our day, the Revised Standard Version still uses "disobedient" here; but "not unfaithful" would make very good English.

The two versions of Wycliffe's translation into English of the Bible illustrate, however, a shift that was beginning to take place[56]. In the earlier one he uses *bilefe*, but in the later this is replaced at many points by the new word "faith", which was just beginning to come into use as the English form of Latin *fides*.

The transition here at work is described more generally in the Oxford English Dictionary as follows:

> *Belief* was the earlier word for what is now commonly called *faith*. The latter originally meant in Eng[lish] (as in O[ld] French) 'loyalty to a person to whom one is bound by promise or duty, or to one's promise or duty itself,' as in 'to keep faith, to break faith,' and the derivatives *faithful*, *faithless*, in which there is no reference to 'belief'; i.e. 'faith' was [equivalent to] fidelity, fealty. But the word *faith* being, through O[ld] F[rench] *fei*, *faith*, the etymological representative of the L[atin] *fides*, it began in the 14th c[entury] to be used to translate the latter, and in course of time almost superseded 'belief,' esp[ecially] in theological language, leaving 'belief' in great measure to the merely intellectual process or state in sense 2 [sc. below]. Thus 'belief in God' no longer means as much as 'faith in God'[57].

By 1611 this transition was virtually complete. In the King James Authorized Version of the Bible of that year the word "faith" occurs 246 times, the word "belief", once.

That is, for the noun. There is, however, no verb in English connected with "faith", as there is in Greek[58] (and, on a more restricted base, in Biblical Hebrew[59]—and, for Islamic scripture, as there is in Arabic[60]). Therefore the English translators kept "believe" as a verb, meaning what it had meant before: to love, to hold dear, to cherish; conceptually, to recognize; actively, to entrust oneself to, to give one's heart, to make a commitment.

This meaning is evinced also in Shakespeare. In his plays, on occasion, our verb still meant what *credo* meant. An instance is in *All's Well That Ends Well* (2:3:159), when the King says to Bertram, "Believe not thy disdain". In this he is acknowledging that that Count does indeed have disdain for the humble-born orphaned girl Helena, but is telling him not to act in terms of it: not to correlate his behaviour with this manifest truth. To believe is to follow through in practice what one recognizes intellectually. Here, "Believe not" names the decision *not* to follow through, the deliberate act of will that rejects what one acknowledges as a fact[61].

Shakespeare's English, however, manifests also more modern developments, along with the more traditional, in his use of the verb "believe"[62]. So far as the noun is concerned, his diction shows too the shift that we have remarked. Even though less overwhelmingly than is the case with the 1611 Bible, yet in his plays the ratio of the use of "faith" to that of "belief" is still impressive: namely, 452 to 15[63].

Of the present thesis, part might be held to be simply this: that the time has come to complete the transition also with the verb. Indeed, that time is overdue. In the three and a half centuries since the King James Authorized Version, the word "faith" has not altogether lost its original spiritual meaning, but the words "belief" and "believe" have. One might therefore urge that "belief/believe" be dropped as religious terms since they now no longer refer directly to anything of human ultimacy. ("Knowledge" does; but that is another story, to which we shall return.) The modern world has to rediscover what "faith" means, and then to begin to talk about that; it must recover the verb, to rediscover what it means to have faith, to be faithful, to care, to trust, to cherish, to be loyal, to commit oneself: to rediscover what "believe" *used to mean.*

This last has, at a linguistic level, been our task. To transpose this from the linguistic to the theological level, and to the personal, the institutional, the socio-cultural, will be a larger task, for coming generations: the rediscovery of living one's life, corporate and individual, in awareness of, quiet confidence in, pledged allegiance to, ardent love of, the transcendent reality in the participation in which the meaning of human life consists. The theologian's or philosopher's task will be the articulation of concepts that make that intelligible and persuasive.

There remains for us here the question of how the change in meaning was effected: the step-by-step transition by which over the centuries the old usage gradually gave way to the new, and the notion of faith became watered down into the notion of what for us to-day is belief. Very large forces were, of course, involved in this; we are speaking of major movements in the development of modern Western civilization. Yet these are reflected, if one look carefully, in the usages of words. It is fascinating to trace the evolution of the meaning of our verb, watching it make the transition. To present this in detail, however, would prolong this present study unduly, and throw its proportions out of balance. Accordingly, I have recently published that particular material elsewhere[64], providing a documented history of the English word "believe", roughly from Shakespeare to the present. Suffice it here to summarize very briefly the chief trends.

The shifts seem to have taken place in extra-ecclesiastical usage most significantly in the seventeenth and eighteenth centuries, with more specifically religious writing on the whole following a century or so behind. (The distinction between religious and secular is not so clear early on as it later becomes.) By the nineteenth century the change was virtually complete. There is evidence, however, that still to-day some religious writers and speakers appear on close investigation to use the term "believe" in religious contexts (not in others) in special senses, which are quite misunderstood by most of their hearers and contribute to, not merely illustrate, present-day confusion.

The long-range transformation may be characterized perhaps most dramatically thus. There was a time when "I believe" as a ceremonial declaration of faith meant, and was heard as meaning: "Given the reality of God, as a fact of the universe, I hereby proclaim that I align my life accordingly, pledging love and loyalty". A statement about a person's believing has now come to mean, rather, something of this sort: "Given the uncertainty of God, as a fact of modern life, so-and-so reports that the idea of God is part of the furniture of his mind".

The difference is drastic. The change did not occur overnight, however. Over the course of some centuries, at least four transitions in the usage of the verb "believe" in modern English may be discerned. Three are towards the impersonal, the non-committal, and the dubious.

First, it appears on inquiry that the object of the verb begins by being almost always a person; it ends by being almost always a proposition. That is, a shift has taken place from the verb's designating an interpersonal relation to its naming a theoretical judgement: from an action of the self, in relation to other selves, to a condition of the mind, in relation to an abstraction. In between these two came an intermediate stage. Between believing a person, in the sense of trusting him or her, having faith in him or her (I-Thou[65], predominant in the fifteenth and sixteenth centuries, strong still in the seventeenth), and believing a proposition, in the sense of agreeing with its ideas intellectually (predominant in the nineteenth and twentieth centuries) came a phase of believing a person's word, then his or her statement, in the sense of trusting that person to be honest and telling the truth (seventeenth and eighteenth centuries). This last still persists—some might say, almost quaintly—among some Roman Catholics, as we have noted. There was also a thing as object, since one may trust not only persons—and promises—but things. (The transition from believing as entrusting oneself to a person or to some thing, to believing propositionally, operated a little more slowly in the phrase "believing in" than in "believing that", so that into the early years of this present century a differentiation between these two could on occasion still be discerned. Indeed, there are to be found a few apologists among whom this still, although rather ineffectively now, survives.)

The change in meaning, in the course of a few centuries, has in itself been monumental enough. A second transformation, however, of another sort, has been equally major: a transition that emerges in not only the object, but the subject, of the verb. It represents a shift from the existential to the descriptive. In the earlier period the verb occurs predominantly in the first person, as "I believe", involving self-engagement, commitment; later on, "he believes", "they believe" and the like gradually become statistically more common, simply reporting particular facts. Thus in Shakespeare, third-person usage is surprisingly rare—in fact, almost absent[66]. (In present-day philosophic analysis, the reverse is the case[67].)

The third transition that can be detected has been again drastic. It is from believing what is true towards utter neutrality, and in more recent times on towards falsity. In Thomas Aquinas, as in the classical Islamic instance (where the term *tasdiq*, used as a characterization of faith, specifically and explicitly designates the recognition or appropriation of truth[68]), the word for faith, as we have seen, names a person's relation to what is in fact and in principle true; and in early modern English this is chiefly the case with Bacon, Hobbes, and (with the word "faith", though no longer so much now with "belief") as late as Locke. It is found to some degree even with Hume. In the 1611 English Bible, the noun "belief" occurs, as we have said, only once, and that is in the phrase "belief of the truth" (II Thessalonians 2:13)—meaning adherence to the truth, allegiance or loyalty to it.

Even after what one believed had tended to become a proposition about something rather than that something itself (*savoir* rather than *connaître*), it was still truth in the sense of a true proposition, and that alone, that was for a time spoken of as being believed. Somewhat later the word came to be applied to propositions regardless of whether they were known to be true or not; then more especially to propositions explicitly uncertain as to whether they were true or not; and presently to propositions that were, by preference, improbable, or even false. This movement can be traced century by century. In one of the major recent American dictionaries, that of Random House, the first entry under the word "belief" defines it as "an opinion or conviction" and proceeds at once to give as an example, *the belief that the earth is flat.* That is, the first illustration of this term that in our day occurs to the compilers (or readers) of this impressive work is of a belief that is erroneous. In other words, the primary connotation of the term in modern usage has come to be with ideas that are false.

One of the differences between secular and religious people nowadays in the English-speaking world is that the term "believe" names different things for each. Religious persons have participated in all these developments no doubt less than have secular persons. Yet unquestionably they have participated: and certainly they have been influenced by them. Let us re-iterate the three trends thus far. The object of faith used to be a person (God and Christ in the Christian case); the object of believing has come to be an idea, a theory. Secondly, the *act* of faith used to be a decision, the taking of a step of cosmic self-commitment; the state (*sic*) of believing has come to be a descriptive, if not a passive, condition. Thirdly, the mood of faith used to involve one's relation to absolutes, to realities of surpassing grandeur and surety; the mood of believing involves one's relation to uncertainties, to matters of explicitly questionable validity.

A fourth development may be noted, somewhat more recent than the others. Indeed, it is still very much in process; we are only groping our way towards being able to handle it conceptually. The growing awareness, in modern times, of other ages and other cultures, and the growing pluralism of our own, have led to a new sophistication about what are increasingly but innovatingly called "belief-systems": sets of presuppositions, or conceptual frameworks through which the world is viewed and in terms of which it is understood. This introduces a new dimension altogether: not only into the faith/belief relation, crucial though that be, but indeed into the development of human intellectuality in general. The present-day articulation of what used to be assumed, the contemporary emergence of varying Weltanschauungen into self-consciousness, signify the turning of a quite new corner. The choice of our word for designating this is also momentous. The notion of "belief" will never be quite the same again.

These various developments have, of course, been intertwined. The third, towards dubiousness and falsity, could hardly have occurred until after the second, when other persons' beliefs rather than one's own became the primary focus of consideration. (Once established, however, this in turn reacted on that, so that even in the first person nowadays, "I believe that such-and-such" normally implies ". . . but I am not sure".) Nor could it occur until after the first, with propositions rather than persons or things as object (persons can be false, but not in the modern sense of truth and falsity). Similarly, the concept of unwittingly "believing" a whole ideational system both derived from and contributed to the notion of others' believing, and to that of unwarranted believing. The modern interpretation of belief is a new, comprehensive, many-faceted, and more or less integrated whole.

Some religious people, as we have remarked, still to-day carry over into their current use of the verb "believe" (less so, of the noun[69]) traces, at least, of earlier patterns, including even the notion of faith. One may suggest that this is anachronistic, obsolete, and probably a lost cause. The Christian Church might be well advised to cut its losses, and to begin again. For however much, for a select few, connotations may be determined by residues of the old meanings, surreptitiously or beleagueredly, yet modern usage even by that faithful few is often dominated, and at least is complicated, confused, disrupted, by present-day conceptions. For most moderns entirely, and for all partially, "believe" to-day has come to mean something quite else.

The role of what it now names—its role in the life of faith and in human life generally—is a novel problem, hardly continuous with ancient pronouncements on quite different issues (even if the actual word "believe" was used in those ancient pronouncements), and hardly amenable to ancient solutions to essentially other problems.

Especially by the new awareness of Weltanschauung has novelty been inculcated (and the novelty of the other developments rendered intractable). Since the emergence of this new awareness, we remarked just now, the concept "belief" will never be the same again. One could also suggest that, with it, the notion "knowledge" itself will soon be in manifest need of recasting. This is so especially of propositional knowledge, recently fashionable; and the aberrant over-simplification involved in propositional views of truth.

Classical Christian, Islamic, Buddhist understandings and expositions of faith, we ourselves have been at pains to insist, did indeed involve in each case what we now call a world-view, which those who do not share may critically analyse and clarify, and may comparatively contemplate. These analyses, clarifications, comparative contemplations, are available to, and perhaps are to-day becoming inescapable for, also those who may inherit, or choose to share, one of them (to participate in its on-going history). What is to be the relation of faith to these conceptual frameworks, or to new patterns of ideas that may be in fashion to-day or be hammered out as humankind proceeds, we leave to our concluding chapter, but also to other occasions and to other writers.

Before we conclude this present chapter, however, with one or two remarks on current trends, we must take note of one more historical development, reaching its zenith in the late nineteenth century: a response from the side of faith to the newly evolving conceptions of belief. Somewhat unwittingly, a position on the relation between the two matters was attained that for a time seemed to serve as a solution. It was more novel than any of those involved were aware; and indeed the historian of religion may regard it as possibly one of the more remarkable emergences in human affairs on this planet[70]. Yet however effective for a time, it presently floundered, and even proved well-nigh disastrous. The West is currently living through the deep confusion and disarray engendered by its short-range viability spiritually.

This was the development that emphasized belief (in the new meanings of that transformed term) as a basic religious category, and envisaged believing as what religious people primarily do. Throughout this study we have urged that faith, rather, is the primary religious category, and the ultimate human quality. This movement did not exactly deny this; but it stressed belief as more or less equivalent, or at least as more closely linked than any other age or group had ever suggested or imagined. Moreover, insofar as it discriminated between them, it posited belief as prior.

This innovating position, although it may have been misconceived and dislocative, yet was hardly either fortuitous or silly. It could hardly have arisen at any other time in world history nor at any other place than Christendom in recent Western cultural development; yet its then emergence may be seen as almost reasonable. It is not merely that the Church had inherited the words "belief" and "believing" from the time when they had indeed designated faith, and was an unconscious participant in the conceptual evolutions by which these had unobtrusively come now to denote quite other matters (as it was participant also in the massive socio-historical process of which those conceptual evolutions were the almost incidental by-product). Equally operative was the major fact noted in our Introduction above that doctrine has characteristically played among Christians, as a form of expression of faith, a quite special role, theology being more central to the Church than perhaps to any other community on earth. One must not under-estimate the extent to which ideational patterns—given the great role of Greek thought in the Church's development—have typically served in the Christian tradition, as other patterns have served in other traditions (and at other levels also in the Christian) to symbolize faith: to structure, to channel, and to sustain it.

In the modern West, therefore, Christian thinkers had a venerable tradition on which to draw. Yet what they constructed was a faith/belief relation that was quite significantly novel. At the very least, in their new pattern one might say that the preponderance of one of the various strands over the others significantly changed. In addition to the long-range background for the prominence of doctrine was the short-range background of the Enlightenment's reconception of rationality.

At the heart of the new system was that belief became self-consciously the yes-or-no passport to faith. For the first time, the predominant question was not even what one believed, religiously, but whether.

For the first time on a grand scale, Christian discussion centred not on transcendent realities, and not on faith, man's relation to them, but on the conceptualizations of both, and on man's relation to those conceptualizations: on believing. The difference was subtle but profound. Presently it ramified.

A new situation arose where, to some significant extent, those who believed the doctrines had faith, and those who did not believe, did not. To some extent also, conversely: those who had faith (at least, in its Christian form) on the whole tended to believe, and those who lost their (Christian) faith did not believe.

This rather bizarre eventuality, for all its brittleness, nonetheless worked for a time. At the operational level it actually was the case that by believing the doctrines, which men of uncontrived faith had formulated in an earlier, less complicated day, persons did in fact find themselves introduced into a world of living faith, did in fact become endowed with that human quality that it had all along been the point of the tradition to inculcate and to nurture. Belief did in historical actuality serve as an avenue to faith. However novel[71], and however precarious, and for however partial a sector of the total Western community, for a while this worked.

Not, however, for long. Rather, doctrinal believing began to disintegrate as an effective expression; and especially it became vitiated as an evocation, an elicitor, an invitation. The short-lived liaison between belief and faith seemed to develop rather into a divorce. We have stressed a discrimination between faith and its conceptualizations; but we have noted also that classically they had been in dynamic interaction. In our century, on the other hand, it would seem that they have fallen apart; this is at least in part because the previous century tied them far too closely together. We speak here specifically of conceptualizations in the form of beliefs in the modern senses; one must remember that those were the only senses available to most, and seemed unavoidable to all. One might ask whether belief so conceived, instead of serving as an avenue to faith, did not rather become some sort of obstacle to it. The twentieth century has seen many persons in the Western world whose potentiality for faith, far from being crystallized around belief, has, rather, been poignantly precluded by it. Instead of being a stepping-stone to faith, religious belief had become a barrier. The Church gave men and women the impression that believing was the price that they must pay; and for the sensitive, that price was too high.

Faith is an almost priceless treasure, and the modern world has been desperate in search of it. But the spectre of having to believe has stood in the way. Early in the century there were some who would have liked to believe but could not. The role of belief in the history of religious life had been turned quite upside down.

A further, and drastic, ramification was that in the resulting confusion, intellectual integrity was in danger. This was disastrous. This is the era that produced the "schoolboy's" devastating quip, "Faith is believing what you know ain't so"[72]. As we remarked above in our Qur'an chapter, the identifying of faith with belief led many in the Church to urge that it was important to say "yes" to the belief question, and many critical thinkers to hold that it was important to say "no" to the faith question. Both were wrong. And both the Church and secular society have suffered sadly from the double error. It was some while, however, before it began to become at all clear that these issues had been badly posed. A society with waning faith, and a Church with waning intelligibility, were exorbitant penalties to be paid.

As the twentieth century proceeded, the ineptitude became gradually more deeply felt, and the consequences more conspicuously damaging, of confusing faith with belief. The crisis is still far from resolved; but we conclude by noting two successive compromises that have been tried. We have mentioned both already in connection with Roman Catholic developments: one, the thesis that faith includes belief but goes beyond it; the other, that faith may be conceived as dispensing with intellectuality altogether.

Each of these has grown out of a recapturing of some vision of the fullness of faith that the short-lived equating of it with belief had radically missed. Yet on careful analysis one may detect that each has subtly perpetuated a covert linking of the two: acknowledging a divergence between belief and faith while at the same time being victims still, in curious inadvertent ways, of their erstwhile coalescing. This is more transparent, of course, in the first movement, but conceivably more dangerous in the second.

That faith is more than belief is a position that has tended to interpret the latter as modern belief in traditional propositions. It has uncritically acquiesced in present-day notions of believing; and has acquiesced also, almost uncritically—or else, apologetically—in inherited statements.

This still gives primacy and absoluteness to earlier and particularistic doctrine, now interpreted in modern contexts—granting such doctrine a veto over entry into the kingdom, even if it acknowledge that once past the gate one has still a stretch to travel. In a different fashion, it misunderstands the faith of Christians in pre-modern ages—as it has been the task of these two chapters to help to make more evident. In still differing fashion, it misunderstands also the faith of most contemporary Christians, a point unfortunately evinced in the gradual waning of this movement and the rise of the next.

Too, it misunderstands believing, as a rational intellectual activity in the modern era. Those of us who are Westerners, whether Christian or no, are still Greeks, and must have our intellectualizations uncompromised, and unrelentingly honest. (Those of us who are not Western have other conceptual traditions on which to draw.) All of us are modern, and must have our thinking both inductive and universal.

Faith is not to be subordinated to belief, nor to anything else mundane. To it, all religious forms are to be seen as at best strictly secondary—as faith itself is secondary to, derivative from, answerable to, transcendent reality and final truth.

Nor is the intellect to be subordinated: neither to faith as conceived, in whatever fashion, nor to anything else—except, again, to transcending reality and truth. The intellect must be answerable to a truth greater than it has yet apprehended. It is making beliefs primary that has tended to depreciate intellectuality—as the critics of the Church have ruthlessly discerned.

As these and other inadequacies began to be felt, in the Church's stance on belief, there emerged the tendency[73] to by-pass the problem rather than to solve it. I have called this tendency anti-intellectualist. For while rejecting belief as integral to faith, it too has been victim of the fallacy that believing represents the role of the intellect in religious life. This movement has seen the awkwardness of belief, in its modern senses, as a major component in the life of faith; but it has envisaged or conceived no other intellectual relation of humankind to transcendent truth. Accordingly, it has ignored or played down, if not outright rejected, *any* intellectual relation.

In our concluding chapter, below, we shall touch briefly on certain alternative concepts that seem to me personally promising for our task: "insight", "understanding", "seeing the point", "recognizing", and the like. Other newer ones may yet have to be forged. During the era that we have been considering, however, the dominant categories in reference to which the intellectual dimension of religious life was considered were essentially two: positively, "believing", and often negatively, in contrast to this, "knowing".

All our concepts are themselves historical. We have pondered "believing" here; but "knowledge" has become similarly problematic. Traditionally it played a major role in religious thinking, including thinking about faith; recently, on the other hand, it came to be omitted from religious considerations. This was during an era in which not only the understanding of religious matters had changed, and the understanding of "believing", as we have examined, but also, and drastically, the conceptualization of "knowing". It is not our task here, manifestly, to analyse this last, nor to sketch its history as a changing idea—beyond calling attention to the fact that the role of ideas in religious life was formulated in terms of (modern) believing, or most recently even of one's being exonerated from believing ("It doesn't matter what you believe, so long as you have faith"), during a specific phase in the recent cultural history of the West when the concept of knowledge was for a time captive of a singularly narrow, and explicitly impersonalist, outlook. The term "knowing" still implies truth—as "believing" once did. Yet the truth to which it relates came to be conceived in quite special fashion (impersonalist, for one thing, and propositionalist for another: both are historically odd, and humanly odd). Also, "knowing" as a concomitant concept was pushed in modern times in quite particular directions—towards the objective, for one (with the preposterous assumption that the only alternative to objectivity is subjectivity); towards the natural sciences, for another, with "knowledge" having become the name primarily or exclusively for a particular (and it increasingly appears, a limited) awareness that we have of the natural world. This among other matters has meant the concept's being moulded into something quite specific (what science knows, and how[74]); and faith is then left either with "belief", or without intellectual dimension.

The sciences, however, give knowledge primarily of the natural world only, of humankind and of the personal only very partially, and especially not of humanity's loftier qualities and involvements: knowing what is higher than ourselves. Poetry and art, the moral life, and everything of "value" was during this disconsolate period thought of, virtually by definition, as a realm not of "knowledge". And history, the study that gives knowledge particularly of man, and especially the history of religion, which might give a knowledge particularly of faith,. were excluded for various reasons—of which "traditional beliefs" constituted one.

The understanding, then, of the intellectual dimension of faith, and the intellectual understanding of faith in general, were hampered positively by the new concept of belief and its misapprehended role, and negatively by the absence of conceptualizations apt for the monumental task of thinking through, in the bewilderments of the modern world, the noblest truths of the human spirit.

What, then, is the relation of faith to intellectually apprehensible truth? I will argue that this is a better formulated question than that of its relation to "belief". The former query we leave unresolved, for the moment, as we bring this historical part of our inquiry to an end. For the modern Western world has as yet not elucidated to itself this relation. To the other question we are bold enough to suggest that we have discovered an answer: faith is not belief, and with the partial exception of a brief aberrant moment in recent Church history, no serious and careful religious thinker has ever held that it was.

Chapter 7

CONCLUSION

As WE bring this study to a close, there could well be some query as to what sort of consideration might constitute a "conclusion". At the highest level, of course, stands an obvious question. If faith has not been and is not belief, then what has it been, what is it? I averred at the start that our aspiration was to contribute to an awareness of the profundity and complexity and universality of that question, not yet to answer it. If our inquiry has made a contribution towards an eventual answer, good. A firmer, or at least a wider, base has been laid, I trust, for on-going inquiry.

We leave aside, then, as beyond our present scope, the question as to the nature of faith, as a basic human quality. We leave behind, as established and now almost trivial, that faith is not belief, is something of a quite different order. Still we are challenged by a question as to belief itself, and more generally the involvement of the mind in the life of faith, in the past and for the future. However far from equivalent the two be, it would be patently absurd to conclude that believing has historically had nothing to do with faith, or to propose that it have no role henceforth. On the contrary: the present-day life of man and society, I have urged, desperately requires intellectual clarification on this very matter. Faith will hardly flourish so long as belief with regard to it continues to flounder. Society will hardly flourish so long as this issue continues unresolved. From a recognition that faith is not belief it follows that the question of the relation between them is more urgent, not less.

Of many observations that might be developed on this, I here propose three. Before propounding them, however, I return to a point of quite fundamental import and priority: namely, that greatly more significant than anything that I myself may be able to suggest in this realm is my pleading that the issue is important, and my urging that others address themselves to it. Our work here is more in the nature of prolegomenon to future thinking in this realm. To elucidate what the relation between faith and intellectuality has been historically in any particular case, is philosophically, shall be Christianly, Islamically, humanly, or whatever—this is a task of sizable proportions, to keep the academic world and the various theological worlds busy for long. Our three observations here are tentative, proffered as interim contributions to what one hopes will be a continuing discussion.

Basic to that discussion will be a recognition of diversity: diversity among communities, and among centuries (and within both). Equally basic will be a recognition that this is a common human problem, to engage us all.

Our first consideration here has to do with faith in global perspective: the fact that faith is now seen to transcend any given form, and manifests itself as fundamentally human. As incidental to this point, we shall be taking note of Western secularism, which has most sorely failed to understand this. Secondly, we shall reflect a little on belief, comparatively, and especially on "belief-systems" as conceptualizable world-views, and on other modes of intellectual understanding. Finally we shall proffer some suggestions on how one may perhaps understand the interrelation between faith generically and its specifically intellectual dimension.

(i) Faith as generically human

First, faith globally. Our modern situation enables man, for the first time, to be significantly aware of the whole sweep thus far of his and her history on the planet. As one looks out over that panorama, one perceives, as observational fact, that humankind is characterized by faith. The history of religion is the history of man. It has been so from palaeolithic times to the present—on every continent, in every culture, in every age.

Perhaps the modern West has in some way been an exception. We shall return presently to this, taking note of recent secularist developments. In the past, however, throughout the world, everywhere and at all times, man has lived by faith, both individually and corporately.

Faith, then, so far as one can see as one looks out over the history of our race, is an essential human quality. One might argue that it is *the* essential human quality: that it is constitutive of man as human; that personality is constituted by our universal ability, or invitation, to live in terms of a transcendent dimension, and in response to it. Certainly the human everywhere is, and from the beginning has been, open to a quality of life in oneself, in one's neighbour, and in the universe that lifts one above the merely mundane and the immediate, and means that one may be always in part but is never totally simply a product or a victim of circumstance. One does not merely react, but rather is open, both individually and in corporate groups, to sources of aspiration, of inspiration, of vision, of obligation, beyond what is given in one's immediate environment.

A true understanding of humankind involves a recognition of our potentiality for faith. One may or may not like to articulate this by saying that man is *homo religiosus*, or is body, mind, *and spirit*. In any case, one must recognize that to come of age is not to grow beyond this, but to appreciate this and to handle it intelligently, constructively. Speculative philosophers may variously interpret this fact, but fact it is, historically observed.

Men and women across the centuries and across the globe are misapprehended if not seen in faith perspective; certainly faith is misapprehended if not seen in historical and global perspective. If part of the truth of man is faith in its unending variety of forms, part of the truth of faith is certainly that very variety, and that universality.

We mean not the variety of external forms. These may rather obscure faith than reveal it. It has traditionally been easy to think of one's own group as having faith (or, as having had it), whereas others, of whose religious life one sees only the outward patterns, the ceremonial practices, the moral codes, the beliefs, are perceived as having merely what have been called religions.

Most religious systems seem quaint, if not silly or even grotesque, to outsiders. It has all too easily arisen, therefore, that others' ideas and practices are deprecated, since the faith that animates and is animated by them has not been discerned. This applies to secularists' views of what they call Christianity, as it used to apply to Protestant assessments of Roman Catholics and *vice versa*, as well as to Christian insensitivity to Hindu, Buddhist, and Muslim positions; and it applies to recent views on earlier generations or ages. By now, however, it is time to move beyond that ignorance.

Now that a world conspectus is available, it is evident that at most times and in most places humankind has been effectively aware that one lives in a world whose greatness transcends one's grasp but does not totally elude one, that Truth, Beauty, Justice, Love beckon one imperiously yet graciously. That awareness we see crystallized in poetry, and art, and philosophy or theology, and ritual, and social structure, and political aspiration. It comprises, in varying degrees of emphasis, an appreciation of the transcendent quality of this world as it is, and a countervailing drive to change it into this world as it ought to be, and a vision of moving beyond both, being beyond both; a recognition of personal transcendence both in oneself and in one's neighbour; a sense of being somehow enabled to realize this in fumbling or in fullest richness. Such awareness has been part, at least, of faith, and it has created most of what has been worthwhile in human history.

Universality, but also variety. I am not affirming that faith is everywhere the same. Nor do I suggest that it is everywhere admirable. To see faith generically is to see it historically in close or remote approximation to its truth. About this basic human quality of *rapport* with oneself and the universe, one may wax fairly optimistic—but not fully so. Over against magnanimity, there has been too a perversity of faith. As many a critic has pointed out, the history of man has also been disfigured by the arrant stupidities, rigidities, fanaticisms of faith. The historian notes, no doubt, the recurrent capacity of men and women of faith across the world to fasten on some expression of their faith, even a perverted one, and in its name to ignore, to suppress, or to demolish not only other expressions but even that of which it itself has been meant to be the symbol. One need hold no brief for *homo religiosus perversus*. The only requirement here is to give heed to the fact, obvious to historical observation, that the perversity, also, appears in a global context. Christians perhaps more than others have stressed that man is a sinner, standing in need of redemption. The condition, however, to which Christians have thus called attention is, as they themselves have recognized, quite world-wide. The Church proclaims itself a congregation of sinners; the proclamation may be unique, but not the fact. Neither the theologian nor the historian finds that all Christians are saints, all others are sinners—nor *vice versa*.

Faith varies. Some have faith that is large, rich, strong, serene, and that renders them generous, courageous, compassionate, patient, noble, creative. Others have a version of faith that is meager, spasmodic, or stunted, rendering them narrow-minded or distracted, unimaginative or bitter, self-righteous or hypocritical. Both extremes of faith, and every gradation between, are to be found, we now can see, in every community across the globe. The historical fact is that faith both in its good and in its unseemly occurrences, its truer and its less true instances, has been found quite across the planet.

Thirdly, apart from magnanimity and perversity, apart from faith as good, as humdrum, and as not so good, there is a further point by which a modern observer cannot but be struck: namely, that human faith has always, everywhere, been limited. Historical criticism shows that the faith of any person, however open it may be to transcendence and the infinite, however much it may be a divine gift, however ideally absolute, yet in actual fact has always[1] been limited by psychological, sociological, and other contextual factors, by the knowledge and the temperament and the situation of the man or woman whose it is. Every person is the child of his or her times; and this truth applies to every person of faith, even though one's having faith is another way of saying that one is not totally a child of one's times. One's faith opens one to what is timeless. Yet so long as one lives on this earth, although faith may enable one to triumph over one's mundane environment, and always enables one to reach beyond it, or is evidence that one has been reached from beyond it, nevertheless it never means that one escapes it altogether. It is always possible for the well-informed historian to see how the shape of faith for every person is related to the particular situation in which that person has lived. This is true of the Christian in third-century Rome or twelfth-century Paris or twentieth-century New York; of the Buddhist in ancient India or mediaeval China or present-day Japan; of the Muslim in classical Baghdad or the modern Soviet Union; of the Hindu in the age of the Upanishads or studying engineering at M.I.T. No two Hindus have the same faith, and no two Christians, and no two centuries.

If the historian is religiously insensitive, he may see no more than this. He may report the specific historical form, and fail to see or to mention the timeless substance. On the other hand, if the historian is studying a person whose faith is of the same tradition as his own, he may then see the transcendent element so vividly that he emphasizes it primarily, and under-estimates, or under-reports, the historical particularity. Muslims may do this of a Ghazzali, Catholic Christians of an Aquinas, Protestants of a Luther, Marxists of a Lenin. A less limited vision, however, offering a comprehensive and fairly readily demonstrable assessment, is that in each particular case faith has been the confluence of both time and what one may wish to call eternity; it is the locus of man's transcendence, a channel of particularized shape by which man has reached, been reached by, a truth that transcends those and all particulars.

In our day a new understanding is possible. It is also imperative. This is so partly because of the new situation for all faith proffered by science and technology, to which much thought has been given. It is so partly because of the new global perspective, equally important but much less pondered. In the past, little attention has been given to a question of faith as a human phenomenon. Most Muslim thinkers have been concerned with Islamic faith; most Christians with faith in (or as one might prefer to say, faith through) Christ; and as we have earlier remarked, even of non-religious thinkers a disappointingly large number have confined their analyses to a quite narrow range: if not to merely external or behavioural observables, at least to a limited sector of humanity's many forms of faith, usually that sector with which they were familiar in their own society, or age, or both. Seldom in past centuries did thinkers address themselves to faith in its global context. Unfortunately, its having become increasingly possible for us to see faith in its generic, human form is due in part to the rise in our day of unfaith. One price that many have had to pay to recognize how much the faith communities of the world have had in common is the discovery of how different from all of them is the bleakness of the modern nihilist.

Christians may differ from Buddhists, or Muslims from Hindus, in ways of which no historian, at least, could fail to see the deeply rooted and widely ramifying consequences. Nonetheless, a new perspective on the religious history of the world, with all its variety, is available from an encounter with that most pitiable of all modern phenomena, the loss of faith in those for whom nothing is worthwhile; for whom life consists of a congeries of disparate items among which they find no coherence; for whom persons appear as things, community is dissolved into structures, and for whom not only God is dead, but order, meaning, and purpose. It used to be that the man or woman of Christian vision found strange the particular order by which Muslims organized their life, the curious symbols in which Hindus encoded the meaning of theirs, the unfamiliar formulae by which Buddhists formulated their vision of life's purpose. The strangeness is still perhaps there; yet the gulfs seem less wide and the bridges to be constructed less venturesome, now that one begins to catch a glimpse of what life looks like to those who have no principle, not even an exotic one, for ordering it, for discerning its meaning, for eliciting and nurturing loyalty to its purpose. Faith in one's fellows, in the universe, and in one's own ultimate destiny has, we now recognize, led to organizing both individual and corporate life in many diverse ways. One need not rush to assert that all are equally good, nor even that all are viable or even fully legitimate. Yet we can begin to discern that all are distinct from the growing inability to see, to feel, to know that life, both one's own and one's neighbour's *is* significant in a final, cosmic way.

Observing the matter in the global context, one might almost be tempted to say that faith differs from faith in seeing the point of life and of the world in differing fashion, and yet also, in the global context, faith differs from un-faith in seeing that life and the universe do, indeed, have a point—a cosmic point; and that man can be grasped by it, and be transported.

One might be so tempted; yet the temptation must be resisted. Once it is phrased so, various reservations may come to mind. The temptation to say what faith is, is strong. Faith can never be expressed in words, however: neither in an aphorism nor in many volumes. In any case, it is not the task of this present work. For the moment our concern is to insist only that, whatever idea of faith one may form, it must be an idea adequate to faith as a global human quality.

Traditionally, the chief obstacles to recogizing faith so were two. One was geographic isolation. The other, especially in Christian and in non-Sufi Islamic instances, was exclusivist theological dogma.

Both these in our day have begun to give way. The former has done so dramatically. Recently the chief obstacle, especially in the West, has been secularist dogma. It is giving way more tardily. An understanding of human faith—indeed, even an ability to sense what it is that one is to understand—involves a coming to terms with Western (and now world-wide) secularism.

For this and for many other purposes, it is helpful to see this secularism in, one may say, both its positive and its negative modes: as a form of faith, and as a form of unfaith.

Faith, as we are using the term, although in most instances it has been linked with what Westerners call religion, is such that it is not always so linked. This is so not only as regards individuals, but also with cultural complexes. To speak more accurately: Westerners do not always call religious those traditions with which faith has been involved. In the particular case of Western civilization, as we remarked in our Introduction, faith has been crystallized chiefly around two traditions, that from Palestine and that from Greece and Rome: the Jewish and the Christian on the one hand, and the socio-political and especially the rational-metaphysical on the other. The latter tradition one may call classical, or humanist. It has also been called secular. For long this tradition was positive and strong, and was a matter of faith. Confusion has arisen when the same term "secular" is now used instead for an absence of faith altogether, for the dismantling of both the West's inherited traditions: the classical-humanist *and* the religious. Unfortunately, the intellectual tradition through which the faith of many of us in the West has been in large part formed seems nowadays in at least as great disarray historically as is the Judaeo-Christian—even though the university can no more operate without faith than can the Church, and the society no more than the person.

The secular tradition to which I here refer, if we are to call it that, in its positive rather than a negative sense, is not that alienated nihilism into which in our day some irreligion threatens to disintegrate. Rather, it has been an orientation of nobility and force, dignity and commitment, coherence and trust, inherited ultimately from the classics of Greece and Rome. We have to do here with a living tradition with its own metaphysical under-pinnings, its own great champions and even martyrs, its own institutions, its own apprehension of or by transcendence, and, for our present purposes, its own type of faith.

Secularism has to be thus positive, and has to be "believed in", in the old sense, if it is to avoid being inert, vacuous, and destructive. It has to be, as at its best it has mightily been, a matter of faith: faith in reason and truth, in justice, and in man. Or one might say: faith through these. Whether in or through, persons were related to these as to ideals transcendentally apprehended and given a pledged allegiance.

This tradition is starkly different from the negative secularism, more recent, that is derived antithetically from a prior "religious" something and is set over against it: the secular in the sense of the profane, the "let's get rid of religion" drive. This kind of secularism is, historically, an excrescence, an addendum. It cannot be defined or understood in itself, but only in relation to what is religious. Quite possibly it cannot survive by itself, but may prove meaningless and absurd, vacuous and short-lived, without a religious substratum on which to dance. It rejects the faith aspects of even the positive secular tradition: metaphysics, for instance, and idealism, and all those concepts and forms that for twenty-five centuries transmitted and nurtured a humanist awareness of transcendent reality, a loyalty to it, a life lived in terms of it. It rejected metaphysics as the "belief-system" of that faith, rejected it in principle as positing a transcendent object of loyalty, whatever it be.

Obviously we cannot, and should not, become involved here in any but the most superficial analysis of modern Western secularism. Indeed, we mention the matter at all only as requisite to elucidate our actual concern: namely, faith as generically human. It would take another book to establish and to explicate the first point, regarding the classical heritage; here we simply record it. Faith, as modern awareness discerns it, has occurred on earth historically in connection with the Jewish, Hindu, Buddhist, Islamic, Christian, and many other traditions and also as the human involvement with the Graeco-Roman heritage in Western civilization. In global perspective, that heritage and its fecundating role in Western life will be seen as one of the major spiritual traditions of our world.

Secondly, requisite for any just appreciation of faith as a human phenomenon is a freeing of oneself from the error to which recent secularist thought has almost inadvertently given rise: namely, the notion that faith is special rather than generic; is extraordinary; is something added on to normal human life.

The truth here is closer to the reverse. Standard man is man of faith. Faith (like its Christian correlatives hope and love, and like courage, integrity, and the other virtues, which it informs) is normal in human life and normative. This is so, however pure or distorted it or they may statistically prove to be empirically in any given situation.

In this perspective, it becomes unclear as to whether the modern West has of late been losing not only its traditional forms of faith, but faith itself. It is involved, perhaps, in no more decisive question. Has this society begun to be an exception to the rule that human beings across the globe, in every culture and age, have individually and corporately lived by faith? No one, perhaps, can glibly rule out two possibilities: one, that modern Western society may be losing its faith; two, that modern Western society may end in disaster. One ardently hopes, of course, that neither possibility is realized. It would be irresponsible, however, to regard either as negligible, or to be insensitive to a possible link between them.

Recent Western awareness has often been unable to recognize the fact of faith's being standard in human affairs, and fundamental. This inability is not only due to a failure (both Christian and secular) to appreciate faith everywhere behind the specifically religious forms—including conceptual—in which it has been overtly expressed. The West has been held back also partly by a failure to recognize the faith that underlies its own positive secular tradition—and partly by its beginning to fall victim to the negative.

Standard man is man of faith; and negative secularity is a strange and sometimes fierce asceticism directed against the spirit, which it can suppress but cannot eliminate. Faith is not something extra in human life, but is essential; secularity is the bizarre addendum, which may or may not work.

Some while ago, in *The New York Times Book Review*[2], there appeared a critique of a novel, presently a best-seller, by the American writer Malamud. The reviewer protested in passing against what he considered a pretentious remark: that "to be Jewish is to be human". He seemed deeply irritated by this. The protest was, I suggest, obtuse. One cannot understand Jews unless one realizes both the truth and the profundity of that quoted observation. For Jews, if not for every man, to be Jewish is indeed to be human. To fail in apprehending this is to misunderstand not only Jews, but humanity.

This may indeed be proffered as one conclusion of this present book.

Let us elucidate it with reference to India. The word "Hindu", as we have seen, is a foreigner's term, not only in origin but more or less until to-day. People in India have not thought of themselves as Hindus. No one in India has ever tried to be Hindu. They have tried simply to be human, to live properly, adequately, truly, as best they could discern how it may be done. To their attempts to do so—since they differ from the attempts of others of us—we on the outside have given a label: "Hindu" (which meant, simply, "Indian"). Indians across the centuries have aspired to be authentically human, in an absolute, cosmic sense. They have known that to be authentically human, to live rightly, is not a whimsical matter, is not merely an historical, circumstantial matter, but is a cosmic one. For to be human, they have recognized and affirmed, is to live a life within the material realm but one on which the realm of spirit impinges. For them to be Hindu has been to be human—not in a grandiose but almost in a casual sense.

I do not mean that it is easy to be human, or that people in India have thought that it was easy. On the contrary: by "casual" here I mean rather that they have taken just the opposite more or less quietly for granted. To be human is a very serious business: a perplexing and teasing matter. Men and women in India and elsewhere find themselves challenged to rise to it—and one must take that word "rise" seriously, as when one characterizes man as a self-transcending being, or affirms metaphysically that we are essentially more than we are accidentally. As someone has remarked, crocodiles have no difficulty in being crocodiles. It seems to require no special effort on their part. Man, on the other hand, has always found that being human *does* require special effort; or special thought; or special grace. For a crocodile, it is easy to be a crocodile; for us, on the other hand, it is easy *not* to be fully human, easy for us to slip away from our true calling. Man can fail to be human, can fail to be him- or herself; and can fail properly to recognize the authentic humanity of one's neighbour, can treat other men and women as if they were less than human.

There is more both to ourselves and to our neighbours than appears on the surface; and if we content ourselves with superficialities we have failed our human calling. If we meet a drunkard in the gutter and see only a drunkard in the gutter we have failed . . . : failed to see that person as he or she truly is. One has failed oneself, too: if we treat fellow human beings so, we have failed to be fully human ourselves. And if we live superficial lives, in terms for instance of money, career, "getting ahead", or as if we were merely organisms reacting to or coping with our mundane environment, then too we are being less than human.

Men and women in India have recognized this since the dawn of history. Their recognition and their response to it are that form of human faith that we call Hindu.

Not quite in a similar, yet in a counterpart, fashion Buddhists have set themselves not a Buddhist ideal but a human or cosmic one. In their understanding, the person whom they therefore called enlightened, "Buddha", disclosed long ago how man as such may best live. In Buddhist eyes, only the Buddha attained this goal, while the rest of us only approximate to it; but the goal is absolute, inherent, is valid for man as man. There are no Buddhist truths, no Buddhist ideals, no Buddhist values; there are only cosmic truths, human ideals, absolute values, which the Buddhists claim to have discerned (not invented).

If there be any truth in what those on the outside call Buddhism, it is not a truth *in* Buddhism. It is a truth in the universe; one to which Buddhists have called attention.

For outsiders, Islam has been the name of a particular religion; for Muslims, it is the generic name of that personal act by which a human being is aligned with the final truth of the universe—and the inherent truth of his or her self.

Similarly, those of us who are Christians proclaim that Christ is both truly God and truly man, is true humanity; that Jesus did not invent but revealed the final word, which is also the original word; and that He is the model, not for Christians, but for man. As we see it, to be truly Christian is not to be something other than human, but to be undistortedly human. Christ offers us the power to become what man was intended to be.

Summing up, then, one may say—speaking in sober observation reporting on the facts—that to be Jewish has been the Jewish way of being human; to be Hindu has been one or other of the various Indian ways; to be Buddhist has been the way of many hundreds of millions of persons; for the Church, Christ died in order that we might be human properly. The various religious systems of the world are not fancy elaborations tacked on to human history as curiosities over and above the standard human. They are, rather, the principal attempts at being human. Put in another way, they are the salient responses to being human. A person is not a human being and then also a Jew, or also a Christian, or a Muslim. One is a human being by being one or other of them[3].

What sort of faith one has is contingent; but to have faith is central.

For the Muslim, the Hindu, the Buddhist, the Jewish, the Christian, and all the others have been various ways in which man has been man. This is part of what is meant by saying that faith in all its forms has been an essential human characteristic. In another wording, the only man or woman there is, is *homo religiosus*. To have faith is to be human, in the highest, truest, sense.

Although this point is universally valid, I have set it forth in, of course, a radically limited way. One cannot speak without using some language; and in a multi-lingual world I have for these particular purposes employed in the above paragraphs a language chiefly of what may appear to be a modified classical humanism. Such language will be adequate only to those readers whose vocabulary this already is, or to those whose perceptivity allows them to translate the argument out of these particularist terms into their own also particularist ones.

The choice of humanist language is not quite arbitrary. For to appreciate this truth about humankind—to recognize faith in its multiformity as a uniform and central human category—is difficult for all Westerners, but perhaps especially in our day for secularists. Christians are precluded from recognizing others' forms of faith as essentially divine, by their inherited theological tradition; but as has been remarked, they have begun significantly to turn that corner. Secularists are precluded from recognizing it as essentially human, by *their* inherited ideology; and have hardly yet begun to turn. Since most of the institutions and operations of modern society are in their hands, the matter is crucial.

Our thesis, of the humanity of faith when seen in global perspective, is in itself simple, yet its implications are elaborate over a wide range of theoretical and practical realms, from epistemology to political science, and from the structure of local school systems to programmes of foreign economic aid. Not only theology is at issue here.

The earlier failure of Christians to perceive faith as authentic in more than one form, expressed in more than one set of beliefs and practices, led to the Thirty Years' War. Western society's response to that cataclysm was not a rising up to pluralism but was rather a moving downwards. It was, once again, obtuse as to the true nature of faith, as human and multiform, and consequently has in its turn proven of short-range viability.

That response was secularist: the view that faith in whatever form is peripheral. The West has devised, as one of its major specialties, the notion that society can be organized on the assumption that faith does not really matter. In our century, it has endeavoured to impose this doctrine on the entire world. The view that either a national or an international order, political, economic, cultural, can be constructed on a negative-secularism base; that when groups of differing faith patterns come together they can collaborate only or best by privatizing or ignoring those patterns and that faith; that what human beings have in common is the non-religious, the non-transcendent—this is the contemporary orthodoxy. It is resented in Asia and will not survive Western dominance. It is developing into tragedy internally in Western life, engendering a pitiably dehumanized society.

Essentially, the view is false; and alas, the modern world is being called upon to pay the price.

Secular humanism, then, is being challenged to revise its understanding of man. This revision will come through an understanding of faith, which it had thought did not need understanding. (It certainly thought that it did not involve self-understanding. Yet to see faith in its diversity as a primal ingredient of being human is to see oneself as well as others in a new light.)

It will be noted that in classical humanist fashion my anthropology here has been metaphysical. To think or to feel that human behaviour may on occasion be inhuman, that people may be "less than human", that, unlike crocodiles, we persons may become or may fail to become our true selves, is to recognize "man" as a transcendent and not merely an empirical concept. Faith bespeaks involvement in transcendence. Any anthropocentrism, then, betrays our human cause if it is not also theocentric —or, to shift to the Buddhist or Greek mode, metaphysical.

To use theological language: the two themes, apparently contrasting, of religion as man's quest for God, or alternatively as God's initiative, His seeking of man, echo through global history. The latter position has been that of the Muslims, of the Bhagavad Gita, of some Buddhist and of most Christian doctrine. It is easier, of course, to aver faith as God's generous gift in an age of faith than, in an era of forlorn confusion, to argue that its absence is simply God's failure to bestow it. Some will perhaps find congenial a formulation that seeks to converge the two themes: for instance, by saying that faith is a response to God's initiative, to His active Self-revelation. In the course of evolution, the emergence of man as distinct from the brutes, man as endowed with the capacity for faith, man as that creature whose nature it is to transcend him- or herself and to be informed by the universe's transcendence: this much can be seen—perhaps poëtically—as a divine gift.

To render the global-perspective point theologically would require another book (forthcoming) and indeed will require a series of books, by many authors. For these one might meanwhile substitute an aphorism, turning to recent Christian terminology and affirming that human history in its totality is *Heilsgeschichte*. The history of man is the history of religion, and the history of religion is the history of salvation by faith.

Faith is man's participation in that *Heilsgeschichte*. Faith, as a global human characteristic, is—or shall we say, keeping to our more strictly historical approach, faith has been—man's responsive involvement in the activity of God's dealing with humankind: that on-going and multifaceted activity. By modern eyes, unless they wear blinkers, that divine activity can be seen as having Hindu and Greek, Buddhist and Jewish, Islamic and Christian, and many another sector.

Faith is man's participation in God's dealings with humankind. The aphorism is inadequate: granted. I still have no desire to put aside my joyous contention that all formulations of faith fail to do it justice—to do justice either to its depth of substance, or to its variety of form. Yet one may suggest that this delineation is more inadequate than false. How else is one to characterize what the historian sees as he or she looks out upon the global history of humankind? The formula, couched in Christian terms, could be translated, without too much effort and with minimal distortion, into Jewish or Islamic or (very differently) into Hindu terms; and while I myself am not enough at home in Buddhist terminology readily to effect that particular translation, I discern that it could be done. It can certainly, of course, be translated back into classical humanist terms: faith is a planetary human characteristic, less or more consummate instances of which have in empirical fact characterized the whole of human history from the beginning; it involves man's capacity to perceive, to symbolize, and to live loyally and richly in terms of, a transcendent dimension to his and her life.

We human beings differ in the depth and richness and vitality, as well as in the contours, of faith. By being human, we all share in common both the capacity for it and also a potentiality always for growth in it.

Faith can be understood better, I am suggesting—and more importantly, man can be understood better—if faith be recognized as an essential human quality, a normal if priceless component of what it means to be a human person.

* * *

This constitutes, then, our first major conclusion. Before we move on to our next, and by way of transition to it, let me note that by this statement I do not glibly mean that faith is "natural". Certainly it is not automatic. Faith is normal: but to abnormality man is naturally prone.

Men and women have normally recognized faith as integral to human truth, the while expressing amazement, exultation, enormous gratitude, and a sense of awesome obligation, that it be so. Christians have set forth in an elaborated doctrine of The Fall their perception of a humiliating gap between humanity in its genuine or pristine, and in its actual, condition—a gap that faith gives access to bridging; and they have seen faith as marvellously available to humankind at a cost that only God could pay—but did pay, by Himself turning human and suffering and dying on a cross. Even the Western philosophic tradition has of course not failed to notice a comparable gap. It is well aware that among human beings irrationality is an empirical fact rampant or at best just beneath the surface, while it has proclaimed over against this threateningly potential or conspicuously actual truth its ideal truth of man as a rational animal. By this it has meant that we are rational metaphysically, essentially, as a norm to which we approximate in practice less than we might, but to which it is our splendid privilege and inherent possibility and imperious duty to aspire to rise. Jews' explanation of their having faith is melodramatic but poignant and awesome. Hindus' is mightily cosmic. Muslims envision faith as primordially human, and man without it as piteously distorted and infinitely wretched, yet utterly dependent for it on God's bountiful mercy. For Buddhists the Dharma is the primary and ultimate truth and reality of the universe, and of human life within it, yet they feel profoundly that they themselves would have missed it had not a phenomenally exceptional figure once attained it and disclosed it in such a way that others of us might in faith enter the stream flowing towards our true home.

It would be untrue to the facts of human history and to the testimony of the vast majority of our race to fail to recognize the planetary universality of faith, and its centrality to the human condition. At the same time it would be drastically unjust to the experience of those same men and women and their self-interpretation over the ages to imagine that such faith was something to be taken for granted.

Faith is neither rare nor automatic. Rather, it is ubiquitously astonishing. It is the prodigious hallmark of being human.

This is so, since to be human is itself something unexpected, unimaginable, full of marvel and mystery. Faith is beyond apprehension because it is the human potentiality for being human. It is our strange dynamic towards becoming our true selves, or becoming divine[4]. Those who have said traditionally that faith is supernatural may in our century be heard by some as affirming that persons are, that personality is, non-reducible, more than mundane; faith is that quality of or available to humankind by which we are characterized as transcending, or are enabled to transcend, the natural order—an order both in and beyond which, simultaneously, it has been normal, we may observe, for men and women to live.

Such an interpretation, however, is clearly controversial. Any given conception of "nature" is an item within one or another ideology or world-view. This, then, carries us into our next section, on believing, or into our concluding one, on its relation to faith. Here it is not our business to champion any particular interpretation; only, if we may reiterate, to urge that any world-view nowadays must be up to interpreting this basic human fact, of faith generically. To accommodate it, Christians may or must extrapolate from their inherited world-view, Muslims, Jews, Buddhists from theirs; secularists must extrapolate from or revise theirs. We cannot live with ourselves or with each other until we have come to terms with this central truth of us both: that faith is a world-wide human quality, primary and ultimate.

(ii) Belief and understanding

Faith is a virtue. Believing is not. To believe is not in itself virtuous: a belief approximates to virtue, if at all, only so far as what one believes is correlated with what is in fact true. It being beyond human capacity intellectually to grasp more than a part of the truth even of small matters, let alone of large, to say nothing of reality as a whole, we do well to maintain humility and charity. Yet also in these realms we must never lose hold of the central import of truth. We know that some potential beliefs are truer than others, and that it matters. Humility, charity, and firm loyalty to truth are virtually prerequisites for understanding here.

To say this, however, is to be involved already with the relation between thought and faith, the topic of our next, concluding, section. Recognizing that truth is inherently important is a matter of faith. Here we wish to give heed rather to believing as such.

Of any term, in any culture or language, in any century, the meaning is a function of the world-view within which it serves and that it helps to constitute and to perpetuate. The development of new meanings for "belief", "believing" in the modern West has been not an independent nor a casual matter, but deeply significant. We have argued that an appreciation of other cultures' or ages' faith requires our seeing their formulations in the light of the basic human fact that words and concepts are culture-specific. The time has come to apply the principle to the modern notion of belief/believing itself.

The awareness now available as to the development of that notion—as partially illustrated, for instance, in the study of our previous chapter, and in the much fuller analysis that I have published elsewhere[5]—makes possible for us all a new self-consciousness in this matter. In the West, one world-view was being superseded by another. We have seen the displacement of the mediaeval Christian by the modern secular; or, as we noted in our Islamics chapter above, of a theocentric by an anthropocentric; more generically, of a transcendence-oriented outlook by an outlook increasingly impervious to anything loftier than the empirical.

Is this last sentence too severe? In science-oriented philosophy and its cultural world-view, with its postulated ceiling on human awareness, the one objective "value" that survived was truth; and when even that began to give, then reality remained (it too is currently crumbling as a concept[6]). In human affairs the one concept still allowed a value connotation not wholly subjective was that of "knowing", "knowledge", designating a human relation—of the mind—to truth or the real. Since the study of history, however, and not only science, gives us knowledge—especially of humanity, of ourselves—that one concept can serve to let us climb back up out of our recent imprisonment.

We now know that all our concepts—not only other people's—are historical. This brings us into a dramatic new era of self-consciousness. The new conception of believe/belief was part, we can now see, of the new Weltanschauung. That new conception explicitly severed any dependable relation between internal conviction and external reality. In significant measure one might almost discern that as a concept it was indeed developed to serve the new non-transcendence-oriented culture (the first such in human history). Its role was expressly to drain the transcendence out of other people's and other eras' perceptions, in order that the new world-view be able to deal with these on its own terms.

This process was in principle not new. Many a classical world-view also had re-interpreted for itself rival outlooks within its own postulated categories—reducing them, that is, by fitting them to its own patterns. In this and in other ways each regularly failed to recognize that those other outlooks too were in touch with *prima veritas* and human wholeness, and even perhaps had seen something that it itself was missing.

"Belief" became in significant part the category of thought by which skeptics, reducing others' faith to manageability, translated that faith into mundane terms. They substituted for an interest in it as faith an interest rather in the exotic mental processes and conceptual framework of those whose lives had been sustained and enriched by it. Therein was wrought a transforming of what had been a noble and open relation into a dubious and closed one. What had been a relation between the human and something external and higher—or, to change the metaphors, into something internal and deeper, but in any case, greater and truer—was transformed by the new thinking into a self-subsistent, mundane operation of the mind. (The concept "know", for example, names a relation of the person to something real; the modern concept "believe" explicitly, pointedly, does not.)

For many, the idea that believing is what religious people do was thus itself a component of their new outlook. To a significant degree, the very concept "believing/belief" had become an integral aspect of the new detranscendentalized ideology: an intellectual instrument for secularizing one's understanding of the human. "Believing" had become a category of thought calculated to denature the religious life.

The concept served as an inherently irreligious interpretation of a phenomenon that it could not authentically appreciate. To imagine that religious persons "believe" this or that is a way of dominating intellectually, and comfortably, what in fact one does not truly discern.

Curiously, the Church did not resist this, unaware of how much the new development of the notion was undermining both its own position, and the faith and general well-being of the society that it was called upon to serve. It not only did not resist, but in fact (this was true especially of the Protestant Church) it allowed itself to collaborate as accomplice—for three reasons. One was that with regard to the religious position of other communities, on which information was beginning to come in, Christians shared with irreligious Western secularists a disparagement of or blindness to their faith. Christians were ready to join with those who saw all religious life as an aberration, in interpreting these other positions non-transcendentally—as mere beliefs. Secondly: as we have stressed, Christians were themselves participant, less or more thoroughly, and less or more consciously, in the secularizing movements of thought that increasingly suffused Western culture. To a significant degree their own minds began to think in these novel and insidiously compelling ways. Or, insofar as they did not do so, they themselves unconsciously or partially or surreptitiously preserved in their own case little or much of the earlier meanings for the terms. This last is connected with the third and most obvious reason: that the actual words "belief" and especially "believe" were, of course, inherited from a time when their conceptual link with truth and with human action, with faith, was strong. The terms were indeed firmly imbedded in the tradition and its most cherished forms.

The modern concept "believe", although inherently alien as a concept to the religious life, was allowed to remain.

The historian notes that this is not the first time that the momentum of a religious tradition has resulted in purely external forms' taking precedence in a changed situation over inner meaning; nor is it the first time that the price to pay for this was high.

In the jig-saw picture that has constituted the novel conceptual world of recent Western culture, an adjacent piece to the "believing/belief" one, and interlocking with it, was another, cut small and lopsided, labeled "knowledge". That piece, as we have noted, seems to serve some moderns well enough for what they know of and through objective science, but in its technical new form is inadequate for what we know interpersonally, for what other cultures and ages have known, for what we to-day know increasingly about human history. Before turning to it, however, we draw attention to the fact, obvious enough once stated, that there is a considerable array of other concepts relatively little used, for a time, in interpreting the religious life of humankind, yet hardly irrelevant.

Among notions in this realm that have recently gained some currency, after being neglected in the nineteenth century, we may first note in particular two, without elaborating them. One is that of symbolizing, in quite recent thought being developed vigorously, without its being yet apparent whether the concept "symbol" will prove strong enough to bear the weight that it is being asked to carry. The other is the highly ambivalent term "myth", pejorative still for many but beginning to be perceived as more major and positive than one used to imagine, particularly as it becomes increasingly felt that the scientific conceptual system is also, strictly, a myth (as perhaps all formulations of truth are, at least insofar as they are not trivial?).

Symbol and myth have been the subject of considerable discourse lately. Once having remarked them, we leave them aside, except to note that they have served, *inter alia*, to take some of the pressures off the "belief" concept, and off the simplistic believing/knowing dichotomy. (Human beings do not exactly "believe" [or disbelieve] a symbol, it is increasingly, and helpfully, recognized—nor even more, a whole symbol-system. Moreover, to come to know what a symbol or a myth—for instance, in the lives of other people—represents better than does a proposition, enlarges the conception of human knowledge in an important fashion.) One does not believe a symbol. Rather, one responds to it, one is more or less successful in seeing what it means (has meant, may mean); in seeing and feeling and being moved by that.

One may, however, go further: to see that the modern concept of believing is inapt also in what has been construed as its proper domain. A serious wrestling with human "believing" around the world frees one from the fallacy of supposing that people believe propositions. Intellectuals translate into propositions what they believe; or propositions induce in people what they then believe. No one, however, has ever believed a proposition. To say so is a short-hand that at times does little mischief, at times much. A person believes (or rejects) what a proposition means —and not in general, but what it means to him or her. In this, propositions are like symbols. May we not say, they *are* symbols[7]?

Leaving these aside, however, I would draw attention to one or two other concepts more directly and even traditionally pertaining to the strictly intellectualist relation of persons to their environment. I suggest that these may to some helpful degree supplement "knowing" and replace "believing", both in general and specifically in religious matters, not least in analysing and interpreting faith, whether one's own or others'. If nothing more, they may serve to illustrate some aspects of our problem.

Among these concepts is, for instance, "understanding". In the study of human affairs, "to know and to understand" must be the twin objectives of intellectual inquiry[8]. It is easy for a person to be ignorant of the data of human history, in general or for a particular sub-process; it requires much effort to come to know, even in small part. Yet to know but not to understand (to know what human beings have done or do, but not to understand them or it) is in its turn all too possible. It is, also, manifestly inadequate intellectually. This is conspicuously so in the history of religion, where knowledge without understanding has been common, and continues into our day. The category of understanding could, I suggest, become of potentially much greater significance than that of believing. It could prove more helpful, more illuminating, even decisive.

There is no earthly reason why a Theravadin Buddhist, for example, should believe in God. For him not to understand the concept of God, on the other hand, as it has played a monumental role in Christian and Islamic and other world history, would be an intellectual shortcoming—minor, so long as he lived within his own community, but potentially more significant once he should come into the company of theists. By "understanding" here I intend his apprehending not what the term "God" means in his own world-view, where it refers to something that perhaps does not exist or is unworthy, but rather what it has meant to those who have used it to denote and to connote a great range of their life in the world, and the universally human reaching beyond the world: their perception both of empiricals and of ultimates.

We are leaving aside until our next, concluding, section the relation of these things to faith. Here we are concerned only with belief as a theoretical concept, and various alternatives at its own theoretical level. Alongside traditional Christians who imagined that their not believing Islamic positions exonerated them from trying to understand them, or Muslims *vis-à-vis* Hindu ones ("why trouble to understand beliefs that are palpably false?"), we have in recent times seen the sorry spectacle also of modern thinkers whose wit and logical acuity were exhausted in adjudicating what they had reduced to others' beliefs while their conspicuous failure to understand constituted a massive intellectual error.

Less dramatically but more poignantly, the problem arose not only between groups but also internally within on-going communities. A preacher who strives to persuade his congregation to believe doctrines put together in by-gone centuries is vastly less effective than one whose sermon enables moderns to understand: who clarifies what those hoary propositions signified in the lives of persons and societies for whom, in the world-view of their times, they were true expressions of the eternal verities. (Even a hostile critic must recognize [*sic*] that and how they were genuine wrestlings with these, or at least with profound and persisting human problems.) It is somewhat pitiful to see modern Christians being asked to believe (or, by inadvertent implication, to disbelieve, or in the recent anti-intellectualist modes, to disregard) erstwhile propositional distillations of wisdom and insight and transcendent truth.

Not to believe ancient doctrines is as old-fashioned and as unintelligent as to believe them (as perhaps linguistic analysts, in their tortured and obfuscated way, dimly sense). The problem lies not in the doctrines, but in conceiving of them as beliefs. This is the modern West's most massive reductionism.

It is not only moderns for whom this is inappropriate. We saw above in our Islamics chapter that classical Muslims did not exactly "believe" the positions that they enunciated or assumed. We noted too that sensitive anthropologists find it uncouth to aver that contemporary primitives "believe" the world-views by which they live.

It is a poor use of language, grossly misleading, to say that St. Thomas Aquinas believed in God in the sense of believing that God exists.

One of the salient advantages for modern usage of concepts such as "understanding", "insight", "seeing the point", "awareness", "recognizing" is that even in the modern world these have not yet been depersonalized. Only a person can understand, or can recognize. Insight and seeing the point take place inside a person's head (or spirit)—or a group of persons'. All these human qualities can be expressed outwardly, empirically—for instance, in written or spoken sentences—but we have not yet lost hold of the fact that such sentences do not themselves constitute what the terms primarily designate, and may succeed in purveying less or more adequately only. My own view is that the locus of truth and knowledge, also, is persons. Yet in any case this is still evident for understanding, insight, and the like; and with the help of such concepts we may move towards restoring thinking in humane terms.

Without ceasing to be empirical and inductive, one must recognize that awareness of truth comes, and will increasingly come from our knowledge of history, and not only of science: from our critical corporate self-consciousness[9] as well as our "objective" knowing.

Shakespeare (but one could equally well instance Aeschylus, or Kalidasa) knew [*sic*] something about persons and the relations among them which was and is worth knowing. He expressed what he knew not in propositions but in poetic dramas of great power and potential effectiveness. It is important whether we are able to recognize [*sic*] through these the truths that he saw. Almost no significant question can be asked about Shakespeare or his plays in terms of what he believed. It is of considerable moment, however, to ask what he saw; what insights his poetry can help us to have; how our understanding of life can be enhanced by our understanding of his understanding of it.

A classical Muslim or mediaeval Jew or early Buddhist not only said that he or she knew, but actually did know, did recognize—and for that matter, a Trobriand Island aborigine "worshipping a fetish", recognizes—something about human beings and their destiny and their relation to themselves and to society and to the universe: something that was and is worth knowing. The former three expressed what they knew in (among other things) reasoned affirmations and myths, which succeeded in communicating it to their fellows, even though they do not communicate it directly to some of us, and perhaps not to their own twentieth-century successors (whereupon some label those propositions "beliefs" and affirm that they used to believe them). We shall never learn what they knew until we can go beyond what we think that they believed.

Our task is to recognize what it was that they recognized. If we are intellectuals and wish to communicate, in turn, our understanding of this to our fellows, our task is then to formulate it anew in expressions of our time and place and group—knowing that as the centuries proceed these too will become out-of-date (without ceasing thereby to have been perhaps true). We need not, indeed, wait: they will be inadequate from the start—as, in a fashion, already the classical formulations were also. No understanding, no insight, can be fully ensconced in a statement. The more profound it be, the truer and more applicable is this observation. Human life is such that there can be no guarantee that any form of words will unfailingly transfer a perception from one person to another. This is far from discouraging. It is the measure of our greatness as persons, and of the richness of human perceptions, not of the littleness of language nor the poverty of our systems. We do better to be impressed by the profundity of human personality and of the world that it inhabits, and by the capacity that nonetheless we all share to learn rewardingly from one another, and by the partial success that somehow communication and understanding can and do achieve—especially if we work at them—than to endeavour to rule out of consideration all those aspects and qualities of human living and of the universe that cannot be transcribed into machine-readable propositions.

Understanding is indeed a virtue; this is primarily so for an intellectual. Nonetheless, are we seeming to evade here the haunting and imperious question of truth? Are we emphasizing a comparativist concern, perhaps unduly ("interesting, no doubt, yet peripheral . . ."), perhaps in the interests of good causes like harmony and peaceful co-operation, or historical sophistication, yet failing to reckon with the intellectual's central task, of assessing rational truth and falsity, or with the Christian's (Muslim's, Buddhist's), of assessing the final truth or falsity of Christianity, Islam, Buddhism? We do well to understand our fellows; yet we must not omit to know the truth.

Such a discrimination, however, reflects an attitude no longer tenable, I would contend. To achieve understanding is to move towards knowing; and, conspicuously in the human realm, all one's knowing of truth limps if one does not understand one's neighbour. (The neighbour may be of another community or another century.) To know separately is to know in inadequate part.

However logical, solipsism—whether of individual or group or era—is not knowledge.

Of our consideration of "belief" above we have in effect summed up the conclusion in a single observation: that this concept in its present form is part and parcel of a particular historical ideology. It can serve only those who are content to live within that ideology and to subordinate to it, or to omit, all alternatives, from the past or in the present or for the future. A concomitant recognition, equally drastic, is that concepts of knowledge and of truth currently dominant in Western society are equally limited, culture-specific, and inadequate: that to move out of its present impasse and to attain a culture, even a vision, less spiritually destitute, less inhuman, less intellectually inadequate, the modern West will require as radical a recasting of its understanding of knowledge and truth as will religious communities of their theologies.

Not merely has "believing" been developed into a category by means of which those who use it may think about other centuries' and other societies' and other persons' religious life without taking them seriously—and even perhaps in part about their own. Also the concepts "knowing" and "truth" have been hammered into new forms in such a way as to dismiss from their imperious realm those other centuries and societies and persons—and in part oneself. This is to dismiss much that surely can no longer be ignored. Yet neither can it be seriously reckoned with, intellectually, until after a change of heart, and of mind. What may induce that change, no one can say; but the comparative historian is inescapably aware of considerations that require and might induce it. The growing disillusionment in the modern world with technocratic life and scientistic ideology may contribute only negatively: may lead not to humility but to despair (the former requires—or is—faith?).

Seen in world-history perspective, the narrowness and insensitivity, indeed the arrogance, of recent Western secular thought, which are illustrated in its notion of knowledge, are understandable, even if sad. The disparagement of other cultures was standard. The disparagement of the past was secured by the notion of progress, the concept of "modern" as significantly equivalent to "better", the sense that previous ages did not know. The disparagement of the personal was achieved through an almost inescapable glorification of natural science, whose knowledge was of the impersonal world of things (so that knowledge of human matters was considered not knowledge unless it were scientific, "objective", amoral, perceiving persons in the manner of things). Past history, and other civilizations, became something that one learned about, but did not expect to learn from. What in the universe and in human life is higher than man, was ruled out of consideration by definition.

It was with this truncated and inhumane view of "knowing" that the new notion of "believing" was correlated and contrasted. The concepts of "reason" and of "truth" were revised, also, to make a coherent whole. (The former was detranscendentalized, the latter depersonalized, denatured.) For a time the new scheme worked well, as have other civilizations' also for a time: more mightily, even triumphantly, than most, although also for a shorter time than many. The inadequacies have relatively quickly shown up, to our corporate sorrow. (Besides, to an extent not widely appreciated, secular modernity proceeded for a good while on the momentum of pre-modern faith and of personal qualities bequeathed and justified by earlier outlooks.) It is not easy, however, to see realities that one's cultural world-view is not calibrated to perceive. It is of the presuppositions of thought that a revision is requisite, if we are to think more truly about the world and our life together.

Obviously it is beyond the scope of this present book, to say nothing of beyond the competence of its author, to tackle the question of that revision. Within our scope, and perhaps even within our competence, is to call attention to the problem, not simply in general but in relation to the specific matter of human faith. (This matter can serve this purpose even as object, let alone as subject, of knowing.) Most human beings have been, and all human beings potentially are, persons of faith. This fact—which it has been our task here to present and to clarify—must be both recognized and understood. So also must be the fact that that faith has been expressed rationally in a diversity of ways. If, in the course of recognizing and understanding these great truths, our theologies or our philosophies prove in need of being revised in order to be able to cope, then we shall have to revise them. (One or two suggestions along the latter line will be adumbrated presently—if only as tentative illustrations of one person's endeavours.) The venture may be urged not merely in the interests of a theory more adequate to interpreting the world that we now know, but more joyously also in that in the process we learn, and provide for, something not only true but also important and good.

The demand upon us is austere; but the reward is large.

An awareness of comparative history makes to the philosopher the same sort of contribution as to the theologian: the compelling vision of diversity, and the ability to see oneself, not only others, in global perspective. At the theological level obviously, but at the philosophic level also, to theorize or to adjudicate about truth within an established conceptual framework without regard to its being one ideational system among others, is to-day naive.

The comparativist issue has become not distinct from or additional to any question of truth, but integral, if not prior, to it. Not only is our world as a whole becoming interpenetratingly complex, integrated in diversity. Also, each person is internally involved, as well as externally. One can no longer be content to talk of differing communities, or differing "languages", if one aspires to be more than parochial or schizoid. Especially is this the case if one's talk be of the relation of God to humankind or of truth to human knowing. If traditionally (and still to-day with scientistic liberals?) a problem was that members of one culture treated as propositions within one world-view (their own) what were in fact the conceptual frameworks or even the propositions of another, in contrast the modern dilemma arises in part, as we saw in the Islamic and the Christian instances, from the fact that the framework of the propositions may be that not only of another culture, but of another era of one's own culture or another dimension of one's own life.

On the one hand, to be a Christian or a Jew, a Muslim or a Buddhist, in the modern world is to be engaged live in comparative culture, having faith whose form was articulated in one outlook while living and to a large extent even thinking in a society informed by another. One may go further, and affirm that to be a human person in modern society—given the dehumanizing and depersonalizing connotations of much of contemporary culture—is to participate in fact in a similar bifurcation. No human being is true to him- or herself who thinks only in objectivistic, thing-oriented, terms. None is true to his or her neighbour who thinks in terms of only one community, one ideology.

Every position has become, in some sort, a world position—but inadequately. Coherence is available to-day neither within nor among conceptual outlooks. It must be constructed.

We do not affirm that no one may legitimately think, any more, within a limited framework. That would be unduly austere, and arrogant. Rather, we suggest only that those who venture to theorize about truth, generically, or about God—to philosophize or to theologize—must move towards doing so in comparativist perspective. In this study I have urged that we must forge for ourselves a new concept for faith; and it turns out that in order to do this we (each group of us) have to modify our conceptual system as a whole, if not actually to forge for ourselves (for all of us) a new one that shall be apt for coping with our modern awareness (both of the natural world and of human history) in its cultural multiformity.

To-day's situation is an historical emergence: it too will pass, unless we bungle our intellectual synthesizing task. Planetary intellectual cohesion need be attained in principle only once. No doubt it will be a pluralistic unity, in which the rich diversity of cultural and ideational forms will be understood by intelligent men and women everywhere within a comprehensive intellectual context that makes coherent sense of that very diversity. It happens to fall to our lot in contemporary history to construct that intellectual context.

For Westerners, there is relatively little in either the Judaeo-Christian or the Graeco-Roman heritage of thought preparing them to handle conceptually this sort of situation; but they are beginning to learn. India has a somewhat more propitious metaphysical tradition, but has been much less historically oriented. East Asia brings various resources to the task, although China has meanwhile opted for its own brand of Marxist singularity. In the Islamic world it is from the Sufi tradition that sophistication is available for this specific issue. In any case, clearly, it is a world problem that humanity will solve, if at all, collaboratively. (It is also a personal problem, for an intelligent cosmopolitan, with which the sensitive will wrestle existentially.)

It is our planetary multiformity that generates the issue and that postulates both the requirement and the validity of a new understanding. That multiformity is, moreover, of both time and place. We all participate in it, in both its dimensions. The intellectual must do so wittingly.

In this sense the question of understanding precedes that of truth. Yet it does not dislodge it. It does, however, render it more complicated, subtle, and contingent than has previously been recognized. In particular, understanding renders obsolete the simple binary classification of true/false. This over-simplification will have to be outgrown—and soon. The position, popular for a time with certain recent philosophers and then others, that propositions (and even that propositions alone) are either true or false, proved inadequate in the light of even a limited comparativist awareness (primarily historical, of inherited theses from an earlier age). It was enlarged for a time to the notion that propositions are first either meaningless or meaningful, and, if the latter, are then either true or false. This, however, can now be seen as a typical instance of a particular world-view, constituting one recent ideology. That ideology derives from, and serves more or less adequately for, achronic natural science, but is grossly ill-suited to accommodate our knowledge of other matters, and must be superseded. The simplistic true/false dichotomy was encouraged in the West not only by recent scientistic rationalism, however, but also, although in less restricted fashion, by the earlier dominant ideology of the Church ("the saved and the dammed"); and even to some degree by classical Greek thought. In each case the view was held for reasons internal to the positions espoused; it was not induced by a consideration of the world scene now available to us. Once this scene is seriously confronted, the ineptitude of the position emerges.

One reason, however, why in the new situation many in the West, rather than dedicating themselves to understanding alien positions, were under compulsion to adjudicate them (as true or false; and usually, then, as false) is that they felt threatened by them. This followed from the fact of their minds' operating within a conceptual system in which, if two statements contradict each other, one of them, it is felt, must be false. Among many Muslims, and many Westerners, whether secularist or Christian, this preconception pressured people into holding their neighbour's view to be false, since otherwise their own would be. This intellectual dogma has wrought incalculable mischief: both towards external deprecation, and towards internal fear.

Understanding awaits its being challenged, and promotes its being modified. In India, for example, a contrasting alternative perceptual disposition has been widespread: that if two statements contradict each other, probably both of them are at least partially false—although also, if each is held by intelligent and sincere persons, especially by large and lasting groups, then probably also both are at least partially true. (More accurately, in India the standard opposite of truth has been not falsity but ignorance. Of ignorance there are, of course, degrees.)

We postpone for a moment a question as to whether one should adopt for oneself and one's own living such an interpretation of logical contradiction. This much may meanwhile be averred, surely: that so far as understanding goes, an outside observer will halt in one's comprehension of, let us say, Hindus and Muslims juxtaposed in India, or The Three Teachings in China, or Buddhist-Shinto relations in Japan, or the difference between the fifth and the fifteenth centuries (or even between the fourteenth and fifteenth centuries) in the Near East, or between town and countryside anywhere, unless one is able seriously to recognize that, for all their logically incompatible variety, each of the positions held had a point—and each of them, no doubt, being human, also left something out.

This, once stated, is perhaps obvious enough. Less obvious, perhaps, is that these considerations apply also to the history of science. Copernicus, in a decisive move that some see as fundamental for the development of modern science, superseded the common-sense notion of the earth's being fixed while the sun revolves around it. He expressed his new discernment in the view (the "belief") that the sun stands still. It, he affirmed, not the earth, is (near) the centre. We now know the sun to be more vagrant than Copernicus thought the earth to be, and no nearer than the earth to the centre of the physical universe. Are we then to say that modern science is based on an insight that was true, expressed in statements that were false?

To say this, although interesting to an historian of religion, illustrates rather the inadequacy of prevailing categories for understanding human discourse. Copernicus's belief was the conceptualization of an insight into reality. The insight was, and remains, valid; the conceptualization, like all ideational activity, was human, finite, and historical. It served in the fifteenth century to enable Copernicus to articulate in his own mind the truth that he discerned. It served in that century, and for a time thereafter, to enable others to attain that true insight. In the twentieth century, it may serve us to attain an insight into the fifteenth century, on the one hand, and into astronomical reality, on the other, if and only if we are able to see beyond the propositions—translating them out of an earlier world-view into our own.

It is naive to suppose, however, that our own is absolute or final. For these considerations illuminate also one's own outlook; and thereby the ultimate questions, of what is true and what is truth[10].

Ideas ("beliefs", even, if for the sake of argument we should concede that term to those still affectionate towards it—especially perhaps in the existential form, "What shall I/we believe?"), are to be not only appreciated, but held responsibly. If we must classify them, a better starting-point (but I stress that phrase) than into "true" and "false" is a prior division of them into two great classes of another sort: namely, other people's (other peoples') and one's own (one's own group's). For this polarity, the fundamental reason is that the moral dimension in the two cases differs. Of one's own affirmations (not those that one has held, but those that one will hold) it is absolutely imperative that they be true. (We shall come presently to that requirement, impossible to evade, impossible to fulfil.) Of others', it is absolutely imperative that they be understood.

We are back here to the crucial distinction—profound logically, semantically, personally—between first-person and third-person usage. In the forms *credo*, "I believe", "I think", the verbs mean something subtly yet profoundly different from what they signify in *credunt*, "they believe", "they think"[11]. Nonetheless, the two in each case are not unconnected (especially for an intellectual). Our suggested dichotomy is proffered here as a helpful first step on the long road back to, and forward towards, coherence—towards their eventual integration in a community (in principle, world-wide) of what *we* know.

The drastic individualism of modern epistemology is one of its crucial weaknesses.

The intellectual problem of the modern world is how to be a relativist without being a nihilist. Or one might say: how to be a pluralist without losing an intelligent, steadfast loyalty to one's own vision. (We reject the facile alternative, of more self-confident thinkers, of being that kind of pluralist who absolutizes one's own position, relativizes only others'—or, dismisses them. This is ruled out by our imperative, that those others' are to be understood, taken seriously.) Our proposed principle of division is a starting-point towards re-uniting the two. For it inherently aims at, conduces to, its own supersession. For one thing, the ability—even the desire—to understand the position of others is a function of one's own position. And dynamically *vice versa*: those who contemplate the diversity of positions with which human history is decorated are impelled to construct an interpretation of truth that will be coherent with what they see. It must be coherent also with what they personally know. The imperative to understand any given utterance includes an obligation to discern (in some degree!) the intricate relation that in varying ways always obtains historically, precariously, subtly among any human being, his or her situation, what that person holds true, and truth itself. This must be correlated, also, with one's own awareness (one's own group's awareness) of truth—and articulation of it.

The polarizing division that I have propounded is manifestly and in principle not final, also in this: that it applies to all of us indiscriminately and simultaneously. No one (group) of us but must—and indeed does—strive to conceptualize, and to state our conceptions (to "believe"), truly. No one (group) of us but deserves the genuine respect of the rest of us. Perceiving, conceiving, articulating our apprehensions, thinking, believing, are something that we human beings do in diverse ways. We therein constitute (potentially) a corporate global community of a now self-conscious intellectual pluralism or relativism pledged, through our several disparate loyalties to truth and our mutual respect for each other, to move severally and jointly closer to that truth, and hence away from the grosser cacophonies of that relativism.

As we have already indicated, once we have successfully coped with our present pluralist challenge, the next stage of human history can then move on to supersede it.

It would be pretentious and distracting to think of outlining here a theory of truth consonant with humanity's diversity of opinions and convictions. That is the task of another book or another writer. Yet it would be delinquent, also, to ignore the matter, pretending that it does not arise. May one, then, with due tentativeness and hesitation, speculate that for a comparativist, the truth may be conceptualized as something that both is immanent within, and transcends, any given formulation of it in any given system. So far as one's own system is concerned, where the immanence is most readily accessible, it is important, of course, to cling fast to that truth and at the same time in due humility to recognize as well the transcendence. The truth of what one believes—even, of what one sees; even, of what one experimentally verifies—is never the whole truth. So far as others' views are concerned, where one can all too easily miss the presence of truth altogether—it being especially easy for an outsider to be aware of those aspects of truth that are, or seem to be, omitted—it is important to recognize the immanence as well as the transcendence: to strive to recognize what of truth there is, couched in the bizarre phrases or moments of an alien view, as well as recognizing that the whole truth is, of course, greater than that.

Might one, then, hazard a definition of belief, or at least an interpretation of conceptualization, whether of faith or of anything else? Any conceptualization (and any formalized awareness, any thesis, any "belief") is an intellectual formulation in the mind of some person or group (and subsequently perhaps, then, in words—but statements and even propositions are always derivative and secondary) of the truth, insofar as that person or group has apprehended it (been apprehended by it). Their apprehension may be good or bad. It will certainly be partial. Yet it may be less or more partial; it may be so inadequate or inaccurate as to constitute almost a misapprehension. Further, the formulation of the apprehension may also be well or badly done. The person or group may have a good apprehension badly formulated, or a poor one or a virtual misapprehension expressed with precision and clarity, or any other combination.

Every specific proposition[12] is formulated in terms of one or another world-view, or general conceptual system. Each world-view may be less or more adequate to comprehending reality in general; and besides, may be less or more adequate for comprehending and expressing the particular apprehension of a specific point.

Since the truth transcends not only what each of us has apprehended, let alone formulated, but also what all of us together have, or can, therefore every observer may in principle learn something of truth from every person—and especially, of course, from every group—in human history, past and present.

Such a relativism is far from nihilism. (In contradistinction from modern "belief", which, we recall, is calculated to sever the relation of persons' ideas to both transcendence and truth, there is postulated here, of course, a transcendent conception of truth. Any other involves, ultimately, either a nihilist denying of truth altogether, or else an absolutizing of one's own system's view of it. The shift from postulate to awareness is discussed in our next section.)

Furthermore, such a view proves itself helpful in two directions. Not only does one thus learn some truth from understanding any "belief" and any "belief-system", without being gullible of any; but also, conversely, such a view of truth in turn promotes understanding. One understands one's fellow human beings better if one sees that they are, like oneself, in pursuit of truth, even when (like oneself) they affirm something that falls short—perhaps woefully short. No sincere statement, no awareness, no belief but is an approximation to truth—however distant, however feeble, however human. Some, no doubt, are less close approximations than are others. Not all can effectively claim our attention and active respect. Persons' whom we meet may. And on a world scale, it would be unintelligent as well as discourteous not to give heed to those few that have been cherished by scores of millions of persons, for many long centuries, and on the basis of which civilizations have been built and sustained. One does well to presume that these are not merely mundanely significant facts but are also significant approximations to transcendent truth.

Moreover, it is well to bear in mind, both for oneself and for one's neighbour, that the curious position of human beings in relation to the historical on the one hand and to the transcendent on the other may mean that any given person may well be, and indeed probably is, in closer touch with transcendent Truth, with God, than are his or her intellectualizations.

This last point, and indeed all recognizing of truth as transcendent, brings us to our next, concluding, section, on the relation of intellect to faith. Both matters had to be introduced here, but remind us that the capacity of human beings to think in ways even approximately true is itself in fact derivative from their personal quality of being able to reach out towards (to be touched by) Truth itself.

(Some would say: Himself.)

(iii) The intellectual dimension of faith

The locus of faith is persons. It is persons, not propositions, not symbols and sacraments—though all such may be channels. The locus is communities insofar as these are personal and not merely institutionalized —although again, an institution may be faith's channel. Moreover, faith is a quality of the whole person. It has, therefore, as many dimensions as has personhood. Accordingly, it has an intellectual dimension. On it we selectively focus because it happens to be the subject of this book, and a major problem in our time (apart from the fact that I myself am an intellectual); but not in order to centralize and to over-emphasize this one facet. The intellect is a human characteristic, and faith a human quality. It over-simplifies only mildly to assert: the role of the intellect in faith is the role of the intellect in human life.

Nonetheless, it may be helpful to specify the intellectual dimension of faith as modern awareness allows this to be perceived. In particular, we may endeavour to draw together into coherent understanding what has seemed to recent consciousness the elemental problem: the manifest diversity of "beliefs" or conceptualizations in relation to faith over the centuries and around the globe. Whatever faith may or may not be, "beliefs" accompanying it have appeared to be many, and odd.

We might begin by noting a handful, chosen not quite arbitrarily but purely for illustrative purposes, of nearly contemporaneous intellectuals who were spokesmen for faith on earth in the early part of this present millennium. Our example comprises the Christian Hugh of St. Victor (ob. 1142), the Jewish poet and essayist Judah ha-Levi (ca. 1080-1141), the Muslim revivificationist Ghazzali (1058-1111), the Hindu philosopher Ramanuja (1017-1137?), the sometime Buddhist neo-Confucian Chu Hsi (1130-1200). In pre-modern times, Jews, uniquely, were accustomed to living as a minority in a cultural world transcending their own (as every group, Marxist, secular-liberal, religious, is a minority in the planetary world of to-day, even though few have come to terms with this difficulty); and Judah had read and his thinking was influenced by some of the writings of the Islamic intellectual Ghazzali. Otherwise, and this is important for our purposes, each of the five lived and thought without having heard of any of the other four; and with the same exception, wrote for readers who would not have heard.

None of them held belief to be faith. More generally, none held that the holding of a given intellectual position (e.g., their own) was a matter of final human destiny, a cosmic criterion. Nonetheless, each held certain matters to be true—and important.

As our millennium draws to a close, we differ from all of them at its beginning in a great many ways. These include our thinking, perceiving ("believing"), and knowing differently from each and yet being aware of and able to appreciate all. We differ also in being aware that our own great-grandchildren will in their turn perceive and know (and "believe"—if that concept survives) differently from us. Yet we can, and indeed must, learn from them. Our ideas in and about faith must comprehend theirs, and be continuous with theirs. We may not dismiss, therefore, what have been called their beliefs. Nor may we neglect their conviction that the truth is important. The intellectual dimension of their faith was—severally and jointly—major. (This, of course, is why we have selected them for consideration here.)

Faith, for these thinkers, is many things. Yet without unduly over-simplifying, perhaps, we may recognize that for them intellectually it includes two salient components: insight and response.

Taking these components one by one, one may aver the history of faith to be a history of insight. There is a difference between knowing that something is true, and knowing its truth, recognizing it. (As a minimal example, one may take the case of propositions. Our distinction pertains in principle to all these, from the simplest on up. "It is warm to-day": in this there is a range of potential knowing, from sheer information to varying degrees of realistic appreciation and sensitive awareness; whether or not one elaborate, by adding either "here" or "in Calcutta", or both.

More abstractly, $e = mc^2$. All informed people know that this last is true, and some even understand it; but few recognize the truth that it expresses.) There is a difference between knowing that a joke is funny (one may be led to infer this from, for instance, the fact that everyone else who hears it, laughs) and personally "seeing the joke". One may believe, for highly persuasive and valid reasons, that Bach's music is beautiful; yet even so one may or may not know its beauty, recognize the truth and glory and poignancy that Bach saw when he wrote it (or that the conductor or performers to whom one is listening may less or more see, and less or more succeed in getting into their execution. Human beings are not incapable, fascinatingly, of validly recognizing more in what they hear than does the person to whom they listen—whether in music or in theology). Two school-children may successfully learn and repeat on an examination a proof in geometry, but one of them may see the point of the argument and the other not.

We are concerned here in principle only with insights that are valid; as well as, of course, with sincerity. It is possible to laugh out of courtesy, even if one does not actually find a story very funny. Yet a true sense of humour goes beyond even the latter, to be genuine not only subjectively but objectively, seeing the mirth of what is truly funny (in the world; not only in stories); and similarly with all intellectuality. To recognize, at least in part, the justice of what is in fact just, the cogency of a logical argument, the goodness of a cup of cold water given in love or the horrendous evil of Auschwitz, the glory of a sunset or of a cherry blossom—these are insights.

These are faith.

For faith, too, intellectually, is insight. It is so on a potentially grander scale, at its best, than any of these; yet it is continuous with them. For the follower, as distinct from the leader, religious faith intellectually is first of all the ability to see the point of a tradition. At the propositional level, religious or otherwise, it concerns an ability that formulations potentially have: that of allowing or inducing those who hear them to move beyond them to the truth with which the person who framed them was in touch.

Each of our faith spokesmen, we have said, affirmed certain matters to be both true and important. Two such affirmations may in particular be singled out as paramount. The first, serving as foundation for all else that they might have to say, was the recognition of transcendence. Not the proposition that transcendence is there: that is my formulation, and it is a gamble whether my readers will share or even appreciate that particular vocabulary, will acquiesce in or find illuminating that late-twentieth-century phrasing. By "transcendence" I mean formally a reality that transcends the immediate mundane. Substantially, in significant part I mean that reality that Hugh and other Christian writers, Judah and other Jewish ones, Ghazzali and other Muslims, Ramanuja and other Hindus, Chu Hsi and other East Asians, have helped me to see: the transcendent reality that, so far as I through their writings am able to ascertain, they saw. In their perception not only of that transcendence, but also of its supreme importance for human life, the five agreed, unwittingly, not only with each other but with virtually all other reputedly wise and respected thinkers in every culture known to man (except in part the recent West). Their insight was of a reality that transcended not only the material world, but—by far—their own apprehension of it. They were unanimous in saying that anything that they might have to say about that reality fell far short of the whole truth.

The second affirmation that each made, each in his own way, was that the transcendent truth that he recognized was not totally transcendent in the sense of being out of reach or altogether unintelligible. On the contrary, each held, in all humility and joyously, gratefully, that he was vouchsafed an insight into that transcendent truth; that he recognized, however partially, a significant truth, one that could be shared with others and that he felt it important to share. Hence his writing.

It is important, said each one, to recognize that truth transcends our insight into it; but each stressed also the importance of the truth that he had been enabled to see.

I personally find no reason to disagree with any of them on any of this.

I may reserve my own judgement as to the ratio, if one may introduce that inapplicable metaphor, between transcendence and the positive insight in each case—or as to the weight that I personally shall give to their several insights in relation to each other (our problem, not theirs). I reserve my own judgement also if any of them inferred syllogistically that if A be true, it then follows that B must be false; this is a matter that I shall use my own best insight into logic (and transcendence) to assess. (Might one call into service here, for judicious and critical use, that other insight expressed in the flamboyant quip, "All religion and all philosophy is true in what it asserts, false in what it denies"?) Insofar, however, as they proclaimed a truth that they saw, I put forth my best endeavour to study their reports and those of persons who have subsequently appreciated them in order to see whether in the reality that surrounds and informs me and my fellows and my world I can see it too.

Insofar as faith is insight, one might venture to suggest that a modern student is either uninformed or unintelligent if he fails to recognize what it was that, however partially, men such as these knew and found important about human life and the universe.

(It is all right, of course, to be uninformed or even unintelligent about such matters, provided that one not make a great case on the basis of it. To proffer an interpretation of the universe and man's place in it, ignoring these men's insights, would seem a whit pretentious?)

Admittedly the modern situation is novel. We live to-day in a world that has been historically modified from that of these five in many drastic ways, including this: that an intellectual, of whatever persuasion, is in danger nowadays of being inadequately perceptive who does not to some significant degree understand the meaning, and one could push on to suggest also the truth, both of what Christians have meant when they affirmed that Jesus Christ is the Son of God, and of what Muslims have meant when they have affirmed that he is not.

If a Christian or a humanist be expected in our day to recognize the truth (however partial) of Islamic theistic and Buddhist atheistic faith, might some not argue that one may surely recognize also the shortcomings, the sorry human follies, the historical failings (and worse), that these and other religious traditions have evinced or allowed? The answer is that indeed one may, although it would be more constructive if the Islamic and Buddhist aspects of this were left to Muslims and Buddhists respectively, while Christians recognized the manifold ways (they have been stridently pointed out) in which their own Church's faith, for all its hold upon ultimate truth, has in historical fact not merely fallen short of its ideal, but found expression in ways that have positively harmed many, both without its walls (most devastatingly: Jews) and within its walls. Further, Christians should observe, the Church has even neglected or formally left out of its highest ideal, until recently or still, aspects of the truth (scientific, for one; the diversity of faith, for another; the relation between love and sexuality; there are more) that others have seen. Moreover, just as religious persons should perceive and acknowledge the enormous achievements of modern secularism, so the irreligious would do well to recognize the devastation, in the depersonalizing of society and the desiccating of individual lives, that their secularist world-view promotes, so large a sector of the truth does it omit. Even science, so promising and so seemingly immaculate a saviour, has for several, of late, been showing itself a potential nightmare, with Hiroshima and polluted oceans, and its apparent drastic incapacity to correlate the human spirit with its world.

Human history demonstrates the desperate ingenuity with which we human beings show ourselves able not only to have limited visions but also to distort, indeed to turn almost upside down, our highest visions, to vitiate even the truth that we have seen. Let none of us deal with this disconsolating awareness by imagining that only other groups, not one's own, are incriminated.

Faith is not only insight, however: it is also, in some ways even more emphatically, response. As we have discovered time and again throughout this study, faith has re-iteratedly been affirmed to involve, or to be, a dedication to living in terms of the truth, and of the good. Effectively this has regularly meant the truth and goodness that one or one's group has seen. (This last truth, this good, is always partial, the historian again notes; although we recall that in principle faith has signified also and always that the truth, and goodness, transcend what one has seen.) Living so, of course, involves will and feeling, deed, community: in short, the total personality, in both social and private aspects, and in both temporal and transcending aspects. Once again we attend here simply to the intellectual dimension, to what has in our day been called "beliefs".

We may consider the matter under again two intertwining headings that we have noted: the truth as seen, and truth transcendent, truth as such. Both have been important. They were so for our five spokesmen, and they are for us.

Faith is a saying "Yes!" to truth; and it would not do to minimize the truth that Christians, or that Muslims, or that any of the others did in fact see and to which in their lives they responded, and in terms of which they and their fellows reared and sustained a civilization. Christian forms of faith were a saying "Yes!" to the truth that they saw in and through Christ (although the almost unitarian Christocentrism of our day is historically recent). Muslim forms were a saying "Yes!" to the truth that they found through the Qur'an (and through other Islamic symbols and patterns); Buddhist forms, to the truth that The Three Jewels specifically enabled them to see. The truth is multi-faceted, and different groups have seen it in differing forms; yet each group was right, surely, in affirming that the truth that they saw was important. No historian can disagree. Each, moreover, has been right in affirming that one must be loyal to the truth that one has seen . . . provided that one go on, as each of our five did, and as we shall elaborate presently, to stress also that the truth is greater than that.

Because of our own intellectualist bias, shared to a considerable extent by our five, we have tended here to write of truth and of response to truth, although as regards both matters we might speak rather of goodness. We may to some degree by-pass (yet not dismiss) that stark problem by thinking of truth as including the truth about goodness (and by recognizing, as did they, that truth is good).

Looking back from our present vantage point to the world situation in the past, none of us can change the firm fact that human beings on our planet at that time perceived reality differently from each other, various groups in the world achieving their own insights and suffering from their own limitations; and presumably none of us wishes to change that fact. Except for Judah ha-Levi (he personally and his community saw and suffered from the violence of such other communities as they knew, the Christian and Islamic), for none of our five was this diversity a primary and acute problem. Yet all were aware of, and to some extent even wrote about, differences, whether intellectual or in the realm of faith. As we have endeavoured to elucidate in this present study, there is one point that none of them did or could realize, with anything like our degree of awareness in these matters. (Ramanuja in some ways approaches it most closely, for synchronic diversity if not diachronic; and from Chu Hsi also the modern world can learn in this realm.) That point is this: that each set forth his delineation of the issues from within and in terms of a distinct conceptual ambiance, at a distinct phase in its historical development—of which it is our modern privilege or burden to be critically and objectively conscious. For no one of them was faith confused with accepting that mediating conceptual complex; yet neither was it understood without it.

What this amounts to is that so far as particularity goes, each proclaimed the truth that he had seen (that had been made apparent to him), and saw faith as in significant part a response to that truth; yet insofar as each presented his understanding also in a particular fashion, he would in principle wish to go beyond this. No one of them but saw a truth that, for all its infinitude or absoluteness potentially, was finite at least in this, that his vision of it was, in the human fashion, finite; and in addition, his report in words and concepts to the rest of us (and indeed, to himself) of what he had seen, was in words and concepts specific of time and place.

This specificity, then, it is our business to go beyond. At least, this is so if we would do justice to their vision. The other particularity, they went beyond themselves. An ingredient of the vision of each, as we have remarked, was the clear awareness that truth transcends their own vision, and that faith involves loyalty also to that very transcendence.

We had noted St. Thomas expressing this point. Faith is saying "Yes!" to the truth. The truth, I believe and contend, is thus-and-so, he spent many years and great ability in expounding. Yet, he went on, *if* I be wrong, I apologize and trust that a more accurate version will be set forth[13]. The sentiment is paralleled not only in each of our five spokesmen, but in general in the writings of any theologians worth their salt.

To a man, they held that faith means loyalty to the truth as such, to reality as such, primarily and overridingly—and to the particular truth/reality that they had seen, and were proclaiming, insofar as and because it came under that mightier heading. Before we explore, as our final problem, the implications of this for us in the twentieth and twenty-first centuries, let us look a little more closely at their conceptualist particularity. Such particularity is part and parcel of the human condition, we to-day know with novel clarity. (Nor must we, in our ability to see or our zest to get beyond the historicism of their expressions of thought, fail to recognize it of our own.) Nonetheless, our five were and have remained notable in no mean part because each transcended the current conceptual tradition of his time and place, seeing its inadequacy especially for a true understanding of human destiny and transcendence and faith. This was not easy for them, and they were criticized for their breadth. Hugh of St. Victor, for instance, startled the Church with his advocacy of the usefulness, for the life of faith, of secular learning. His views contributed to the development of the University of Paris (which means, also, to the Western university as such), and paved the way for St. Thomas a century later, who took Hugh's advice and brought to bear on his understanding of faith all the resources available to him for that momentous task. These resources included, of course, those proffered to him by the Church, its sacraments and its teachings and its devotional life; but they included also the untrammeled use of his brilliant and powerful, independent mind. (He was attacked for being too independent, for being too rationalist, for being an intellectual not nearly subservient enough to accepted Church positions.) They included also the insights of teachings of whatever non-Christian civilizations he was aware of, specifically of course Greece and monumentally Aristotle. (He was criticized for that, too. There were many Christians at the time for whom it was not at all obvious that a right understanding of God and of man's relation to God which is faith, is attainable through a "synthesis" of Christian and "pagan" thought; whereas to him it was obvious that one excludes from this great undertaking nothing that one knows.) Less self-consciously, he was influenced by Islamic culture, in subtle ways and overtly by Ibn Rushd ("Averroes"); he was accused in his day of, and has had to be defended in ours for, being an Averroist.

Similarly for the others. Judah wrote a book on comparative religion. Ghazzali studied deeply each of the major movements in his world—theological, revolutionary, skeptical; Islamic and extra-Islamic—and is great because he struggled through to produce a personal and public synthesis (which, daring at the time, in later centuries became itself established). Ramanuja, although less influenced by Buddhist thought than had been his major predecessor Sankara, developed a theology that could almost be called a theistic theory of comparative religion. Chu Hsi, China's "great synthesizer", again a bold innovator in his time whose thought later became an orthodoxy, excluded from his critical interpretation of man's place in the universe none of the traditions known to him in the China of his day (whether indigenous or from outside).

Indeed, is there not something not merely petty, but from the spiritual (faith) point of view skirting blasphemy, and from the intellectual ("belief") point of view skirting irresponsibility, in approaching an issue of this seriousness with anything less than the fullest range of data, method, and preparation? Of late we have seen the introvert isolationisms of a range of disparate "religions" each in principle excogitating an intellectual vision for itself in exclusivism from the others and in contradistinction from scientific or secular knowledge. This, although ostensibly traditionalist in each case, is a relatively recent innovation (although it is not without roots in a curious Western particularity as well as, of course, in earlier geographic and historical dispersal). It has been the mark of an age of waning faith.

Of fundamental importance, it has been the thesis of this book to stress, is that faith for us should be continuous with that of earlier ages. In the first instance, continuity means for Christians continuity with faith in its Christian forms, for Muslims in its Islamic, and so forth. Disastrous, however, both intellectually and spiritually, has been the monumental error of seeking similarity of belief—or as much of it as can be salvaged or contrived—rather than similarity of faith. We might amuse ourselves with an aphorism: that while one's faith, as many have averred, is given by God, one's belief is given by one's century or one's group. The quip is, of course, gross: not least because of the ambiguity that we have uncovered in the term "belief". It certainly applies in large measure to belief as presupposition, conceptual framework. (An observant traditionalist theologian, even, could hardly disagree?) Yet this has been so "in large measure" only, since man's mind is capable, as is his and her spirit, of recognizing transcendence, in and through the mundane. Belief also, therefore, transcends. Faith being an awareness of transcendence and a response to it, its intellectual dimension has included such reaching out beyond the given as one's mind can manage. Certain outstanding or "creative" intellectuals, of great faith, do so manage in part—as our five illustrate.

If our faith to-day is to be continuous with faith in the past, or even if our conception of faith is to do justice to it, then we must widen, not narrow, our appreciation of its involvement with ideas.

Persons of faith, the history of religion makes manifest, have not "believed" any one thing. Yet it does not at all follow that ideas can be set aside, to let faith wallow innovatingly in sentimental a-rationality. It belongs to faith (as our five bear eloquent witness) to move upwards, not downwards, intellectually from the past: faifthfully to comprehend more, not less. It turns out that the ideas of intellectuals of faith in the past can help us in this, not prove a barrier, if we give truly close heed to what they have in fact been saying.

It is no part of faith to believe what other centuries appear to have believed, to accept the ideas or the world-views by which they lived their lives. It is, however, part of faith, anyway for an intellectual, to take those ideas seriously—at least the leading ones among them. It is part of faith to understand them. This is so especially, certainly, for the leading ideas of one's own community in the past. It is so also nowadays, sc far as feasible, for those of other communities across the globe; and especially, certainly, it is so for those of one's neighbours.

Certainly for the Christian, whose salient commandments are to love God and to love one's neighbour, such understanding is incumbent.

(One must, as Christ saw, understand what "neighbour" means in those inherited injunctions; and nowadays also, what "God" means.)

Ideas are part of this world, of its transient flux; they are human constructs. Yet at their best they may serve as windows through which we may see beyond them, may see truth. What have been called religious truths are at their best never more than mundane conceptualizations; but also are at their best never less than important clues to a reality that others have known, and that we may know. Ideas do not capture knowledge; but if we are sensitive and fortunate, they may be instrumental to it.

First, we have seen that, throughout, conceptualizations have been, and have aimed at being, of faith generically. Chu Hsi never thought about Chinese or East Asian or Confucian faith, but about human—however much he may have done so in a Chinese way, or an East Asian or Confucian (yet a New-Style Confucian), and in a twelfth-century way—and so for all groups and all ages (until our own).

Secondly, all concurred in asserting that that faith is not only a recognizing but a saying "Yes!" to truth; and one might ask to what extent implicit in this was a tacit addition, "—whatever it be". Classical spokesmen affirmed, as we have seen, that even ultimate truth is not totally out of touch with human living; and they set forth their apprehensions in particular patterns. Insofar as their modern successors have been tempted to imagine, or have been pressured into imagining, that faith is assent and loyalty not to truth as such, but to those inherited patterns, one may concede that into these latter went two components. First, that faith is assent and loyalty to truth; and second, that truth is *x* (or *y*; or

. . .). A question, Which of these two did they regard as more important, verges on the unmanageable. For they could hardly conceive that the two could be separated. (The parallel is exact to asking any modern scientific liberal or scientist: Which is more important, to believe in science, or to believe in truth?) Which *we* should regard as more important for them is, however, a question not merely manageable, but one to which an answer is relatively clear. A Christian or a Muslim (for whom the explicit concept "faith" has been crucial; for some of the others the query would have to be worded differently but the substance would remain) may be conceived as asked to choose between two theses:

i. Faith, intellectually, is assent to truth, whatever it be;
ii. Faith, intellectually, is assent to *x* (in the one case; *y* in another; *z* . . .), whether it be true or not.

It is fully evident how any modern would and should respond; and also, how any classical Christian or Muslim would, such as those mentioned living at the beginning rather than the end of this millennium.

This is not sheer conjecture on our part. For instance, both traditional Christians and traditional Muslims tended to think of the other group as persons who had chosen the second alternative—persons whose loyalty was to *y*, or to *x*, whether it was true or not, and who therefore *did not have faith*. To give assent to a belief that is not true was not, and is not, "faith". In Christian (mis)understanding, Muslims were characterized by belief, of course, but not by faith—and *vice versa*. The modern tendencies to use the term "belief" indiscriminately, for any religious position regardless of whether it be oriented to truth or not, and to fabricate or to accept a word "faiths" in the plural, are irresponsible and obfuscating.

Faith is not belief in a doctrine. It is not even belief in the truth as such, whatever it be. It is "assent" to the truth as such, in the dynamic and personal sense of rallying to it with delight and engagement. It is the exclamation mark in saying not merely "yes" but "Yes!" to the truth when one sees it. It is the ability to see and to respond.

Faith is, among other things, an attitude; and for intellectuals, an attitude to truth. It involves, among other matters, the will; and for intellectuals, the will to know and to understand. It requires—or confers—among other virtues, integrity; and for intellectuals, the utmost intellectual honesty. Among different persons, as well as among different communities and different centuries, the element of understanding and particularly of conceptualizing has played differing roles in faith, and by intellectuals has been envisaged as playing differing roles. Yet insofar as conceptualizing be involved at all, it must, we may affirm, if it is to be *faithful*, be *the closest approximation to the truth of which one's mind*[14] *is capable.*

In its intellectual dimension, faith is first of all recognition of truth, insight into reality; and its conceptualization (the "belief" that goes with it) must on the one hand be sincere, subjectively, a close approximation to what one personally apprehends (is apprehended by), and on the other hand be valid, not only in the objective sense of being a significantly close approximation to Reality, to final Truth, but also in the dynamic and demanding sense (thus linking the subjective and the objective) of the closest approximation possible.

Some might counter that the concept of revelation seems to be left out of consideration in this understanding. The *concept* of revelation, however, has been part of the human response to what might be termed the fact of revelation, which in turn has yet to be understood and explicated for our day. Earlier conceptions of it have become for us observed items in historical conceptual frameworks, of which we are objectively conscious; and thus they can no longer serve us in innocence, to be either accepted as presupposition or rejected as untenable. Besides, the understanding and the explication for our day must be more comparativist and historical than have served in earlier times. In any case, we leave the conceptualizing of revelation to another volume, on theology; we return to our issue here, of faith.

One's conceptualizing of faith, and of the universe perceived from faith, if it is itself to be faithful, must be the closest approximation to the truth to which one is capable of rising (being raised): this may serve as a formal definition (along with the formal consideration that it must be demonstrably continuous with faith in the past)[15]. This position *is* continuous with that of each of the five thinkers mentioned, and perhaps with the history of faith, and of interpretations of faith, globally. At the very least, it takes those positions seriously. At the end of the current millennium, we have a deeper awareness and more richly documented recognition that man's ideas and especially the propositions setting them forth are at best an approximation to truth, never truth itself, are an approximation conditioned by one's milieu. For all that, they are an approximation potentially allowing the *person* whom they serve to live in less or more close approximation to truth itself, to live truly.

Each of our five was more intelligent than most of us, and at least equally dedicated to truth; to say nothing of the richness and depth of their several faith, in its other dimensions. Yet our formulation seems perhaps legitimate as a comprehensive historical characterization of their diverse positions on the matter before us. It is part of faith—it is faith's intellectual dimension—that one's ideas be as true, as valid, as at all one can manage.

Faith, let us remind ourselves, involves loving not only truth but all goodness—God—and loving one's neighbour. Even in relation to truth it means living loyally in terms of such truth as one knows, and of that truth towards which one's particular tradition and situation encourage and enable one to reach out. To isolate its intellectuality, therefore, is an abstraction, no more; yet intellectuals traffic in abstractions, and these are not unimportant. Yet even in the intellectual realm, we return thus to the classical positions. Faith, so understood, even in its intellectual dimension, differs from ordinary knowledge in at least two ways. The first is that, on the side of what is known, transcendence is recognized: one knows what one knows but knows also that there is more to be learned, and more than one's "interests" dictate and than one's situation makes possible, and certainly than one has yet ascertained. The second, on the side of the knower, is that the will is involved: the will to know—and the firm, unwavering resolve that one's apprehension shall, however inadequate, be the closest approximation to that ever elusive truth that one is or may yet become capable of attaining, or of being vouchsafed.

There is, therefore, a certain tentativeness or humility about faith conceptions—which for a time the word "belief" used perhaps reasonably to connote. In its recent development, on the other hand, that abused term was manoeuvred into denoting a quite other condition: one in which the intellectual loyalty of the person of faith was envisaged as being to a truth—or even, to a doctrine—lower than what he or she knows, rather than higher.

Our interpretation of conceptualizing pertains both to oneself and to one's neighbour. The requirement that one's own ideas be true is a moral demand; the requirement that others' be understood is a moral demand also. Both requirements belong to the intellectual dimension of faith, which also provides us with the arena in which to meet them. It belongs to faith to see and to rejoice that our interrelations as persons require and constitute this mutuality. It belongs to faith, secondly, to respond, rejecting the older notion that my business with regard to others' "beliefs" is to judge them. Faith intellectually is, further, the ability now to recognize (what in our preceding section was but postulated) a truth or reality lying behind and also transcending any given perception or expression, beyond any "belief". Thus it is faith, in a form appropriate to our day, that enables one to cope intellectually and personally with pluralistic relativism—with, for instance, truth as that to which all accounts of it approximate—so that acceptance of diversity enriches rather than undermines one's own apprehension of truth.

The "closest approximation available", which faith requires of us all, may for a villager, or other non-intellectual, be the ideas purveyed to him by his culture or his religious organization—preferably, by that institution or group within his culture whose faith is most genuine and serious:

including their faith in, dedication to, intellectual truth, as well as in and to moral righteousness and human virtue. If, on the other hand, one be oneself an intellectual—especially, of course, an intellectual leader of a community of faith, but also if one be but a lone inquirer puzzled, searching for an answer to the modern question, "What shall I believe?"—then the issue becomes more delicate. Faith without works is dead; and while conceptualizing may be no more salient a "work" than various others, yet intellectually faith without that highest approximation is vacuous.

If *credo* and *amana* do not mean "to believe", as classically they demonstrably did not, then how a Christian or a Muslim should conceptualize the world becomes (once again) an open question. (It still presses.) There is no reason in principle why in the modern world a Canadian and a Thai should believe anything different—although also there is no reason why they should not continue to have differing loyalties, and even differing perceptions of the world. (In principle, if both were intelligent and informed, each would have a perception of the world and would understand that the other has a differing perception, and even would understand that other differing perception. In principle, each would know the world as something that is perceived in Canadian and in Thai ways.) Similarly, there is no reason, in the modern world, why *in principle* an intelligent and informed Jew or Muslim and an intelligent and informed Christian, and indeed an intelligent and informed and sensitive atheistic humanist, should understand differently (should have different beliefs). Yet also there is no reason why they should not continue to live in terms of differing symbols and differing coherences of symbols.

In practice, of course, our world will not cease to evince differences of conviction, as Christians also differ among themselves, and Thais among themselves, and similarly Jews, and scientists. Nevertheless, presumably we can in principle learn from each other.

Our immediate loyalties may diverge, as may the ways in which we nurture them, as well as the extent to which each of us can move from a self-regarding to a self-transcending living, as faith entails. Yet those were not absurd who held that reason is in principle universal, and that in the intellectual realm humankind converges. Truth is ultimately one, although the human forms of truth and the forms of faith decorate or bespatter our world diversely. Our unity is real transcendently; whether history will so move that we approximate it more closely actually in the construction on earth of a world community, not merely a world society already virtually with us, is a question of our ability to act in terms of transcending truth, and love.

Allow me to close somewhat as we began, and in consonance with a note that I have sounded more than once. It may now be recognized as harmonious with the general theme of our submission. The ideas that I have propounded in the course of this inquiry are—like all conceptualizations pertaining to faith and to human transcendence—human, limited, and inadequate. They are more so than some, no doubt, and much more than would be appropriate to the greatness of our theme. The significance of our study, however, will lie not in the "rightness" or "wrongness" of such ideas so much as in the validity of the vision that they are an attempt to conceptualize, and in the contribution that one may hope that this work may have made to calling attention to an important problem, and enabling perhaps some readers to see areas where truth lies waiting to be discerned. It is not of primary importance that readers agree with any particular thing that I may have said; my attempts, however resolute and careful, to recognize and especially to articulate truth are all too incipient. My fundamental plea, rather, would be that theologians and laymen of various communities, and humanists, and scientists, address themselves to a matter that is in our day demanding attention and promises richly to reward it. That matter grows out of the profundity of our being human, seen now in historically rich and variegated ways.

It is our common human involvement, increasingly shared and sharable, and persistently crucial, in the mystery of that manifest reality our involvement in which I have called faith.

Notes and References

COMMENT ON THE NOTES AND REFERENCES

THE NOTES in this work are in many cases elaborate and ramifying; some are technical. Many will, I trust, be found decidedly illuminating, and some perhaps even entrancing (as I myself have often found the data to be). Yet I have at times wondered (also about my earlier study, *The Meaning and End of Religion*) whether maybe they might be studied only by those who have the time, energy, and interest to read the book at least twice. The most obvious pattern then would be to read the text through first, uninterrupted; if engaged by the argument to the point of feeling it worth thorough investigation, assessment, and pondering, one would then re-read it, pausing at each referred point to explore the evidence on which it is based, the justification for this particular interpretation of the data, or in some cases qualifications, elaborations, or collateral considerations. In a few cases it might, I suppose, happen that a reader would know before he or she started that a book on this particular subject is worth reading, or perhaps requires reading, twice, in which case that reader might the first time consider the underlying evidence at each point as it arises; yet in that case he or she, that reading once completed, should then go back and read through the text without reference to the notes, in order to perceive and to assess the over-all argument as a coherent whole.

Another consideration has to do with the diversity of fields touched on. Some might feel the documentation overly fastidious. Our thesis is, however, radical; and the matters treated, crucially important. One must not advance new interpretations of deeply cherished positions lightly. I have long contended that any one religious tradition, and even the faith that it inspires and expresses, can be understood better when seen in the context of the others (the comparativist's basic but bold principle). Those closely familiar with each, however, or with a sub-field of any, can be induced to acknowledge, and perhaps even to see, that new understanding only if it can be shown to pertain legitimately to, and indeed to grow out of, the data that pre-eminently they themselves know. Accordingly, the section here on Aquinas is argued in such a way that Christians in general and Thomists in particular may see its point and assess its validity; that on Hindu positions, so that Hindus and Sanskritists may; and so on. The former may not be interested in the full documentation and analysis for the latter, and *vice versa.* The Islamic theologian may find the main presentation of the Christian Church Fathers' views on faith more engaging than the precise references that support and explain this. Yet such references are requisite in each case so that various groups may feel themselves drawn in, and so that also the cogency of each part of the over-all thesis may be weighed. The whole should be convincing, presumably, insofar as the several parts are; as well as *vice versa*. Also, readers should feel themselves engaged through those matters with which they are personally acquainted or where their own personal involvements are at stake.

Furthermore, of course, I myself hope to be alerted if I have gone wrong in detail at any point.

NOTE: *In bibliographic citations I refer, of course, in each case to the edition used by me; but in certain cases give in addition specifications of other editions—for instance, for historical purposes, of an earlier original. I give the date, publisher, or other such data in square brackets in instances where I have not myself seen those other editions; or occasionally, usually of recent works, may have seen them but prefer to use a subsequent, sometimes author-revised, version.*

Chapter 1

1 The notion that it implies goes back much further in Christian thinking, especially to St. Augustine; but the actual phrase *Fides quaerens intellectum* ("faith in quest of intellectual understanding") was popularized in the Middle Ages when St. Anselm (ca. 1033-1109) propounded it as the somewhat informal name coined for an essay ("I did not judge it worthy of being called a book"—*opusculum . . . nec . . . dignum libri nomine . . . iudicabam*) which is known to modern scholarship by the "more appropriate" (or: "more convenient") (*aptius*) title by which he officially launched it after it had already begun to circulate privately: namely, *Proslogion. S. Anselmi Cantuariensis Archiepiscopi Opera Omnia . . .* recensuit Franciscus Salesius Schmitt, 6 voll., [Vol. 1, Seckau, 1938] Edinburgi: Nelson, 1946-1961. The *Proslogion* is 1:89-122. See esp. *Prooemium*, 1:[93]-94; the quotations adduced in this note are from p. 94.

2 Certain theologians, especially Christian and Islamic, might be inclined to pause here, wondering whether priority should not be recognized as rather with God. God, however, is not a religious category nor a human category. The idea of God is; but that is not the same thing. And the idea of God, although one of the most monumental and consequential matters in human history, certainly, no historian could doubt, yet has been neither geographically universal nor historically stable. Indeed, to the idea of God faith has been prior, in various senses: the idea has owed both its origin and its persistence to the human capacity for faith. God Himself, as distinct from the human idea of God (and the theist is vividly aware of how awesomely distinct), is not a religious or a human category; to think of Him as an ontological category, even, though an improvement, the sensitive theologian would find hardly satisfying. In any case, so far as this world is concerned, the world of human affairs, the religious history of the race, the statement in our text stands: the fundamental religious, human, category is faith. On the religious matter, both the believer and the atheist, as well as the observer in open inquiry, may agree. The theologian who affirms that God has entered human history, and that His acting in human history is that history's most significant fact, may agree that He has been active in and through the life of faith.

3 This has been explicitly the case since Schleiermacher. A modern example: "The function of systematic theology is to make clear the meaning and significance of Christian faith. . . . Theology . . . analyses Christian faith as it actually exists" (Gustaf Aulén, *Den allmänneliga kristna tron*, 5th rev. edn., Stockholm/Lund: Svenska Kyrkans Diakonistyrelse, 1957, pp. 11-12; my translation). Must one not ask whether another of its functions is to decide whether and on what grounds it should restrict itself to the investigation of "Christian" faith? That decision once made, Aulén claims to be "scientific"; the decision itself is probably unconscious rather than arbitrary. Although he, if challenged, would probably defend it on theological grounds, I could in turn argue on explicitly Christian theological grounds that the decision is un-Christian, as well as arguing that it is out-of-date and irrational. It is in-

teresting that he uses the adjective "Christian" with "faith" but not with "theology". I envisage a day when the reverse will seem more natural.

4 That faith has an object is a manner of speaking that was introduced in Christian thought mid-way in the latter's historical development; the notion "object" has gradually changed its meaning over the centuries since, and more recently the phrase has accordingly begun to give way to certain other conceptualizations. This matter is explored somewhat in a companion study to this present volume: Wilfred Cantwell Smith, *Belief and History*, Charlottesville: University Press of Virginia, 1977, chap. III, esp. pp. 94-95 and notes 40-44, pp. 127-130.

5 "Faith is faith in *x*" is a formula that I have found to be surprisingly widespread. It unfortunately presumes that one either already knows, or is not greatly interested in, what faith as such, faith as a human quality, is, and it indicates only where it is directed. A Christian, an Islamic, and a Buddhist example: (i) faith was faith in Christ, for the early Church, the major Swiss scholar Cullmann has published a recent book to show; this is the thesis of his entire study, and is stated explicitly more than once; (ii) a classical and authoritative Islamic Tradition (*ḥadīth*): "What is faith? Faith is your having faith in God and in His angels and in . . ."; (iii) Buddhist: "What faith is this? It is the faith by which one has faith in the four *dharmas*". References are as follows:

(i) Oscar Cullmann, *Les premières confessions de foi chrétiennes*, Paris: Presses Universitaires de France, 2e édn., 1948, passim (see esp., e.g., pp. 22, 40f., and "*Conclusion*", 52f.). The work nowhere addresses itself to the question as to what faith itself might be; this would appear to be taken for granted as presumably clear.

(ii) *mā al-īmān qāla al-īmān an tu'mina bi-llāhi wa bi-malā'ikatihi wa bi-* . . . —the *ḥadīth* is found in the standard collections; I quote from the *Ṣaḥīḥ* of al-Bukhārī, where it is in *Kitāb al-īmān, ḥadīth* 47; I have used the Cairo edition with the commentary of al-Kirmānī, 'Abd al-Raḥmān Muḥammad, ed., al-Maṭba'ah al-Bahīyah al-Miṣrīyah, 1358/1939, vol. 1, p. 194. The speaker is said to be the angel Gabriel (Jibrīl). Cf. also Qur'ān 24:62 and 49:15.

(iii) *katamā śraddhā yathā śraddhayāścaturī dharmānabhiśraddadhāti*—Śāntideva, *Śikṣāsamuccaya*, xviii; I have used the Bibliotheca Buddhica edition, C. Bendall, ed., St. Petersburg, 1898-1901 [vol. 3], p. 316, line 15. (My translation differs slightly from that in Cecil Bendall and W. H. D. Rouse, transs., *Śikshā-Samuccaya: a compendium of Buddhist doctrine compiled by Śāntideva, chiefly from earlier Mahāyāna Sūtras*, London: John Murray, 1922 [Indian texts series], p. 283.).

6 Similarly for the Qur'ān, the Bhagavad Gītā, and others. See Wilfred Cantwell Smith, "The Study of Religion and the Study of the Bible", *Journal of the American Academy of Religion*, 39:[131]-140 (1971).

7 The Psychology of Religion has, of course, focused on "the human side of these involvements", in another fashion than that here pursued. There is much to learn from its work. It will appear as we proceed, however, that the present orientation is rather different.

8 These sentences appeared first in the present writer's Introduction to the section on Religion in the *Propaedia* of the New Britannica III: Wilfred Cantwell Smith, "Religion as Symbolism", *The New Encyclopaedia Britannica*, Chicago &c, 1:500.

9 I have toyed with the idea of attempting over the next several years a series of volumes on faith in the Islamic instance, in the Hindu, in the Buddhist, and even perhaps in the Christian: anthologies setting forth historically and critically major participants' self-understandings on this matter.

10 Wilfred Cantwell Smith, *The Meaning and End of Religion: a new approach to the religious traditions of mankind,* New York: Macmillan, 1963; Mentor paperback, New York: New American Library, 1964; San Francisco: Harper & Row, 1978; London: S.P.C.K., 1978.

11 This is an historian's and observer's comment. Theologically, within the community a question was canvassed long and sharply as to whether faith is a yes-or-no matter—one either has it or one does not—or whether, rather, it varies in quantity or quality. See, for example, the particular discussion of Sa'd al-Dīn al-Taftāzānī, *Sharḥ al-'Aqā'id al-Nasafīyah* (in the Cairo edition of Dār Iḥyā al-Kutub al-'Arabīyah—'Īsá al-Bābī al-Ḥalabī, n.d. [1335?/1917?], pp. 128-130). In general, the literature is conveniently summarized in Louis Gardet, *Dieu et la destinée de l'homme* (G.-C. Anawati [et] Louis Gardet, *Les grands problèmes de la théologie musulmane: essai de théologie comparée*), Paris: Vrin, 1967 (Étienne Gilson et Louis Gardet, edd., Études musulmanes, IX), pp. 375-376 ("La foi peut-elle croître et diminuer?") and pp. 377-379 ("Les 'degrés' de la foi"), and in Toshihiko Izutsu, *The Concept of Belief in Islamic Theology: a semantic analysis of* îmân *and* islâm, Tokyo: Keio Institute of Cultural and Linguistic Studies, and Yokohama: Yurindo, 1965 (Nobuhiro Matsumoto, ed., Studies in the Humanities and Social Relations, 6), pp. 179-193. The Ṣūfīs definitely recognized varying faith in themselves and in the community; apart from many of them recognizing, as the non-Ṣūfī Muslim seldom was willing or able to do, faith outside the community, in other than Musulmān forms. Unfortunately, a critical history of Ṣūfī concepts of and discussions on faith has not to my knowledge been written.

Returning to the outside observer's standpoint, one may note the illuminating portrayal by a sensitive anthropologist of what may well be termed three salient varieties of faith of Muslims evinced in an Indonesian town: Clifford Geertz, *The Religion of Java*, Glencoe, Illinois: Free Press, 1960 (the three "variants" are set forth under the headings of *abangan*, *santri*, *prijaji*); and for the same writer's comparison of modern Muslim religious life in north-west Africa and south-east Asia, as two variant forms of Islamic faith, see Clifford Geertz, *Islam Observed: religious development in Morocco and Indonesia*, New Haven and London: Yale University Press, 1968 (The Terry Lectures, 1967). Indonesian writers have responded to Geertz's presentation instructively; as one example among several, see Harsja W. Bachtiar, "The Religion of Java: a commentary", in *Madjalah Ilmu-Ilmu Sastra Indonesia*, 5:85-118 (1973).

12 This, like the last, is formally an historian's comment, from the outside. Hindus themselves have spoken less in terms of types of faith, our concept, than of varying "ways", rather (*mārga* and the like): the way of knowledge, the way of adoration-faith, the way of action (*jñāna, bhakti, karma*). For the varying life-stages, *āśrama*, the conceptual analysis is again somewhat different. A Hindu would hardly resist my formulation here, however. (And explicitly in the Bhagavad Gītā: "Faith is of three kinds" [*trividhā bhavati śraddhā*—17:2]; but this is rather different, the three not being equally worthy. That faith varies from person to person is, however, clear.)

For Gītā text used, see our chap. 4, ref. 5.

13 In traditional Catholic thought, the oneness of faith tends to be strongly emphasized. An instance of this (cf. below, our chap. 5, reff. 110-112) is St. Thomas Aquinas, *Summa Theologiae*, 2:2:4:6—although he does allow in passing that as with any other virtue, so here on the part of the *subject* there is of course individual diversity (*est una fides: . . . ex parte subiecti . . . fides diversificatur. . . . ex subiecto individuatur*). In the late twentieth century, on the other hand, with the growing personalist movement, while the oneness of faith is certainly not abandoned, yet increasingly emphasis is being given among Church thinkers to this individual diversity. An example is Rahner, who speaks for instance of *die verschiedensten Gestalten des Glaubens* ("the most diverse forms of faith") among Christians.

References: For Thomas's major work, here and throughout this study I have used the following edition: *S. Thomae Aquinatis doctoris angelici Summa Theologiae, cum textu ex recensione Leonina*, Petr[us] Caramello, ed., n.p. [sc. Turin and Rome]: Marietti, 3 voll., 1952-1962. My reference above, "2:2:4:6" signifies *Pars* Secunda Secundae, *quaestio* 4, *articulus* 6; and so throughout. The passage quoted is found at vol. II, page 32. All subsequent citations from this work (abbreviated as *Summa Th.*) will give both the traditional specification of *pars, quaest., art.*, and the volume and page number of this Caramello edn.

Karl Rahner, *Im Heute glauben*, Einsiedeln: Benziger, 1965 (Hans Küng, ed., Theologische Meditationen, 9), p. 10 (Karl Rahner, *Faith Today*, Ray and Rosaleen Ockenden, transs., London & Melbourne: Sheed & Ward, 1967 [Hans Küng, ed., Theological Meditations, 9], p. 4).

14 The work mentioned in our ref. 4 above.

15 Illustrative is the following poem reputedly composed on the occasion of the great annual festival of the Grand Shrine at Ise, the most sacred place of Shinto: a simple, moving poem that for many centuries has been popular and significant among wide sections of the Japanese people:

> What it is
> That dwelleth here
> I know not;
> Yet my heart is full of gratitude,
> And the tears trickle down.

This has been attributed to the major poet, the priest—or sage—Saigyo

(Saigyō Hōshi or Saigyō Shōnin: 1118-1190 A.D.), but the ascription was not unchallenged in mediaeval times and about it modern criticism is quite skeptical. The item is not included in perhaps the only English translation of Saigyo's verse, *The Sanka Shu*, "*The Mountain Heritage*", trans. H. H. Honda, [Tokyo]: Hokuseido Press, 1971, but is found, I am told, in various editions of the Japanese text of this poet's works, often with its authenticity as his explicitly queried. I have cited above the English version given in W. G. Aston, *A History of Japanese Literature*, New York: Appleton, 1899 (Edmund Gosse, ed., Short Histories of the Literatures of the World), p. 263. The Japanese original evidently runs:

nanigoto no
owashimasu ka wa [*owashimasu oba* / *owashimasu to wa*]
shiranedomo
katajikenasa ni
namīdi koboruru

(One may note that *katajikenasa* could mean "awe" as well as "gratitude", I am told.)

16 Ancient Egyptians were generally religiously devout, and often theologically sophisticated; but in these matters never deliberately systematic. Two modern historians, after stating rather boldly that our present-day conception of a religion ("of course") makes systematic *beliefs* about divinity primary and basic, go on: "Il en allait tout autrement de l'antique religion égyptienne: pour comprendre son essence, il faut renverser les termes de la conception moderne. Sa base n'était pas la croyance, mais le culte . . . : le fait de rendre hommage à un dieu de tel nom, reconnu et proclamé seigneur et maître de tel endroit. La religion égyptienne était essentiellement l'adoration de fait des dieux. . . . Il était toutefois impossible d'adorer ainsi des dieux sans se former une opinion sur leur nature et, l'abondance des formules théologiques inscrites sur les monuments le prouve, sans raisonner sur leurs attributs et sur leurs relations entre eux. Mais il faut remarquer que, si actives, si variées et si touffues même qu'aient été les spéculations des théologiens, elles n'ont jamais . . . codifié la croyance. . . . Les recueils les plus répandus . . . ne furent que des compilations de formules pratiquement utiles aux particuliers. . . . Leur importance secondaire par rapport à l'essence de la religion égyptienne est assez démontrée par le fait qu'ils apparurent et disparurent successivement sans que cette religion subît la moindre altération. Il est à noter également que les exposés théologiques ne se soucièrent jamais de controverse . . . et qu'enfin les documents ont permis de donner simultanément de la religion égyptienne —et avec des raisons sérieuses à l'appui—, des explications contradictoires. . . . C'est qu' à l'égard du culte ce que nous appelons le dogme faisait figure d'interprétation privée, variant selon les lieux, les milieux, et même dans certains cas les individus. . . . Le roi animait . . . le culte partout, mais . . . il laissait partout la théologie au soin des sacerdoces locaux. Ceux-ci avaient élaboré une mythologie, une cosmogonie, une histoire sacrée. Ils avaient leurs idées sur la nature de leur dieu. Leur doctrine rayonnait suivant la notoriété de

leur temple. . . . Mais elle n'était en somme que l'opinion collective des premiers des fidèles qu'étaient les prêtres. . . . Elle laissait donc le champ libre à d'autres opinions chez ceux qui se coudoyaient aux abords du même temple et pratiquaient aussi authentiquement les uns que les autres la même religion: fétichistes ou symbolistes, anthropomorphistes ou partisans de la spiritualité de la nature divine, polythéistes, hénothéistes ou monothéistes à nuances diverses, tenants de l'historicité des mythes ou de leur interprétation soit allégorique soit naturiste. Toutes ces croyances, qui ne peuvent s'exprimer qu'en dogmes contradictoires, ont en fait trouvé place, les unes à côté des autres, dans la religion égyptienne et laissé leurs traces dans ses écrits" (Étienne Drioton et Jacques Vandier, *Les Peuples de l'orient méditerranéen*, vol. 2, *L'Égypte*, Paris: Presses Universitaires de France, 4ème édn., 1962, pp. 61-63. When these authors say that belief was not the "base" of this religious life, they are of course right; yet the cult was, more strictly, also not the base, but in our terms the primary expression (as belief was then a secondary) of the real base: namely, the faith of those Egyptians, whose "adoration" of the gods is after all not self-explanatory. Faith is clearly logically prior to the cult, just as in turn the cult was, as is here clarified, prior to their theologies. The points that are fundamentally interesting are that the Egyptians chose to worship at all, along with the question as to what effect their worshipping had on their lives, their persons.

17 It is evident that systematic theology developed in Christian history only gradually. In origin it is plainly secondary to Christian faith. The earlier Church believed certain things, no doubt one may say; but for a while it lived, and lived forcefully, without systematizing those beliefs.

18 Classical and mediaeval Muslims devoted much energy and skill to rationalizing and systematizing the expression of their faith; but what chiefly they rationalized and systematized was moral obligation, in great patterns of jurisprudence (*fiqh*) or law (*sharī'ah*), and only secondarily—or less—conceptual propositions, in *kalām* or dialectical theology. This last was impressively done, but never became central to Islamic religious life; and it was widely suspect, being resisted especially by the Ḥanbalī school of law. In fact, theology has been not even a secondary expression of Islamic faith, but takes at best a tertiary place after the moral-legal (*sharī'ah*) and the mystic Ṣūfī (*taṣawwuf*, organized institutionally since about the fifth Islamic century [twelfth A.D.] in great orders [*ṭarīqah*]). By the conservative schools of jurisprudence, *kalām* was attacked. By the Ṣūfī movement, it was not resisted so much as disdained or ignored. Illustrative of the more outspoken hostility is a work "Discrediting Theology and Theologians" (*Dhamm al-kalām wa-ahlihi*) by Anṣārī al-Harawī (1005-1089), who was both a Ṣūfī and a Ḥanbalī legist. (The table of contents of this work and substantial extracts from it have recently been published, along with a French translation, in S. de Laugier de Beaurecueil, *Khwādja 'Abdullāh Anṣārī . . . mystique hanbalite*, Beyrouth: Imprimerie Catholique, 1965, pp. [204]-221.) See also and especially the later vigorous leader Ibn Taymīyah (1263-1328), alluded to in our statement in the text. He quotes from the former thesis of Anṣārī just mentioned

(e.g., see *Majmū'at fatāwá shaykh al-islām . . . ibn Taymīyah*, ed. Faraj Allāh Zakī al-Kurdī, Cairo, 1329 [= A.D. 1911], vol. 5, from p. 274 line -1), and develops several diatribes of his own. Probably his most outspoken stricture is found in his belligerent Fatwá *al-Ḥamawīyah al-Kubrá*, which includes an attribution to Satan of the original inspiration of the movements in Muslim thought resulting from the translation into Arabic of the writings of the Greeks in the second Islamic century. The treatise culminates in vigorous rejection of theology (*kalām*). For this work I have used the edition in Muḥammad Ḥāmid al-Fiqī, ed., *Nafā'is*, [Cairo]: Maṭba'at al-Sunnah al-Muḥammadīyah, 3rd edn., 1374/1955, pp. [85]-166; see esp. pp. 99, 166. Again, to the outstanding thinker and authoritative spokesman of the Islamic establishment the Imām al-Shāfi'ī (767-820), founder of the Shāfi'ī School of Islamic Law, are attributed a caustic denunciation of theologians (*ahl al-kalām*) and a poem in which various matters, by implication including theology, are dubbed of Satanic inspiration (*wiswās al-shayāṭīn*). This denunciation, the poem, and various other lively condemnations of Islamic theologizing are cited by, for instance, an anonymous commentator, recently identified as perhaps 'Alī ibn Muḥammad ibn Abī al-'Izz al-Ḥanafī, in his commentary on the *'Aqīdah* of the influential and highly respected third/ninth-century Egyptian jurisprudent and traditionist Abū Ja'far Aḥmad al-Ṭaḥāwī. See Abū Bakr, ed., *Sharḥ al-'Aqīdah al-Ṭaḥāwīyah*, Dimashq: al-Maktab al-Islāmī, 3rd edn., n.d., pp. 10-11. (For the authorship of the work, see the editor's introduction, *d-h* [sc. pp. iv, v].) The condemnation of theologians by al-Shāfi'ī became current; it too is quoted by Ibn Taymīyah, op. cit., p. 166; by al-Ghazzālī (see just below); and by many others, until to-day. Remarkable also is how popular the strictures of Ibn Taymīyah continue to be in our own day. The Fatwá mentioned is constantly being reprinted; it keeps re-appearing off the presses of Cairo not only as one item in this author's collected or selected treatises, but also as an independent pamphlet.

It should be remarked, however, that on other occasions Ibn Taymīyah and other critics are more discriminating in their assessments of the theological enterprise, and express their reservations, however substantial, in more measured tones, decrying rather its excesses or such developments within it as diverge from scripture and the received norms (from "orthopraxy"). For a statement of the position on this matter of the central and massively influential thinker (one might almost say, theologian) Abū Ḥāmid al-Ghazzālī (1058-1111), including the remark that while the Qur'ān is like food, profitable for everyone, *kalām* is like medicine, profitable for some but deleterious for most people, see his *Iljām al-'awamm 'an 'ilm al-kalām*. For this work I have used the edition in an anthology: Muḥammad Muṣṭafá Abū al-'Alā', ed., *al-Quṣūr al-'Awālī li-l-imām . . . Abī Ḥāmid . . . al-Ghazzālī*, Cairo: Maktabat al-Jundī, 2nd edn., 1390 [= A.D. ca. 1970], vol. 2, where the passage mentioned is found on p. 88. A synopsis of his yes-and-no views on the subject, stating the pros and especially the cons, and including his quoting of the Shāfi'ī stricture mentioned above, and others, is found also in his *magnum opus* entitled *Iḥyā' 'ulūm al-dīn*, in Section 2 of Book 2 of the first Quarter. My edition is that of the

Lajnat Nashr al-Thaqāfah al-Islāmīyah, Aḥmad Ibrāhīm al-Sarāwī, ed., Cairo, 16 voll., 1356-1357 [= ca. 1937-1938], where this is 1:161-180; see esp. pp. 163-171 (re al-Shāfi'ī, pp. 163-164; re medicine, p. 168). Cf. Nabih Amin Faris, trans., *The Foundations of the Articles of Faith, being a translation with notes of the Kitāb Qawā'id al-'Aqā'id of al-Ghazzālī's "Iḥyā' 'Ulūm al-Dīn"*, Lahore: Ashraf, 1963, pp. [13]-53 (esp. pp. 16-35, and specifically, pp. 17f., 28).

19 Probably the three chief figures to be considered for this matter are Maimonides, Mendelssohn, and Schechter. One might with Wolfson wish rather to trace the development back to Philo of Alexandria (see Harry Austryn Wolfson, *Philo: Foundations of religious philosophy in Judaism, Christianity, and Islam*, Cambridge, Mass.: Harvard University Press, and London: Oxford University Press, 2 voll. [1947], 4th printing, rev., 1968. Note especially chapp. 3, 10, and 12 and particularly 1:164-165 and 2:208-211). Even Wolfson, however, sees the role of Philo as significant primarily within the history of Western philosophy (where for him it has been of massive consequence) rather than in the history of Jewish religious life.

It would then hardly be misleading to see our issue as stemming from the innovation of the twelfth-century Maimonides (Rambam, Mōsheh ben Maimôn, Mūsá ibn Maymūn), for whom the final purpose of life, and of the Law, is to know (*lêdha'*). Specifically, he articulated faith in thirteen affirmations, in propositional form. "This systematic formulation . . . triggered a long, sometimes acrimonious debate concerning the role of dogma in Judaism" (Isadore Twersky, ed., *A Maimonides Reader*, New York: Behrman House [1972], p. 402). The debate is not yet over. Mediaeval Jewish resistance to the idea of such formulating (or to this particular formulation) was outspoken. Yet the propositions themselves, later called *'ᵃqārîm*, were in due course incorporated in the liturgy, where in somewhat revised form they remain until to-day (*The Authorised Daily Prayer Book of the United Hebrew Congregations . . . , with a new translation by the late Rev. S. Singer*, Nathan Marcus Adler, ed.; new edn., Israel Brodie, ed., London: Eyre and Spottiswoode, and New York: Bloch, 5722 = 1962, pp. 93-95; cf. pp. 3-4 for a poetic affirmation, the *Yigdal*).

In eighteenth-century Germany, Moses Mendelssohn, leading spokesman for the movement incorporating the Jewish community for the first time into the general intellectual life of what had been Christendom, set forth that Jewish beliefs are but the universal recognitions of all rational men (*Vernunftwahrheiten*). It is Jewish laws, rather, that are distinctive. Revelation is of prescriptions and proscriptions, and of historical truth, but not of doctrinal. "We have no belief-statements that are contrary to reason or above it" (supplementary to it?), he wrote (in a letter of July 23, 1771, published in *Monatschrift für Geschichte und Wissenschaft des Judenthums*, Leipzig, 8:172-174 [1859]: *Wir haben keine Glaubenssätze* [עקרים] *die gegen die Vernunft oder über dieselbe seien* [p. 173]). (From this we might conclude that for Enlightenment Jewry there is human philosophy, but not Jewish theology. More generally, if one were to accept the traditional Christian or Western [also Islamic] distinction between philosophy and theology, one might say that the former has on occasion impinged on the development of Jewish religious life and its articulation, significantly if not centrally, whereas the latter hardly.) For a time, the slogan "Judaism has no dogmas!" was current among many Jews.

Mendelssohn's position is worked out principally in his *Jerusalem, oder über religiöse Macht und Judenthum*, 1783; I have used the edition in the one-volume *Moses Mendelssohn's sämmtliche Werke*, Wien: Schmidl-Klang, 1838, pp. 217-291. See especially pp. 261-266 (the word *Vernunftwahrheiten* just cited is p. 262 of this edn.). Further, a recent editor has brought together and published in English two or three other excerpts bearing on the matter before us, entitling them "A Religion Without Dogma?". See Alfred Jospe, ed. & trans., *Jerusalem; and other Jewish writings by Moses Mendelssohn*, New York: Schocken, 1969, pp. 137-138. The volume includes, as the title indicates, also an English version of *Jerusalem*, pp. [9]-110.

By the end of the nineteenth century the situation had again changed. This was so especially as regards a sense of the universality of theism; or even, its credibility. "Judaism has no dogmas" was by then no longer a triumphant rationalist affirmation, as it had been in the preceding (largely deistic) phase of Western-European history. In 1889 Solomon Schechter published two articles, "The Dogmas of Judaism" in *The Jewish Quarterly Review* (London, 1:48-61, 115-127), reviewing the situation and advocating a more positive Jewish attitude to creeds. This essay has continued influential; it was republished in S. Schechter, *Studies in Judaism*, New York and London: Macmillan, 1896, pp. 147-181, again in Solomon Schechter, *Studies in Judaism: First Series*, Philadelphia: Jewish Publication Society of America [and London: A. & C. Black], [1905, 1911], 1945 and again in his *Studies in Judaism: a selection*, New York: Meridian books, and Philadelphia: Jewish Publication Society of America, [1958], 1960, 1962, pp. 73-104. A synopsis appeared also in Norman Bentwich, ed., *Solomon Schechter, Selected Writings*, Oxford: Phaidon Press—East and West Library, 1946 (Hugo Bergmann, ed., Philosophia Judaica: Selections from the writings of the most eminent Hebrew thinkers in English translations), pp. 40-43.

In the twentieth century, and especially the latter part of it, the rise and at times agonizing poignancy of a question of religious belief as a Jewish concern, and the rise of Jewish theology as a newly recognized if still problematic category, have been complicated but major. A careful study of these recent developments would be highly illuminating. The general thesis of this book, with its identifying of faith classically as a foundational quality of life and its exploring of belief recently as an historically emerging religious problem, could be illustrated richly from the Jewish instance. This matter has, alas, not been pursued here. I have collected a certain range of data on both parts of this, and also on the conceptualizing of faith and on belief in the Far East, particularly in the Chinese case. In both instances my preliminary study has indeed indicated clearly that our general thesis, substantiated in this present work from other parts of the world, would be corroborated and enriched, certainly not contradicted, from these two traditions. I leave to others, however, a developing of these aspects of our inquiry.

An investigation of the Jewish dimension of our total problem would involve a word-study of the terms "belief" and "believe" in Jewish writing in English, in modern times, and "faith" there (and quite recently, "doubt"). Over past centuries it would consider the Hebrew terms *ᵉmûnāh* and *biṭṭaḥôn* (generally), *dᵉvēqûth* (the Hasidim), etc., plus Jewish use of Arabic terms like *iʿtiqād*, *īmān*, *muʾmin*, etc.

Moreover, specifically in the Maimonides matter and the thirteen "Principles", it would consider the formal conceptual status given at various stages to the affirmations; for instance, whether they appear as principal clauses and statements of fact or as subordinate clauses, and in the latter case subordinate to what verbs or concepts. On the basis of what preliminary inquiry I have done, there seems to have been a movement over the centuries, which it would be rewarding to investigate more thoroughly, somewhat paralleling what we do investigate for the Christian case below (esp. our chap. 6): a gradual transition from truths, which one may or may not know, to propositions that one does or does not believe, with an intervening phase of formulations articulating faith, for those of faith. In the Prayer Book to-day, the thirteen occur as subordinate clauses, objects of believing (in English), of faith (in Hebrew; *ᵃnî maʾᵃmîn be-ᵉmûnāh shᵉlēmāh she- . . .*). Maimonides, on the other hand, more often either uses "to know" (*lêdhaʿ*), to recognize, to realize, or else makes the presentations in simple affirmative form.

In the Chinese case, careful historical studies not only of *hsin* but also of various other terms, especially *ch'eng*, would demonstrably prove rewarding. In Japan, the subtle difference between *shinjin* and *anjin* as the chief conceptualization for faith in Pure Land thought proved at one point historically significant, to cite one example.

I mention the Far Eastern matter here in order to apologize for not covering it in this book, as I apologize for not covering the Jewish. Both are too relevant to our study, as well as too important in themselves, to be omitted without apology. (Equally relevant, even if my tendency is to think of them as finally less important, are the "primitive" cultures studied by anthropologists. On them Needham's corroborative study on the concept "belief" is decisive [below, our chapter 3, ref. 3].)

For Maimonides I have used the following editions. For *al-Sirāj*, written in Arabic—his youthful Commentary on the Mishnah, in which he first set forth the propositions—: for the original Arabic, in Hebrew characters, Yôsēph . . . Dāwidh Qâphaḥ, ed. and trans., *Mishnāh, ʿim Pêrûsh Rabbênû Mōsheh ben Maimôn, māqôr wᵉthargûm . . .* , 6 voll., Yᵉrûshālayim: Môsad Hā-Rabh Qûq, 1963-1968. (A translation into Hebrew is given in parallel columns.) See vol. [4] (*Sēder Nᵉzîqîn*), pp. 210-217. A translation into English (by Arnold J. Wolf, 1966) is found in, for instance, the above-mentioned Twersky *Reader*, pp. 417-422 (cf. 402-423). To introduce the affirmations Maimonides here chose the word *qāʿidah*—support, basis; literally, that on which something sits. This Arabic was rendered in Hebrew by the closely equivalent Biblical term *y^esôdh*. They are, he says (in the standard Islamic Arabic of the day), *uṣūl sharī'atinā*. (In the Hebrew translation by the modern editor, Qâphaḥ, above, this is given as *'iqārê tôrāthênû*. For our purposes, with their concern for conceptions prevailing over the centuries, the mediaeval Hebrew translations, rather, are significant; for this I have consulted *Masekheth Sanhedrîn min Talmûdh Babh^elî, 'im Pêrûsh Rash'î . . . w^e . . . w^e . . . û-Phêrûsh ha-m-Mishnāyôth li-hā-Ramb'am* . . . , Niyû Yôrq: M^eôrôth, 5719 [= 1959] which turns out to be a photographic reprint of an 1892 Vilna edn. Here *y^esôdh* is re-iterated; but *uṣūl sharī'atinā* is rendered rather as *'iqārê dāthēnû*—folio 11 *recto* [= p. 21].)

He repeated the "fundamentals" and discussed them in his later great work the Mishneh Tôrāh, or Yādh ha-Ḥ^azākhāh, for which I have used Moses Hyamson, ed., *The Mishneh Torah by Maimonides, Book I, edited . . . with introduction, . . . notes and English translation*, New York: Bloch, 1937. (Selections from this translation also in Twersky, pp. 43ff.) Here, the first of the "positive commandments" (*mizvōth '^aṣēh*), injunctions, moral obligations, is "to know" (*lêdha'*) (that God is there—Hyamson, p. א5, cf. 5a; also ב19, 19b); the first book is "The Book of Knowing" (*sēpher ha-m-maddā'*); and our affirmations are the first matter to be discussed (pp. א34, 34a ff.). These last are introduced with the general assertion that the foundation of the foundations (*y^esôdh ha-y-y^esôdhôth*) and the pillar of the sound sciences (*'ammûdh ha-ḥokhmôth*) is to know (*lêdha'*) that . . . (there is a First Being &c); although in general the theses are set forth affirmatively without introductory qualification. Collectively they are headed *y^esôdhê ha-t-Tôrāh* (pp. ב19, א34). Note further such remarks as that knowledge of [*y^edhī'ath*] this matter is a *mizvāh* (p. א35). The difference between "knowing" and "believing", religiously, is examined at some length below; esp. our chapp. 3, 5, and 6.

For the Guide, written in Arabic, parts of which are also remarkably relevant to our considerations, I have used for the original text the recent critical edition in Arabic script: Ḥusayn Atā'ī, ed., *Dilālat al-Ḥā'irīn, ta'līf al-ḥakīm al-faylasūf Mūsá ibn Maymūn* . . . Ānqarah: Maṭba'at Jāmi'at Ānqarah, 1972 [*sic*]/ Hüseyin Atay, ed., *Delâlet'ü l-Hairîn Filozof Musa ibn Meymun el-Kurtubî* . . . , [Ankara]: Ankara Üniversitesi Basımevi, 1974 (Ankara Üniversitesi İlâhiyat Fakültesi Yayınları, 93).

For the two major mediaeval Hebrew translations: Aryēh Lêb Sh^elôsberg (sc. Léon Schlosberg), ed., *Sēpher Môrēh N^ebhûkhîm* [on the half-title page, more accurately and less traditionally, *Môrēh ha-n-N^ebhûkhîm*], *ḥibb^erô bi-l-shôn 'ar^ebhîth . . . Rabbēnû Mōsheh b/R Maimôn, w^ene'taq li-l^eshônēnû ha-q-q^edhôshāh 'al y^edhai . . . Rabbî Y^ehûdhāh b. Rabbî Sh^elōmōh al-Ḥ^arîzî . . . 'im he'ārôth meṣkālôth* . . . [Sh.] Shayy'er [sc. Simon B. Scheyer], [London, 3 voll., 1851-1879] Tēl Ābhîbh: [Môsadh hā-Rabh Qûq], n.d. [ca. 1963?]. *Sēpher Môrēh N^ebhûkhîm, l^e-hā-rabh hā'^elōhî . . . Mōsheh ben Mayymôn . . . b^e-ha-'^athāqath hā-Rabh R. Sh^emû'ēl ibn (Abhen) Tîbbôn, 'im ṣ^elōsāh pêrûshîm . . . ^Ephôdhî, Shēm Ṭôbh, b. Q^ereshqāsh, w^e . . . Rabbênû Dôn Yizḥaq*

Abhrabhan'ēl . . . , Ḥēleq Rîshôn, [W]Wârshâ: Yiẓḥaq Gôld^{e}mân, 1872.

For an English translation: Moses Maimonides, *The Guide of the Perplexed, translated with an introduction and notes by* Shlomo Pines, *with an introductory essay by* Leo Strauss, [London & Chicago]: The University of Chicago Press, 1963.

See, for instance, chapp. 33-35 and particularly chap. 50 of Book 1—in the four versions mentioned, respectively pp. 76-87, 118-119/ pp. 123-140, 180-182 (note: in this edn., these are designated chapters 32-34, 49, rather)/ folios 51v-56r, 69r-70v/ pp. 70-81, [111]-112. (Cf. also Twersky *Reader*, pp. 257-265). The opening and closing sentences of chap. 50 are especially germane and revealing. It is engaging to note in the former that Maimonides's word *iʿtiqād* (conviction, a binding of oneself [sc. to a position; as a theological term, to a conceptualized position]) is rendered by al-Ḥ^{a}rîzî as ^{e}*mûnāh*, by ibn Tîbbôn as *'^{a}mānāh* and by Pines as "belief"; further, by Friedländer as "faith" (*The Guide of the Perplexed of Maimonides, translated from the original text and annotated by* M. Friedländer, London: Trübner, for the Society of Hebrew Literature, 3 voll., 1881-1885). In the various editions, pp. 118 (Atay), 180 (Schlosberg-Scheyer), folio 70v (Goldmann), p. [111] (Pines), 2:171 (Friedländer).

20 We are following here the positions set forth in my earlier study *The Meaning and End* . . . (our ref. 10 above), chapter 7, "Faith", where the analysis is elaborated. At the time of writing that book I had not yet discovered that the doctrinal expression of faith has predominantly characterized the Christian Church over only a relatively recent sector of its history, as is developed below in this present investigation and elaborated in a separate study (cf. our ref. 4 above). The results of these new inquiries modify the details but corroborate the central thesis of that earlier analysis.

21 Cf. the now famous remark of the anthropologist Marett, that "savage religion is something not so much thought out as danced out". The larger passage in which this occurs reads as follows, with reference to the turn of the century: ". . . when I began to write, certain representative theories dominated the entire field of Comparative Religion, . . . theories . . . in my judgment too intellectualistic, too prone to identify religion with this or that doctrine or system of ideas. My own view is that savage religion is something not so much thought out as danced out; that, in other words, it develops under conditions, psychological and sociological, which favour emotional and motor processes, whereas ideation remains relatively in abeyance". R. R. Marett, *The Threshold of Religion*, second edition revised and enlarged, London: Methuen, 1914, pp. xxx-xxxi. This passage does not seem to be found in the first edn., London, 1909.

22 The ancient Egyptians have already been cited above (reference 16) as an instance where cult took precedence over theology. The classical Roman situation goes further: there, religious life was oriented in such a way as to give primacy to rite not only over doctrine (ideas organized into propositions) but over the gods and goddesses themselves (as conceptualized entities). Ritual and cult were in some ways more significant, more holy, than the

divine beings. In the words of a major scholar: "The *numen* for the Roman is expressed not in the figure [sc. of the god], but in a succession of acts, in which it [sc. the *numen*] encounters man" —Franz Altheim, *A History of Roman Religion*, translated by Harold Mattingly, London: Methuen, 1938, p. 181. This passage, and the chapter in which it is found, seem to have been added in the English version; they do not appear in the shorter German original of this work: Franz Altheim, *Römische Religionsgeschichte*, Berlin & Leipzig: Walter de Gruyter, 3 voll., 1931-1933 (Sammlung Göschen). The Latin word *religio* itself designated the cultic pattern. In this outlook the Romans diverged, especially in earlier times, from the Greeks, whose more elaborate mythologies represented the gods and goddesses vividly and with more emphasis.

23 Adumbrated in some of my earlier published writings, the thesis is set forth fully in an as yet unpublished lecture delivered as the presidential address to the Humanities and Social Sciences Section of the Royal Society of Canada, 1973.

24 This was written before the recent surfacing in the United States of widespread disillusionment with the scientific enterprise, not only on the outside but among scientists themselves. In 1974 the American Academy of Arts and Sciences devoted an issue of its quarterly, *Daedalus* (vol. 103, no. 3) to this disillusionment and reflection upon it (under the title *Science and Its Public: the changing relationship*, Gerald Holton, guest ed., Boston, 1974). The opening word of the title of the opening article is "faith". The entire volume is impressive and highly instructive, illustrating the matter considered in this paragraph of our text; but most explicitly the author of this opening article ponders the faith of the public in science and the faith of scientists in themselves and their own endeavours, and the possibility of the waning of such faith. (Edward Shils, "Faith, Utility, and the Legitimacy of Science", op. cit., pp. 1-15. Cf. further our chap. 5 below, ref. 51.)

Chapter 2

1 This statement I have not been able to track down to its source. If any reader can supply a precise reference, I should be grateful.

2 The time during which this was a salient religious issue in Western life was relatively short: chiefly, the eighteenth and especially the nineteenth centuries, and to some degree on into the twentieth. This historicity is explored somewhat in later chapters below, and in my companion volume *Belief and History* (op. cit. above, our chap. 1 here, ref. 4).

3 On this a preliminary bibliography of secondary studies would include the following items:

de la Vallée Poussin, "Faith and Reason in Buddhism", in *Transactions of the Third International Congress for the History of Religions*, Oxford: Clarendon Press, 1908, 2:32-43.

B. M. Barua, "Faith as in Buddhism", in *Sir Asutosh Mookerjee Silver Jubilee Volumes*, Calcutta: Calcutta University Press, vol. 3—*Orientalia*, Part

3, 1927, pp. [237]-256. This is reprinted (in a slightly modified and curiously curtailed form, under the title "Faith in Buddhism") as chapter xii in Bimala Churn Law, ed., *Buddhistic Studies*, Calcutta & Simla: Thacker, Spink, 1931, pp. [329]-349.

N. Dutt, "Place of Faith in Buddhism", *Indian Historical Quarterly*, 16: [639]-646 (1940).

Edith Ludowyk-Gyomroi, "The Valuation of Saddhā in Early Buddhist Texts", *University of Ceylon Review*, 5/2:32-49 (1947).

David Snellgrove, "Theological Reflections on the Buddhist Goal of Perfect Enlightenment", *Bulletin, Secretariatus pro non Christianis*, [Vatican] #17 (1971—6th year), pp. 76-98. See esp.: "Faith as the basis of all religious practice", pp. 88ff.

Graeme MacQueen, "The Concept of Faith in Early Buddhism": unpublished seminar-paper, Harvard University (Center for the Study of World Religions), autumn, 1972.

4 He did not deny the existence of God or the gods, but rejected their traditional significance.

5 Edward Conze, *Buddhism: its essence and development*, [Oxford: Bruno Cassirer, 1951]; New York: Harper Torchbooks, 1959, p. 40.

6 These include Winston L. King, *Buddhism and Christianity: some bridges of understanding*, Philadelphia: Westminster, 1962, pp. 29ff., 45-50, 56-63; Huston Smith, *The Religions of Man*, New York: Harper, 1958, p. 112; and others. Perhaps the most thorough treatment is that given in a study with the appropriate term "paradox" in its title: Robert Lawson Slater, *Paradox and Nirvana: a study of religious ultimates with special reference to Burmese Buddhism*, Chicago: University of Chicago Press, 1951, esp. chapp. 3, 4. See also, for a descriptive and interpretive account of the history of Western views, Guy Richard Welbon, *The Buddhist Nirvāṇa and its Western Interpreters*, Chicago and London: University of Chicago Press, 1968.

7 This word in both its Sanskrit and its Pali forms has had in Buddhist history a prodigiously elaborate development of meanings, moving far beyond its original or later connotations in extra-Buddhist Sanskrit. We are here concerned only with the meaning, for Buddhists, of a (the) cosmic absolute, hinted at in the sense in which the term is used to verbalize for Buddhists one of their Triratna (the Three Jewels): that Dharma to which a Buddhist goes for refuge. See s.v. *Dhamma* in *The Pali Text Society's Pali-English Dictionary*, T. W. Rhys Davids & William Stede, edd., Chipstead, Surrey: Pali Text Society, Part iv, 1923; see specially the "Note" there to section B.I.(a), pp. 171f., and section C, pp. 172f. More generally, the chief Western studies of this concept have been those of the Geigers and Stcherbatsky. More particularly, recent studies are an unpublished doctoral thesis and a journal article by my former student John Carter. References are as follows:

Magdalene und Wilhelm Geiger, *Pāli Dhamma: vornehmlich in der kanonischen Literatur*, München: Bayerischen Akademie der Wissenschaften, 1920 (1921, 1922). (Abhandlungen der bayerischen Akademie der Wissenschaften; Philosophisch-philologische und historische Klasse, Band xxxi, 1.)

Th. Stcherbatsky, *The Central Conception of Buddhism and the Meaning of the Word "Dharma"*, London: Royal Asiatic Society, 1923 (Prize Publication Fund, vol. VII).

John Ross Carter, "*Dhamma*: Western Academic and Sinhalese Buddhist Interpretations: a study of a religious concept", doctoral dissertation, Harvard University, Cambridge, Mass., 1972 (original in Widener Library).

John Ross Carter, "*Dhamma* as a Religious Concept: a brief investigation of its history in the Western academic tradition and its centrality within the Sinhalese Theravāda tradition", *Journal of the American Academy of Religion*, 44:661-674 (1976).

8 I am aware, of course, that the response of thoughtful Buddhists to this present thesis will be significant. To suggest some equivalence or convergence between a particular Buddhist conception and the Western category of the divine will be recognized by Westerners, particularly theists, as endeavouring to ascribe to the former concept the highest possible attribution, and to elevate Western appreciation of it. This is what may give rise to some Christian or Jewish resistance; insofar as there is Buddhist resistance, it is because to Buddhists, "God" is too limited, too demeaning a concept to apply to their ultimates. This sort of difficulty is, of course, inherent in all speculating about a possible convergence (even asymptotic) or parallel between the reference of human concepts from radically divergent ideational systems. To deal intellectually with this sort of problem is one of the tasks for coming times, in our increasingly pluralistic world. We return to it at a theoretical level briefly in our concluding chapter, below.

9 For example: Piyadassi Thera, *The Buddha's Ancient Path*, London: Rider, 1964. (Cf. his comment, p. 9, on the title.)

10 Saṃyutta-Nikāya, 12:65 (II:1:7:5):21 = 22. The original Pali will be found in Léon Feer, ed., *Saṃyutta-Nikāya: Part II, Nidāna-Vagga*, London: Oxford University Press for the Pali Text Society, 1888, p. 106. A fuller and more precise translation of the passage is given by Mrs. Rhys Davids [Caroline Davids] in her *The Book of the Kindred Sayings (Saŋyutta-Nikāya) or Grouped Suttas: Part II, the Nidāna Book (Nidāna-Vagga)*, London, New York, etc.: Oxford University Press, n.d. [sc. 1922] (Pali Text Society translation series #10), pp. 74-75. I have cited it rather in her somewhat synopsized version presented in her earlier essay, *Buddhism: a study of the Buddhist norm*, London: Williams & Norgate, and New York: Henry Holt, n.d. [1912?] (Home University Library of Modern Knowledge), p. 34.

11 See, for example, among recent Christians, Paul Tillich, *Systematic Theology*, Chicago: University of Chicago Press, 3 voll., 1951-1963, esp. 1:235ff. A comparable issue was raised in classical Indian thought; there the point was articulated not in terms of using one verb rather than another, but rather in terms of both affirming and negating, or neither affirming nor negating, a concept of being or existence for what is ultimate, Brahman. The speculation that primordial reality precedes both being and non-being, existence and non-existence, goes back to Ṛg-Veda 10:129:1. In the Upaniṣads see, for instance, the Taittirīya 2:6, Chāndogya 3:19:1 and 6:2:1, Kaṭha 2:3:13 (sc. 6:13).

Further, the Bhagavad Gītā (13:12) avers that Brahman is called "neither existent nor non-existent" (neither being nor not being—*na sat tan nā 'sad ucyate*). Śaṅkara's commentary on the Upaniṣad passages just mentioned is of interest, but I have found particularly illuminating—and relevant to students of Tillich—the disquisition on this matter to which he is prompted in his commentary on this Gītā verse (*Śrīmadbhagavadgītā Śrīśaṅkarabhagavatpādācāryaviracitena bhāṣyeṇa sahitā*, Dinkar Vishnu Gokhale, ed., Poona: Oriental Book Agency, 2nd. rev. edn., 1950 [Poona Oriental Series No. 1], where the passage is pp. 197-199; cf. *The Bhagavad-Gîtâ with the Commentary of Srî Sankaracharyâ translated from Sanskrit into English by* A. Mahâdeva Sâstri [1897], 5th edn., Madras: V. Ramaswamy Sastrulu, 1961, pp. 344-348).

As in the Christian case, so in the Islamic, the general position has been that God is; philosophically, He is the one necessarily existent being, all else that exists being created by Him, its existence derivative from His. Nonetheless in both instances there have been some exceptions. One may cite the atypical thesis of Sijistānī: "It becomes obligatory to separate (*dūr kardan*) existence from Him who brought existence into being, the Creator. . . . Thus it is proper [to say] that 'necessary Existence' does not apply in any fashion whatever to the Creator" (as if "He were in need of being"). (Abû Ya'qûb Sejestânî, *Kashf al-Maḥjûb* [*Le Dévoilement des choses cachées*], *traité ismaélien du IVme siècle de l'hégire: texte persan publié avec une introduction par* Henry Corbin, Teheran: Institut Franco-Iranien, [et] Paris: Adrien-Maisonneuve, 1949, p. 14 of Persian text, lines 2-3, 4-5, 4 [my translation]. See further Part 1, §6 in general: ibid., pp. 12-14. This work appears not to have survived in its original Arabic, but only in the above Persian version.)

He goes on to say (in the next section: p. 14, especially lines 10 and 15-17), that "The Creator is not a thing and not no-thing; He is not limited and not non-limited; He is not qualified and not non-qualified; He is not in a place and not in no place; not in time and not not in time; He does not exist and does not non-exist".

In the Buddhist case, there was elaborate development of the thesis of the (originally Hindu) *catuṣkoṭi* ("four alternatives") rejection: the denial of all four of "P is Q, P is not Q, P is both Q and non-Q, P is neither Q nor non-Q". This may strike some Westerners as a *via* almost fulsomely, yet meticulously, *negativa*; it was cheerfully applied in speaking of the being or existence of most transcendent matters, including Nirvāṇa, life after death, the Buddha; but it seems not to have been said, to my knowledge, of Dharma, of which, on the contrary, rather it is proclaimed that "it has been, it is, it will be" (*bhūtvā bhavati bhaviṣyati*). Ultimate reality is felt in later Buddhist thought generally, however, to transcend both being and non-being. On this matter and its relation to Western orientations see a recent article of Masao Abe, "Non-being and *Mu*: the metaphysical nature of negativity in the East and the West", *Religious Studies*, 11:[181]-192 (1975).

For the *catuṣkoṭi* denial with regard to the matters mentioned and some others, see, for instance, Majjhima-Nikāya, *suttas* 63, 72 and Nāgārjuna, *Mūlamadhyamakakārikās*, chap. 25; English translations by, respectively, Henry

Clarke Warren in his *Buddhism in Translations: passages selected from the Buddhist Sacred Books and translated from the original Pāli* [Cambridge, Massachusetts: Harvard University Press, 1896 (Charles Rockwell Lanman, ed., Harvard Oriental Series, volume 3)] New York: Atheneum, 1963, pp. 117-128 ("Questions which tend not to edification"); and Frederick J. Streng, *Emptiness: a study in religious meaning*, Nashville and New York: Abingdon, 1967, pp. 215-217. Cf. also the latter part of ref. 17 below.

12 Saṃyutta-Nikāya, 12:20 (II:1:2:10):3. (My translation.) The original Pali will be found in Feer, op cit. (our ref. 10 above), p. 25. For another translation see Mrs. Rhys Davids, . . . *Kindred Sayings* . . . (op. cit., our ref. 10 above), p. 21.

13 Mrs. Rhys Davids, *Buddhism*, (op. cit., our ref. 10 above), p. 33.

14 Udāna, 8:3. (My translation.) The text will be found in Paul Steinthal, ed., *Udânaṃ*, London: Oxford University Press for the Pali Text Society, 1885, pp. 80-81. The term that I have rendered "a way of transcending" and, the second time, "a transcending", is the Pali *nissaraṇam*. In my first draft I used "escape", and toyed with "refuge": the latter is the standard translation for the central Buddhist concept *śaraṇa* (Sanskrit) from which this term is not actually derived but was felt to be. Both "escape" and "refuge" are given in the Pali Text Society dictionary (op. cit.) for the compound *nissaraṇa*, but these are low on their list; other meanings given, with more priority, are "going away", "departure", "leaving behind". Since I use the word "transcend" almost literally—basically, "to climb beyond", "to pass beyond" (cf. its sister-terms "ascend", "descend")—I have felt that it perhaps communicates more accurately what the Pali here envisages.

Other translations are available in D. M. Strong, trans., *The Udāna; or, the Solemn Utterances of the Buddha*, London: Luzac, 1902, p. 112, and in F. L. Woodward, trans., *The Minor Anthologies of the Pali Canon. Part II. Udāna: Verses of Uplift, and Itivuttaka: As It Was Said*, London: Oxford University Press, [1935], 1948 (Sacred Books of the Buddhists, vol. 8), p. 98.

Some will perhaps feel that I am pressing the argument unduly, since "the unborn . . ." here is primarily Nirvāṇa; though the Buddha's exposition of this teaching is called *dhamma* in the introductory part of this same paragraph (repeating the first part of 8:1—cf. Steinthal, p. 80). I hope that I may not seem to have confounded *dharma/dhamma* with *mārga/magga* as the path leading to Nirvāṇa; *dharma* as the law or truth about, or reality of, both the path and the goal somehow transcends this. Although I have tended to render *dharma* as "moral law", one must be on guard against succumbing to a duality of moral and intellectual: in the Buddhist view, to live morally involves living intelligently, and truth and goodness converge. (The first item even in the Eightfold Path is Right Views—a fact that impinges entrancingly on the general thesis of this present book.) For the fact that truth and reality are conjointly comprised in the concept *satya/sacca*, see for instance Richard A. Gard, ed., *Buddhism*, New York: [George Braziller, 1961] Washington Square Press, 1963 (Richard A. Gard, gen. ed., Great Religions of Modern Man), p. 95.

15 From the Metta Sutta ("Lovingkindness discourse"); a somewhat free translation of verse 7 and part of verse 8. This sūtra occurs twice in the Pali Canon: in the Sutta-Nipāta (where it is 1:8) and in the Khuddaka-Pāṭha (9:7). The original Pali will be found, in the former case, as verse 149 (and 150) in Dines Andersen and Helmer Smith, edd., *Sutta-Nipāta*, [London]: Oxford University Press for the Pali Text Society, [1913], 1948, p. 26; and in Lord Chalmers, ed. & trans., *Buddha's Teachings, being the Sutta-Nipāta or Discourse-Collection*, Cambridge, Massachusetts: Harvard University Press, and London: Oxford University Press, 1932 (Charles Rockwell Lanman, ed., Harvard Oriental Series, vol. 37), p. 36. The latter gives a facing English translation, p. 37; cf. also E. M. Hare, trans., *Woven Cadences of Early Buddhists*, London: Oxford University Press, [1945], 1947 (The Sacred Books of the Buddhists, vol. 15), p. 24. I have used rather a rendering that is in a sense a paraphase of verse 7 influenced by and indeed incorporating something from the next verse, which elaborates the sentiment; a rendering legitimated also, perhaps, by the commentaries (Buddhaghosa, for instance, glosses *mānasam* as *mettaṃ mānasam*. See *The Khuddaka-Pāṭha, together with its Commentary Paramatthajotikā I*, Helmer Smith, ed., from a collation by Mabel Hunt, London: Luzac, for The Pali Text Society, 1959, p. 248).

This sūtra (popularly called also the Karaṇīya Metta Sutta) is widely popular in Buddhist lands; new editions, translations, commentaries abound in, for instance, present-day Sri Lanka. A Christian comparativist's comment: "It is the Buddhist 'Thirteenth Chapter of First Corinthians' " (E. A. Burtt, ed., *The Teachings of the Compassionate Buddha*, New York: New American Library, Mentor Books, 1955, p. 46).

16 Documentation for this once widely famous remark is not altogether firm. The editors of a recent dictionary of quotations have managed to proffer only the following entry: "Ernest [sc. Ernst] Haeckel, the great German philosopher [sc. philosophizing biologist], was asked what he thought was his most bothersome question. He said, 'The question I would most like to have answered is, "Is the universe friendly?" '—Anonymous"; *The Encyclopedia of Religious Quotations*, Frank S. Mead ed. & comp., Westwood, New Jersey: Revell, 1965, p. 459. The earliest citing that I personally have tracked down, also attributed without exact reference, and deviating slightly in wording but not in substance from the above, is from 1933.

17 Visuddhi-magga, 16:68. The Pali original will be found in Henry Clarke Warren, ed., Dharmananda Kosambi, rev., *Visuddhimagga of Buddhaghosâcariya*, Cambridge, Massachusetts: Harvard University Press, and London: Oxford University Press, 1950 (Walter Eugene Clark, ed., Harvard Oriental Series, vol. 41), p. 431. I have cited the translation of I. B. Horner in Edward Conze, ed., *Buddhist Texts through the ages* [Oxford: Bruno Cassirer, for the Royal India, Pakistan and Ceylon Society, 1954], New York: Harper & Row—Harper Torchbooks, 1964, p. 100. The word *dhamma* is not in the original (which reads *Paṭipattiyā vañjhabhāvâpajjanato*). This passage occurs within a discussion as to whether Nirvāṇa is to be deemed non-existent because it is inapprehensible (*anupalabbhanīyato*—sc. by the mind, like a self-

contradictory concept; verse 67), to which the answer is that it is attainable (*upalabbhati*) through the appropriate means (*upāyena*—sc. by following the Buddhist Path).

18 Immanuel Kant, *Kritik der praktischen Vernunft* [Riga: Hartknoch, 1788], 1:2:2:4, "Die Unsterblichkeit der Seele als ein Postulat der reinen praktischen Vernunft", and 1:2:2:5, "Das Dasein Gottes als ein Postulat. . . ". I have used the edn. of Benzion Kellermann [Berlin: Bruno Cassirer, 1914, Ernst Cassirer, ed., Immanuel Kants Werke, Band v], Hildesheim: Gerstenberg, 1973, pp. 132-134, 134-143. Cf. Immanuel Kant, *Critique of Practical Reason and other writings in moral philosophy*, Lewis White Beck, ed. and trans., Chicago: University of Chicago Press, 1949, pp. 225-227, 227-234: "The immortality of the soul as a postulate of pure practical reason", and "The existence of God as [id.]".

19 This word "hold" is inherently appropriate. The word *dharma* is from the Sanskrit root *dhṛ* (*dhārayati*), "to hold" (transitive and intransitive). Buddhists often say about it that "it holds". One example among many: the major commentator Buddhaghosa already mentioned (our ref. 15 above) writes (in his *Papañcasūdanī* . . . , 24:7 [= 4:68]), *dhāretī ti dhammo* (J. H. Woods and D. Kosambi, edd., *Papañcasūdanī Majjhimanikāyaṭṭhakathā of Buddhaghosâcariya*, London, New York etc.: Oxford University Press for the Pali Text Society, Part 1, 1922, p. 131). Moreover, at the present time ordinary Buddhists in Sri Lanka if asked about *dharma* will often spontaneously respond with a hand gesture beautifully signifying this assurance, my former student Dr. John Carter has reported to me.

20 Étienne Lamotte, *Histoire du bouddhisme indien, des origines à l'ère Śaka*, Louvain: Publications universitaires—Institut orientaliste, 1958 (Université de Louvain, Institut orientaliste: Bibliothèque du *Muséon*, vol. 43), p. 26.

Chapter 3

1 My *Belief and History* (above, our chap. 1 here, ref. 4), esp. its chap. II.

2 And, more fully, that additional volume, noted in our preceding reference just above.

3 An example of a modern anthropologist stopped up short by an awareness that conventional concepts of "believing" are inadequate to what it is his task to describe: Rodney Needham, *Belief, Language, and Experience*, Oxford: Blackwell, and Chicago: University of Chicago Press, 1972. This brilliant, learned, and at times poignant work came into my hands only after my *Belief and History* (our previous two reff., just above) was complete, and this present study virtually so. It covers some of the same ground, and is of major importance for our argument, although its concern is the relation of belief primarily not to faith, as is ours, but to intellectual, philosophic, understanding: it is much more impressive in this realm than things done by recent professional philosophers. Some sense of the range of views and uncertainty of categories among present-day scholars generally in the anthropology

field is available from Robert A. Hahn, "Understanding Beliefs: an essay on the methodology of the statement and analysis of belief systems", followed by a critique from fellow anthropologists, in *Current Anthropology*, 14:207-229 (1973)—the discussion including a plaint from Needham (p. 225) that Hahn, in typical anthropologist fashion, has ignored philosophic writing on the topic. For a perhaps somewhat strident comment on some modern-day analytic philosophers' positions on belief in the religion field, see chap. 1 of the present writer's work just referred to.

4 Many moderns, of course—but this is a radically different matter—have felt religious beliefs to be inept and illegitimate, the while regarding believing as the characteristic and decisive religious category. They have gone on then to suppose that faith is also inappropriate. Both believers and non-believers are thus in diverse ways misled by confusing belief with faith.

5 Op. cit. (our ref. 1 above), chap. III, where it is shown that the words "belief", "believing" are misrenderings in modern English of the scriptural text, and suggested that the Bible will have to be retranslated so as accurately to present in English what it has to say.

6 Below, our chap. 5, *Credo*. . . .

7 *'arafa,* and especially *'alima.*

8 The verb *'arafa* occurs 20 times in its Ist form, and its various derivatives (*ta'ārafa*, *ma'rūf*, etc.) a further 48 times. The verb *'alima* occurs 382 times in its Ist form, and its various derivatives 401 times. For these and subsequent calculations I have made use of the admirable Qur'ān concordance of Muḥammad Fu'ād 'Abd al-Bāqī, *al-Mu'jam al-Mufahras li-Alfāẓ al-Qur'ān al-Karīm*, Cairo: Dār al-Kutub al-Miṣrīyah, 1364 [= 1945 A.D.]. Citations from the Qur'ān, and verse numberings, I throughout give from the official edition printed in Cairo under royal patronage, 1342 h./1923 A.D., and many times reprinted. Its text covers 826 pp. I have used the edition of the Government Central Press, Hyderabad-Deccan (India), 1938, in two volumes. All translations from Arabic are my own.

9 *i'taqada*. The root *'aqada*, "to tie a knot", either literally or in the figurative sense of binding a person by a legal or moral commitment, making a binding engagement, occurs seven times in the Qur'ān: twice as the verb and five times as a noun. The words *'aqīdah*, *'aqā'id* do not occur. Furthermore, I have found in working on mediaeval *kalām* texts that the VIIIth form *i'taqada*, which does not occur in the Qur'ān but is introduced into theology later, along with *'aqīdah*, *'aqā'id*, in the sense of "creed", begins there by meaning not "to believe" something but rather more literally to bind oneself, to commit or to pledge oneself to, to take on the engagement of living in accord with a given position; and that only gradually across the centuries does it eventually acquire the more neutral meaning of "to believe" something intellectually. This last comes quite late in the mediaeval period and is perhaps not common until early modern times. That even into the twentieth century a residue has persisted of the personalistic engagement involved in this concept, as explicitly distinct from the neutrality of mere "believing" (*ra'y*), is evidenced in an interesting article, which considers the

matter more from a political than a religious viewpoint (to use modern or Western terms): Aḥmad Amīn, "al-Ra'y wa-al-'Aqīdah", which appeared first in the journal *al-Risālah*, Cairo, October 16, 1933 and is reprinted in Aḥmad Amīn, *Fayḍ al-Khāṭir* [Cairo, 1938-1955], 5th edn., Cairo: al-Nahḍah al-Miṣrīyah (Lajnat al-Ta'līf), 1965, 1:1-3.

10 On this concept in the Qur'ān, see the general discussion in my *Meaning and End* . . . (above, our chap. 1 here, ref. 10), chap. 4, § vi, with reff. 88-111 (pp. 108-115, esp. 111-115; Mentor edn., pp. 99-105, 101-105)—although that discussion is oriented primarily to the correlative term *islām*, only secondarily to *īmān*. To the bibliography there given, the following studies of these two concepts in the Qur'ān should now be added: Abdul Khaliq Kazi, "The Meaning of *Īmān* and *Islām* in the Qur'ān", *Islamic Studies: Journal of the Islamic Research Institute, Pakistan*, 5:[227]-237 (1966); and Muhammad Abdul Rauf, "Some notes on the Qur'anic use of the terms islām and imān" [*sic*], *The Muslim World*, 57:94-102 (1967). In addition, although they deal only with *islām* and not with *īmān* as terms, yet the following may be noted as significant for our purposes here for engaging with, and in the second case for demurring to, my earlier interpretation of that term set forth above: L. Gardet, ISLĀM, "I. Definition and theories of meaning", in the new edn. of *The Encyclopaedia of Islam*, Leiden: Brill, and London: Luzac, 1960- (in process), fascicules 63-64 [vol. 4], pp. 171-174 (1973); and Isma'īl R. al Fārūqī, "The Essence of religious experience in Islam", *Numen*, 20:[186]-201 (1973). See also: Jane I. Smith, "Continuity and Change in the Understanding of *'Islām'* ", *The Islamic Quarterly*, 16:[121]-139 (1392/1972).

Regarding the term *īmān*, those who know Hebrew will recognize in that language this same root—used in the Bible in relation to faith chiefly also in the corresponding *hiph'il* form האמין (*he'ᵉmîn*)— and its corresponding nouns אמת (*'ᵉmeth*) and (chiefly post-Biblical) אמונה (*'ᵉmûnāh*).

11 This sentence is from my own earlier work, *The Meaning and End* . . . , mentioned in the preceding ref. just above; p. 112 (Mentor edn., p. 103).

12 *fa-lammā jā'ahum mā 'arafū kafarū bi-hi*, Qur'ān 2:89. Similarly, in 16:83: "They know [*sic*] the benefaction of God, and then disown it, most of them being rejectors" (*ya'rifūna ni'mata-llāhi, thumma yunkirūnahā, wa-aktharuhumu-l-kāfirūna*).

13 *wa-jaḥadū bi-hā wa-stayqanat-hā anfusuhum*: Qur'ān 27:14. *hā* here refers to *āyātunā* in the preceding verse: sc. *āyāt Allāh*. Another example is Qur'ān 2:34, ". . . and he [Satan] refused, in pride; becoming one of those who reject" (*abá wa-stakbara wa-kāna mina-l-kāfirīn*). Cf., similarly, Qur'ān 15:31. The idea that Iblīs (Satan) did not believe is, quite simply, ludicrous.

14 *ẓulman wa-'ulūwan*—27:14.

15 This characterization represents much of the theological discussions generally, where words such as *idh'ān*, *qubūl*, *taslīm* are common. In choosing this wording, however, I had in mind in particular a passage such as the following from one of the most widely received of mediaeval commentators: Faith "is that appropriation of truth by the heart that reaches the point of decision and compliance"—Sa'd al-Dīn al-Taftāzānī, in his commentary

(*Sharḥ*) on the *'Aqā'id* of Najm al-Dīn al-Nasafī. I have used the following editions: Istanbul: Yūsuf Ẕiyā, ed. 1326 [= ca. 1908], and Cairo: Dār Iḥyā' al-Kutub al-'Arabīyah ('Īsá al-Bābī al-Ḥalabī), n.d. [sc. 1335? (= ca. 1917)]. This passage is found on pp. 157, 128 respectively. The Arabic reads: . . . *annahu* [sc., *anna al-īmān*] *al-taṣdīq al-qalbī alladhī balagha ḥadd al-jazm wa-al-idh'ān*. For the translation, see my article "Faith as *Taṣdīq*" mentioned in ref. 34 below. For bibliography on the matter in the development of Islamic theology in general, see ref. 32 below. It should be remarked that the Istanbul edn. mentioned was published in a volume comprising two sets of pagination, the second part of the book consisting of a super-commentary on Taftāzānī's presentation; all our references throughout this present study, with the exception of ref. 31 below where the two parts are compared, are to the first sequence of page-numbers.

16 It is charming to note the curious co-incidence that the fourteenth-century theologian Taftāzānī, just mentioned (our preceding ref.), writing in Arabic, feels constrained to resort to Persian to explain faith, introducing the word *giravīdan*, just as modern existentialists writing in English resort to the French terms *s'engager*, *engagement*; with the further fact of the French word *gage* and the Persian word *girav* being exact equivalents, as designating the stake pledged, or held by a third party, in a wager, or contract. See Taftāzānī, *Sharḥ* (our preceding ref.), p. 152/125: *wa-bi-l-jumlah huwa al-ma'ná alladhī yu'abbaru 'anhu bi-l-fārisīyah bi-ḳirawīdan*—"In fine, it is the meaning that is expressed in Persian by *giravīdan*/*s'engager*".

17 Also the counterpart *āmīn* in Arabic itself, used similarly.

18 In the Qur'ān itself there is a verse that seems clear in making faith a matter of willed choice on man's part: "The truth is from your Lord; let him who so wills, accept it, and let him who so wills reject it" (*al-ḥaqqu min rabbiḳum, fa-man shā'a fa-l-yu'min, wa-man shā'a fa-l-yaḳfur*—18:29). There are many other verses in the scripture, however, in which a seemingly differing position is presented, in that the will active in human faith or its contrary is divine. Indeed it may be noted that of the verb *shā'a*/*yashā'u*, "to will", used 236 times in the Qur'ān, the subject in far and away the overwhelming majority of cases is not man (as in the verse that we have cited) but rather God on high. This is true in general, and is so also in the matter of faith: verses in which it is asserted that God guides whom He wills [*sic*] and leads astray whom He wills (e.g., 35:8, reversing the order: *fa-inna-llāha yuḍillu man yashā'u, wa-yahdī man yashā'u*). In accord with this, in the discussions in later Islamic life on the act of faith, what was canvassed tended to be not the question of whether or how man's will is involved in it as over against his intellect (although that issue did arise: cf. ref. 20 below), so much as whether and how that will is involved alongside of God's—and how far and in what sense and fashion in that involvement it is what the West calls "free". Given the two types of presentation in the Qur'ān, Muslims have had occasion not to suppose simplistically that between human free-will and a divine control of events there is a straight either/or polarity. In any case, their at-

tention and consciousness have been drawn to the matter of God's willing much more vividly, emphatically, than to man's.

So far as later theological discussion is concerned, one may note as illustrative not of the divine/human willing problem but of the human willing/ratiocinative problem, a passage such as one in Taftāzānī in which, in the course of arguing against the notion that faith is belief, or even knowledge, mere intellectual recognition of a truth but without concomitant self-commitment, he moves very close to affirming that it is rather an act of will but then draws back, evidently hesitant to make it altogether voluntary (*Sharḥ*, edd. citt., our ref. 15 above: Cairo, p. 129, lines 19ff.; Istanbul, p. 159, lines 1ff.). On the former subject more generally, see W. Montgomery Watt, *Free Will and Predestination in Early Islam*, London: Luzac, 1948, for the first some centuries; and especially Gardet, *Dieu et la destinée* . . . (above, our chap. 1, ref. 11), Part 1, chap. 2, "La production des actes humains libres", pp. 45-77 (also s.v. *ikhtiyār* in Index). This last should be supplemented by Gardet's article IKHTIYĀR in *The Encyclopaedia of Islam* (above, our ref. 10, this chap.), 3:1062f. (1971). See also our next ref., just below.

Despite the theoretical discussions, however—especially but not only those of outside observers—and their tendency to focus on certain terms (the verb *shā'a*, the noun *ikhtiyār*), there was in Islamic life by way of other concepts room for and indeed emphasis on human willing which have been major. Especially important here perhaps is the concept *nīyah*, "intention",—a form of willing, surely—that was integral to every act of faith. See below, our chap. 4, ref. 46.

19 One example from among many: "Faith is an illumination injected by God into the hearts of his servants, a gift and a present from Him" (*al-īmān nūr yaqdhifuhu Allāh fī qulūb 'abīdihi, 'aṭīyah wa-hadīyah min 'indahu*)—Ghazzālī, *Fayṣal al-Tafriqah*. The immediate context of this passage, it may be remarked in passing, is an argument against such theologians as regard faith as primarily a theological matter, of conceptualist subtlety. "He who imagines that what conduces to an awareness of faith is rational discourse, sheer proofs, distinctions set out in order—to put it bluntly, he is aberrant", he says in his preceding sentence; "rather, faith is . . ."—and there follows the statement that we have quoted. We might paraphrase him here as averring in these two sentences that *īmān* means not belief but faith.

(The exact reference: Muḥammad Abū Ḥāmid al-Ghazzālī, *Fayṣal al-Tafriqah bayna al-islām wa-l-zandaqah*. In the edition of Sulaymān Dunyā, Cairo: Dār Iḥyā' al-Kutub al-'Arabīyah—'Īsá al-Bābī al-Ḥalabī, 1381 h./1961 A.D., p. 202.)

On this issue in general, the discussions were nuanced. The opposite of faith, in Islamic thought, being not its absence but active rejection, *kufr*, the nub of the problem, recognized as serious, was whether that *kufr*, the infidel's infidelity, should be deemed God's doing or man's free choice. That faith itself, on the other hand, is from God was taken virtually for granted on all sides. All blessings (*ni'am*) are from God; and among all blessings this is the chief. The word *tawfīq*, sometimes translated "grace" (more literally, God's "conforming, rendering conformable"), was one of the theological terms used in this connection. Within this consensus there was indeed the canvassing of a question as to the createdness of faith. Those who held it to be a created thing were affirming that each person's faith is directly brought into being by God, while those who held it to be uncreated might be interpreted as seeing a person's faith as his or her participation, if we may use that Platonic language, in a pre-existent quality of God Himself. See Gardet, *Destinée* (our chap. 1, ref. 11 above) pp. 69-71, 99-107, and s.vv. in index for *tawfīq* and *luṭf*, and his "Annexe: La grâce divine", pp. 101-103; see also Izutsu, *Belief* (our chap. 1, ref. 11, above), chap. II: "Creation of *îmân*", esp. pp. 204-214 (although Izutsu tends to dismiss the uncreatedness argument as not very serious).

20 *al-īmān maʻrifatun*. This characterization, of faith as a knowing of something, is found in the authoritative Tradition (*Ḥadīth*) attributed to the Prophet, in one of the collections compiled in the third Islamic century (9th A.D.) (Ibn Mājah, *Sunan*). It was said to have been professed also (in more specific form—*al-īmān al-maʻrifah bi-llāh . . . wa . . . bi-l-rasūl*) by the prominent and authoritative legist Abū Ḥanīfah, in the preceding century (al-Ashʻarī, *Maqālāt*, 1:138-139). In more strictly theological circles, however, it was propounded by early thinkers and groups and schools that presently were superseded and even denounced as heretical—the point being that faith must be recognized as *more* than knowledge (never less) even in its intellectualist component as a relation to the truth. The position rejected was attributed particularly to the second-century figure Jahm ibn Ṣafwān (ibid., 1:279: *al-īmān huwa al-maʻrifah bi-llāh faqaṭ*); to the Murji'ah school at large, to which he was said to pertain (ibid., 1:132-144); and to the Qadarīyah movement generally, or some parts of it (Taftāzānī, *Sharḥ* [our ref. 15 above], Cairo, p. 129). Recent critical scholarship finds more problematic the position of individual figures such as Jahm, and the relation among him and the movements mentioned: the niceties of who propounded the various positions, to what "sect" each belonged, and indeed even what constituted a named "sect", require more precision than has been traditional (see the articles of Watt and Pessagno specified below). In any case, the formulation "faith is knowledge", manifestly reflecting a movement of thought at one time current, did not find lasting favour (cf. our next ref.), on the grounds, as we have said, that it was seen as inadequate. Yet that faith has to do with what one knows continued strongly affirmed, or else was quietly taken for granted (see our ref. 34 below).

References are as follows: Abū ʻAbd Allāh Muḥammad ibn Yazīd al-Qazwīnī Ibn Mājah, [al-] *Sunan*, Muḥammad Fu'ād ʻAbd al-Bāqī, ed., [Cairo]: Dār Iḥyā' al-Kutub al-ʻArabīyah—ʻĪsá al-Bābī al-Ḥalabī, 1372/1952, vol. 1, p. 26 (Muqaddimah, *bāb* 9, #65). Abū al-Ḥasan ʻAlī ibn Ismāʻīl al-Ashʻarī, *Maqālāt al-Islāmīyīn wa-ikhtilāf al-muṣallīn—Die dogmatischen Lehren der Anhaenger des Islam*, Hellmut Ritter, ed. (Hellmut Ritter, ed., Bibliotheca Islamica, 1), 2 Bde., Istanbul: Maṭbaʻat al-Dawlah—Staatsdruckerei, and Leipzig: Brockhaus, 1929-1930. W. Montgomery Watt, article D̲JAHM B. ṢAFWĀN, *The En-*

cyclopaedia of Islam (our ref. 10 above), 2:388 (1965). J. Meric Pessagno, "The Murji'a, īmān and Abū 'Ubayd", *Journal of the American Oriental Society*, 95:382-394 (1975).

21 Of this particular formula, by the mediaeval period Taftāzānī can write: "Our scholars are agreed that this is wrong" (*aṭbaqa 'ulamā'unā 'alá fisādihi—Sharḥ* [our ref. 15 above], Cairo, p. 129, Istanbul, p. 152).

22 "Those to whom we have given the Scripture know it as they know their own children; yet there is a group from among them that indeed hide the truth, knowingly" (*alladhīna ātaynāhumu-l-ḳitāba ya'rifūnahu ḳamā ya'rifūna abnā'a-hum, wa-inna farīqan minhum la-yaḳtumūna-l-ḥaqqa wa-hum ya'lamūna*)—Qur'ān 2:146. The first half of this verse is repeated at 6:20, which in its differing second clause goes on to indicate rather that of those who thus know (*sic*), some to their own destruction do not respond with faith, do not make the act of faith (*alladhīna ḳhasirū anfusahum fa-hum lā yu'minūna*). Cf., further, reff. 12, 13 above.

23 Wilfred Cantwell Smith, *The Faith of Other Men,* New York: New American Library, 1963, pp. 58-59; Mentor books, 1965, p. 55. New York: Harper & Row—Harper Torchbooks, 1972, pp. 58-59.

24 The chief verses for this group are as follows: 2:46, 230, 249 / 12:42 / 17:102 (but cf. 17:101) / 18:53 / 24:12 / 37:87 / 38:24 / 41:48 / 69:20 / 72:12 / 75:25, 28 / 83:4. In these instances, one could argue that a concept "believing" does indeed appear; it is not, however, a religious category, is not commended, is quite casual and of no final importance. It is not something that Muslims characteristically do, or are supposed to do.

Of particular interest is 45:32, *in naẓunna illā ẓannan*: "We believe it a mere belief", "we imagine that it is only imagination". Here the verb, being used in the first person, seems at a superficial level therefore to avoid the manifestly pejorative quality of its cognate object. At a deeper level, however, the verb as well as the noun is here negative, rather than neutral, expressing the disdain not so much of the speakers for themselves (unless, as it imaginatively were, retroactively) but of the Qur'ān for men stupid and perverse enough to have voiced such blasphemous fallacies. Altogether the verb is found in the first person fourteen times in the Qur'ān, yet in almost all these cases, even, it is nonetheless pejorative in some such sense.

25 Pagans' veneration of God is characterized by Calvin as according to a conception *par la folle & estourdie vanité de leur esperit. . . .* Consequently, he says, *ilz adorent, non pas le Dieu éternel, mais les songes & resveries de leur cueur au lieu de Dieu.* [Jean Calvin], *Confession de la Foy . . . extraicte de l'Instruction dont on use en l'Eglise de* [*Genève*] [n.p., n.d. (sc. 1537)] in Albert Rilliet & Théophile Dufour, edd., *Le Catéchisme français de Calvin publié en 1537: réimprimé pour la première fois d'après un exemplaire nouvellement retrouvé . . .* , Genève: H. Georg, 1878, p. 5.

26 In the Qur'ān, as we have seen, even those who reject are depicted as rejecting that which explicitly they know; let alone, those who accept. On the former, cf. above, ref. 22; on the latter, so firmly is this taken for granted, that in the great majority of cases the verb *āmana*, to accept, to have faith, is

used without further specification (especially in the frequent phrase *yā ayyuhā-lladhīna āmanū*). No "object" is indicated. In later Islamic theology, the point is worked out quite explicitly that faith, while not itself knowledge (cf. above, ref. 20, and below, ref. 33), is oriented to the same matters: that it is *li-mā 'ulima* (in what is known) or *li-mā 'alima* (in what one knows). Cf. Smith, "Faith as *Taṣdīq*" (our ref. 34 below), its reff. 31-33, 49, and esp. 61-62.

In the mediaeval Christian case, as we shall consider in our discussion below of St. Thomas Aquinas (our chapter 5; see esp. pp. 85-86, at reff. 69-76), a divergence on this point emerges. There too faith was considered a relation of the person to truth, as were the various kinds of knowledge. Yet the truth to which one is related in faith, being not derivative but primordial, not complex but simple, so far transcends those truths that are comprehensible to our minds here below that lesser sorts of knowledge are indeed correlated with it, yet knowledge of the highest sort is, despite revelation, in principle available to humankind only *in patria*, not *in via*. (That lesser knowledge is called *notitia*, or is served by verbs like *cognosco*, while that of the ultimate is *scientia* or involves other forms of the verb *scire*—which might be translated "knowing and understanding", even perhaps "comprehending".) Accordingly faith becomes a mundane precursor to that final transcendent apprehension. Faith is in orthodox Christian thought in this sense less than knowledge, while in "orthodox" Islamic thought it is more than knowledge, even though in both cases all faith and all knowledge are relations to the same object, truth (reality). Between the two visions it could prove highly rewarding to have a sensitive exploration of the differences—and of the similarities. The former could be instructive; the latter, too, are significant. Such an essay might, for example, find not only that faith is in the one instance less than one kind of knowledge, in the other instance more than another kind of knowledge, but even that in the Islamic case this had manageably to do with a differential use in later centuries of the two Qur'ān terms for knowing: namely, *'alima* and *'arafa*. Some sort of comparability might thus emerge between some facets of this aspect of the Christian position and some facets in Islamic life of thinking expressed in terms of *'irfān* (and in some contexts also *ma'rifah*) and other forms from this root rather than or as well as *'ilm*. Thus it has been reverberatingly asserted, "The task of humankind is not to know God but to obey Him", the asserter the while nonetheless patently holding that persons know (*'alima*) what constitutes that obedience (he himself was one of the *'ulamā'*, those who "know" such things) and know such metaphysical matters as that God must be obeyed. Thus perhaps his divergence from Aquinas on the relation of faith to knowledge is less than might have been supposed.

27 To Arabic *ẓanna*, Greek *dokēsis* comes closer than does *doxa* or *endoxon*. (Yet that there is, for Plato, a difference of ontological status between the object of *doxa* and that of *epistēmē* [e.g., *Republic*, end of Book 5:477b-480a], is also relevant to our discussion.)

28 The form of the statements is usually something of this sort: they *ẓanna x*, whereas in fact, *y*. We may see that "believe" here does make a possible translation; yet one misses the flavour of the presentations if one omits from

a rendering the recognition that *ẓanna* is in fact a pejorative. Here are some illustrative verses:

"They *ẓanna* about God other than the Truth, the *ẓann* of the times of ignorance" (Qur'ān 3:154).

"About it they have no knowledge; rather, a following of *ẓann*!" (4:157).

"The majority of them do not follow anything but *ẓann*. Verily, *ẓann* is no substitute for Truth!" (10:36). This last clause is repeated more than once (cf. 53:28); as usual, the English translation seems sadly feeble in comparison with the forceful and pungent rhetoric of the original: (*inna-ẓ-ẓanna lā yughnī mina-l-ḥaqqi shay'an*!)

"You *ẓanna* that God was not aware of much of what you were doing" (41:22). Again, the ridicule implicit in this denunciation will be appreciated only by those who have some sense of the vividness of the Qur'anic imagery and the almost devastating presentation of God's awareness of all that men do.

"That is your *ẓann* which you *ẓanna* about your Lord—and it has ruined you (*ardāḳum*)" (41:23).

Often, the word appears in verses along with radically pejorative terms (*al-sū'*, *ḳādhib*, *ḳāfir*, and the like). There are, it is true, some cases where the *ẓann* of men about God is simply wrong, though there is a little or no disdain: for example, in 12:110, where "they *ẓanna* that they had been betrayed, but We (God) rescued them". One might render this, they imagined—they had reached the sorry point of imagining—that all was lost. . . . There is actually one verse (34:20) where this root converges with *ṣ-d-q*, truth—but it is Iblīs here, the Devil, about whom the Qur'ān is speaking. The passage might be taken in various ways, and indeed there are variant readings; one could suggest, "And Satan verily made come true against them his *ẓann* [we might almost translate it here "his machinations"], for they follow him, all but a few of those who have faith". One may note here once again the polarity over against faith (*mu'minīn*).

Cf. ref. 39 below.

29 To say that Muslims *āmanū bi-l-jinn* (had *īmān*, faith, in *jinn*) would mean something that is palpably false, almost heinous. It is not at all a reasonable statement. Linguistically, however, and intrinsically, it would not be totally impossible, absurd. The assertion earlier in our paragraph stands, about believing rightly: in the Qur'ān the object, expressed or tacit, of *āmana*, "to have faith", is always right, is the truth, is worthy of recognition, insofar as a dimension of intellectual awareness is at issue. It is not quite strictly the case, however, that in the more usual sense, not of "believing" but of putting one's faith in, responding in commitment towards, it is unfailingly used of doing so properly. In the total number of occurrences there are perhaps one-quarter or one-third of one percent of instances where the word is indeed used for a misplacing of one's faith, of one's allegiance. Thus in 29:52 woes are pronounced upon those who turn their backs on God and opt instead for vacuity (*alladhīna āmanū bi-l-bāṭili wa-ḳafarū bi-llāhi, ulā'iḳa humu-l-ḳhāsi-rūna*); and, perhaps less strikingly, in 40:12, on the Day of Judgement the divine abhorrence is proclaimed against those who when God was invoked

alone had said "No!", but who would respond positively, in faith, to Him in conjunction with imputed partners (*idhā du'iya-llāhu waḥdahu, kafartum, wa-in yushrak bi-hi tu'minū*). Thus, perverse persons may, atypically, be said to have faith in wrong things. Nonetheless, given the extreme rarity of these usages, it remains the case that the verb *āmana* in the Islamic semantic field—and even more the generic, *al-īmān* (note the generic definite article)—is linked to truth and goodness, indeed to God, and should be linked to nothing unworthy. It would not—quite—be linguistically impossible to say that Muslims had *īmān* in *jinn*, yet to say it would be grossly inept.

30 *mubīn*. Cf. our ref. 37 below.

31 This is an over-simplification; more strictly, one might aver that they were hardly conscious of believing anything finally important, anything in which a modern (outsider or Muslim) would say that they had faith. The verbs *dhahaba ilá* and *ra'á*, common in the classical and mediaeval Arabic theological literature, could perhaps be translated as "believe" in modern times without distortion. That *i'taqada* has come to mean "believe" only gradually, and perhaps not even yet quite fully, is indicated above, at our ref. 9.

The matter is illumined perhaps if we consider carefully a definition of faith such as that propounded by the twelfth-century Najm al-Dīn 'Umar al-Nasafī, in the course of a general theological statement which proved perhaps the most widely accepted of any in the Muslim world. He wrote, *al-īmān huwa al-taṣdīq bi-mā jā'a min 'inda Allāh*: Faith is the integral appropriation of the truth that comes from God. From this characterization a Christian, a Jew, and many a Hindu would hardly wish to dissent. It is an Islamic definition of faith, not a definition of Islamic faith. It is a statement about faith generically; it was not meant to be, was not proffered as, a statement of Islamic faith—indeed, it is not possible to translate the concept "Islamic faith" into classical Arabic.

No doubt the person who wrote this sentence and the Muslim who read it "of course" understood the truth that comes from God to be in the Qur'ān. *But he does not say so.* If a modern outsider wishes to affirm that the mediaeval Muslim believed this, then the statement in our text stands: that he was not conscious of believing it. (His and his society's taking this for granted, as axiomatic, self-evident, to the point of omitting it from their definition of faith, is vastly more significant than has latterly been recognized.) Not only were they not conscious of believing it; furthermore, had they been conscious of believing it, then they would not have believed it, one may realize on following the matter through reflectively. Had each seen it as a belief of oneself and one's culture, rather than as an evident (*mubīn*) truth, then it is not clear that they would have formulated their faith in this way, nor have been in any different case from their modern uncertain successors.

Had a classical or mediaeval Muslim been conscious of believing that there is no God but God, that Muḥammad is the Apostle of God (cf. above, our ref. 23)—had he been self-consciously aware that these were beliefs in his mind, part of his particular Weltanschauung—then he would hardly have been able to attest to this Islamic affirmation at all, it being in the first instance, as we have remarked, a statement about the universe, not about his subjective intellectual framework.

Let the position not be misunderstood; let no one imagine me to be suggesting a total subjectivizing of faith or of how we may best envisage it. On the contrary! Faith is a personal relation to truth. The faith of a mediaeval Muslim does not deserve to be called faith, either by his standards or by ours, insofar as that to which he was related was not Truth, was not God, was not Reality (*al-ḥaqq*); nor insofar as the channel through which his relation was mediated was not oriented to ultimates. Since, however, the truth, Truth, God, as he well knew and we must remember, transcends by far him and everyman—including us!—, we may, more profitably perhaps than the West has recently been wont to do, think in terms of approximations to Truth, mediations themselves finite and in part mundane of absolutes of and by which all human apprehensions are partial. Of those apprehensions, in turn, all propositions are only partially adequate objectifications. We must, then, learn to reckon adequately with conceptual patterns too, the tacit presuppositions in terms of which those overt propositions have meaning, in terms of which various groups among us severally articulate in words and concepts such Truth as we know. We return to these questions further below, in our concluding chapter.

(There is a variant reading in the Nasafī text, above, with *jā'a bi-hi* in place of *jā'a*, especially in versions from later centuries with commentaries and glosses. This would modify the form of our argument somewhat, but not its substance.)

I have used the following edition: William Cureton, ed., *'Umdat 'Aqīdat Ahl al-Sunnah wa-al-Jamā'ah/Pillar of the Creed of the Sunnites: being a brief exposition of their principal tenets, by Háfidh-uldín Abú'lbaraḳát Abdullah Alnasafi; to which is subjoined, a shorter treatise of a similar nature, by Najm-uldín Abú Hafs Umar Alnasafi*, London: Printed for the Society for the Publication of Oriental Texts; sold by James Madden & Co., 1843. (It is on this short treatise that Taftāzānī's commentary [*Sharḥ*: above, our ref. 15] is written; this passage, in its variant form, and with his exegesis, is there found p. 126/153.) [The elusive Cureton edn. did not prove available to me for checking this reference; I have verified it against the version at the end of the Istanbul edn. of the *Sharḥ*, p. 109 of the second round of pagination, the Khayālī *ḥāshiyah*, where the same wording is found, over against the reading with the *bi-hi* addition, p. 153 of the first round.]

32 On the understanding of faith in classical and mediaeval Islamic theology, the salient monographic treatment by a Muslim is that of Ibn Taymīyah in the fourteenth century. Otherwise, the literature is scattered in a vast number of less or more incidental, yet highly important, passages. I know of no over-all study by a present-day Muslim scholar. With regard to outsiders' secondary interpretations, I have recently written two articles (reff. 34, 35 below) on specific phrases used in explication (*taṣdīq bi-l-qalb* and *'amal bi-l-arḳān*), and one or two other studies not yet published. For the two best studies of the general position, preceding our discrimination between faith and be-

lief, see Izutsu, *Belief . . .*, and Gardet, *Dieu et la destinée . . .* (both, our chap. 1 above, ref. 11). See also the latter author's article ĪMĀN in the new edn. of *The Encyclopaedia of Islam* (above, our ref. 10, this chap.), 3:1170-1174. One might also perhaps note the review of *Dieu et la destinée . . .* in the *Journal of the American Oriental Society*, 92:377-381 (1972).

Among earlier studies of a more general sort, the excellent work of A. J. Wensinck, *The Muslim Creed: its genesis and historical development*, Cambridge [England]: at the University Press, 1932, should not go unmentioned.

Of Ibn Taymīyah, *Kitāb al-īmān*, there have been a number of modern editions; mine is [Zahīr al-Shāwīsh, ed.], *al-Īmān*, ta'līf Shaykh al-Islām ibn Taymīyah, [Bayrūt]: al-Maktab al-Islāmī, [1381], 2nd edn., 1392 [h.; = 1972 A.D.].

33 A concept of "knowledge" is found (and is prized) in virtually all human cultures, as designating a relation of the mind to truth. A further relation of the total person to truth is conceptualized in all major civilizations, under a term usually rendered "faith", it becomes apparent once one looks into the matter. This concept designates that particular quality of the human condition when not only the mind but the whole personality is involved in the relation to truth—feeling as well as intellect, and overtly also speech, and also other behaviour (or at least a readiness, a disposition, to act). One may know the truth but say its opposite; this is a lie, is faithless, in most cultures. Similarly one may know the truth but not be affectively engaged by it; let alone not actively engaged by it. The convergence of Buddhist, Hindu, Christian as well as Islamic positions on this understanding of faith is striking.

Cultures or civilizations or centuries that differ among themselves as to whether *x* or *y* is in fact true, may nonetheless converge in their concept and definition of knowledge. Similarly, they may converge to a remarkable degree, and in fact have converged, in their concept and definition of faith. In recent Western history, differences of opinion as to what is true have disrupted consideration of the former concept less than of the latter.

That one's relation to truth that is faith differs from, transcends, one's relation to it that is knowledge, is discussed above, at ref. 20; the matter is pursued a little further at ref. 26.

34 This is the Arabic word that was centrally used in classical and mediaeval Islamic interpretations of what faith is. To a careful elucidation of its denotations and contextual connotations in various centuries I have devoted a technical article addressed to scholars knowing Arabic and have published also a general presentation interpreting this concept and discussing its implications for Western culture in a paper offered to humanists and philosophers/theologians at large. For the latter see "A Human View of Truth" in John Hick, ed., *Truth and Dialogue: the relationship between* [sic] *world religions*, London: Sheldon (P. R. Baelz, gen. ed., Studies in Philosophy and Religion, 2), and with a somewhat differently worded title, *Truth and Dialogue in World Religions: conflicting truth-claims*, Philadelphia: Westminster, both 1974, pp. 20-44 (cf. pp. 156-162); published also in *SR: Studies in Religion / Sciences religieuses*, 1:[6]-24 (1971). The more technical article is "Faith as *Taṣdīq*" in Parviz

Morewedge, ed., *Islamic Philosophical Theology*, Albany: State University of New York Press, forthcoming.

35 Whether bodily action—"action with the limbs" (usually, *jawāriḥ*; sometimes, for the sake of rhyme, *arkān*)—should be included in the definition of faith was a moot point in Islamic theology, Muslims being teased by the faith-and-works problem no less than Christians. That a Muslim must "act with his limbs" as well as recognize with his mind and resolve in his will so to act, no one questioned. The problem was for a time acute, however, as to whether his so acting was rightly considered a result of his faith, or a part of it. (That *arkān* in these contexts means "limbs"—rather than, as is sometimes felt, "the [five] pillars [of Islām]"—is shown in my article "*Arkān*", in Donald P. Little, ed., *Essays on Islamic Civilization presented to Niyazi Berkes*, Leiden: Brill, 1976, pp. [303]-316.)

36 Muslims, and those familiar with the scholarly literature, will recognize this paragraph as an interpretative summary of the standard Islamic discussions. Cf. the secondary materials mentioned in ref. 32 above.

37 In the Islamic outlook the Qur'ān is the revelation not of a mystery so much as of something now lucid. The word *mubīn*, "clear" (or: "making clear"), occurs 119 times in the scripture (which means, on an average of more than once per *sūrah*/chapter). In addition, other forms of the verb (not counting, of course, the preposition *bayna*, but including *bayyannā*) occur a further 138 times.

38 Cf. our reff. 12, 13 and esp. 22 above.

39 Might one translate this into Arabic as *ẓanna*, perhaps?

40 Not by all. The Ṣūfī poet and mystic, on the one hand, stressing movement more than system, meaning more than form, person more than pattern, has been sensitive to faith wherever it be found, and has given expression to his humane—and divine—vision, especially in Persian, with an eloquence and passion perhaps unmatched in any other literature. The systematizer, on the other hand, whether conceptually (*mutakallim*) or morally-legally (*faqīh*), has been largely exclusivist.

41 The West is just beginning to recognize that it is hardly in a position to adjudicate on the truth of others' presuppositions and patterns until it has made more progress towards reckoning with its own. Considerable work towards dealing with other cultures' systems has been done by "scientific", "objective" circles in the West, such as cultural anthropology; but such thinking has usually done little with its own presuppositions in self-aware critiques, self-critical awareness. In philosophy, Kant indeed introduced self-criticism, recognizing that the categories of Western thought are not induced from the external world, but did not have the global perspective to see the matter in an historical and comparative context. More recently, one may, in illustration, as one among others of signs of an incipient reckoning with this challenge, refer perhaps to such analysis as Martin Heidegger, "Die Zeit des Weltbildes", in his *Holzwege*, Frankfurt am Main: Vittorio Klostermann, 1950, pp. 69-104. (An English translation of this, omitting the substantial supplementary notes [*Zusätze*, pp. 89-104], appeared in the short-lived [1950-1951] Chicago quar-

terly *Measure: a critical journal*, 2:[269]-284, Marjorie Grene, trans.) Another example is the Needham work mentioned above (our ref. 3). A good deal more thinking, however, will be required before we have attained much sophistication—as we go on to say in the next paragraph of our text—in the exhilarating, perilous, new task of formulating ideas in the ever dynamic and variegated situation within which we now know that we live and that all human thinking necessarily takes place. The historical and comparative awareness now available to us presumably makes this in principle possible. We shall return to these issues briefly in our concluding chapter, below. Yet I stress that our task in this present study, on the relation of faith to such formulations, is to call attention to the gravity of these conceptual problems, rather than as yet to solve them; and in the interim to suggest that humankind's awareness of the Truth, in the past and still to-day, in classical Islām and in Western or Westernized modernity, may outrun its capacity to form propositions that embody that truth in any but transient and culturally specific and always vulnerable ways. If we do not attain a universal theory as to the relation between truth itself and truth articulated in the midst of the relativity of human life and history, we may at this stage at least achieve a greater sympathy for the articulations of other ages and civilizations, and also for their faith, their more personalized apprehension of truth, whatever its conceptualized articulation. We may also gain some understanding of, even sympathy for, their conviction or instantiation that, of these two, faith is perhaps both logically and axiologically prior.

Chapter 4

1 Also, *vice versa.* I do not at all mean that a new conception of religious faith should be subordinated to current views on other matters! On the contrary, the recent incapacity of the modern intellect to understand faith, and to understand human beings as fundamentally persons of faith, has meant that contemporary ideas on many other matters are to that extent inadequate. A proper understanding of humanity will involve a revised comprehension certainly of the social sciences and to some degree even perhaps of the natural (as is, indeed, beginning to be increasingly widely recognized—for instance, to take one illustration: by that growing group for whom Roszak is spokesman. See, e.g., Theodore Roszak, *Where the Wasteland Ends: politics and transcendence in postindustrial society*, Garden City, New York: [Doubleday, 1972], Doubleday Anchor, 1973). See further our concluding chapter, below.

2 The remark is one that I myself developed some years ago in my class lectures before I learned to drop terms such as "Hinduism", as I was working my way towards some appreciation religiously of the Indian and the world scenes. It is the validity of what the formulation is trying to say that makes that formulation itself finally inadequate. I am not sure whether a comparable point is being made by the striking opening remark, perhaps pardonably exaggerated, of another observer: "We of the Occident are about to

arrive at a crossroads that was reached by the thinkers of India some seven hundred years before Christ"—Heinrich Zimmer, *Philosophies of India*, Joseph Campbell, ed., New York: [Pantheon Books, 1951 (Bollingen Series, xxvi)], Meridian Books, [1956], 1959, p. 1.

3 Of the various concepts in Hindu thought that may be correlated with the Western category of faith, the chief are represented by the three Sanskrit words *viśvāsa*, *āstikya*, and *śraddhā*. Of these three the first is mentioned below (our ref. 57), and the second we discuss; it is the third, however, that will chiefly occupy us. (On *bhakti*, a fourth term, designating one specific form of faith among Hindus, cf. below at our ref. 25.) A book-length study of each of these words and concepts and their history is desirable. Other notions also should be simultaneously considered, as potentially tributary to an eventual global concept of faith. (I would not exclude concepts such as *niṣṭhā*, *āsthā*, *bhāva*, even, in some of their uses. Certainly the Vaiṣṇava *prapatti* idea is germane. Historically it would seem that whereas *śraddhā* was in classical times the chief concept in India more or less counterpart to our present concerns, in mediaeval centuries it was to some considerable degree supplemented or superseded by other terms designating the same or a nearby reality.)

On the concept *śraddhā*, the focus of our present inquiry, certain investigations have already been done, by Indian, Japanese, and especially German scholars. In chronological order:

Mrinal Das Gupta, "Śraddhā and Bhakti in Vedic Literature", *Indian Historical Quarterly*, 6:[315]-333 and [487]-513 (1930).

Hans-Werbin Köhler, "*Śrad-Dhā* in der vedischen und altbuddhistischen Literatur", unpublished doctoral thesis, Göttingen, 1948. (Consulted in microfilm.)

Paul Hacker, "Über den Glauben in der Religionsphilosophie des Hinduismus", *Zeitschrift für Missionswissenschaft und Religionswissenschaft*, 38:51-66 (1954). (Hereafter, Hacker, 1954.)

G. Dumézil, "Credo, etc." being *Quaestiuncula Indo-Italica* 6 in *Hommages à Léon Herrmann*, Bruxelles-Berchem: Latomus, Revue d'études latines (Collection Latomus, vol. 44), 1960, pp. 323-329.

Paul Hacker, "*śraddhā*", *Wiener Zeitschrift für die Kunde Süd- und Ostasiens und Archiv für indische Philosophie*, 7:151-189 (1963). (Hereafter, Hacker, 1963.)

Minoru Hara, "Note on two Sanskrit Religious Terms: *Bhakti* and *Śraddhā*", *Indo-Iranian Journal*, 7:[124]-145 (1963-1964).

K. L. Seshagiri Rao, *The Concept of Śraddhā* (*in the Brāhmaṇas, Upaniṣads and the Gītā*), Patiala: Roy, 1971.

I am greatly indebted to the work of these scholars, and of course esp. for their having brought together for study various passages in which the term occurs, from a vast literature in which I myself am far from being competent. I have allowed myself, however, to differ from their interpretations and translations, as will be evident as we proceed to those familiar with their writings.

The following brief (73 pp., plus notes) Basle University thesis came into my hands too late to be used in the preparation of this work; but it appears not to require a modification of our conclusions: Gouriswar Bhattacharya, *Studies in the Concept of Śraddhā in Post-Vedic Hinduism*, Berlin: Dissertationsdruckstelle, 1971. (The author at a few points argues for linking the Sanskrit concept more closely than would I with "belief" and "doubt", though without inquiring closely into the significance of these English terms.)

On *śraddhā* as a term, and its etymology, cf. this chap., our ref. 35 and below, our chap. 5 reff. 25, 26.

On *āstikya* and other relevant words I am not aware of particular studies, except the interesting but for our purposes only tangentially relevant article: J. C. Heesterman, "On the Origin of the Nāstika", in G. Oberhammer, ed., *Festschrift für Erich Frauwallner*, Wien, 1968, pp. [171]-185 (= *Wiener Zeitschrift für die Kunde Süd- und Ostasiens und Archiv für indische Philosophie*, Band XII-XIII, 1968-1969: Beiträge zur Geistesgeschichte Indiens).

4 Represented most notably by the root *man-* (*manyate*), "to think"—cognate with English *mind*, Latin *mens*, etc. (Cf., however, below, our ref. 23.)

5 We say "not usually", but may cite exceptions. From the root *man-*, mentioned in our preceding note, the derivative *māna* (false opinion of oneself —remarkably like the English "conceit", from "conceive") is overtly derogatory. Further, the terms *vikalpa, kalpana*, used in Buddhist and Vedānta polemics, and which might here be rendered as "fancying", "imagining" (not unlike the English "fiction"), come close in meaning and usage to *ẓanna* in the Qur'ān case. (So does the verb *śaṅk-* [*śaṅkate*] in some of its uses.) A belief, one might almost contend, is at this level just a human mental construct, so that anything that can be simply "believed" is but a mundane fabrication. One begins to touch here on the issue elaborated below in our chapter 6, that a religious position becomes a belief only when viewed from the outside as false. The notion of thinking becomes downgraded when it is explicitly or tacitly contrasted with that of knowing.

Of the root *man-* mentioned above, one significant occurrence is Bhagavad Gītā 7:24:

> *avyaktaṃ vyaktim āpannaṃ*
> *manyante mām abuddhayaḥ*

Some read this passage pejoratively; Edgerton, for example, translates: "Fools conceive Me . . ."; and Zaehner, similarly: "Fools think of Me . . .". In line with my remarks later in this chapter on *buddhi*, I would take *abuddhayaḥ* here as meaning "those who are not aware" or ". . . not perceptive", but would interpret this as applying to most of us (cf. two verses further on: *māṃ tu veda na kaścana*—"But no one knows Me") and would see the line as stating rather that persons not apprehending the Lord as He truly is, beyond depiction, think of Him as reduced to depicted or depictable form. Telang gives "The undiscerning ones" for *abuddhayaḥ* here. About this verse Hill observes: "commentators vary widely in their interpretations". That *manyante*, however, is here depreciatory seems clear; it is parallel with *ajānanto*, "they do not know", in the latter half of the verse.

References:

Bhagavad Gītā, translated and interpreted by Franklin Edgerton, *Part 1: text and translation*, Cambridge, Mass., Harvard University Press, and London: Oxford University Press, 1944 (Harvard Oriental Series, vol. 38). This is the edition used throughout this present study for the transliterated Sanskrit text; passages are cited from it by chapter and verse, not by page number.

R. C. Zaehner, *The Bhagavad-Gītā, with a commentary based on the original sources*, [Oxford: Clarendon Press, 1969], paperback edn., New York: Oxford University Press, 1973, pp. 70, 253 (this translation appeared first in *Hindu Scriptures*, R. C. Zaehner, trans. and ed., London: Dent, and New York: Dutton [Everyman's Library], 1966, p. 281, where this passage had been rendered rather, "Fools think I am . . .").

The Bhagavadgîtâ: an English translation and commentary by W. Douglas P. Hill, [London: Oxford University Press, 1928], 2nd ed., Madras &c: Oxford University Press, [1953], 3rd imp. 1969, p. 129n. Kâshinâth Trimbak Telang, trans., *The Bhagavadgîtâ* . . . , Oxford: Clarendon Press, 1882 (F. Max Müller, ed., Sacred Books of the East, vol. 8), p. 76.

6 *jñāna*. The word is cognate with the Greek term *gnōsis*, and with Latin *gnosco, cognosco*, English *know*, etc.

7 We are speaking here primarily of the *jñāna mārga* generally, and especially Advaita. The term *jñāna* is used also in Viśiṣṭādvaita and by *bhaktas*. For these last some modification in our phrasing would be apt, although not in our argument. For them also, the salvation-knowledge attained is not conceptual: even if a servant-master, beloved-lover interrelation of some sort persist eternally, it is not a subject-predicate polarity.

8 Verbs such as *prati-ī-* (*pratīyati*), *ava-gam-* (*avagacchati*); nouns such as *pratyakṣa* and, as considered later in this chapter, *buddhi*. The term by which the sense of validity is most vividly expressed is perhaps *sākṣātkṛ-* (. . . *-karoti*): more or less, "to see with one's own eyes". I have taken these because they have on occasion been translated as "believe" by modern scholars. Passages in which these terms are used are, for instance, cited by Hacker, 1954 (our ref. 3, above), pp. 60-63. One of the most illuminating is analysed just below in our next ref. 9. *Avagacchati* is noted in ref. 53 below.

9 Illustrative is a passage from Vātsyāyana's commentary on the work of logic Nyāya Sūtras discussing the meaning of words; explicitly this comprises those words that speak of mundane empirical matters and those of transcendent reference. In the passage it is indisputably clear that the author holds—and his wording inherently implies—that the transcendent sphere is real, not imaginary; that what seers (*ṛṣi*), prophets and the like have had to say about it is in fact true; and that he presumes that his readers will of course agree. His whole argument would collapse if what these people are talking about were simply something that they believe to be there. To use terms like "be-

lieving" is not to translate Vātsyāyana's text but to paraphrase it in the language of the modern skeptic (or apologist).

Accordingly, I should render the opening clauses of Vātsyāyana on sūtra 1:1:8 as follows (the Sanskrit original is given at the end of this present note, below): "That [sc. word] of which the referent is seen here [in this world], is *dṛṣṭārtha* ('[word] of visible referent'); that of which it is perceived (apprehended) yonder [in the other world], is *adṛṣṭārtha* ('of invisible referent'). This, indeed, is the distinction between the statements of sages (*ṛṣi*) and those of mundane people." I would therefore take the liberty of regarding as quite misleading, not to say wrong, a translation such as the following modern version (though it is by a Hindu): "That 'Word' of which the thing spoken of is perceived in this world is called '*Dṛṣṭārtha*'; while that of which the thing spoken of is *only believed to exist* in the other world is '*Adṛṣṭārtha*'. [His footnote: '(1) That which speaks of things directly perceived by the Speaker, and (2) That which speaks of things only known to him indirectly, by means of Inference for instance.'] These are the two divisions under which are included all the assertions of sages and ordinary men." (Emphasis mine.) The use of "*the* other world" (rather than "another world") here is inconsistent, and the whole tenor of the English collides with what has been said in the preceding sūtra (1:1:7) and the commentary on it (and particularly with the word *āpta* there and its exegesis by *sākṣātkṛta*—see below).

The term that I have rendered here by "is perceived" or "is apprehended" is *pratīyate.* The context makes it fully clear that the author, Vātsyāyana, by this word intends something of that sort. The object of the verb (the subject of its passive mood, here used; that to which "the word", *śabda*, under discussion refers) is invisible, explicitly, but it is certainly not unreal. What is perceived, discerned (*pratīyate*, *geglaubt*) is apprehended (*āpta*), not fancifully imagined—even if it take a seer sage, *ṛṣi* ("Übermensch", "Seher") to grasp the invisible (the root *āp-* means "to reach, to obtain, to lay hold of").

The passage runs as follows:

> (Nyāya-Sūtra 1:1:7) *Āptopadeśaḥ śabdaḥ.* (Vātsyāyana ad loc:) *Āptaḥ khalu sākṣātkṛta-dharmā yathā dṛṣṭasyārthasya cikhyāpayiṣayā prayukta upadeṣṭā* . . . . (1.1.8) *sa dvividho dṛṣṭādṛṣṭārthatvāt.* Vātsyāyana: *yasyeha dṛśyate 'rthaḥ, sa dṛṣṭārthaḥ; yasyāmutra pratīyate, so 'dṛṣṭārthaḥ. Evam ṛṣi-laukika-vākyānāṃ vibhāga iti. Kim arthaṃ punar idam ucyate. Sa na manyeta dṛṣṭārtha evā 'ptopadeśaḥ pramāṇam arthasyāvadhāraṇād iti. Adṛṣṭārtho 'pi pramāṇam arthasyānumānād iti.*

I have used the following edition: Vināyaka Gaṇeśa Āpaṭe, ed., *Śrīmad-Vātsyāyana-Muni-kṛta Bhāṣya Śrī-Viśvanātha-Bhaṭṭācārya-kṛta vṛttisametāni Śrī-Gautama-Muni-praṇīta Nyāyasūtrāṇi*, Pune: Ānandāśrama Mudraṇālaya, 1844/1922 (Ānandāśrama Saṃskṛta Granthāvaliḥ, #91), pp. 24-25. The English translation that I have cited: Gaṅgānātha Jhā, *Gautama's Nyāyasūtras (With Vātsyāyana-Bhāṣya) translated into English with his own revised notes*, Poona: Oriental Book Agency, 1939 (Poona Oriental Series #59), pp. 30-31.

10 I do not wish to suggest that once such a concept were constructed and

applied, it would find in Hindu history no material on which to work. This present study is an inquiry not into belief among Hindus, nor the religious role of belief; I feel, as observed earlier, that for our consideration of the faith/belief question one does better to begin with other concepts and from the side of faith, as attempted in small part in this chapter. Nonetheless, an historical study on believing among Hindus could presumably prove highly instructive—provided it avoided being "over-simplified, and inappropriate", by first clarifying a number of distinctions within the modern English-language notion of believing. Grist for this particular mill, if anyone wished to set it a-turning, would be such matters as that some Hindus, certainly, have held the views of other Hindus to be wrong; at times, indeed, dangerous (even though those persons who held them might be recognized as nonetheless somehow attaining through them some sort of truncated vision or beatitude?). Again, one sect—for example the Gauḍīya Sampradaya Vaiṣṇavas, to cite one instance somewhat at random—might forbid its own novices to listen to the alternative interpretations of another sect. (Nonetheless, they perhaps did not disapprove of members of other sects' listening to those other interpretations and even adopting them?) Again, on the matter of believing in a modern Roman Catholic sense of one person's accepting the word of another—as distinguished from a more unmediated knowing—and the regarding of this as good, sects might be cited (the same illustration could serve) whose novices were expected to adopt on trust a truth taught by, or made available through the teachings of, a particular community until such time as they came to see or to experience that truth for themselves (by *anubhava* and the like). (It is not clear to me, however, that this process was conceptualized, so as to make believing a self-conscious activity, or belief a category.)

On the controversial question as to whether Hindu acceptance of diversity of belief was as substantial traditionally as modern repute would have it, cf. our ref. 17 below, on "neo-Hinduism". On terms that might be rendered "believing", cf. our reff. 4, 5 above.

I repeat: an historical study of believing among Hindus and its role religiously would be most welcome.

11 This slightly quizzical point is taken up a little in our reff. 13, 20, 24 below.

12 The modern West, although proud of its basic operating principle in law that a man is presumed innocent until shown to be guilty, in the religious realm tends rather to feel, consciously or unconsciously, that a religious position is presumably false, or at least is suspect, unless it can be proven correct. This skeptical position is perhaps due ultimately at least in part to the West's markedly "either/or" outlook, with its theoretical implications of dichotomous truth and falsehood, with mutually exclusive doctrines (and its practical implications of internecine strife).

Illustrative of the Indian position is the corollary of a remark of Śabarasvāmin (quoted in Hacker, "Über den Glauben", 1954 [our ref. 3 above], p. 64) in his commentary on the Mīmāṃsā Sūtra (the indirect reference is to 1:1:2) that every item of knowledge is valid so long as it is not contradicted by another. Cf. further below, in our concluding chapter.

13 The validity of this generalization is greater on the positive than on the negative side. An exception to it might seem to be that relatively small group whose *nāstikya* was formulated to their own satisfaction in the negation, *para-loka nāsti*: "the world beyond does not exist" (this is how the sentence, doubtless, was usually heard?), or "there is no world beyond" (sometimes from the side of the speaker?). Even this is a whit problematic, since it is not clear what, conceptually, they were denying—as is illustrated by the Mīmāṃsā position mentioned in our text and in our next note, and as is hinted in our double translation here (cf. also our ref. 24 below). In any case, we may leave that aside for the moment, remarking that normally the case was different: Sanskrit writers were prone to using the term *nāstika* polemically, not of oneself but of opponents said (sometimes gratuitously) to believe certain negatives: that there is no moral retribution in another life or another world, that the Vedas are not true, or the like. In both cases, one may note, it is others' positions, not one's own, that are objectified as theories and depreciated, a simultaneity that we have observed also elsewhere. Thus in both cases it is a matter of disbelief, rather, that is at stake. Although believing is not what religious people characteristically do, not believing may yet characterize the irreligious (or, the apparently or allegedly irreligious)—disbelief being the rejection by the latter of what they conceive the former to "believe". What a modern would call differences of *belief*, consciously affirmed, obtained within what was recognized as the *āstika* complex, and by no means only or even primarily between it and "outsiders". We observed above in our Islamics chapter how, while belief and faith are not identified, disbelief and un-faith regularly are; and as we shall see in our Christian chapters below, it is such rejection that generates in modern times the notion of religious believing. For Hindus, cf. further below, reff. 15, 24.

14 For instance, one radical commentator from this school is quoted (—by Hacker, "Über den Glauben", 1954 [our ref. 3 above], p. 53, with referenece to Śālikanātha, "Prakaraṇapañcikā [Benares 1903], S. 101ff.") as saying that the ideological content is but supplementary (*adhyāhāra*) to the commandments, and the example is given of the word for "Heaven" for which it is necessary to "supply" (root *adhi-ā-hṛ-*) a meaning in order for the sacrificial ritual in which this occurs to become meaningful; but "happiness" or "success", he says, will serve as that meaning in this context. More generally, this school is more moralist than ideationalist. The practical orientation of this outlook has been a good deal more prevalent in Indian religious life than has perhaps been much recognized in the West. I know of no study comparing the Mīmāṃsā instance of this religious mood with its Jewish and Islamic instances.

15 I have used "atheistic" rather than "atheist", but even it may be too strong; perhaps "godless" would be a better adjective. The connotations of Western terms become involved here, given the well-nigh ineluctable sense that an atheist is repudiating something. The Sāṃkhya school was not en-

gaged in denying anything, and any negative attribute tends to misrepresent its position.

16 Cf. my *Meaning and End of Religion* (our chap. 1 above, ref. 10), pp. 63-66 and 256-259; Mentor edn., 1965, pp. 61-64 and 249-253. The beginnings in late mediaeval Indian usage of the term "Hindu" are explored in the Bengal case for the Gauḍīya Vaiṣṇavas by my former student Joseph T. O'Connell, peripherally in his unpublished doctoral dissertation at Harvard and more systematically in "The Word 'Hindu' in Gauḍīya Vaiṣṇava texts", *Journal of the American Oriental Society*, 93:340-344 (1973).

17 The famed "religious tolerance" of Hindus, their acceptance in principle of pluralism as something not merely inescapable but right and proper, has become explicit as a formulated affirmation only gradually and especially perhaps in relatively recent times, in a form that some Western scholars differentiate by naming "neo-Hinduism". Perhaps involved in this emergence (of the formulation, not of the phenomenon) has been a reaction to modern Western impingements. The spirit of recognizing religious life as polymorphic is, however, ancient in India, even though a full history of this matter also remains to be written. (It should take the form of tracing the interplay over the centuries of two contrastable strands in the Hindu complex, a particularist and a universalist? Their varying force and predominance and mutual impingement through various times and places and in relation to various sectors of life have been fascinating, and continue to be dynamic.)

I have not succeeded in ascertaining who coined the term "neo-Hinduism". The earliest use that I have thus far found for it is D. V. Athalye, *Neo-Hinduism: an exposition of Swami Vivekananda's conception of Vedantism* (*Yoga philosophy*), Bombay: Taraporevala, 1932 (Library of Indian Wisdom). This author in fact uses it somewhat incidentally only, outside his title. He speaks of Vivekānanda's dream of a revived and purified evolving Hinduism, of adjusting "the old Hinduism" (p. 23) to modern times; and apart from his title seems to use the word "Neo-Hinduism" twice (both, p. 24) to designate this new form of "this Faith of the Aryans" (p. 22), while admitting that the subject of his monograph "disliked the appellation of 'Hindu' and 'Hinduism' forced upon us by the ancient Persians" (p. 24) and quotes him as saying, "I always use the words 'Vedantism' and 'Vedanta' " (p. 25) rather. There is no suggestion in the book that the term is original with Athalye, nor that it was known to Vivekānanda.

Among Western writers it is the erudite Hacker, perhaps, who espouses the term most earnestly and has pressed hardest, in various of his writings (see references at the end of this note), a distinction between it and what he calls *der historische Hinduismus*. He affirms: "The Neo-Hindu dogma of the equality of all religions, however much it may find support in certain Hindu traditions, yet first arose at the beginning of the nineteenth century out of the ideology of the European Enlightenment" (1961, p. 399; cf. 1957, p. 179). His data have to be reckoned with, certainly; yet it is difficult not to be left feeling that the writing is a whit tendentious, the mood begrudging: he speaks of *die pseudovedāntische Ethik in den Neuhinduismus* (1961, p.

394), calling this an historical curiosity and a logical impossibility (ibid., p. 396), and generally suggesting that the development is, in effect, illegitimate.

This position, though it must be taken seriously, reflects not only a Western Christian's reservations about India, but also a Protestant Christian's reservations about creative religious development as the historical process proceeds. His sense is that the classical is the pure, that early centuries in any tradition are closer to the truth (of that tradition) than are later ages. This is a none too appropriate way for envisaging the rich and never-ending dynamics over the centuries of India's religious life? Neo- has been the "Hinduism" of each century now for the last thirty-five.

References: Paul Hacker, "Religiöse Toleranz und Intoleranz im Hinduismus", *Saeculum: Jahrbuch für Universalgeschichte*, 8:167-179 (1957), and "Schopenhauer und die Ethik des Hinduismus", ibid., 12:366-399 (1961). (The phrase that we have cited, *der historische Hinduismus*, contrasting with modern or neo-, is found, e.g., 8:179 and 12:366, 396.) Further, Paul Hacker, "Der Dharma-Begriff des Neuhinduismus", *Zeitschrift für Missionswissenschaft und Religionswissenschaft*, 42:1-15 (1958).

For a different view, developed also by an outside classicist historian and an equally major Sanskrit scholar, see J. Gonda, *Viṣṇuism and Śivaism: a comparison*, London: Athlone, 1970 (Jordan Lectures, 1969), chap. v, "The Mutual Relations of the Two Religions", pp. [87]-109, and esp. pp. 95 ff.

An explicit stressing of a pluralist vision for the first time in the early nineteenth century could have been a reaction to, rather than a borrowing from, Europe, it could be countered.

18 Hacker, almost in the very terms of my work just mentioned (our ref. 16 above) calls it an affirmative posture towards a tradition-complex: "*Âstikya ist vielmehr bejahende Haltung gegenüber einem Überlieferungskomplex*" ("Über den Glauben", 1954 [our ref. 3 above], p. 53).

19 They did not become books until many centuries had past; and never became merely books, until read by objectivist ("unbelieving") students or the like from outside India. Scriptures are misunderstood by outsiders as the observable entities that are mundanely available to those outsiders—just as an imaged deity may be misunderstood as the material "idol" or form that for the outsider is visible and for the worshipper is suggestive. Besides, "the Vedas" in India were never a specifiable and concretely definite class of writings. I should like to see a word-study of the concept *veda* in Hindu literature: I feel confident that a sensitive investigation of usages would prove greatly illuminating. (A first illumination could come from a discrimination between singular and plural.)

20 These last three paragraphs may seem to go too far, given the classical Indian polarity between, on the one hand, those who for all their diversity accepted the "Vedic" tradition and, on the other hand, Buddhists, Jains, materialists, and the like who did not. Over against the standard Western interpretation, however, of this situation and this word, which interpretation rests on (and incorporates) a sophisticated relativistic skepticism, I have thought it

legitimate to present the "Hindu" interpretation as it would be felt by those within that tradition. In principle, I think it fair to affirm that *āstikya* has been what is here set forth, even though in practice this vision was challenged and those holding it knew that it was challenged.

21 Sāyaṇa as he comes to the term *śraddhā* in its various forms in various passages, explains it in various ways: chiefly, as *ādarātiśaya* and as the somewhat parallel *bahumāna* (both these have to do with paying great attention or respect; we will return to these below, at our ref. 49; cf. our ref. 56) and the later much canvassed *viśvāsa* (confidence, trust; cf. below, our reff. 36, 57). He uses also other explanatory terms (cf. our reff. 51, 63, 73 below). Occasionally, however, he exegetes with *āstikya-buddhi* (e.g., on the Atharva-Veda, ad 6:122:3 [below, our ref. 84] and 11:9:9 [cf. Das Gupta, our ref. 3 above, p. 319]). Similarly Mahīdhara uses this last term for *śraddhā* in commenting on the Vājasaneyi-Saṃhitā of the White Yajur-Veda, ad 8:5 (his vol. 1, p. 365) and ad 19:30 (his vol. 2, p. 993); and Uvvaṭa, in his commentary on the latter passage, gives *āstikya* (ad 19:30; vol. 2, p. 993).

For these last two writers I have used the following edition: *Śukla-yajur-veda-saṃhitā, Vājasaneyi-mādhyandina-śākhīyā, Śrīmad-Uvvaṭācārya-viracita-mantrabhāṣyeṇa, Śrīmat-Mahīdharācārya-viracita-veda-dīpenaca-Sahitā*, Paṇḍita Śrī Rāma Sakala Miśra Śarma, ed., Benares: H. D. Gupta & Sons—Chowkhamba Sanskrit Book Depot, 4 voll., 1912-1915.

22 An example: in his commentary on Bhagavad Gītā 17:1 (introducing the Gītā's chapter on types of *śraddhā*), Śaṅkara exegetes quite simply: *śraddhayā āstikyabuddhayā*. Similarly in his commentary on the Kaṭha Upaniṣad ad 1:1:2, he writes: *śraddhā 'stikyabuddhiḥ*. Hacker ("*śraddhā*", 1963 [our ref. 3 above], p. 159) uses the term *üblich* for Śaṅkara's choice of *āstikya-buddhi* as explication of *śraddhā*. For reference to several other Śaṅkara passages, see Hara (our ref. 3 above), p. 141. Both Hara and Hacker (locc. citt.) list other commentators also who make this same equation.

I find it not without interest, under the heading of how classical texts have been understood by those who read them, in addition to their authors' intent, that the early-nineteenth-century religious thinker and reformer Rām Mohan Roy, claiming to follow Śaṅkara in his interpretation, translates *śraddhā* in the Upaniṣad text cited as "compassion". Radhakrishnan in effect gives an engaging rendering of or illumination to *āstikya-buddhi* by his note *ad loc.*: "*śraddhā*: *faith*. It is not blind belief but the faith which asks whether the outer performance without the living spirit is enough". (Indeed, for any reader, that the boy came to "believe" [for *śraddhā 'viveśa*—Upaniṣad, loc. cit.] is, in this particular context, quite inappropriate.)

I have used the following editions. For the Gītā commentary of Śaṅkara, ed. cit. (our chap. 2 above, ref. 11). For the Kaṭha Upaniṣad and commentary, the edition in the Ānandāśrama Sanskrit series, #7: *Kāṭhakopaniṣat saṭīkādvayaśāṅkarabhāṣyopetā* . . . , Vaijanātha [Kāśinātha] Rājavāḍe, ed./Mahādeva Cimaṇāj Āpaṭe, publ., Pune: Ānandāśrama Mudraṇālaya, Śaka 1810/1889 A.D.; p. 7. Rammohun Roy, *Translation of the Kuth-Opunishud, of the Ujoor-Ved, according to the Gloss of the celebrated Sunkuracharyu*, n.p., n.d. [sc. Calcutta, 1819], p. [1]. S. Radhakrishnan, *The Principal Upaniṣads, edited with introduction, text, translation and notes*, London: Allen & Unwin, 1953, p. 595.

23 More accurately: with what Westerners may call the mind. The etymologically cognate Sanskrit term, *manas*, is in Indian thought a different organ, lower on the scale of human faculties. The distinction between the two has been important in India, as have the lack of that particular distinction in the West, and the making of others, as for instance between *ratio* and *intellectus*. Any person's or culture's view of the human mind is a function of his, her, or its total Weltanschauung, and *vice versa*. The Greek contribution to Western civilization, that reason is that quality of human beings through which they are linked with transcendence or ultimacy (more accurately: that reason is a quality of transcendence or ultimacy in which human beings, alone among living things, participate) has no exact counterpart in Indian thought, which in this matter is in some ways more comparable with recent Western outlooks (as well as, in many ways, less). Hence my imprecise elaboration here of the term "mind" with three other concepts. Cf. our reff. 35, 67, below; also our chap. 5 below, ref. 41.

24 That *āstikya-buddhi* is more positive than "belief" is demonstrated by the fact that *nāstikya* is also a belief but could not (by religious men) be called a *buddhi*. It is (for them) not a perception, but a failure to perceive; not a "recognition" but a blindness. *Āstikya-buddhi* conceptualizes a person's capacity to see that what is there is indeed there; the concept *nāstikya* denominates the position of that man who, surrounded by a transcendent reality, is insensitive to it. The *nāstika* is he who says "no" to the truth.

If a person uses this last word of him- or herself, of course, something different is meant by it. It is important to realize that differences of religious perception logically precede talk about such differences. This constitutes one of the chief problems for modern comparative-religion studies: a problem little recognized, and certainly not yet solved. Inherited terms may, and in the case of divergence of position almost must, mean something different to the person who uses them and the person who hears them. Our modern task is to forge concepts that will serve both of these persons (and then statements that will be intelligible and even acceptable to both)—and eventually, all. In the meantime, I am endeavouring here simply to adumbrate the meanings of these terms to Hindus—meanings, that is, appropriate to one who would use *āstika* of himself and *nāstika* only of someone else. As suggested in our ref. 13 above, a notion of "believing" would be more nearly involved in the reverse case.

For further exploration of the significance and innuendos of the word *buddhi* in its relation to faith, see below, our ref. 79.

25 To aver that *śraddhā* is "faith" as if equating the two without qualification would be unduly over-simplified, as will be made clear in the sequel; this is not what is intended in this wording. A serious question could be raised as to whether the concept *bhakti* is not a closer, richer, more cogent parallel to extant English-language notions of "faith" in its deepest senses (not as

belief, but as the quality of man's life in relation to God) than is any other Hindu concept, and especially than *śraddhā*. Should not it rather than this latter have been the primary focus of our attention in this study? The question demands care. The first consideration is that if the question were rather phrased, should not it *as well as* "śraddhā" be pondered, then the answer is clearly "yes", at least in theory. In practice, we do not wish to extend this present study, and do not pretend that it is exhaustive. Furthermore, the similarities mentioned between *bhakti* and English "faith" are evident, and have long been noted; major studies, even comparative studies, although they should unquestionably continue and greatly develop, have well begun. Of the considerable literature in this realm probably the best known is Otto's study, originally written in German, delivered as lectures in Sweden, and published first in Swedish, of which an English translation presently appeared. [Rudolf Otto, *Christianity and the Indian Religion of Grace*, Madras: Christian Literature Society for India, 1929.] The following year an enlarged version appeared in the original German, and thence in English with the title reversed: *Die Gnadenreligion Indiens und das Christentum, Vergleich und Unterscheidung*, Gotha: Leopold Klotz, 1930, and München: C. H. Beck, n.d.; *India's Religion of Grace and Christianity, compared and contrasted*, Frank Hugh Foster, trans., London: Student Christian Movement, 1930, and New York: Macmillan, 1930. Another example: Kurt Hutten, *Die Bhakti-Religion in Indien und der christliche Glaube im Neuen Testament*, Stuttgart: Kohlhammer, 1930 (E. Littmann und J. W. Hauer, edd., Veröffentlichungen des orientalischen Seminars der Universität Tübingen: Abhandlungen zur orientalischen Philologie und zur allgemeinen Religionsgeschichte, erstes Heft).

Of *śraddhā*, on the other hand, theologically sensitive studies in modern times, and especially of a comparative sort, are hardly to be found; I have felt that one might make a contribution, if only by calling attention to this rewarding area. The very similarity between *bhakti* and Western Christian, especially Protestant, interpretations of the life of faith (as well as the significant divergences) means that for the moment perhaps more is to be gained for fresh perspectives, and especially towards a generic concept for comprehending differences, by looking further afield. (Nonetheless, anyone, and especially theologians, writing on Christian, and especially Protestant, faith specifically, as distinct from generic conceptualizing, must surely take *bhakti* seriously if they are to write intelligently and intelligibly in modern times. See, e.g., John B. Carman, "Is Christian Faith a Form of Bhakti?", *Visva-Bharati Journal of Philosophy*, 1968, pp. 24-37 [2-15].)

Secondly, and more decisively: *bhakti* is definitely one of the Hindu forms of faith. Being explicitly one among others, and therefore specific, it does not so readily lend itself as a potential counterpart for the explicitly generic notion of faith for which we are seeking. Christian conceptions of faith have in practice been specific also, yet in principle universal: the Christian concept has classically never recognized itself as of one form of faith among others, as we shall be noting in our next chapter. Only in the nineteenth century did this begin, haltingly; and by that time the English-language term "faith" was also beginning to denote other forms as well as the Christian—even in Christians' own usage. It seems reasonable, accordingly, to use the English word "faith" for the new concept that the modern world will construct; whereas in Sanskrit other terms than *bhakti* will have to play this role. *Bhakti* has no such history, and no such probability of expansion, it being inherently aimed at specifying faith in one particular form as distinct from others. And it must continue to do so. (It is certainly notable that in its specificity it has been significantly closer to many specifically Christian understandings of faith than has any other concept in India, and than have most others in the world—even though Christians in India have generally chosen rather the term *viśvāsa* [our ref. 57 below] to render their own concept.)

Thirdly, and still more significantly (but also, more controversially), *bhakti* is inherently a relational term (its root *bhaj-* means "to participate", also to partake and to partition) and a theists', explicitly designating a sharing relationship with God; whereas we are concerned to attempt to satisfy the manward side of such relationships. *Bhakti* is a bilateral concept; we are concerned with a human quality, one that makes such relationships possible. It could be argued that a carrying through of our investigation will ineluctably lead to concepts such as *bhakti*, on this very score: that faith is nothing if not faith in some *x* (cf. our chap. 1, ref. 5 above). Perhaps. This may be finally true; but our preliminary endeavour is to elucidate not that "in *x*" but faith itself as a prior or distinguishable concept. This is precisely because, just as in India *bhakti* has been one "way" among others, so in human history at large faith has in fact appeared in many forms—and, it has been thought, with many "objects". The faith of early (Theravādin) Buddhists, as sought in our second chapter above, would hardly be called *bhakti*.

That having been said, let us however also call attention to the fact that although one may say that *bhakti* is a form of faith, one may *not* quite say that *bhakti* is a form of *śraddhā*. (The latter comes closer to being fractional to the former.) This demonstrates, if proof were needed, that *śraddhā* is a component of generic faith (as it is of specific *bhakti*), but is not that generic faith itself. Agreed. Ours is not a study of Hindu faith, nor of its self-understanding; except partially (cf. at our ref. 31 below). As indicated in the opening sentence of this note, our avowal that *śraddhā* is faith was not meant to equate the two so that the converse could also have been said, that faith is *śraddhā*.

On the relation between *śraddhā* and *bhakti*, see further below, our reff. 63-67.

On *bhakti* as the name given to an historical movement, the bibliography is very large; see §vi, "The Way of Devotion" in the chapter of Norvin J. Hein, "Hinduism" in Charles J. Adams, ed., *A Reader's Guide to the Great Religions*, New York: Free Press, and London: Collier Macmillan, [1965], 2nd edn., 1977, pp. 126-140. For a study of *bhakti* as a word and concept, see ref. 3 above and J. Gonda, "Het Begrip bhakti", *Tijdschrift voor Philosophie*, 10:[607]-660 (1948); and especially Part 1, "Etymology and semantics of *bhakti*", pp. [9]-23, 32-44 of Mariasusai Dhavamony, *Love of God according to* Śaiva Siddhānta, *a study in the mysticism and theology of Śaivism*, Oxford: Clarendon Press, 1971, which also has a good bibliography (p. [11], fn.), to which should now be added the section on "bhakti" in Suvira Jaiswal, *The Origin and Development of Vaiṣṇavism*, Delhi: Munshiram Manoharlal, 1967, pp. [110]-115; and Adalbert Gail, *Bhakti im Bhāgavatapurāṇa: religionsgeschichtliche Studie zur Idee der Gottesliebe in Kult und Mystik des Viṣṇuismus*, Wiesbaden: Harrassowitz, 1969 (Helmut Hoffmann, ed., Münchener indologische Studien, Band 6).

(Not pondered in this note, nor in others later on the matter, because I have not investigated the question, and yet probably decidedly worth investigating, is that the relation between *śraddhā* and *bhakti* as concepts in India must be understood also historically. My preliminary impression is that for many centuries, through and beyond the classical period, the salient notion was *śraddhā*; in mediaeval times *bhakti* was popularized, and to-day its name is perhaps the more current term in the realm that concerns us.)

26 Of course, one is not in a position to assert that in fact no Hindu has even written a study on *śraddhā*; but it does seem fair to suggest that no prominent Hindu thinker seems to have done so, or at least none is generally so recognized or reputed. No systematic, analytic, interpretive monograph has become well known in Sanskrit nor, so far as I am aware, in the mediaeval Indian languages. In modern English, in Western academic form, three Hindu writers figure in the bibliography given above at ref. 3. Of these, the double journal-article of Das Gupta (op. cit.) deals chiefly with the concept *bhakti*, but she does devote six pages (316-322) as well as part of her title to *śraddhā*; the doctoral dissertation of Seshagiri Rao was undertaken at my suggestion.

Unlike Hindus, the Buddhist movement in India allegedly produced one major work on this matter; but the allegation is dubious—although Indian Buddhists did indeed adopt and elaborate the term and concept *śraddhā* (Pali, *saddhā*) for their own purposes. Chinese sources state that an important Buddhist work on faith, one that has been highly influential in the history of that country and in Japan and is indeed a basic Mahāyāna text—namely, *Ta-ch'eng ch'i-hsin lun* ("great-vehicle faith-generating treatise": generally known in the West as *The Awakening of Faith in Mahāyāna*)—had a Sanskrit counterpart. Indeed a Sanskrit title, *Mahāyāna śraddhotpāda śāstra*, has been reconstructed for it, and widely accepted. One of two Chinese statements (one made in 597 A.D. by Fei Ch'ang-fang in his catalogue of Buddhist works *Li-tai san-pao chi*) averred that the work was a translation into Chinese from Sanskrit, the original being by Aśvaghoṣa (traditionally taken to be the famous first- or second-century Sanskrit court poet, a Buddhist convert of that name); this interpretation gained wide currency in East Asia. The other statement (made in the seventh century A.D. by Tao-hsüan, in his Lives of Eminent Monks,

Hsü kao-seng-chuan) averred that it was translated from Chinese into Sanskrit, by a leading Buddhist scholar well known for his translations in the reverse direction, Hsüan-tsang (602-664 A.D.), who " 'circulated it throughout all of India' " (Yoshito S. Hakeda, trans., *The Awakening of Faith attributed to Aśvaghosha translated, with commentary*, New York & London: Columbia University Press, 1967, Introduction, pp. 5-9: the quotation from Tao-Hsüan is from p. 9. Hakeda's Bibliography on this whole matter, pp. 119-122, is the most useful that I have seen). In any case, if this Buddhist work was ever extant in Sanskrit it has not survived nor has any Indian reference to it ever been found: it has clearly been unknown among Hindus. (There is some reason to believe a Sanskrit text more likely to have existed perhaps in Khotan than in India.)

27 Book 10, hymn 151.

28 Hacker, who has made the most thoroughgoing studies of the concept to date, calls faith "die selbstverständliche Voraussetzung" of all Hindu religious life ("Über den Glauben", 1954 [our ref. 3 above], p. 52). He goes on to indicate that by "faith" here (*der Glaube*) he intends both *āstikya* (*āstikya-buddhi*) and ("more often"—p. 55) *śraddhā*. Cf. further at our ref. 42 below.

29 And as *la foi*, *der Glaube*.

30 As should be expected, modern Hindu writers are particularly ready to feel hesitations about an equivalence with "faith" partly because of their special sensitivity to the Hindu overtones, partly because they are sometimes no more penetrating in their appreciation of the subtleties and depths of this Western term than are Westerners of Hindu spiritualities. Thus Das Gupta remarks that "authorities . . . would translate it, rather misleadingly, by the word 'faith' " (her "Śraddhā . . ." [our ref. 3 above], p. 316); and Seshagiri Rao, more cautiously, that "modern scholars, both Indian and Western, generally take *śraddhā* to mean 'faith' " but that it is "misleading to translate the word uniformly and without any qualification by the English word 'faith' " (his *Concept* [our ref. 3 above], pp. 2, 186). Hacker writes, on the one hand: "Das Wort, das in der philosophischen und religiösen Hindu-Literatur den Glauben meist bezeichnet, ist *śraddhā*" (his "*śraddhā*", 1963 [our ref. 3 above], p. 151), and on the other hand: "Wir müssen damit rechnen, dass *śraddhā* etwas ist, wovon wir keinen Begriff und wofür wir kein Wort haben" (ibid., p. 162). My suggestion here is that we would do well to make good this latter deficiency, by enlarging our conceptualizations.

31 However integral, it remains partial only. Of other Sanskrit terms that are germane, we have already mentioned a couple: especially *viśvāsa*, in addition to *āstikya*, and have considered *bhakti* (see above, our reff. 3, 25 and below, ref. 57). The "divergences" mentioned above are chiefly that *śraddhā* on the whole designates one step only in the life of faith. It would be wrong to see it as more; yet also, as less. It has to do with faith in human life more as a transforming act than as a transformed condition; it is more like *credo* than like *fides*, in the Christian case; more like *īmān* as a verbal noun (*maṣdar*) than as a generic or stative or abstract noun, in the Islamic case

(or, one might say, more like *īmān* in Arabic than like *īmān* in Persian or Urdu; or, one might also say, once the life of faith is under way, perhaps more like *nīyah*, even, than like *īmān*: cf. below, our ref. 46); it is more like *shinjin* than like *anjin*, in one of the Japanese Buddhist cases. We suggested in our opening chapter that "faith" might be tentatively taken as that human quality, whatever it be, that has (a) given rise to, and (b) been elicited, nurtured, and shaped by, the religious traditions of the world; *śraddhā* has perhaps more to do with (a) here than with (b)—though its continuity over time is a function of (b).

32 Seshagiri Rao, *Concept* (above, our ref. 3), p. 1.

33 Cf. Hacker, "*śraddhā*", 1963 (above, our ref. 3), p. 151 (et passim).

34 "[B]ehind all religious activities . . . the indispensable attitude is that of *śraddhā*. It is this attitude that gives an action its religious character. . . . *śraddhā* is the core of all religious endeavour"—Seshagiri Rao, *Concept* (above, our ref. 3), pp. 162, 163. "[D]ie *śraddhā* das eigentlich Religiöse am religiösen Tun des Hindu ist"—Hacker, "*śraddhā*", 1963 (above, our ref. 3), p. 157. These comments are induced by a consideration of the same Bhagavad Gītā passage: namely, 17:28, a verse that we, with reference to its negativity, adduce below, at our ref. 47.

35 I have written "almost without equivocation"; the word "almost" is out of deference to two recent scholars who (independently of each other?) have disputed a part of this otherwise well established etymology. All linguists are agreed that *śraddhā* in Sanskrit and in Vedic is from a primitive Indo-European **ḳred-dhē*, with cognate forms appearing in similar religious usage in Avestan, Old Persian, Latin, Old Irish, and certain other widely distributed dialects; and that **dhē* is indeed "put". The question is only as to whether *śrad-/*ḳred* is "heart". Most scholars have been persuaded that it is, seeing this Sanskrit form (rather than *hṛd*—see below) as directly cognate with the corresponding term for "heart" in virtually all languages of the Indo-European family (e.g., Greek *ḳardia*, Latin *cord-*, Lithuanian *šird-*, German *Herz*, English *heart*, etc.). The regular classical Sanskrit word for "heart" is, however, not this but *hṛd* (with *hṛdaya* and *hārd-*). The question in its detailed technicalities is intricate; I have had in mind the possibility of writing a journal article going into the etymological niceties. I have decided that neither is the matter worth pursuing carefully here, nor does my thesis in this present study need to be significantly affected because of these new considerations that are being adduced. For in effect the revisionist etymology could be seen as arguing that the first part of our compound (**ḳred-*, set forth as an otherwise unknown term) meant "heart" originally not in the literal anatomic sense, designating the visceral organ, but rather in the figurative sense in which we are using it here; that the compound signified "putting one's heart on" metaphorically, not actually. The new contention, then, even if it be etymologically valid, hardly modifies the argument that we are building upon the term. The metaphorical use of "heart" is so world-wide and so established in religious usage (not only in the Indo-European languages but also in Chinese [*hsin*], Japanese [*ḳoḳoro*],

the Semitic [*qalb*, *lēbāb*/*lēb*, etc.] among others) that one might almost wonder whether it is even legitimate to call the metaphysical sense metaphorical, as if it were secondary. (In the Christian case, cf. Christ's saying [based on Aramaic, but then made public in Greek and become current in all the languages of Europe], "Where your treasure is, there will your heart be also" [Matthew 6:21 = Luke 12:34]; and for one of many Islamic instances, cf. our ref. 59 below.) In English, there are two separate words, "mind" and "brain" to designate the metaphysical and the anatomical facets of our thinking (not all languages have counterpart pairs), and the relation between the two has been canvassed; there are not two different words, however, for the metaphysical and the physical aspects respectively of what we designate by "heart". (Nor do all languages, by any means, make the distinction on the metaphysical level between "mind" and "heart", between thinking and feeling: in the cultural history of the world it has probably on the whole been much more common that the word for anatomical "heart" has been used also for "mind". How parochial is the Romantic distinction, the polarity, between mind and heart—however much that distinction, even that polarity, have in their own realm played a profound and significant role. It is interesting to speculate on the untranslatability of Bourdillon's forceful poem, "The Night Has a Thousand Eyes"! (Cf. also below, our chap. 5, ref. 41.)

For the potentially four thinkables, mind, brain, organ of feeling, organ of pumping blood, relatively few languages have four distinct terms. Most coalesce at least two of them into one concept, or one name, and many do this with three; but which two or which three are conceptualized or verbalized together varies with the culture and the century. Too, the links between and among them vary. Aristotle linked the first and the fourth; India, China, the Islamic world, and often the West have tended on occasion to interrelate the first and the third; the modern West homonymizes the third and the fourth but does not converge them in its thinking, which tends towards approximating rather the second and third; and so on. And of course other anatomical items have been and continue to be conceived as involved.

Of the two recent dissenters from the received etymology as to heart, Benveniste has advanced the additional consideration that semantically inherent in the term **ḳred* (underlying Sanskrit *śrad*) is a notion of reciprocity: so that in placing **ḳred* one lends, rather than gives, one's support, confidence, loyalty to a deity or person in the sense of expecting or requiring a return. That this expectation or requirement of a reward is linguistically intrinsic in the actual term and inescapable, rather than a culturally or religiously added element, is stated rather than evidenced in the article, and to me seems unproven; although it is an interesting suggestion.

Pokorny, who enters *śraddhā* and its cognates under the Indo-European word for "heart", only to go on to remark that it does not properly belong there (without giving his reasons), in effect admits in passing that in the Zarathushtrian case the Avestan form of our word (*zrazdā*: "faith") was felt by those who used it to mean "putting the heart on", "giving one's heart to", although he feels that they were wrong in doing so, saying that they themselves connected it with their word for "heart" (*zërëd*) by "folk etymology" (p. 580).

See Julius Pokorny, *Indogermanisches etymologisches Wörterbuch*, Bern & München: Francke, 2 Bände, 1959-1969, 1:579-580; and Émile Benveniste, *Le vocabulaire des institutions indo-européennes; 1, économie, parenté, société*, [Paris]: Éditions de Minuit, 1969, chap. 15, "Créance et croyance", pp. 171-179. The standard etymology, with which I also have (tentatively) aligned myself, pending further investigation, is set forth, with bibliographical references, in Manfred Mayrhofer, *Kurzgefasstes etymologisches Wörterbuch des Altindischen* . . . , Heidelberg: Carl Winter Universitätsverlag, several volumes, 1956- , in process, Lieferung 22, 1970, [3]: 386-387. Mayrhofer writes, "es ist unnötig, ein anderes Etymon für **ḱred°* zu suchen", but in an added footnote takes note of the 1969 Benveniste thesis as something implicitly too recent for him to wrestle with. "The Night has a Thousand Eyes" by Francis William Bourdillon; e.g., in Arthur Quiller-Couch, ed., *The Oxford Book of Victorian Verse*, Oxford: Clarendon Press, 1925, p. 744. For Aristotle on the physical heart as the seat of the intellect see John I. Beare, *Greek Theories of Elementary Cognition from Alcmaeon to Aristotle*, Oxford: Clarendon Press, 1906, pp. 328-331.

See further below, our ref. 38 and our chap. 5, reff. 25, 26.

36 E.g.: 1:55:5 / 1:103:3 / 1:103:5 / 1:104:7 / 8:75:2 / 10:147:1. Also, in a famous Indra hymn it is found in one form of the refrain: *śrad asmai dhatta sa janāsa indraḥ* (2:12:5). For this the translation "Believe in him; he, O men, is Indra" (Das Gupta, "Śraddha . . ." [above, our ref. 3], p. 320 as well as earlier scholars) strikes me—in the current sense of "believe"—as incongruous. (It would be possible to see it as merely ambiguous, if "believe" here were perhaps to be taken in the old way as meaning "have faith and confidence in": not like "believe in fairies" but like "believe in hard work".) Surely, as the last three words imply, and indeed proclaim, his existence is quite taken for granted. Is the meaning, rather, not reasonably well expressed by taking the words literally, so that the point is one of urging that Indra be taken seriously. Put your heart on him; pay heed to him; make him your concern, the focus of your attention.

The full verse is as follows:

yaṃ smā pṛcchanti kuha seti ghoram
utem āhur naiṣo astītyenam
so aryaḥ puṣṭīr vija ivā mināti
śrad asmai dhatta sa janāsa indraḥ

Ṛg-Veda 2:12:5

With regard to Indra's existence being presupposed: it is straightforward enough to read the words *naiṣo asti* here as meaning not "he does not exist", but "he is not present", "he is not to hand", along the lines of *kuha seti* in the first line (cf. Heesterman, "Origin" [our ref. 3 above], pp. 180, 181). Indeed, to read them otherwise might (given the tenor of the whole poem) be dubbed a turn-of-our-century bias?

Sāyaṇa ad loc. exegetes *śrad asmai dhatta* as *viśvāsam atra kuruta*. This may be rendered as "place confidence in him". (For further discussion of *viśvāsa*, cf. below our ref. 57).

For both text and commentary, both here and in subsequent citations hereafter, I have used F. Max Müller, ed., *Rig-Veda-Samhitâ: the Sacred Hymns of the Brâhmans, together with the commentary of Sâyanâkârya*, 2nd edn., London: Oxford University Press, 4 voll., 1890-1892, except that in the case of vol. 2 only the unrevised first edn. was available to me (*Rig-Veda-Sanhita . . . Sayanacharya*, London: William H. Allen, 1854), and in that case I have accordingly checked all passages cited here also against the edition of vol. 2 of the Vedic Research Institute, Tilak Mahārāshtra University: *Ṛgveda-saṃhitā, śrīmatsāyaṇācāryaviracitabhāṣyasametā*, n.p.: Vaidika-Saṃśodhana-Maṇḍala, Śaka 1858/1936 A.D. The passage from the Indra hymn cited is to be found in vol. 2, pp. 469-470 (=Tilak, vol. 2, p. 47), and the other passages, respectively: 1:279-280; 1:455; 1:455-456; 1:459; 3:517-518; 4:463-464.

For further discussion of Vedic occurrences, and a somewhat different interpretation, cf. Hermann Oldenberg's remarks in his article "Vedische Untersuchungen", §4, *śraddhā*, in *Zeitschrift der deutschen morgenländischen Gesellschaft*, 50:448-450 (1896), and in his *Die Religion des Veda*, [Berlin: Hertz, 1894], 3 und 4. Auflage, Stuttgart & Berlin: Gotta, 1923, pp. 373, 566-567; and, more recently, Köhler, "Śraddhā . . ." (our ref. 3 above). These see the enthusiasm that is *śraddhā* as perceived by the priests in quite non-transcendentalist terms (enthusiasm for the ritual, expressing itself in a crass generosity towards its functionaries). In other religious communities too, faith has sometimes been perceived by the interested as measurable in terms of support, even financial support, for the religious establishment; yet I doubt that the word "faith" has ever *meant* simply that to anyone. (One may prefer, therefore, the more sensitive wording of Bloomfield: "The *s*raddhâ is 'faith, religious zeal,' that makes the sacrificer liberal to the priests"—rather than that it *is* that liberality—in his commentary on Atharva-Veda 9:5:7:5 [a "Prayer to appease . . . the demon of grudge and avarice": pp. 172-173], in Maurice Bloomfield, trans., *Hymns of the Atharva-Veda together with extracts from the ritual books and the commentaries*, Oxford: Clarendon Press, 1897, [F. Max Müller, ed., The Sacred Books of the East, vol. 42], p. 424.)

37 Most strikingly, of course, in the hymn to Śraddhā, 10:151; and otherwise 1:102:2 / 1:108:6 / 7:32:14 / 8:1:31; also in a more complex compound (*śraddhāmana*) 2:26:3 / 10:113:9. The past participle *śraddhita* occurs 1:104:6.

38 In post-Vedic Sanskrit, *śrad* is never found except in our combination with *dhā*. The traditional view would hold that in all other contexts it was replaced (and indeed, with one exception—Ṛg-Veda 8:75:2 [ed. cit. (our ref. 36 above), vol. 3, p. 518], where it is problematically associated with *kṛ*—that it had already been replaced in Indo-Iranian) by the alternative forms *hṛd* (and its related forms *hṛdaya* and *hārd-*). As we have seen, it has recently been argued (cf. our ref. 35 above) that the latter constitutes not an alternative form, but is *the* Sanskrit word for "heart" in the literal anatomical sense (and, one must add, in most metaphorical or metaphysical senses). The

fact is that neither *śrad* nor *hṛd* in Sanskrit is altogether clear, etymologically; let alone the relation between them. The primitive-Indo-European word for "heart", namely **k̑ered*, **k̑erd*, **k̑hērd*, etc. (our ref. 35 above) would have come out in Sanskrit as *śard* or *śṛd*. *Śrad* is close to this, but not precisely right. The *hṛd* forms are presumably from a primitive form **ghṛd-*, **ghērd*, for which there is no other evidence and which Pokorny calls a *Reimwort* (*Wörterbuch* [our ref. 35 above], p. 580) for the other. Similarly, Dandekar calls *hṛd* "merely a rhyme-word" for what "properly speaking . . . should have been *śṛd*": see R. N. Dandekar, "Hṛd in the Veda", in Vishva Bandhu [sc. Shastri], ed., *Siddha-Bhāratī, or, the Rosary of Indology: Presenting 108 original papers on Indological subjects in honour of the 60th Birthday of Dr. Siddheshwar Varma*, 2 voll., Hoshiarpur: V. V. R. [sc., Vishveshvaranand Vedic Research] Institute, P & P [sc. Printing & Publication] Organisation, I, 1950 (Vishveshvaranand Indological Series, 1) pp. [137]-142, esp. p. 141; cf. also p. [137], fn. 1.

39 Cf. our ref. 49 below. See Seshagiri Rao, *Concept* (our ref. 3 above), p. 177 ("Laukika"); and the dictionaries.

40 The elaborate and complex studies of this concept (our ref. 3 above), especially those of Hacker, are of course valuable, indeed immensely helpful, and it would be churlish to criticize them; yet they seem to me to have become unduly complicated by including the object of *śraddhā* in the consideration of the various usages and then exploring the resultant modalities of faith in their intricate variety, in such a way as to obscure what is common to all and is relatively simple. In favour of my thesis here that the notion is inherently simple, stands the fact, otherwise strange, that Indian thinkers over the centuries have indeed taken it for granted, have tended to treat it as a relatively self-evident, self-explanatory notion. If, as I suggest, *śraddhā* means just what it says ("to put the heart on"), then the point ceases to be puzzling that it has been used so widely and with so little analytic scrutiny.

Seshagiri Rao does say (the first sentence of his "Conclusion"; *Concept* [our ref. 3 above], p. 176): "In our investigation, we have seen that the etymological or derivative meaning of the word *śraddhā* (*śrat*, heart; and *dhā*, to place; that is, the placing of one's heart on something) continues to be relevant throughout". He goes on, however, without developing this. One might even remark that the two elements on which he does then concentrate—to long for a desired end, and to trust an appropriate means thereto—might have been synthesized by saying that *śraddhā* is to put one's heart on something in the sense not of desiring passively, inertly, but in the more apt sense which the English phrase also tends to imply, of desiring actively, of desiring-and-going-after. To set one's heart on a prize is not merely to reflect quietly that it would be nice to have it, but more resolutely is to orient oneself towards winning it.

Hacker's typology of ritual *śraddhā*, intellectual *śraddhā*, etc., has clearly been influenced by his prior mental association of faith with intellectual content (an association from his modern Christian heritage), and the Western tendency to define faith in terms of its object. This comes out in that his first article on this subject was on faith in Hindu thought, starting with the Western concept and treating various Sanskrit terms that more or less correspond to it, and only subsequently did he turn to the Hindu term itself, using an Indian word as his starting point. (Hacker, 1954: "Über den Glauben" [*sic*] "in der Religionsphilosophie des Hinduismus"; but 1963: "*śraddhā*". [Above, our ref. 3.] He comments in the second sentence of his latter article about this difference.) It comes out also in his remarking in the later study that intellectualist faith we in the West understand readily; but that it is all the more difficult for us to understand ritual faith (1963, p. 158). I would suggest that neither is the one so easy, nor the other so hard. If we can understand *śraddhā* at all we can understand it in all its Hindu forms. For it is not (as the concept "faith" has misleadingly tended to become recently in Christendom) a primarily intellectualistic concept.

41 About half-way along in its history thus far the Western Church developed a view of faith as one of the "virtues", following classical conceptualizations, with the further view, then, of it and them as having each a particular "object" in a scholastic sense now foreign to the language and thought of most moderns; in recent times a speaking of faith's having an "object" has continued (although not other virtues'), with the meaning having developed in drastically new fashions. This important matter is considered somewhat in my *Belief and History* (above, our chap. 1 here, ref. 4); see esp. pp. 94-95.

42 Cf. Hacker, 1954 (our ref. 3 above), p. 52: "Denn Glaube ist für den Hindu zwar die selbstverständliche *Voraussetzung* für jede intellektuelle, emotionale oder rituelle Beziehung zur Gottheit oder zum Heile, aber er ist noch nicht diese Beziehung selbst". He goes on in the next sentence, however, to quote with approval Lacombe's characterizing it as an *ausseres Mittel*, which I would find a whit misleading if one allowed oneself to interpret this as a "means", instrumentally. Lacombe's wording is *moyen extrinsèque*; does this, or the German, lend itself to a less utilitarian, more "mediating" sense than that English term? Lacombe's full discussion tends to support our present thesis: see Olivier Lacombe, *L'Absolu selon le Védânta: les notions de Brahman et d'Atman dans les systèmes de Çaṅkara et Râmânoudja*, Paris: Geuthner, 1937, pp. 348-350. Admittedly, Lacombe notes that *śraddhā* is not a participation in God—is not *jñāna*; and in effect too, this signifies, is not *bhaḳti*. In the Christian terms that he also adduces, his argument amounts to noting that it is more like *credere* than like *fides*. Yet he sees it as involving explicitly a sincere conversion of the soul, and as eschewing any selecting for oneself of spiritual means (or, intermediaries).

43 My paragraph in the text here is perhaps too anthropocentric; too traditionally Western? Its phrasing may seem to postulate an atomistic individualism, and to suggest too unilaterally that faith is something that man takes the initiative in launching. I prefer to stress that it is a quality of his and her life, or person (of their humanity). There is a question, answered variously within each tradition, as to whether man's relatedness to a transcendent other follows upon, or is a function of or is correlated with, or precedes, his transcending of himself, and/or his capacity to transcend himself; and indeed

whether the distinction between other and self here is not itself misleading. Any conceptualization that we generically achieve must allow such questions to be canvassed. On this entire matter, although my understanding of Heidegger is feeble, yet perhaps it is not unfair to see some parallel between the *śraddhā* concept and one of that thinker's major concerns: the primordiality of man's relatedness. Heidegger sees man not as a separate being who enters into relationship with the world around him; rather, he sees that relationship as original, with man and Being each constituted by the inherent quality of being interrelated, for which the philosopher struggles to find words. He launches as a technical term ("as little translatable a key term as Greek *logos* or Chinese Tao"—p. 101) the virtual coinage *das Er-eignis* (100ff; cf.: "Das Ereignis vereignet Mensch und Sein in ihr wesenhaftes Zusammen"—p. 103). He speaks also of the "Zusammengehörigkeit" of man and Being (90ff.); of "ein Zueinander" (96), of "einander an-gehen" (99), "einander in ihrem Wesen erreichen" (102), "einander übereignen" (97; cf. 94, 95), and of "diese Übereignung" (97), "ein . . . Vereignen und Zueignen" (100). Indeed he defines man in terms of this "relationship of responding": "Der Mensch *ist* eigentlich dieser Bezug der Entsprechung. . . . Im Menschen waltet ein Gehören zum Sein" (94). (For him, a philosopher despite himself in the Greek tradition, man's relation to reality is primarily through rational thinking, *Denken*; indeed, the *Zusammengehörigkeit* mentioned above is introduced first as between Thought and Being, and the whole lecture begins with a fragment of Parmenides on the identity of *νοειν* [*noein*] and *εἶναι* [*einai*]. In India, the relation of man to reality is certainly affirmed in terms of knowledge, yet hardly of thinking, and other ways for man's realization of that relation are also canvassed.)

(These quotations are all from his 1957 lecture "Der Satz der Identität", Freiburg, in Martin Heidegger, *Identität und Differenz*, Pfullingen: Günther Neske, 1957. I have used the German text in Martin Heidegger, *Identity and Difference*, [edited], translated and with an Introduction by Joan Stambaugh, New York, Evanston and London: Harper & Row, 1969, pp. [77]-146.

Turning in quite another direction, might one also tease oneself with speculating on a possible comparability at some level perhaps between this general point and the Buddhist *anatta* doctrine?

44 In what follows, only a few passages will be cited to which this interpretation is illustratively applied. The statement in the text is based, however, on reading, in addition to other passages that I have come upon myself, also each of the Sanskrit passages assembled in the studies listed at our ref. 3 above. This includes all instances where the term occurs, in any of a variety of forms, in the Ṛg-Veda, and especially (Hacker) in mediaeval philosophic texts and commentaries. I have found no instance where a notion of "putting the heart" is not relevant and appropriate; and several instances where it has seemed to me more apt for shedding light than other translations proffered. A detailed full-length study of *śraddhā* passages, setting forth this thesis and exploring its technical and other implications, is something to which I have had hope of perhaps some day turning my hand.

45 For "Faith as ultimate concern", and more elaborately and precisely, "Faith is the state of being ultimately concerned" (respectively, the title of the opening section, and the opening sentence, of this work), see Paul Tillich, *Dynamics of Faith*, [New York: Harper, 1957] (Ruth Nanda Anshen, ed., World Perspectives Series, vol. 10), New York: Harper—Harper Torchbooks, 1958, p. 1. (See also the entire first chapter, "What Faith Is"). See also Paul Tillich, *Systematic Theology*, Chicago: University of Chicago Press, 3 voll., 1951-1963, 3:129-138, esp. pp. 130-134. There is ambiguity in Tillich's usage as to whether the phraseology intends concern with what is in fact ultimate in the universe and human life—namely, God—or with what particular persons rightly or wrongly actually concern themselves with surpassingly. He himself recognizes this ambiguity: on the subjective and objective meanings of the terms or the formal and material definitions, see ibid., 3:130. On faith as, rather, just plain concern, "caring", see our ref. 50 below.

46 In the Islamic case, for instance, the observance of all prescriptions and full participation in all proper Islamic life, when done without faith (without *īmān*), are designated *nifāq* (usually translated "hypocrisy"); the person who acts appropriately but does so without faith is *munāfiq*. This is a heinous sin, for which the unequivocal recompense is Hell fire. The Word of God is fundamentally an imperative, and man's role is to obey; yet to act obediently without faith is utterly vapid. Another way of phrasing this might be to say that the primary and ultimate command to mankind is to have faith, to be faithful, to live oriented and committed to the service of God (ultimate reality, Truth); the detailed additional injunctions then take on significance only in relation to that general and prior orientation. Accordingly, with regard to those specific acts of obedience, another parallel in the Islamic case that might be propounded is to the concept rather of *nīyah* ("intention"). The Islamic scheme is so unified that it tends to be in terms of the over-all coherent whole that acceptance and rejection are conceptualized—in, respectively, *īmān* and *ḳufr*; this is a situation that presents a certain degree of typological divergence from the Hindu more atomistically articulated complex. Accordingly, while an individual action Islamically can be executed with or without *īmān*, yet another parallel to the specific situation envisaged in the Gītā verse quoted in our next note is perhaps provided in the Islamic precept *al-a'māl 'alá al-nīyah* ("deeds depend upon intention"), crystallizing the thesis that the religious validity of any action is a function of the (purity of) intention with which it is performed. If one's heart is not in it, a Muslim might well say, in accordance with this precept, any *'amal* (deed) is, to use the Gītā term, *asat*, bogus. Indeed, I find an entrancing exactitude of similarity between the Arabic maxim just cited and the Bhāgavata Purāṇa dictum that the merit reward of an act is in proportion to faith (*śraddhānurūpaṃ phalahetuḳatvāt*: 8:17:17). Comparable instances from other traditions come readily to mind, also.

References: The Islamic precept cited (also in the forms *innamā al-a'māl bi-l-nīyah* and . . . *bi-l-niyāt*) is found in virtually all the Ḥadīth collections and all the law books, as well as regularly elsewhere. As would be expected, Ghazzālī's is one of the engaging treatments: he has devoted to the topic Chapter 1 (*fī al-nīyah*) of Book 7 (*kitāb al-nīyah wa-al-ikhlāṣ wa-al-ṣidq*—"Book of Intention, of Sincerity, and of Truthfulness") of Part 4 of his *Iḥyā'*, where he develops what might be called a virtually sacramentalist position, with the man of faith's every act on earth performed in vivid relation to God. My edition is Abū Ḥāmid al-Ghazzālī, *Iḥyā' 'Ulūm al-Dīn*, Cairo: Lajnat Nashr al-Thaqāfah al-Islāmīyah, 16 voll. in 5, 1356-1357 h. [=ca. 1937-1938 A.D.], where this section is pp. 2694-2717 (=14:154-177). In English, see the article (1935) of A. J. Wensinck, s.v. NĪYA in the first edn. of *The Encyclopaedia of Islām*, Leiden: Brill, and London: Luzac, 4 voll. & Suppl., 1913-1938, 3:930-931; reprinted in H. A. R. Gibb and J. H. Kramers, edd., *Shorter Encyclopaedia of Islam*, Leiden: Brill, 1953, pp. 449-450.

For the Bhāgavata Purāṇa, I have used the 1866 A.D. edition of Bombay: Gaṇapati Kṛṣṇajī, 1788 (Śaka). An English version is available in J. M. Sanyal, trans., *The Srimad-Bhagbatam of Krishna-Dwaipayana-Vyasa, translated into English prose from the original Sanskrit text*, Moti Jheel, p.o. Dum Dum (Bengal): Datta Bose & Co., n.d., 3:179, who renders this, "The measure of recompense must suit with the measure of reverence cherished for me"—with which as a statement Ghazzālī (understanding "me" differently, of course) would heartily agree.

47

aśraddhayā hutaṃ dattaṃ
tapas taptaṃ kṛtaṃ ca yat
asad ity ucyate pārtha
na ca tat pretya no iha
(17:28)

Literally: "Without *śraddhā*, oblation made, something donated, austerity practised, something done, such is unreal (untrue, non-existent), it is said, O son of Pṛthā: such a thing is nothing—neither hereafter, nor here".

(On the form of this verse, we may note in passing that it illustrates two points developed below, our ref. 61. First, the *śraddhā* compound is the first word, and receives marked emphasis thereby; second, it is in the instrumental case, is being used adverbially.)

48 A Christian analogy, whose parallels and whose divergencies are both provocative, comes also to mind, from the famous thirteenth chapter of I Corinthians. There, however, it is *agapē* (ἀγαπη), "charity", rather than the usual Christian term for faith (πιστις [*pistis*]) that St. Paul uses, when he says: "Though I bestow all my goods to feed the poor, and though I give my body to be burned, and have not charity, it profiteth me nothing . . ." (I Corinthians 13:3).

It is interesting to speculate on the degree to which a comparison might be entertained between what "charity" used to mean and what *śraddhā* has meant. To be related to a person in charity is to recognize that person as of high intrinsic worth, and to treat him or her as of high worth. (Latin *caritas* is from *carus*, valued, cherished, dear in the sense of high-priced, literally precious). Cf. our next two reff. *Agapē* has come to be translated recently rather as "love", although then a distinction allows itself to be drawn between it and *erōs* (ἔρως); might one toy then with comparing that distinction with a distinction between *śraddhā* and *bhakti*? On an element of "desire" in *śraddhā*, however, cf. below, our ref. 56; and *bhakti* can be thought of as the state of union to which the devotee (aspirant?) aspires. Yet one may note that some Hindus have dissented from making a distinction between *śraddhā* and *bhakti* (cf. below, at our reff. 63-65); and some Christians, from polarizing ἀγαπη and ἐρως (for instance: M. C. D'Arcy, *The Mind and Heart of Love—Lion and Unicorn: a study in Eros and Agape*, London, Faber and Faber, [1945], 1947; esp. chap. 2 "Eros and Christian Theology", pp. 54-83).

49 Sāyaṇa exegetes our term with such notions as *bahumānaṃ kuruta* and *ādarātiśaya*. The former, *bahumāna*, is "attaching great importance to, having major regard or respect for, having a high opinion of". The latter word is a compound of *atiśaya*, "pre-eminent", "surpassing", "outstanding", and *ādara*, "respect, regard, notice; care, trouble, interest". Thus the idea of *śraddhā* as paying attention to, being concerned with, is heightened with superlatives. Illustrative examples: ad Ṛg-Veda 1:103:5 and 3 respectively. Müller edn. (above, our ref. 36), vol. 1, pp. 456, 455. The latter recurs at 1:108:6 / 8:1:31 / 10:151:3, etc. (vol. 1, p. 474 / 3, p. 231 / 4, p. 470).

50 Cf. Mayeroff, "On Caring", *International Philosophical Quarterly*, 5: [462]-474 (1965). This engaging article was subsequently expanded into a short book: Milton Mayeroff, *On Caring*, New York: [Harper & Row, 1971 (Ruth Nanda Anshen, ed., World Perspectives, 43)], Harper & Row, Perennial Library, 1972. In any age other than our own, and in any culture other than the Western, this sensitive and humane exposition would have been quite self-consciously and explicitly what in any case I should propose considering it to be unconsciously, humanistically: namely, an analysis (partial, no doubt, as ever; yet serious and illuminating) of faith. In the book, there is towards the end a brief sub-section "Faith" (pp. 83-85); although quite incidental, it does have the merit in passing of speaking of this quality not in relation to the beliefs of other centuries or other cultures but as an essential human characteristic. Similarly, what the author calls "caring" and I should call "faith" is here (as has been the case in other centuries and other cultures) presented in relation to humankind and to knowledge; in contradistinction from the latter, and supplementary to it. (As with classical accounts in other cultures and centuries, a relation to belief is not canvassed.) The concept "faith" having got somewhat lost in his culture, he can write that caring "has been the subject of very little philosophical reflection", as he does in his second sentence (he discriminates between what he himself intends by the term ["an important way of living"] from Heidegger's *Sorge*—p. [462] of the journal article, fn.; and does not consider other ages or civilizations). This follows his important opening statement: "Caring like knowing . . . is an activity whose understanding is central to the understanding of man" (ibid., p. [462]).

51 In Bhagavad Gītā 4:39 we read:

śraddhāvāṃl labhate jñānaṃ
tatparaḥ saṃyatendriyaḥ

Tatparaḥ (literally: having that as ultimate) means that one is concerned only with that (Edgerton [above, our ref. 5] translates "intent solely upon it"); and *saṃyatendriyaḥ* (literally: with the sense-organs drawn in tight, held under close control) means that one suppresses interest in other, potentially competing, claims upon one's attention. Supreme knowing, these lines may be rendered as affirming, is attained by a person with that sort of faith.

The former word, similarly, is found at a less reflection-oriented level when Sāyaṇa on Atharva-Veda 6:122:3 exegetes *śraddadhānāḥ* with *karmānuṣṭhāna-tatparā* (below, our ref. 84; as we shall see, we may render him as averring here that the man of faith is he for whom the performance of ceremonial works is of primary importance or concern).

With this Gītā verse, and with Ghazzālī's *nīyah* (our ref. 46 above), might one compare Kierkegaard's "Purity of heart is to will one thing"? (This was one of his "Edifying Addresses" [*Opbyggelige Taler*, København, 1847]; I do not read Danish and have consulted Søren Kierkegaard, *Purity of Heart is to Will One Thing: spiritual preparation for the office of confession, translated from the Danish with an introductory essay by* Douglas V. Steere, New York: Harper's, [1938], 1948; Harper Torchbooks, 1956.)

52 *anyatramanā abhūvam*. This scriptural quotation is as usual not identified by Śaṅkara himself. Actually the phrase (as indeed its entire context) is found twice: as Śatapatha Brāhmaṇa 14:4:3:8 and as Bṛhadāraṇyaka Upaniṣad 1:5:3. Of the Brāhmaṇa, however, this (final) sector occurs in the Mādhyandina recension (*śākhā*) only, not in the Kānva; and it is the latter with which Śaṅkara was familiar (on which he wrote his commentary—as he did on this Upaniṣad). Accordingly, we may take it that he is referring here to Bṛh. Up. 1:5:3. For it, I have used the edition in the Ānandāśrama Sanskrit Series, #15: *Bṛhadāraṇyakopaniṣat . . . Śāṃkarabhāṣyasametā*, Mahādeva Cimaṇājī Āpaṭe, ed., Puṇe: Ānandāśrama Mudraṇālaya, Śaka 1813/1891 A.D. For the Brāhmaṇa: Albrecht Weber, ed., *The White Yajurveda*, Berlin: Ferd. Dümmler, and London: Williams and Norgate, 1855; Part II, The Çatapatha-Brâhmaṇa, p. 1055. For the full Śaṅkara passage, the reference is given in our next note, immediately below.

53 And specifically, with a mind that is distracted by external sense objects. Our whole paragraph paraphrases a passage (given below) in the commentary of Śaṅkara on Chāndogya Upaniṣad 6:12:2. This Upaniṣad has a section (chap. 6, parts 8-16), each part of which culminates in a refrain that includes the now world-famous asseveration *tat tvam asi*: "That which is this subtle essence—that, this all has as its soul. That is truth/reality. That is the Soul. That art thou . . . ". (Some prefer to translate *ātman* here as Self rather than Soul.) One of the parts sets forth that the great banyan tree grows from the invisible subtle essence underlying the seed, and immediately before the above refrain it concludes: "Good child, have *śraddhā*" (*śraddhatsva somya*).

The verse as a whole reads as follows: *Taṃ hovāca yaṃ vai somyaitam aṇimāna na nibhālayasa etasya vai somyaiṣo 'ṇimna evaṃ mahānyagrodhas tiṣṭhati śraddhatsva somyeti* (—6:12:2). Śaṅkara's exegesis of the final clause runs as follows:

> *śraddhatsva somya sata evāṇimnaḥ sthūlaṃ nāmarūpādimatkāryaṃ jagad utpannam iti. yady api nyāyāgamābhyāṃ nirdhārito 'rthas tathaivety avagamyate tathā 'py atyauta-sūkṣmeṣv artheṣu bāhya-viṣayāsaktamanasaḥ svabhāva-pravṛttasyāsatyāṃ gurutarāyāṃ śraddhāyāṃ duravagamatvaṃ syād ity āha śraddhatsveti. śraddhāyāṃ tu satyāṃ manasaḥ samādhānaṃ bubhutsite 'rthe bhavet tataś ca tad arthāvagatiḥ. "anyatramanā abhūvam" ityādi śruteḥ.*

For text and commentary I have used the following edition, in the Ānandāśrama Sanskrit Series, #14; *Chāndogyopaniṣat . . . Śaṃkarabhāṣyasametā . . .*, Vināyaka Gaṇeśa Āpaṭe, ed., Pune: Ānandāśrama Mudraṇālaya, 1856 Śaka/1934 A.D.; pp. 373-374. (Other texts read *saumya* rather than *somya.*) A literal translation of the passage is available in Ganganatha Jha, *The Chāndogyopaniṣad* (*a treatise on Vedānta philosophy translated into English with the commentary of Śaṅkara*), Poona: Oriental Book Agency, 1942, pp. 347-348.

The use here two or three times of *avagam-* (to arrive at, to obtain, to come to know, to comprehend) with *dur-avagam-* (difficult to grasp), and the general tenor of the passage, illustrate that the point under consideration is taken as valid, not uncertain, and its truth is recognized, not opined. The point at issue is not of believing it but of understanding it. Cf. our earlier discussion, above, our reff. 8, 9. This is one of the rare instances where *śraddhā* is construed with an *iti* ("that") clause.

54 Bhagavad Gītā 4:40 follows the verse quoted above at our ref. 51 (on those with faith who attain), by contrasting the opposite case, of those without faith who fail:

> *ajñaś cā 'śraddadhānaś ca*
> *saṃśayātmā vinaśyati*
> *nā 'yaṃ loko 'sti na paro*
> *na sukhaṃ saṃśayātmanaḥ.*

Saṃśaya here is usually translated as "full of doubt", "doubting" (so Edgerton, Zaehner, opp. citt. [our ref. 5 above]); but the root *sam-śi* means to be in doubt not in the sense of doubting as distinct from believing, primarily, but rather to hesitate, to be irresolute, to be confused (literally, to lie together).

Of *saṃśayātmā* (*-manaḥ*) here, then, an almost literal translation is the modern psychiatric term "ego-diffusion". This verse might be rendered: "He who is without awareness, and without faith, is ego-diffused, he perishes: Neither the mundane nor the transcendent world is [his], nor happiness". Hence our next sentence in our text.

55 To live without faith is to live with a congeries of interests in disarray, of concerns none of which is, as Tillich might say, ultimate.

56 The suggestion of desire in *śraddhā*, noticeable in some current secular usage, is from time to time made explicit also in religious. One example: Sāyaṇa on Ṛg-Veda 1:103:3 (ed. cit. [above, our ref. 36], vol. 1, p. 455) expounds *śraddadhānaḥ* as *ādarātiśayena kāmayamānaḥ*, "desiring with surpassing interest". Comparably, this same commentator, on the Taittirīya Brāhmaṇa, uses the word *abhilāṣa*, "desire" (so Das Gupta [above, our ref. 3], p. 318, although she gives *abhilāsa* for *abhilāṣa*). The word *śraddhā* is frequently associated also with the verb *iṣ-*, *icchati*, to seek, search after, desire. Two examples are Sāyaṇa on Ṛg-Veda 10:113:9 (ed. cit., vol. 4, p. 379) and on Śatapatha Brāhmaṇa 2:2:2:5 (Rao, [above, our ref. 3], p. 22). Another is Bhagavad Gītā 7:21, *bhaktaḥ / śraddhayā 'rcitum icchati*, where it is no less probably *icchati* than *arcitum* that *śraddhayā* modifies ("a devotee seeks with faith worshipfully to praise"). Further, in the Śaṅkara passage given above (our ref. 53) from his Chāndogya commentary, it could be argued that a notion of desiring (as well as of paying attention) is not absent, as is hinted for instance by the words *āsakta* (the contrasting orientation of being attached to worldly affairs) and *bubhutsite 'rthe* (the "desired" object).

57 From Sāyaṇa on, the explanation is not uncommon of *śraddhā* by *viśvāsa* (Sāyaṇa on Ṛg-Veda 2:12:5—cf. our ref. 36 above). Cf. also Mahīdhara on the Vājasaneyi Saṃhitā of the Yajur-Veda, 8:5 and 19:30. (Rao [above, our ref. 3], p. 5; Das Gupta [ibid.], p. 318). *Viśvāsa* is confidence, trust in, reliance upon, fearlessness about. Mahīdhara's further comment, then (ad 18:5—locc. citt.) that *śraddhā* is *paraloka-viśvāsaḥ* may be rendered as: faith is one's ability to count on the transcendent. (Etymologically, one might almost aphorize that faith is one's ability to breathe freely in an environment of transcendence . . . !)

For a rather different relation to *viśvāsa*, cf. our comment on the important Rāmānuja definition of *śraddhā* below, our ref. 82; although there *viśvāsa* has a proposition as object, and comes closer therefore to "believing", or perhaps "recognizing". *Viśvāsa* was the term chosen by the Christian missionaries to render their concept of faith; whether the choice was a wise one or not is an entrancing question. Perhaps (cf. our next two chapters below) by the time this rendition was being made, faith was on its way to being conceptualized in the West as belief, as well as *viśvāsa*'s being on *its* way towards "belief" also in India.

58 Indeed, the "Conclusion" of Seshagiri Rao's investigation (above, our ref. 3) is, in brief, that *śraddhā* "comes to mean: (i) a longing of the heart or yearning for some end; and (ii) confidence or trust in some 'means' which can lead to the desired end. . . . both these implications are inherent in and integral to the concept. . . . To take either of these meanings (viz, desire or confidence) and leave the other is to deprive the concept of its special significance in Indian religious thought . . . *śraddhā* involves both a desire for a goal and confidence in an appropriate means to reach it" (p. 176).

59 Twice in the Bhagavad Gītā this quite charming point is tacitly made,

of the linkage between faith and cheeriness, the contrast between *śraddhā* and *asūya*:

> *ye me matam idaṃ nityam*
> *anutiṣṭhanti mānavāḥ*
> *śraddhāvanto 'nasūyanto*
> *mucyante te 'pi karmabhiḥ*
>
> *ye tv etad abhyasūyanto*
> *nā 'nutiṣṭhanti me matam*
> *sarvajñānavimūḍhāṃs tān*
> *viddhi naṣṭān acetasaḥ* (3:31-32)

Again:

> *śraddhāvān anasūyaś ca*
> *śṛṇuyād api yo naraḥ*
> *so 'pi muktaḥ śubhāṃl lokān*
> *prāpnuyāt puṇyakarmaṇām* (18:71)

Asūya is ill-will, anger, is the attitude of rejection (like Islamic *kufr*: not any mere "disbelief" or even indifference, but a definitely "anti-" mood), but can also mean (as most interpreters take it here) murmuring, begrudging. The term tends to be used in cases where out of some vice such as jealousy a man is unhappy at the good fortune of another, or is deprecatory of what is in fact worthwhile. It is not, then, an altogether neutral term, but tends to imply a negative attitude to a positive object. Admittedly, the explicit contrast here in chapter 3 of the Gītā is between, on the one hand, persons of faith who are (also? or, therein?) *an-asūya*, non-complainers, and who follow the teaching, and, on the other hand, persons (presumably without faith, and with *asūya: abhyasūyān*) who do *not* follow it. Nonetheless implicit is an absence of applause for any who might follow the teaching but do so in a vexed or recalcitrant fashion: without *śraddhā* and with, instead, *asūya*. At least, I get from these passages the clear suggestion that a person who followed the Lord's teaching but did so not cheerily, but "murmuring", irked that the truth is the way that it is, would fall short of *mokṣa* (liberation/salvation). The grudging belief (even: recognition) of some religious men that something is true but one wishes that it were otherwise, that something is good or incumbent but one wishes that it were not, may be compliance but it is not yet faith. Faith is in part the capacity to rejoice that ultimate truth, transcendent reality, is as it is. An interesting contrast is the rare, and indeed rather deliberately paradoxical use of πιστις [*pistis*] in one passage in the New Testament for the devils who also recognize the truth but tremble: και τα δαιμονια πιστευουσιν και φρισσουσιν (James 2:19). They are not *anasūya*, though they have πιστις. They do not have *śraddhā*, I am suggesting; just as Christian orthodoxy has held that they do not have saving faith. (This New Testament passage is touched on again in our next chapter, below, and is discussed at length in my *Belief and History*.)

The *anasūya* or rejoicing element in faith has its witnesses in other communities also. A parallel understanding is suggested by, for instance, certain Islamic positions, exemplified in Ibn Taymīyah: "Faith is not constituted merely by assent and commitment, but these must be accompanied by 'works of the heart'. Thus . . . loving what God has commanded man to do and disliking what He has forbidden are among the special characteristics of faith".

A similar position is set forth by Aristotle, for whom virtue involves a being delighted with what is good, and not merely the doing of it. Moral virtue, he affirms, has to do with what one finds pleasurable and what painful. (*Nicomachean Ethics,* 2:3—1104b). He offers as an illustration: ". . . he who refrains from bodily pleasures, and who is happy in doing just that, is a temperate person, whereas he who is bothered by it is self-indulgent. Again, he who stands firm against things that are threatening and is glad to do so, or at least is not pained, is a brave person, whereas he who is pained is a coward" (loc. cit., lines 5-9).

As often in these matters, the classical Chinese instance sets forth rather a graded evaluation: "The Master said, To prefer it is better than only to know it. To delight in it is better than merely to prefer it" (*The Analects of Confucius*, 6:18, Waley trans.).

References: I. Bywater, ed., *Aristotelis Ethica Nicomachea*, Oxonii: E. Typographeo Clarendoniano (Scriptorum Classicorum Bibliotheca Oxoniensis), [1894], 1962, pp. 26-27. Ibn Taymīyah: *al-īmān* (above, our chap. 3, ref. 32), p. 290. Arthur Waley, trans., *The Analects of Confucius*, [London: Allen & Unwin, 1938], New York: Random House, Vintage, n.d., p. 119.

60 It needs to be stressed, perhaps, that this, although I have called it a "facet" of the general position, is explicit only on occasion and becomes then *śraddhā* in one particular orientation rather than generally. One might call it, then, one type of faith (among others). As clear an illustration of it as any is Bhagavad Gītā 17:17:

> *śraddhayā parayā taptaṃ*
> *tapas tat trividhaṃ naraiḥ*
> *aphalākāṅkṣibhir yuktaiḥ*
> *sāttvikaṃ paricakṣate*

("This three-fold asceticism, executed with pre-eminent faith by persons not desirous of fruits, disciplined, is named *sāttvikā* [truly spiritual]").

This passage is crucial in illustrating that *śraddhā*—and indeed *śraddhā* of the most excellent type (*parayā* here)—characterizes, at least on occasion, men unattached to the fruits of their actions, men seeking no reward. This, therefore (and the spirit of the passage is hardly exceptional), dissuades me from accepting without more ado the view (e.g., as advanced by Seshagiri Rao in our ref. 58 above, and others) that *śraddhā* inherently involves a conviction that a given means will lead to a given end that is desired. (Contrast, however, our citation at ref. 82 below of Rāmānuja, where the instrumentalist word *sādhana*, "means", is indeed used.) Some might hold it theoretically possible, perhaps, to construe *aphalākāṅkṣin* in the Gītā verse above as *aphala/ākāṅkṣin*, "desiring fruitlessness", as well as *a/phalākāṅkṣin*, "not desirous-of-fruit"; but I find this quite unlikely. There would seem to me a tension between the view that *śraddhā* is the confidence or trust or even the belief that the ritual act or whatever will "work", and the often-observed position that precisely this attachment (non-detachment) vitiates it. Faith is the capacity to recognize and to live sincerely in terms of cosmic purposes rather than one's own.

61 In the Bhagavad Gītā, I calculate that when used as a noun, our term occurs in the preponderant majority of instances (almost three to one) in the instrumental (adverbial) case ([*a-*]*śraddhayā*: 6:37 / 7:21, 22 / 9:23 / 12:2 / 17:1, 17, 28); and further that its occurrence in adjectival compounds ([a-] *śraddadhāna*, *śraddhāvān*, etc.: 3:31, / 4:39, 40 / 6:47 / 9:3 / 12:20 / 17:3, 13 / 18:71) is again more than three times as frequent as its use as a noun except instrumentally, adverbially. Striking also, I find, is the frequency (over half) with which the term occurs as the first word in the verse or hemistich in which it is found; its use is emphatic.

62 Taking it as if it were an item, integrated in each different system, is what has puzzled and, if I may suggest so, misled several modern observers, who have had to interpret it therefore in a variety of ways so as to let it be a coherent ingredient in each disparate pattern within the Hindu complex: intellectualist, devotionalist, ritualistic, mystical, or whatever. (The relevance of this consideration for the comparative study of religion generically bears pondering.)

63 Another way of putting this point would perhaps be, that some Hindus have used the term *śraddhā* to verbalize also what they and other theists mean by *bhakti*. Madhusūdana's commentary on Bhagavad Gītā 7:21 is cited for an equating of the two (Hacker, 1963 [above, our ref. 3], p. 151). Similarly Sāyaṇa on Atharva-Veda 4:30:4: "*śraddha* is *bhakti*" (*śraddhā bhaktiḥ*). Viśvabandhu et al., edd., *Atharvavedaḥ (Śaunakīyaḥ) sa ca padapāṭhena ca Sāyaṇācāryakṛtabhāṣyeṇa . . . saṃpāditaḥ*, Hoshiarpur: Vishveshvaranand Vedic Research Institute, 4 parts in 5 voll., 1960-1964 (Vishvesharanand Indological Series, 13-17), 1:519.

64 This is a common view, against which careful scholars feel impelled to write. Hacker speaks of "Die hin und wieder begegnende Behauptung, die *śraddhā* stehe besonders der Bhakti nahe" (1963, p. 151), and Das Gupta is at pains to write that "even [*sic*] in later [sc. post-Vedic] literature *śraddhā* is not always used synonymously with *bhakti*" (p. 322). This latter writer had dismissed Sāyaṇa's equating of the two (our previous ref., just above) as "obviously inadmissible" (Das Gupta, p. 319, fn. 1). Hara, similarly: "The two terms are often treated as synonymous, but a careful philological study will show their fundamental difference" ("Note", p. [124]. For Hacker, Das Gupta, and Hara here, see our ref. 3 above.)

65 An identifying of *bhakti* with *śraddhā* is expressly denied in, for ex-

ample, Śāṇḍilya, Bhaktisūtra 24, on the grounds that *śraddhā* is common (*naiva śraddhā tu sādhāraṇyāt*)—to *jñānins*, *karmins*, *yogins*, as well as *bhaktas*, whose way is superior to these (verse 22). All religious persons have *śraddhā*, only the best have *bhakti*, is the argument here. Besides this, it is further contended, to identify *śraddhā* and *bhakti* would lead to an infinite regression (*tasyāṃ tattve cānavasthānāt*—verse 25): as the commentators (e.g., Svapneśvara) explain this, the point is that *śraddhā* is a subordinate or ancillary part (*aṅga*) of *bhakti*. Similarly to this last, the late-mediaeval *bhakta* Rūpa Gosvāmī makes *śraddhā* an *aṅga* of *viśvāsa* (cf. our ref. 57 above) on the way towards *bhakti*. The Śaṅkara characterization cited in our ref. 67 just below might be seen as implying that, contrariwise, *bhakti* is subordinate to (is *aṅga* of) *śraddhā*.

References: *Śrīḥ Bhakti Mīmāṃsā, Śrī Śāṇḍilya Ṛṣi praṇītā . . . Ācārya Svapneśvara viracitena Bhāṣyeṇa saṃyutā* . . . Bombay: Śrī Veṅkaṭeśvara Mudrāyantre Ankitā, 1809 Śaka/1944 Saṃvat, pp. 15-16. For Rūpa Gosvāmī: Bon Mahārāj, ed. & trans., *Śrī Rūpa Gosvāmī's Bhakti-Rasāmṛta-Sindhuh: Sanskṛta text with Devanāgarī script, with transliteration in English, and English translation with comments*, Vrindaban: Institute of Oriental Philosophy, n.d. [sc. 1965], vol. 1, p. 201.

66 This goes back to the Gītā (e.g., 6:47—*śraddhāvān bhajate yo mām*, "he who with faith is devoted to me"); and is standard in much of later *bhakti* literature. See Rao (our ref. 3 above), p. 174; cf. Hacker, 1963 (ibid.), pp. 154-155. Cf. our reff. 63-65 just above.

67 *śraddhā . . . āstikyabuddhir bhakti sahitā*. This formula occurs in his exegesis of Bṛhadāraṇyaka Upaniṣad, in the section (3:9:20-25) where it is being set forth that the visible forms, life-generative matter, the truth (*satyam*), and also faith (3:9:21) are dependent upon, are firmly supported by, dwell steadfast in (*pratiṣṭhitāni bhavanti*) the heart—and indeed, the heart alone (*hṛdaye hy eva*). Ed. cit. (above, our ref. 52), p. 484. (It may be noted that "heart" here is explicitly interpreted by Śaṅkara as what Westerners would call the mind: namely, the two discriminated organs *buddhi* and *manas* together—ibid., p. 483, commentary on 3:9:20. Cf. above, our reff. 23, 35.)

68 "The Uncommitted" is the title of a recent study of American undergraduates (Kenneth Keniston, *The Uncommitted: alienated youth in American society*, New York: Harcourt, Brace & World, 1965). There would seem little question but that, if this book were to be translated into Sanskrit, the most telling rendering of its title would be, precisely, *Aśraddhāvantas*.

69 As mentioned above, there has been a secular (*laukika*) use of *śraddhā* as well; it has not been investigated by scholars but would presumably be relevant here. Modern scholarly interest in *śraddhā* religiously has confined its attention explicitly to the term as used in religious texts (cf. the bibliography at our ref. 3 above). One may wonder whether this has not perhaps introduced a religious/secular split into the inquiry that reflects present-day concerns rather than classical and mediaeval Indian usage. If not speculating as to whether inquiry might show a divergence of meaning in the two spheres

hardly to have obtained, I have at least a hunch that a comparative study of all usages, religious and secular, would prove rewarding. It is not clear to me from looking at usage in religious literature that writers conceived the human quality of *śraddhā* to be of an inherently distinct sort when operating in the religious sphere. This too would explain the absence of Hindu treatises specifically on *śraddhā* as a religious matter, despite its importance religiously. The putting of the heart on this or that is something that people naturally do; religious writers concerned themselves with the all-important "what" in the religious case, but noted in passing that that "what" is nonetheless not activated into significance for men and women "if their heart is not in it". The modern writers who have explored religious *śraddhā* have been instigated, clearly, by the Western concept of "faith" with its (almost) exclusively religious orientation. This point is becoming invalid, however, I would suggest, even in the West, when faith is coming to be lost not only in the religious sphere but also in the secular. Cf. our reff. 50, 68 above, and the penultimate paragraph of this present chapter, below. Between the secular and the religious, in the modern West, stands philosophy, where a loss of faith in transcendence has not only brought the metaphysical tradition, some would say, to an end but has made its past formulations appear "meaningless".

70 "*śraddhā* or faith, is not acceptance of a belief. It is striving after self-realization by concentrating the powers of the mind on a given ideal. Faith is the pressure of the Spirit on humanity, the force that urges humanity towards what is better. . . . Cp. Plato: 'Such as are the trend of our desires and the nature of our souls, just such each of us becomes'" (and there is a footnote reference to *Laws*, 904c)—Radhakrishnan, in *The Bhagavadgītā: with an Introductory Essay, Sanskrit text, English translation and notes by* S. Radhakrishnan, London: Allen & Unwin [1948], 5th Impr., 1958, p. 343. He is commenting here on the Gītā verse (17:3) that is discussed at our next reference.

The Greek whose translation he cites here reads (from Book 10 of the *Laws*): *ὀπῃ γαρ ἀν ἐπιθυμῃ και ὀποιος τις ὠν την ψυχην, ταυτῃ σχεδον ἑκαστοτε και τοιουτος γιγνεται ἁπας ἡμων ὡς το πολυ.* I have used the Scriptorum Classicorum Bibliotheca Oxoniensis edition, Ioannes Burnet, ed., *Platonis Opera*, Oxford: Clarendon, 5 voll. [1900-1907], vol. 5, 1962 imp. On the "striving" matter he might equally well have cited the Athenian's preceding remark to the Cretan, Clinias (903c): "of these [various parts of the universe as a totality], one also, dull fellow, is thine own part, which, however little it be, yet is striving towards the whole, ever facing in that direction; but thou hast forgotten . . ."—*ὡν ἑν και το σον, ὠ σχετλιε, μοριον εἰς το παν συντεινει βλεπον ἀει, καιπερ πανσμικρον ὀν, σε δε λεληθεν* . . . (Burnet, op. cit., 903c).

71 Bhagavad Gītā 17:3:

yo yacchraddhaḥ sa eva saḥ

72 I have not succeeded in tracing the exact source of this English verse,

which lodged itself in my consciousness when I heard it long ago as a boy. The Platonic doctrine that each human being tends towards becoming what he or she loves has been developed into a strong strand running through some of the history of Western and especially Christian thought and life. Our particular wording seems to be a direct translation from the version of the German-Polish mystic Johann Scheffler, who wrote under the pseudonym Angelus Silesius. In his *Cherubinischer Wandersmann* [1675; rev. edn. of Ioannis Angeli Silesii, *Geistreiche Sinn- und Schlussreime*, Wien: J. J. Kürner, 1657], entry 200 of Book 5 reads (in a modernized-German text, to which alone I have had access):

Mensch, was du liebst, in das wirst du verwandelt werden.
Gott wirst du, liebst du Gott, und Erde, liebst du Erden.

Angelus Silesius, *Sämtliche poetische Werke*, Hans Ludwig Held, ed., München: Carl Hanser, 3te Aufl., 3 Bde., 1949-1952, 3:163. (A different English rendering is found in Angelus Silesius, *Selections from* The Cherubinic Wanderer, *translated with an introduction by* J. E. Crawford Flitch, London: Allen & Unwin, 1932, p. 131, entry 100; cf. p. 225.)

73 Aitareya Brāhmaṇa (Pañcika 7:10:4 = Adhyāya 32:9:4): *śraddhā patnī satyaṃ yajamānaḥ. śraddhā satyaṃ tad ity uttamaṃ mithunaṃ, śraddhayā satyena mithunena svargāṃl lokāñ jayati.*

The imagery of the opening four words here is of the ceremonial Vedic sacrifice, performed by a priest in the presence of a couple; normally, the wife must be present, but the husband is called the *yajamāna*, the "sacrificer" in the sense of the one who pays for the proceedings and on whose and whose wife's behalf it is done, to whose benefit it redounds. I would translate, then: "Faith is the wife, truth the husband at whose behest the sacrifice is performed. Faith, truth: that is the supreme conjunction. With faith and truth coupled, one wins the heavenly worlds". (This passage occurs in a section where the problem is being discussed of what happens in the ritual if a man's wife has died or has become unavailable.)

A link between *śraddhā* and *satyam*, faith and truth, although not usually presented with such dramatic force, yet is a suggestion that, even if occasional and minor, is recurrent in the literature. Such a link is apparent already in the Ṛg-Veda: cf. 1:108:6 and 9:113:2, where the two terms are found in juxtaposition. Further, in Bṛhadāraṇyaka Upaniṣad 6:2:15, one reads *ye cāmī araṇye śraddhāṃ satyam upāsate* (ed. cit. [above, our ref. 52], pp. 777-778), which has been variously translated: of the two accusatives, one or other is, presumably, the object, but the remaining one can then be in apposition to it or taken adverbially. One possible way of taking it is, "And also those who in the forest revere (esteem) *śraddhā* as truth". Hume, on the other hand, (see below), offers "and those too who in the forest truly worship faith", and Radhakrishnan (also see below), "and those too who meditate with faith in the forest on the truth". This last follows Śaṅkara.

More teasing, Sāyaṇa in his commentary on Ṛg-Veda 1:55:5, interprets *śrad* as equivalent to ("a name for") truth (*śrad iti satyanāma*—edn. cit. [above, our ref. 36], vol. 1, p. 280). The one occurrence in Sanskrit of the word *śrad* without *dhā-* (namely, Ṛg-Veda 8:75:2: *śrad viśvā vāryā kṛdhi*, a somewhat perplexing construction) also elicits from Sāyaṇa the explication: *śrat satyāni, kṛdhi kuru* (ed. cit., vol. 3, p. 518)—that is, to "do *śrad*" means to do those things that are true. Similarly, Uvvaṭa and Mahīdhara in their commentaries on the Vājasaneyi Saṃhitā of the White Yajur-Veda, ad 8:5 and 19:30, again interpret *śrad* as synonymous with "truth" (*satyanāma*). (Miśra edn. cit., our ref. 21 above, vol. 1, p. 364 and vol. 2, p. 993.) Also, Das Gupta ([above, our ref. 3], p. 321; cf. Rao [ibid.], p. 5) cites the early grammarian-commentator Yāska (his *Nirukta* 3:13 with reference to *Nighaṇṭu* 3:10; cf. also *Nirukta* 9:30 with reference to *Nighaṇṭu* 5:3) as setting forth this same position. I must confess that I do not clearly understand what is being affirmed in this equivalence. These points might perhaps be interpreted as offering some support for something like the Pokorny-Benveniste thesis (above, our ref. 35)?

This much, at least, one may take from all this: that the tradition has encouraged Indians to associate the two ideas, *śraddhā* and *satyam*: to think in terms of their giving their heart to, directing their faith towards, what is true and genuine.

Apart from this link, there is the other convergence, of faith with knowledge, of which also the note is heard, though quietly. An example: in Chāndogya Upaniṣad 1:1:10 it is said, of those involved in religious observances, that some do so knowing what they are doing, others not so knowing; and it goes on to state that what is done "with knowledge and with faith" (also, with *upaniṣad*; we may for the moment leave that unexplored) is better: implying that faith accompanies knowledge, either in the sense of being in some fashion equivalent to it (understanding what one is doing) or, more probably, as an added quality. As in the New Testament (cf., for instance, I John 4:16, where "having faith" follows upon "knowing"; see my *Belief and History*, p. 84), and as in the Islamic case (above, our chap. 3, esp. at reff. 15, 26), so here (and Śaṅkara, our ref. 79 below), faith is not a believing what one does not know, but a doing or becoming something in relation to what one does know. This may here mean nothing more than knowing plus paying close attention (cf. above at our reff. 49-53) to what one knows; the order of the two remains significant. In full: one acts with knowledge, faith, and *upaniṣad* (*vidyayā karoti śraddhayopaniṣadā*). The last term is hardly univocal, and need not detain us, but the general sense is that in performing any ritual observance, one should know what it means, should take it seriously (or take it to heart; appropriate it interiorly, plan to act upon it?), and (perhaps?) should indeed meditate upon it in total reverence. Some could argue, given the full verse, that knowing is here seen as involving these two.

Quotations are given as from the following editions. Ānandāśrama Sanskrit Series #32, Kāśīnātha Śāstrī Āgāśe, ed., (Hari Nārāyaṇa Āpaṭe, publ.,) *Aitareya Brāhmaṇam, Śrīmat Sāyaṇācāryaviracitabhāṣyasametam* . . . , Pune:

Ānandāśrama Mudraṇālaya, 2 voll., Śaka 1818/1896 A.D., vol. 2, p. 830. Robert Ernest Hume, *The Thirteen Principal Upanishads, translated from the Sanskrit with an outline of the philosophy of the Upanishads*, London, &c: Oxford University Press, [1921], 2nd edn., revised, [1931], 1971, p. 163. S. Radhakrishnan, *The Principal Upaniṣads*, (above, our ref. 22), p. 314. Chāndogya Upaniṣad: ed. cit. (our ref. 53 above). Of the Aitareya Brāhmaṇa there is an English translation as follows: Arthur Berriedale Keith, *Rigveda Brahmanas: The Aitareya and Kauṣītaki Brāhmaṇas of the Rigveda, translated from the original Sanskrit*, Cambridge, Massachusetts: Harvard University Press, 1920 (Charles Rockwell Lanman, ed., Harvard Oriental Series, vol. 25); this passage is p. 297.

74

dṛṣṭvā rūpe vyākarot satyānṛte prajāpatiḥ
aśraddhām anṛte 'dadhāc chraddhāṃ satye prajāpatiḥ

—Vājasaneyi Saṃhitā of the White Yajur-Veda, 19:77 (Miśra edn. cit., our ref. 21 above, vol. 2, p. 1027.)

75 *śraddhayā tat-kathāyāṃ ca kīrtanair guṇakarmaṇām*—Bhāgavata Purāṇa 7:7:31. I have used the following edition: Śrimadbhāgavata Bhāṣā Tīkā, Varāṇasi: Paṇḍita Pustikālaya Rājādaraṇāja—Saumarurām Gauriśaṃkara Prays ["Press"] [1952], f. 113. For elaboration of the meaning, see below, our ref. 77.

76 "Amahl and the Night Visitors". RCA Victor Records, LM 1701. New York, 1952.

77 All tales are false, vacuous, unreal, that are not told to the glory of the Lord; that speaking alone is true, that alone is for our well-being, that alone is auspicious, in which He is being spoken of, is being extolled; what is sung in praise of the Lord is alone joyful, beautiful, ever new, that alone is the perpetual great feast of the mind; that alone dries up men's ocean of affliction —we are told in Bhāgavata Purāṇa 12:12:48-49. This illuminates, explains, *śraddhā kathāyām* (ibid., 7:7:31; our ref. 75 above), a phrase the spirit of which is surely better rendered by a modern Hindu translator as "a reverential hearing of the recital" (J. M. Sanyal) than by "believing in the stories" (cf. the use of *glauben*, if this be what is intended by that word in a German rendering of the passage).

I press this point a little, this being a minor but illustrative instance of the major matter of moment for our world, as to the distinction between faith and belief even in regard to "stories".

References: Bhāgavata Purāṇa, edn. cit. (our ref. 75 above). For the English cited: J. M. Sanyal, trans., *The Srimad-Bhagavatam of Krishna-Dwaipayana Vyasa, translated into English prose from the original Sanskrit text*, 3rd edn., Calcutta: Oriental Publishing Company, n.d., vol. 3, p. 33. (Cf. 2nd edn., vol. 5, p. 283, for 12:12:48-49.) Paul Hacker: " 'der Glaube an die Geschichten' (an den Mythus von Viṣṇu)", in his *Prahlāda: Werden und Wandlungen einer Idealgestalt—Beiträge zur Geschichte des Hinduismus*,

Teil 1, Wiesbaden: Franz Steiner, for the Akademie der Wissenschaften und der Literatur in Mainz, 1959 (Abhandlungen der Geistes- und Sozialwissenschaftlichen Klasse, 1959-Nr. 9), p. 661 [p. (145), 43].

78 In an address (The Massey Lectures, 2nd series) given over the Canadian radio network CBC, 1963. Subsequently published as Northrop Frye, *The Educated Imagination*, Toronto: Canadian Broadcasting Corporation, 1963, p. 24, and Bloomington: Indiana University Press, 1964, p. 64.

79 *buddhi . . . niścayātmikā.* —from the *Sarvavedāntasiddhāntasārasaṃgraha*, previously attributed to Śaṅkara but now thought to be one of his pupils, rather; verse 210. The full couplet runs:

> *guru-vedānta-vākyeṣu buddhir yā niścayātmikā*
> *satyam ity eva sā śraddhā ni dānaṃ mukti-siddhaye.*

Each of the subsequent seven verses, also, includes the term *śraddhā*, and the whole is worth careful reading. A translation of the full passage will be found in Hacker, 1954 (above, our ref. 3), pp. 56-57—but again, I take the liberty of asking to be allowed to dissent from his rendering, especially of the first part of verse 210 as "Glaube ist die entschiedene Meinung dass die Aussprüche des Lehrers und der Upaniṣaden wahr sind". I should prefer "entscheidende" to "entschiedene", but am especially unhappy about "Meinung" with a *dass* clause: the Indian author is speaking here about a recognition of truth, not about an opinion on problematic propositions. At least, I offer my interpretation in our text as a more accurate rendering of the meaning of the Sanskrit as understood both by the person who wrote it and by most Hindus who over the centuries may have read it. Literally: "That awareness of the words of the teacher or of the scripture (Vedānta) whose essential quality is resolve, decision—that is *śraddhā* . . . ".

Śaṅkara himself, similarly, at one point remarks that it would on the face of it be impossible for those who know (*sic*) what they ought religiously to do but do not do it, to be called persons "endued with faith" (*śraddhayā 'nvitāḥ*)—his Gītā commentary, ad 17:1.

In my translation of the *āstikya-buddhi* definition of faith presented above, perhaps my word "awareness" is a whit too passive, *buddhi* implying rather something of an active or deliberative judgement, a process with a coming to a conclusion, passing a verdict. Yet the objective validity of that conclusion, the rightness of the verdict, are here presumed. Reverting, then, to our earlier, literalist, metaphor, maybe one should speak of awaking to these truths rather than awakeness to them: if not simply an awareness of how things are, maybe a coming to a recognition of that. The word "realization" might, then, serve: faith is here being presented as that decisive realization that the words of one's spiritual teacher or of the sacred books are indeed true. "Decisive" here means: leading to decision—a responsive, self-involving engagement.

This is no negligible definition of faith. And one may be forgiven for finding not without interest the fact that it could be appropriated as its stands by Christians, Muslims, Jews, Buddhists, and others. In the Islamic case, for instance, the almost exact convergence of this with classical Muslim expositions of faith as *taṣdīq* (above, our chap. 3, ref. 15) is arresting.

References: For the *Sarvavedāntasiddhāntasārasaṃgraha* I have used the following edition: H. R. Bhagavat, ed., *Minor Works of Śri Śaṅkarācārya*, Poona: Oriental Book Agency, [1925], 2nd edn., 1952 (Poona Oriental Series, #8), where this passage is p. 148. For Śaṅkara's Gītabhāṣya, edn. cit. (above, our chap. 2, ref. 11), where this passage is p. 240; cf. in the Eng. trans. cit. (ibid.), p. 427.

80 Matthew 7:24, 26. Explicitly, in the Gospel parallel the differentiation is in terms of the overt behaviour, and I do not wish to minimize that; but I am suggesting that positive overt behaviour presumably presupposes on the part of the person who, "like a wise man", undertakes it, a prior attitude of self-commitment, a decision to get involved. It is this to which the Vedāntins and many other Hindus give the name *śraddhā*.

81 See above, our chap. 3, reff. 15, 16.

82 Rāmānuja, commentary on Bhagavad Gītā 17:2: *yatra rucis tatra śraddhā jāyate śraddhā hi "svābhimataṃ sādhayaty etad" iti viśvāsapūrvikā sādhane tvarā*. "Where there is something attractive, there śraddhā is generated. Given the confidence that a particular religious path does indeed lead to one's goal, *śraddhā* is then one's eager setting out upon that path". More literally: "*śraddhā* is the eager pursuit of a (religious) system, a prior element in which [eagerness] is the confidence that this [system] will effectively lead to one's goal".

On the first five words, compare the Gospel: "Where your treasure is, there will your heart [*sic*] be also" (Matthew 6:21 = Luke 12:34).

I have used the following edition: *Śrīmad Bhāratāntargatā Śrīmad Bhagavadgītā Śrīmad Rāmānujācāryakṛtabhāṣya sametā*, Kalyāṇa-Muṃbarha: Śrī Kṛṣṇādāsātmaja Gaṃgāviṣṇu, 3rd edn., Śaka 1824/1959 Saṃvat, p. 261 (but see caveat below). English translations will be found in A. Govindāchārya, trans., *Ṣrī Bhagavad-Gītā with Ṣrī Rāmānujāchārya's Viṣishtadvaita-commentary, translated into English*, Madras: Vaijayanti Press, 1898 ("Faith is indicated where there is a display of enthusiasm shown for a work lovingly undertaken with the belief that the object for which it is undertaken will be successfully fulfilled"—p. 502) and in Johannes Adrianus Bernardus van Buitenen, *Rāmānuja on the Bhagavadgītā: a condensed rendering of his Gītābhāṣya with copious notes and an introduction, Academisch Proefschrift . . .*, 's-Gravenhage: Ned. Boek- en Steendrukkerij, n. d. [1953?], p. 159 ("A man has faith in that act for which he has a preference. Faith is the zeal in executing the means to fulfil a desire; so it presupposes confidence"). For a German version see Hacker, 1963 (our ref. 3 above), p. 159.

Regarding the Sanskrit text, it should be noted that I have not felt it requisite to accept this editor's punctuation; other modern scholars seem to treat *vāsanā ruciśva*, here set forth as the last two words of this sentence, as rather the first two of the sentence following (thus, as correlates of *śraddhā* rather than as further predicates of it). It would mean too elaborate an excursus to tease out the meanings involved in the one reading: it changes nothing in what we have proposed, but adds to it an unlikely, even if engaging, possible new predication. The relation of *vāsanā* to faith is no doubt a significant question; for a comment in passing, see below, our next chap., ref. 41.

83 Or, being; or, believing; or whatever.

84 The affirmation "persons full of faith enter [or: serve] this [heavenly] world" (*etaṃ lokaṃ śraddadhānāḥ sacante*) is found in Atharva-Veda 6:122:3 and (with slight variation of context) 12:3:7. As he comes to the first of these passages Sāyaṇa exegetes *śraddadhānāḥ* as *śraddhāvantaḥ āstikyabuddhiyuktāḥ karmānuṣṭhāna tatparā janāḥ*—"persons of faith who are fully endowed with *āstikya-buddhi* and for whom the carrying out of the ritual actions is their chief concern" (cf. our ref. 51 above). Similarly, according to Das Gupta ([above, our ref. 3], p. 320), Sāyaṇa "in another place in the same text"—which I have not succeeded in locating—explains *śraddhā* in almost the same terms, as *tad-anuṣṭhāna-viṣayā āstikya-buddhiḥ*. Das Gupta, evidently as a modern skeptic about ritualism, takes this latter phrase (or both phrases) as signifying "a belief in the efficacy of ritualistic worship" (loc. cit.), whereas the same Sanskrit words could equally well be rendered as an awareness, or recognition, of its propriety, or obligatoriness. Actually, a literal translation would be "that positive awareness that manifests itself in the performance of" those ritual actions, which is then another instance, presumably, of *śraddhā* as a faith that actively engages, a theoretical knowing that eventuates in doing. This might be seen as constituting one more example (cf. also our ref. 9 above) for the modern hermeneuticist of an interpreter's draining the transcendence out of another man's, or era's, position before apprehending it.

References: *Atharvaveda*, edn. cit. (ref. 63 above), vol. 2, p. 836; vol. 3, p. 1466.

85 *Śraddhā* is the first step on the path to any worthy goal, including that of understanding: the concern, the intent, to know precede knowing. For Śaṅkara, cf., e.g., above, at our ref. 53; for Thomas Aquinas, cf. below, our chap. 5, at reff. 52, 53; for John Locke, cf. my *Belief and History* (above, our chap. 1 here, ref. 4), its p. 83, at ref. 19. One may compare also the ὀρεξις [*orexis*] of the famous opening sentence of Aristotle's *Metaphysics* (980:21): Παντες ἀνθρωποι του εἰδεναι ὀρεγονται φυσει—"All human beings are so constituted that they are moved to reach out towards knowing". This too is faith. (W. Jaeger edn., Oxford: Clarendon Press, [1957], 1963, [Scriptorum Classicorum Bibliotheca Oxoniensis], p. 1.)

Chapter 5

1 The substance of our first sentence in the text, that "the faith of Muslims classically would be rightly understood . . . as something different from their belief, . . . although not unrelated to it", was held by classical Muslim theorists, in theology; in addition to this one must note that many of the Ṣūfī mystics in their own way set forth a position that approaches our second sentence as well. In fact, it is in no insignificant part from a study of their writings, particularly their poetry in Persian (and to a less extent, in Urdu), that I have myself

come to the understanding developed in the thesis of this book. Nonetheless, it would be irresponsible to make a statement of the kind in our second and fourth sentences without engagement. Accordingly, I may be permitted to remark that I tested this suggestion by presenting the substance of much of the material constituting our Islamics chapter above to a predominantly Muslim audience, of high intellectual calibre and sophistication, as part of the Iqbal Memorial Lectures, 1974, at the University of the Punjab, Lahore, Pakistan, along with a comparative presentation of some of the counterpart Christian material on "belief" (now incorporated in our chapter 6 below); and did not fail to learn from the reception accorded. These lectures have now been published in *Al-Hikmat*, Lahore, 6:[1]-43 (1975).

2 It is only by becoming in part Hindu that a Westerner is enabled to be both Christian and Muslim at the same time, one may aphorize. (The quip is only half facetious, and may not be at all irreverent. Cf. also my *Questions of Religious Truth*, New York: Scribner's, and London: Gollancz, 1967, chap. 4.)

3 Chapter III, "The Bible", in my *Belief and History* (above, our chap. 1 here, ref. 4). The argument is developed there that it is a mistranslation to render any word in the Christian scriptures by the English terms "belief", "believe", those concepts not being found in the Bible. The parallel between that chapter, on the Bible, and our chapter 3 here, above, on the Qur'ān, is not fortuitous.

4 The presentation given here is based primarily on the first ("Procatechesis") and the last five (the "Mystagogae"; more especially the first three of these) of the twenty-four lectures that are extant. For the text, I have used, for the *Procatechesis*, the following convenient edition: *St. Cyril of Jerusalem's Lectures on the Christian Sacraments: The Procatechesis and the Five Mystagogical Catecheses*, F. L. Cross, ed., London: S.P.C.K., 1951; and for the *Mystag.*, the recent critical edition in *Sources chrétiennes* (C. Mondésert, dir.): Cyrille de Jérusalem, *Catéchèses mystagogiques: introduction, texte critique et notes de* Auguste Piédagnel, *trad. de* Pierre Paris, Paris: Éditions du Cerf, 1966. For lectures 1 to 18 following the "Procatechesis", of which 1, 3, and 5 are particularly relevant, I have used the text of W. C. Reischl and J. Rupp, *Cyrilli Hierosolymarum archiepiscopi opera quae supersunt omnia* [Monaci: Lentnerianae, 2 voll., 1848-1860] photocopy reprint, Hildesheim: Georg Olms, 2 voll., 1967. Based on this last-mentioned version of the text, an earlier English partial translation is reproduced in Cross; one more recent and complete is available in *The Works of Saint Cyril of Jerusalem*, Leo P. McCauley and Anthony A. Stephenson, transs., Washington, D.C.: Catholic University of America Press, 2 voll., 1969-1970 (The Fathers of the Church: a new translation, Roy Joseph Deferrari, Bernard M. Peebles, edd., voll. 61, 64). About the authorship and other related matters, see the Introductions to these works (also the "Introduction to the Mystagogical Lectures" in the latter: 2:143-151), and the General Introduction to the "Selections from the Catechetical Lectures" in William Telfer, ed., *Cyril of Jerusalem and Nemesius of Emesa*, London: SCM, and Philadelphia: Westminster, 1955 (The Library of Christian Classics, volume 4), pp. 19-63.

5 The terms used are ἀποταξις [*apotaxis*] and συνταξις [*syntaxis*] respectively, and the verbs ἀποτασσω [*apotassō*] and συντασσω [*syntassō*]. (One example: *Mystag.* 1:8, lines 10, 11 [*Piédagnel*, p. 96].) The former term signifies "taking leave" (a striking New Testament instance is Luke 9:61, "I will follow thee, Lord; but first let me bid farewell to those at home"), "quitting", "cutting oneself off from"; and the latter, "joining", "aligning oneself with", "pledging allegiance to". In the counterpart Latin formula, for the former the verb *renuntio* was used: "to refuse", "to disclaim", "to renounce". (Some writers [cf. our ref. 17 below] used the alternative noun forms ἀποταγη [*apotagē*], συνταγη [*syntagē*].)

It is entrancing to note that in the Semitic-speaking world the concept of abjuring in these Christian formulae is expressed in the translations by the root *ḳ-f-r-*. That term, used for "repudiating" here, is the same term that served (as we have seen: above, our chap. 3, esp. at ref. 12 and the following paragraph in the text) in the Islamic case to denominate the infidel's rejecting of God's claim upon him or her. See, as one example, the Syriac version of Theodore of Mopsuestia's *Liber ad Baptizandos*, vol. 2, chap. 3 (Homily 13, §5): *ḳāpar (')nā' b-Sāṭānā'* (see reff. below). We argued in our Islamics chapter above that the concept of so-called "atheism" in Muslim thought presupposed belief exactly as does the concept faith. This is now confirmed. One does not abjure the Devil without believing in him in the modern sense.

Of this work of Theodore, the Syriac text has been published, most conveniently by Mingana along with an English translation, and in facsimile with a more rigorous translation in French by Tonneau, as follows: "Commentary of Theodore of Mopsuestia on the Lord's Prayer and on the Sacraments of Baptism and the Eucharist", being vol. 6 of *Woodbrooke Studies: Christian documents edited and translated with a critical apparatus by* A. Mingana, Cambridge [England]: Heffer, 1933, and *Les Homélies catéchétiques de Théodore de Mopsueste: reproduction phototypique du MS. Mingana Syr. 561 . . . traduction, introduction, index par* Raymond Tonneau . . . *en collaboration avec* Robert Devreesse, Città Del Vaticano: Biblioteca Apostolica Vaticana, 1949 (Studi e Testi, 145). The passage cited is from Mingana, p. 166, line 22 (Eng. trans., p. 37—cf. p. 174, lines 1, 5, 8; pp. 43-44), and in Tonneau, [p. 372] folio 94r, lines 21-22 (Fr. trans., p. 373—cf. [p. 388] folio 98r, line 23, and [p. 390] folio 98v, lines 2, 6; pp. 389, 391).

6 *Mystag.* 2:4, lines 2f. (Piédagnel, p. 110): ὡς ὁ Χριστος ἀπο του σταυρου ἐπι το προκειμενον μνημα.

7 *Mystag.* 2:4, lines 15f. (Piédagnel, p. 112): το σωτηριον ἐκεινο ὑδωρ και ταφος ὑμιν ἐγινετο και μητηρ.

8 *Procat.* 2, lines 3-5 (Cross, p. 1): και κατεβη μεν το σωμα, και ἀνεβη· ἡ δε ψυχη οὐ συνεταφη Χριστῳ, οὐδε συνηγερθη.

9 The word used is *christoi*. "Having therefore become participant in Christ, you are quite properly called 'christs' "—Μετοχοι οὐν του Χριστου γενομενοι, χριστοι εἰκοτως καλεισθε [*Metochoi oun tou Christou genomenoi, christoi eikotōs kaleisthe*]: *Mystag.*, 3:1, lines 4f. (Piédagnel, p. [120]). (One is re-

minded of the German usage, of calling each Christian *ein Christ.*) A little later on in this lecture they are called χριστιανοι [*christianoi*]—"Christians" or "Christian" or "Christ's": *Mystag.*, 3:5, line 2 (Piédagnel, p. 128). One might translate the earlier word "anointed".

10 *Mystag.*, 4:8, lines 12-15 (Piédagnel, p. 142). Those who had been baptized did ceremonially wear white garments for the first week following the rite.

11 *Mystag.*, 4:9, lines 10f. (Piédagnel, p. 144)—quoting II Corinthians 3:18.

12 The history has been much studied. Collections of documents are: E. C. Whitaker, ed., *Documents of the Baptismal Liturgy*, London: S.P.C.K., 1960; August Hahn, ed., *Bibliothek der Symbole und Glaubensregeln der alten Kirche*, 3te Auflage von G. Ludwig Hahn [Breslau, 1897], photographic reissue, Hildesheim: Georg Olms, 1962 (esp. 2te Abtheilung, "Die Taufsymbole der alten Kirche", pp. 22-159). Among recent secondary studies may be mentioned: Joseph Crehan, *Early Christian Baptism and the Creed: a study in ante-Nicene Theology*, London: Burnes Oates & Washbourne, n.d. [sc. 1950] (Bellarmine Series, xiii); J. N. D. Kelly, *Early Christian Creeds*, London, New York, Toronto: Longmans Green, 1950, 3rd edn., 1972; G. W. H. Lampe, *The Seal of the Spirit: a study in the doctrine of baptism and confirmation in the New Testament and the Fathers*, London, New York, Toronto: Longmans Green, 1951 (esp. chapp. 4, 6, 8, 11); Alois Stenzel, *Die Taufe: eine genetische Erklärung der Taufliturgie*, Innsbruck: Felizian Rauch, 1958 (Hugo Rahner, Joseph A. Jungmann, edd., Forschungen zur Geschichte der Theologie und des innerkirchlichen Lebens 7/8).

13 ". . . baptism involved becoming Christ's man"; footnote: "That is involved in baptism 'in the name of Christ' ". Arthur Darby Nock, "Hellenistic Mysteries and Christian Sacraments" [1952], added to the paperback edition of his *Early Gentile Christianity and its Hellenistic Background*, New York and London: Harper & Row, Harper Torchbooks, 1964, p. 125.

14 "In baptism we are incorporated into salvation history"—"In der Taufe werden wir . . . in die Heilsgeschichte hineingestellt". Oscar Cullmann, *Heil als Geschichte: heilsgeschichtliche Existenz im Neuen Testament*, Tübingen: J. C. B. Mohr (Paul Siebeck), [1965], 2nd edn., 1967, p. 236; English trans. (of the 1965 edn.) "drafted by Sidney G. Sowers and afterwards completed by the editorial staff of the SCM Press", *Salvation in History*, London: SCM Press, 1967, p. 258. The phrase "decision for Christ" (*Entscheidung für Christus*) is found ibid., p. 305 (Eng. trans., p. 330). He speaks not only of incorporating oneself—also "aligning oneself" (*hineinzustellen*; *einzureihen*) —but also of the *decision* so to incorporate, so to align (German, pp. 298, 299, 306; Eng. trans., pp. 322, 324, 331); cf. "decision of faith" (*Entscheidung des Glaubens*, pp. 297f.; Eng., p. 322). The concept *Heilsgeschichte* popularized by Cullmann and often associated with his name, goes back, as he himself points out (p. 56, fn.; Eng., p. 75), to the nineteenth century.

15 One example from Cyril, among many: στρατευσοι ὑμας ἑαυτῳ, ὁπλα περι βαλων—"may He enlist you as a soldier in His services, investing you with the armour . . .": *Procat.* 17, lines −5f. (Cross, p. 11, our ref. 4 above.)

Cf. *Procat.* 10, in full (Cross, p. 6). Also, in the very opening paragraph of his first lecture: *στρατειας κλησις*, the roll-call for military service: *Procat.* 1 (Cross, p. 1). Also, he uses *παραγγελια, παραγγελλω*, "(to give) battle orders", frequently (e.g., *Procat.* 11, line 1; 17, line 1 [Cross, pp. 6, 11]). In other writers, both Greek and Latin, similar imagery abounds: the Christian is the *miles*, soldier, of God, there is regularly reference to the *militia Christi*, the *militia sacra*, etc. An example: *vocati sumus ad militiam Dei uiui*—"We were summoned (or: invited) to military service under the living God": Tertullian, *Ad Martyras*, 3:1. Baptism was the act of joining that army of God, as the remainder of Tertullian's sentence (cf. our next ref., just below) makes explicit. Text used: *Quinti Septimi Florentis Tertulliani Opera*, Turnholti: Brepols, pars 1, *Opera Catholica* . . . , 1954 (Corpus Christianorum, series latina, 1), p. 5 (E. Dekkers, ed.).

16 The Christian swore an oath of allegiance to God and Christ, and was beholden then to remain faithful (*sic*) to that oath. The seven words immediately following on the quotations from Tertullian given in our preceding ref., just above, are: *iam tunc, cum in sacramenti uerba respondimus*—we became soldiers in God's army "at that very moment when we answered the words in our oath of allegiance" (*Ad Martyras*, 3:1). Another example is the same author's query, in *De Corona* 11:1, as to whether it be legitimate for Christians to enter the military service of the state at all, "to take an oath of allegiance to a mere human being over and above the oath of fidelity to God", as a recent rendering translates *humanum sacramentum diuino superduci.* Edwin A. Quain in *Tertullian: disciplinary, moral and ascetical works*, trans. by Rudolph Arbesmann et al. (Roy Joseph Deferrari, ed., *The Fathers of the Church: a new translation*, vol. 40), p. 255. For the Latin text, I have used the Corpus Christianorum edition of Aem. Kroymann in Tertullian, *Opera* (our preceding ref., just above), pars II, *Opera Montanistica*, 1964, p. 1056.

On the use of the term *sacramentum* in Tertullian generally, see, most recently, Dimitri Michaélidès, *Sacramentum chez Tertullien*, Paris: Études augustiniennes, 1970 (with bibliography). (This author develops, in addition to the oath notion in *sacramentum* and its military connotations, also the legal notion of a guaranteed surety or solemn undertaking to stand responsible.) See, however, also Ernest Evans, ed., *Q. Septimii Florentis Tertulliani De Baptismo Liber: Tertullian's Homily on Baptism, the text edited with an introduction, translation and commentary*, London: S.P.C.K., 1964, pp. xxxviii-xl.

17 At more than one place in the early literature on the rite, both Greek and Latin, the point is made that, both God and the baptizand entering into a solemn agreement or pact or covenant at the latter's baptism, God cannot conceivably but be faithful to His side of the contract: He may be utterly counted upon to stand fast by His pledge—come high water or Hell. The human contractor thus is on the one hand assured as to the total unshakable reliability of the affair, and is on the other hand exhorted to remain himself or herself faithful also in turn. In this connection God is called *πιστος* [*pistos*],

"faithful", just as is the Christian—for instance, by Cyril (*Procat.* 6 [Cross, p. 4]), who uses this symmetry to suggest a divinization of the human participants. It is then ridiculous, were it not merely anachronistic (see our next chapter below), to translate πιστος here (but I would say: almost anywhere) as "believer" (as R. W. Church does [Cross, p. 44]). That God is a believer surely goes without saying!

Another example, among many: in some recently discovered and published preparatory lectures on baptism by the fourth-century St. John Chrysostom, the rite is regularly denominated a contract or treaty (συνθηκαι [*synthēkai*]), explicitly compared with the formal written engagement that must be drawn up when "someone wishes to entrust his goods (or: affairs) to someone else" (the word for "entrust" here being ἐμπιστευσαι [*empisteusai*]). Again (cf. ref. 5 above), the central element in the act is stated as the double matter of one's renouncing or repudiating (ἀποτασσομαι [*apotassomai*]) the Evil One, Satan, and aligning oneself with or enrolling under the orders of (συντασσομαι [*syntassomai*]) Christ. The renunciation (ἀποταγη [*apotagē*]) and the adhesion (συνταγη [*syntagē*]) together are seen to constitute the baptizand's contribution or input into the formal contract; it is interesting that the word used in connection with the extravagant return on this from God's side, the treasure-trove of goods that He entrusts (*sic*) to His servant in exchange, is in its turn ἐμπιστευει [*empisteuei*]. Indeed, the verb πιστευω [*pisteuō*] itself is used of God's *committing* to him who has entered His service, through this ceremony, goods not perishable and corruptible but spiritual and heavenly. That is, in this act the person commits his life to God, and in return is committed by God with supernal rewards. πιστις is the act of pledging, dedicating, and here describes this act both on God's part and on man's.

Another example of the use of contract language in the presentation of baptism is Theodore of Mopsuestia, a generation or two after Cyril. For instance, in the course of a paragraph or two in a sermon to candidates, he speaks five times of the rite in terms of "our contract and our engagements" "your engagements and promises", etc. (*Liber ad Baptizandos*, vol. 2, chap. 2 [Homily 12, §26-27]; cf. that chapter, passim). The sermon has not survived in its original Greek, and accordingly we do not know his actual wording; in the Syriac, the terms are *tanway, tawdīṯā'/tawdᵉyāṯā', qᵉyāme'*.

In Latin, the word *pactum* was used (e.g., *Retinete semper pactum, quod fecistis cum Domino*—"keep ever in mind the pact that you made with the Lord": Niceta of Remesiana, *De Symbolo*, 13 [Burn edn., p. 51]), and also *pactio* (e.g., [*pactio*] *in qua creditur Deo in nomine Trinitatis*: Justinian of Calencia [Migne, 96:158]). More generally, cf. "Baptism as a contract", being chap. 5 of Crehan, *Baptism* (above, our ref. 12), pp. 96-110. On the continuing use in English, into our own day, of the terms "promises", "covenant", "vows" in the Anglican Prayer Book in characterizing baptism, cf. below, our ref. 39.

References for this note are as follows: Jean Chrysostome, *Huit catéchèses baptismales inédites, introduction, texte critique, traduction et notes de* Antoine Wenger, Paris: Éditions du Cerf (C. Mondésert, dir., Sources chrétiennes, no. 50 bis), 2e édn., 1970. The term συνθηκαι [*synthēkai*], "contract", "covenant" is used passim, the entries in the index, p. 278, constituting a highly partial list. The first quotation given above is from 2:17, p. 143: Καθαπερ γαρ ἐν τοις βιωτικοις πραγμασιν ἐπειδαν ἐμπιστευσαι τις βουληθῃ τινι τα αὐτου πραγματα, γραμματεια ἀναγκη συντελεισθαι μεταξυ του ἐμπιστευομενου και του ἐμπιστευοντος. In addition to the frequent pair ἀποταγη, συνταγη [*apotagē, syntagē*] (and specifically ἀποτασσομαι σοι, Σατανα . . . και συντασσομαι σοι, Χριστε [*apotassomai soi, Satana . . . kai syntassomai soi, Christe*], 2:20, 21 [p. 145]), the polarity "to be set free from . . . , to attach or to dedicate oneself to" (ἀπαλλαττεσθαι, προσνεμειν [*apallattesthai, prosnemein*]) is also used (2:18 [p. 144]). Underlying our sentence in the statement above about the return from God's side is a passage from 2:21 (p. 145): Εἰδες ἀγαθοτητος ὑπερβολην; Τα ῥηματα δεχομενος παρα σου μονον, τοσουτον ἐμπιστευει σοι πραγματων θησαυρον. The use of πιστευω for God's action towards human beings is found in the conclusion of the sentence first quoted above: τον αὐτον δη τροπον και νυν, ἐπειδη μελλετε πιστευεσθαι παρα του των ἁπαντων δεσποτου οὐκ ἐπικηρα πραγματα οὐδε φθαρτα και ἀπολλυμενα ἀλλα πνευματικα και ἐπουρανια (2:17 [p. 143]). Chrysostom is himself, it would seem, a trifle caught up short by his own use of this word in this context, for he goes on to explain that the notion of *pistis* having to do with our apprehension of transcendent realities is also involved: his next sentence reads, Δια γαρ τουτο και πιστις λεγεται ἐπειδη οὐδεν ὁρωμενον ἐχει ἀλλα παντα τοις του πνευματος ὀφθαλμοις κατοπτευεσθαι δυναμενα—"One speaks of *pistis* also for the following reason: that it has to do not with anything visible but rather with all those things that are able to be descried with the eyes of the spirit" (2:17 [p. 143]—here even a cognitive element in πιστις is to be translated not by "believing" but as "recognizing"; cf. below, in our next chapter).

For Theodore of Mopsuestia, see the ednn. cited above (our ref. 5): Mingana, p. 162, lines 5-6, 6, 16-17 and p. 163, lines 2, 5 (English, pp. 33, 34); Tonneau, [pp. 362, 364, 366] folios 91v, lines 24, 25; 92r, lines 11, 24-25; 92v, line 2 (French, pp. 363, 365, 367).

A. E. Burn, *Niceta of Remesiana: his life and works*, Cambridge [England]: [Cambridge] University Press, 1905, "Libellus Quintus de Symbolo", pp. 38-54.

Justinian of Calencia, *Liber de Cognitione Baptismi* (6th cent.); available in the annotated commentary of Ildephonsus of Toledo (7th century), *Liber Annotationum de Cognitione Baptismi*, in J.-P. Migne, ed., *Sanctorum Hildefonsi, Leodegarii, Juliani . . . Opera Omnia . . .* (J.-P. Migne, ed., Patrologiae Cursus Completus . . . series latina, . . . tom. 96), Paris, 1862, coll. 111ff.

18 For instance, in Cyril, *Procat.* 6, last four lines (Cross, p. 4, our ref. 4 above): "If it were the days of your wedding that are now before us, would you not be disregarding everything (else) and be engaged with preparations for the festivities? Since, rather, you are about to consecrate your soul to your heavenly bridegroom, will you not leave aside mundane things in order to attain spiritual ones?" Another example is from the very opening paragraph of this first lecture, where he touches on this motif among others (*Procat.* 1

[Cross, p. 1]). In other Christian writers also, Greek and Latin, the analogy was not infrequent.

19 The very opening paragraph of the opening lecture sets the tone: included in it are the words ἐπιθυμια, προθεσις, προαιρεσις, διανοια [*epithumia*, *prothesis* (bis), *proairesis*, *dianoia*]; and these are re-iterated throughout. Further: "God seeks nothing other from us than a good intention (or resolve)"—Οὐδεν γαρ ἀλλο παρ' ἡμων ζητει ὁ θεος, εἰ μη προαιρεσιν ἀγαθην: *Procat.* 8, opening line (Cross, p. 5). Again, the verb θελω [*thelō*], "to will", "to purpose", is in constant employ (one example: ref. 23 below). Note the close parallelism of θελειν [*thelein*] and πιστευειν [*pisteuein*], *Procat.* 8, line 3 (Cross, p. 5). Again, between the person with faith (πιστος [*pistos*]) and the one without (ἀπιστος [apistos]) the distinguishing characteristic that he notes is again intention, resolve (προαιρεσις [*proairesis*])—*Procat.* 6, lines 14f. (Cross, p. 4). Since this last term refers literally to the choosing of one thing over another, I suppose that one might translate it here and in §8 quoted above as "one's sense of priorities", a good προαιρεσις being "getting one's priorities straight" or the like—except that the implication of deliberate choice and of somewhat steadfast acting upon one's values is too strong for it to signify merely "having" the right values, to use the modern jargon. In any case, at issue are the questions of what one chooses and of the strength, courage and resolute persistence to will, and to sustain, that choice.

Similarly, while Cyril recognizes that there may be some hypocrites among those presenting themselves for baptism—men who do so because they are interested in some of the women of the group, for instance—even here he characterizes their hypocrisy not in terms of their not believing, but morally (*Procat.* 5 [Cross, pp. 3f.]). He asks such persons to go ahead with the ceremony, hoping (that is, he is asking them to hope) that it will become real for them—not in the sense that it will change their minds and that they will come to believe, but that it will change their hearts: that they will "die to sins, and live to righteousness: from this day forth, live!" (loc. cit.; Cross, p. 4).

Some modern Christian thinkers, especially Roman Catholics, are somewhat embarrassed by the voluntarism that saturates Cyril's presentation—an example: Stephenson, *St. Cyril* (our ref. 4 above), 1:70, fn. 6, he approaching the whole matter from the viewpoint of subsequent orthodoxy. He is right, however, in noting that Cyril's conception of faith as a primarily, and indeed thoroughly, moral quality, however distinct it be from present-day conceptions, does not therein entail any particular answer to a question as to whether it be God-given or anthropogenetic.

Another fairly vivid instance of the use of προαιρεσις is *Catech.* 2:5, last sentence (Reischl and Rupp, 1:46): "The only requisite, finally, is resolute purpose"—ζητειται δε λοιπον ἡ προαιρεσις. Telfer translates: "All we have to seek for is the will to be saved" (Telfer, *Cyril and Nemesius*, p. 85); although the Roman Catholic McCauley's rendering is a good deal more cautious: "the proper disposition is a requisite condition" (*St. Cyril*, 1:99). Similarly, Church translates *Procat.* 8 cited at the beginning of this note as, "God seeks nothing else from us, save a good purpose" (Cross, p. 44); but McCauley, "God requires of us only one thing, sincerity" (1:77). (For all these reff. see our ref. 4 above.)

20 Above, our ref. 18.

21 Θεος ἐκαλεσε, συ δε ἐκληθης: *Procat.* 9, last sentece (Cross, p. 6).

22 δωμεν ἑαυτους . . . ἱνα ὁ θεος . . . δωῃ ἡμιν μετανοιαν σωτηριας: *Procat.* 9, last five lines (Cross, p. 6).

23 Ἐαν δε τα μεν χειλη σου λεγῃ το θελειν, ἡ δε καρδια μη λεγῃ . . . : *Procat.* 8, lines 4f. (Cross, p. 5).

24 Δυναται γαρ ὁ θεος και τον ἀπιστον πιστοποιησαι, ἐαν μονον δῳ την καρδιαν: *Procat.* 17, lines 11-13 (Cross, p. 11).

25 I say "it seems" since, as we saw above (our chap. 4, ref. 35), there has been some recent challenge to the received etymology. There is no question whatever, from any corner, but that Latin *credo* and Sanskrit *śraddhā* are originally the same word. What has come in question is whether the first part of the compound is from proto-Indo-European **ḳred-* etc. meaning "heart", or whether in both cases it comes from a nearly but not quite convergent original form of uncertain meaning, said to have been perhaps more specifically religious. (In another phrasing, we might say that it may fundamentally have designated "heart" not in the sense of the seat of human feelings generally but "heart" in the specific sense of the seat of religious commitment, religious involvement.)

26 This *do* is not *dō, dāre* . . . (Greek διδωμι [*didōmi*]), "to give", but rather a third-declension verb **-do* (Greek τιθημι [*tithēmi*]), "to put, to set, to place". It survives in Latin only in compound verbs, but in quite an array of these: *abdo, abdere, abdidi, abditum*, "to put away, to secrete, to conceal"; *condo -dere -didi -ditum*, "to put together"; *trādo* (for *transdo*) *-dere -didi -ditum*, "to hand over, to give up, to surrender, to betray"; and so on. (Although etymologically *dō* [to give] and **-do* [to place] were discrete words in Latin, psychologically and culturally they were sometimes felt, and treated, as converging. Cf. *Oxford Latin Dictionary*, Oxford: Clarendon Press, 1968- , in process, fascicule 3, 1971, p. 566, column 2, lines 2-3; also *Thesaurus Linguae Latinae*, Lipsiae: Teubner, 1900- , in process, vol. 5, part 1, fascicule 7, 1914, column 1659, lines 28-29 and fascicule 8, 1928, column 1701, lines 30-33.)

27 "Whatever other uses they may have been put to in the course of history, the true and original use of creeds, their primary *raison d'être*, was to serve as solemn affirmations of faith in the context of baptismal initiation"—Kelly, *Creeds* (our ref. 12 above), p. 31.

Similarly, the Roman Catholic Crehan, in his *Baptism and Creed* (our ref. 12 above), p. 135, makes much the same point, saying that modern studies (which he cites) have "put it beyond all doubt".

(The Kelly passage goes on to qualify the statement quoted by saying that while it is generally true, it is "subject to certain reservations" (p. 31), which do not affect our argument here: they are considered below, in our ref. 34.

In addition to, and in some sense perhaps over against, his book on *Early Christian Creeds*, this author has another and different book on doctrine:

J. N. D. Kelly, *Early Christian Doctrines*, London: Adam & Charles Black, 1958 [and New York: Harper, 1959; 4th edn., London: Black, 1968].)

28 There are two main points involved here. One is that the ceremony of baptism was not envisaged, either by those administering it or by those undergoing it, as a movement from non-belief to belief. The second is that the word *credo*, specifically, did not designate such a movement. The latter point will be dealt with below, our ref. 32. (That the Greek term πιστευω [*pisteuō*], although not equivalent to *credo*, also did not designate a movement from non-belief to belief, is developed a little at our ref. 31 below.) The first point has been the burden of our chapter thus far, with Cyril's description of and commentary on the rite as illustrative; but we elaborate it somewhat at our ref. 35 below, illustrating the thesis also from other writers lest it be thought that Cyril was in any way atypical in this matter. The evidence is so general and indeed so overwhelming that it would be tedious to adduce it, were it not that modern preconceptions of the role of belief in Christian life (and especially modern notions of its crucial role as what distinguishes Christians from others), and modern translations of the creeds, have stood in the way of its being perceived. Even the scholars in this field would appear to have failed to notice that something that they take so decisively for granted is in fact not there in the material that they study.

29 The principal verbs in the classical creeds are performatives: "I hereby commit myself to" (or: "I hereby pledge allegiance to"). In Greek, there are in the various forms of the so-called Apostles' Creed *no other finite verbs.* Even those who might strive to translate πιστευω [*pisteuō*] or *credo* here by "I believe" are confronted with the fact that its object is in no instance a proposition. There are nouns or adjectives used appositionally (or attributively) with the first Person of the Trinity (*πατερα, παντοκρατορα, ποιητην*—"Father, ruler of the universe [or: all-powerful?], maker"); and in the case of the second Person, nouns, adjectives, and participles similarly (*Ὑιον . . . μονογενη, τον κυριον . . . τον συλληφθεντα . . . γεννηθεντα . . . παθοντα . . . θανοντα* . . .—"Son . . . unique [later: only-begotten], Lord . . . conceived . . . born . . . having suffered . . . having died . . .", etc.). In Latin about half, and in English almost all, the participles emerge as relative clauses with finite verbs (*qui conceptus est . . . descendit . . . ascendit* . . .—"who was conceived . . . suffered . . . was crucified . . . [buried?] . . . descended . . . rose"). Of these descriptive qualifications, the number increased gradually as time went on: for instance, in the successive forms of the Apostles' Creed. In the Nicene Creed (325 A.D.) there is one finite verb in a subordinate clause (*δι' οὗ τα παντα ἐγενετο*—"through whom all things came into being"), and if the anathemata be counted, a second performative (*ἀναθεματιζει*—"the universal Church hereby declares anathema". The object of this last verb is such-and-such persons; in and by the pronouncement the Church constituted them as in that status). In the Nicene-Constantinopolitan Creed (381 A.D.? fifth century?) one further finite verb, in the future tense, appears, once again in a subordinate clause: *οὗ της βασιλειας οὐκ ἐσται τελος* —"of whose reign there will not be an end". And parallel with the introductory verb πιστευομεν [*pisteuomen*] two further principle finite sen-

tences are added: ὁμολογουμεν . . . προσδοκωμεν [*homologoumen . . . prosdokōmen . . .*]—"we confess . . . we look forward to . . .". Again in Latin a few of the Greek participles become relative clauses. None is or ever becomes a proposition, however.

These facts and developments may be seen in either or both of two ways. One is their defining and "doctrinal" function, specifying orthodoxy and excluding heresy, a function whose gradual development over the centuries, and whose use especially after the Constantinian establishment, are considered below, e.g., at our ref. 38. The other way of understanding the development is to consider the matter in relation to a parallel phenomenon that is historically earlier, and more germane to the baptismal role of early creeds. The usage is illustrated in the closely parallel formulae, also explicitly performatives, of exorcism. It was customary for the early Christians to exorcise evil spirits by a solemn and ceremonial pronouncement of the type: I adjure thee, O demon, "in the name of the Son of God, first-born of all creation, born of a virgin, become a suffering human being, crucified under Pontius Pilate . . . dead, risen from the dead, ascended to Heaven", to leave the afflicted person.

See, as an example of this, the second-century Justin Martyr, *Dialogue*, 85:2, also 30:3 (full reff. below). Cf. already Acts 4:10. In the third century, Origen says explicitly that the power (ἰσχυω [*ischyō*]; elsewhere also δυναμις [*dynamis*] is used) that Christians are seen to have over demons is due to the invoking of the name of Jesus with an enumeration of the events of His life (*Contra Celsum* 1:6).

From a pronouncement such as these a modern may, no doubt, *infer* several things about the "beliefs" of those early Christians who made it: their beliefs about devils, about power and what we to-day might call magic, about a relation between language (especially formalized language) and spiritual force, about Christ, and so on. Most of this (all but the last) they shared with, and indeed had taken over from, the surrounding culture, both Jewish and Greek. Nonetheless, the utterance has not been understood (nor properly translated) if by moderns these inferences are substituted for, or confused with, its explicit meaning. It has not been understood unless the modern can move beyond these inferences about belief, using them as presuppositional ground-work on which to reconstruct a solemn and dramatic action and the meaning that it had for those involved. The adjuration was not understood by the person who uttered it, nor by those who heard it, whether the man or woman "possessed of a devil" or the bystanders, as an expression of belief; and we have not understood it either if we focus on what it implied and miss what it meant. We see here in operation a first-century way of perceiving the world; but the historian's task is to understand both that world-view and specifically what was going on within it. (And the translator's task is to translate what is written. No word in the adjuration formulae means "to believe"—just as no word in the baptismal formula does.)

A positive instance of this use of an appositional formula to solemnize a moral obligation at the moment of its being incurred (or bestowed) can be found already in the New Testament: "I charge you before God, who gives life to all things, and before Christ Jesus, who witnessed before Pontius Pilate the good confession, that you keep the Commandment . . ."—I Timothy 6:13f. Again, the descriptive clauses here are, in the Greek, not finite verbs but participles. They are evidence for, but not statements of or about, what the speaker "believed".

To return to the Creeds: It might by some be thought that the interpretation of πιστευω [*pisteuō*] and *credo* as a self-engaging commitment, a pledging of allegiance, is persuasive for the three persons of the Trinity, and the Church, but that with the later phrases, such as "the remission of sins", "the life everlasting" and the like, this is more problematic, the modern mind finding itself impelled towards substituting propositions for these, and towards substituting for a performative a notion like believing. If this be a temptation, then one should consider the late-fourth-century *Apostolic Constitutions* presentation of the baptismal formula on these very points. The wording of the pronouncement of the baptizand in that exposition is as follows: "I renounce the Devil . . . and align myself with Christ. I *pisteuō* and am baptized (or: have myself baptized—*baptizomai*) into one God . . . and into the Lord Jesus Christ . . . ; and I am baptized into the Holy Spirit . . . into the resurrection of the flesh and into the remission (or: the getting rid of) sins and into the kingdom of the heavens and into the life of the era that is coming"—*Constitutiones Apostolorum* 7:41:2, 3, 4, 5, 7, 8. (For the Greek, see below, at the end of this note.) It is inescapable that *baptizomai* here is a performative (in the next sentence, the author calls its action "this promise" [42:1]) and inescapable that the noun phrases that function as its object (that "into which one is baptized") are not propositional.

(For another illustration of the non-propositional quality of "the remission of sins" phrase, this time from the baptism of infants, see below, our ref. 32.)

The earliest formal ecclesiastical statement in which a few (still not many) propositions do appear—to the discomfort recently of the Church—is the *Quicunque vult*, ca. fifth century, the so-called Athanasian Creed ("actually, neither Athanasian nor a creed"). For it in this connection, see my *Belief and History*, chap. II, ref. 31 (pp. 109-110).

References for the above: *Bibliothek der Symbole und Glaubensregeln der alten Kirche*, August Hahn, ed., 3te Auflage, G. Ludwig Hahn, ed., Breslau, 1897; I have used the Hildesheim: Georg Olms, 1962, photographic reprint. The successive forms of the Apostles' Creed are given pp. 22-36. The Nicene Creed, Greek, pp. 160f.; Latin, p. 162. The Nicene-Constantinopolitan Creed, Greek, pp. 162-165; Latin, pp. 165f. The Athanasian Creed, pp. 174-177.

For Justin, *Pros Tryphōna Dialogos*, I have used the modern edn. of the Greek Church: *Bibliothēkē Hellēnōn Paterōn kai Ekklēsiastikōn Syngrapheōn, tomos 3tos, Polykarpos . . . Ioustinos* (*meros* á), Athēnai: Ekdosis tēs Apostolikēs Diakonias tēs Ekklēsias tēs Hellados, 1955, where the passage here translated is found pp. 288, line 40 and 289, lines 1-5; cf. also 30:3, p. 234, lines 10-12. A recent translation (but one that comes close to missing the force of the participles) will be found in Thomas B. Falls, trans., *Saint Justin Martyr*, New York: Christian Heritage, 1948 (Ludwig Schopp, ed. dir., The Fathers of the Church, a new translation), pp. 283, 192.

For Origen, I have used the edn. in the series Sources chrétiennes, ##132, 136, 147, 150: Origène, *Contre Celse: introduction, texte critique, traduction et notes* par Marcel Borret, Paris: Éditions du Cerf, 4 voll., 1967-1969. The passage in question is found in vol. 1, p. 90, lines 5-7 of this para. (translation on facing page); cf. similarly 1:22 (ibid., p. 130, lines 6ff.).

Franciscus Xaverius Funk, ed., *Didascalia et Constitutiones Apostolorum*, Paderbornae: Schoeningh, 2 voll., 1905, 1:444, 446, 448. The passages read: *Ἀποτασσομαι τῳ σατανᾳ . . . και συντασσομαι τῳ Χριστῳ· και πιστευω και βαπτιζομαι εἰς . . . ἀληθινον θεον . . . και εἰς τον κυριον Ἰησουν τον Χριστον . . .· βαπτιζομαι και εἰς το πνευμα το ἁγιον . . . εἰς σαρκος ἀναστασιν και εἰς ἀφεσιν ἁμαρτιων και εἰς βασιλειαν οὐρανων και εἰς ζωην του μελλοντος αἰωνος. . . . την ἐπαγγελιαν ταυτην.*

On exorcism in general (something in which the early Church "believed", without knowing or saying that it believed in it, just as did its surrounding society), see the suggestive, though not fully satisfactory, article of C. H. Ratschow, "Exorzismus: I. Religionsgeschichtlich" in *Die Religion in Geschichte und Gegenwart: Handwörterbuch für Theologie und Religionswissenschaft*, Tübingen: J. C. B. Mohr (Paul Siebeck), 7 voll., 1957-1965, vol. 2 (1958), coll. 832-833 and bibliography. On it in specifically Christian usage, see W. Michaelis, "Exorzismus: II. Im Urchristentum", ibid., coll. 833-834, and Leclercq, "Exorcisme, exorciste" in Fernand Cabrol et Henri Leclercq, et al., edd., *Dictionnaire d'archéologie chrétienne et de liturgie*, Paris: Letouzey et Ané, 15 voll., 1907-1953, vol. 5 (1922), coll. 964-978. A little more recently but less fully, the little posthumous work of Reginald Maxwell Woolley, *Exorcism and the Healing of the Sick*, London: Society for Promoting Christian Knowledge, 1932.

30 Whether it would be, and not merely seem, ludicrous depends on the meaning (to-day) of "believe", a drastically equivocal word—one that we investigate in its own right in our next chapter, below. We said above in our Islamic chapter (at its ref. 31) that classical and mediaeval Muslims were hardly conscious of believing anything very significant. They believed much, in one of the present-day senses of that word: namely, in the sense of their minds' operating within an intellectual world-view that they themselves did not recognize as such, as one human ideology among others, conceptually objectifiable and obtaining at one phase of its (also conceptually objectifiable) historical development. If they had had a word to designate such believing, they did not and could not apply it to themselves. Similarly it is vastly truer to the facts than either modern Christians or modern critics of the Christian movement have begun to discern that the early Christians were hardly conscious of believing anything. (An example: they did not know that they believed in a devil.) We shall concern ourselves below, later in this present chapter, with Christian believing in the Middle Ages; for the early period we leave that realm of inquiry aside, since it impinges only indirectly

on the two matters before us, the term *credo* and the baptism ceremony.

31 There are three matters involved here: (i) neither did the Church use the Greek root *pist-* for this; (ii) linguistically, it employed other terms than these two when speaking about the range of issues and conceptual relations that we to-day signify by "belief", "believing", (iii) substantially, insofar as it concerned itself explicitly with that other range of issues, it did so at times and in relation to matters other than those addressed by *credo*, and other than baptism. My thesis about *credo*, particularly in this negative aspect that it did not designate a concern with belief, is so divergent from what has become (recently) received opinion, that each of these points has to be considered somewhat carefully. This present note will touch on (i), and on the relation between *pist-* and *credo*; although a careful, or even minor, treatment of that relation is both beyond the scope, of course, and in some ways outside the concern of this chapter. Points (ii) and (iii) are treated in our reff. 34 and 35 below, respectively. Further evidence as to what *credo* did positively mean and how it was positively used is discussed a little in our next note just below, ref. 32.

As indicated, we propose no substantial inquiry here into the (many) uses of *pist-* by Christians outside the baptismal service. Within that service, beyond what has already been said one may note that in some of the formulae in official use the three verbs συντασσομαι, πιστευω, βαπτιζομαι [*syntassomai, pisteuō, baptizomai*] were to be solemnly pronounced in immediate succession to each other *in that order*: I range myself on the side of, I pledge commitment to, I am baptized (I have myself baptized). Of course, all three words here imply the Christian conceptual or theological framework (as does the preceding ἀποτασσομαι [*apotassomai*] used for repudiating the Devil, and indeed as does the whole service—just as we saw in the Qur'ān case that *ḳafara* and *āmana*, conceptualizing faith and infidelity, both presuppose belief). Yet I cannot see how the second of our three specifically can be interpreted as here meaning, even in part, an explicit conceptual belief, or even a recognition—or else it would have to come first, not second. I confess, therefore, to not finding fully clear one part of Theodore of Mopsuestia's commentary (our ref. 5 above) on this formula. His interpretation (*Ad Baptizandos*, vol. 2, chap. 3; Homily 13, §14) is future-oriented, speaks of promises, hope, and the like, and yet he correlates the second verb here with Hebrews 11:6 in a way that I admit to not quite understanding. (I commend the passage to any reader inclined to dispute my general interpretations.) The correlation throws perhaps more light on the Hebrews passage (cf. my *Belief and History*, pp. 73, 75, 77-80) than it does on the baptism formula?

What Theodore himself understood by the first of these three verbs he has just explicated clearly in a way that leaves no room for doubt as to the resolute pledging quality and future-oriented sense of the matter: ". . . when you say 'I engage myself before God' you show that you will remain steadfastly with Him, that you will henceforth be unshakeably with Him, that you will never separate yourself from Him, and that you will think it higher than anything else to be and to live with Him and to conduct yourself in a way that is in harmony with His commandments" (Mingana trans., p. 44). The existence of God is here patently (and calmly) presupposed. The author then goes on to discuss what he calls an appropriate "addition" to this: namely, *wa-mhaymen (')nā'* (transparently, πιστευω [*pisteuō*]). Any proposed interpretation of what he means by this must be consonant with the fact that his remarks here *follow* the explication just enunciated, and are proffered to those who are to pronounce the verb clause in question *after* they have affirmed the preceding one presumably with the understanding that he has just propounded.

Perhaps, it could be suggested, he is taking πιστευω here as a transcendental "recognizing" and "acknowledging", in a conjoined intellectual and moral sense (cf. later in this present note, and ref. 36 below); although even so the order of our three words still troubles me.

The interpretation proffered by Mingana (p. 44) is more conformable to currently received notions of faith as belief but less coherent with the preceding steps in Theodore's argument and the context generally. Tonneau's rendering (more faithful, I feel, to the to me not fully clear Syriac) leaves indeterminate what *croire à* (p. 391, line 21) signifies, except that propositional belief seems excluded by the two concluding (i.e., immediately following) clauses. Perhaps "to resolve to live (or simply: to live) one's life in terms of" would make the passage intelligible?

Another usage of πιστος [*pistos*] illuminating for our purposes was its serving almost as a past participle to mean "he who has taken the plunge", a baptized Christian as distinct from those Christians (*sic*) who had not yet made that ceremonial move. The latter group included the *catechumenoi* (cf. our ref. 35 below), a formal and even ceremonialized class, in some areas going about in public with a cross on their foreheads, whose members might well and indeed almost certainly did "believe" and might well be and surely often were faithful. Thus for this πιστος neither "believer", the modern concept, nor "faithful", a standard meaning otherwise in Christian usage, can serve as a translation. The term designated specifically a person who had, in baptism, been consecrated (or: had consecrated himself). See also the use of this Greek verb by St. Chrysostom above, our ref. 17.

Although negatively Greek πιστευω and Latin *credo* agree in not meaning "believe", positively nonetheless they were, in Christian usage, at first not full equivalents. In the New Testament our verb occasionally means "to commit, to entrust" ("Jesus did not commit Himself to them"—Ἰησους οὐκ ἐπιστευεν αὑτον αὐτοις: John 2:24; etc.), as it does in the Chrysostom passage just adduced (from our ref. 17 above). Regularly also, of course, it means "to trust". Nonetheless, a cognitive component—not of "believing", but of "recognizing"—is in general more common in Christian Greek for it than it is in early Christian Latin for *credo*. The "trust" component of the Greek Christian concept for faith turns up in Latin primarily in *fides* (sometimes used with the verbs *fido, confido,* also), on which term see below. *Credo* in early Christian Latin, in distinction from this, clustered its meanings primarily around its central usage in baptism and the creeds (Greek συμβολον [*sym-*

bolon]). Until to-day the Roman Church has kept alive a distinction between faith and the act of faith (*credo* and *fides*), unlike Protestants, for whom Latin has been a less important language (and—to a lesser extent—Greek, in which this distinction is not verbalized, a more important one).

Later developments, however, were of course intricate and complex. The Latin-speaking Church, having chosen *credo* as its term for self-commitment and the oath of loyalty at the heart of the baptism service, presently then carried this word also into its Latin translations of the Bible (and of the Greek Fathers) as its standard rendering of the verb designating the having of faith (πιστευω) in all the latter's occurrences, not just the performative one. For the noun "faith" (πιστις), on the other hand, there existed in Latin no cognate to *credo*. *Fides* (culturally already linked somewhat with *credo*, but cognate ultimately rather with πιστις) was to hand and was chosen. (It is an etymologically rather curious word: see below.)

Fides was personified as a goddess in ancient Rome, and there was an important temple to her. Dius Fidius was another god, or a name or aspect of Jupiter. The term *fides* characterized relations among men (perhaps also among the gods) and between men and god; both she and Dius Fidius personified and divinized (recognized the transcendent quality of) the virtue of good faith, fidelity, and of respect for promises and pacts, and especially oaths.

The history of Roman Catholic thought has been distinctive partly because of its having two conceptual expressions for, respectively, the noun and the verb pertaining to faith: for the personal state or quality and for the act. Ultimately it is this bifurcation in the Western Church's conceptualization that has made both necessary and possible our present inquiry into the polarity faith/belief.

For a consideration of πιστευω in the New Testament, and specifically that it never means "to believe" there, see my *Belief and History*, chap. 3. A conclusion of that analysis is that insofar as there is a cognitive propositional usage of or component in πιστευω it signifies not "believing" but "recognizing" (cf. our ref. 36 below).

Other references: For the baptismal formula cited: *Constitutiones Apostolorum*, 7:41:3, 4, Funk, edn. cit. (our ref. 29 above), p. 444. Theodore of Mopsuestia, *Ad Baptizandos*, Mingana edn., p. 166, lines 23-24; Eng. trans., p. 37—Tonneau edn., [p. 372] folio 94r, line 24; French, p. 373. For Theodore's commentary on the middle word, Mingana, pp. 174, line 16 to p. 175, line 1; Eng., p. 44—Tonneau [p. 390] folio 98v, line 15 to [p. 392] folio 99r, line 1; French, p. 393.

On our Latin terms etymologically see *inter alia*, A. Meillet, "Traitement de *S* suivie de consonne" and id., "Lat. *crēdō* et *fidēs*", both in *Mémoires de la société de linguistique de Paris*, 22:211-218 (1922); Georges Dumézil, "*Credo* et *fides*" in his *Idées romaines*, [Paris]: Gallimard, 1969, pp. [47]-59, esp. pp. 55-59. On *fides* as a deity, see, e.g., Georges Dumézil, *Archaic Roman Religion . . .* , Philip Krapp, trans., Chicago and London: University of Chicago Press, 2 voll., 1970, 1:81, 144-146 (and cf. bibliography, p. 144 fn.

6), 180, 198-200, 280; 2:397, 400-401. (This last work was published first in French [Paris: Payot, 1966] but our reff. here are to the English which is in this instance more authoritative, having been "revised and annotated by the author" [verso of title-page]). See further our ref. 66 below.

32 We may cite a few instances where the dedication denotation of *credo* emerges as particularly manifest. One way of seeing it is by taking note of time sequence (as with πιστευω [*pisteuō*], in the preceding reference 31 just above). Justinian of Calencia we have already mentioned as one of those who call baptism a contract; but he refers to it actually as a double transaction: first, the formal agreement of a rejecting of the Devil, and second (*sic*), that of a dedication to God (*duae autem sunt pactiones. Prima, in qua diabolo renuntiatur. . . . Secunda, in qua creditur Deo.* Ildephonsus, in Migne, 96:158 [our ref. 17 above].) It would be totally unreasonable to translate *credo* here in such a way as to aver or even to imply or to include that the baptizand came to believe in God only *after* he had ceremonially repudiated Satan.

Another comparable illustration is involved in the telling use of the past tense of our verb. Niceta of Remesiana, also cited above, urges that the baptised Christian, whenever the Devil may tease him or her with a temptation to be frightened or greedy or lustful or angry, may turn the tables on the Devil and boldly threaten him back, asserting, "I (have) rejected thee, and I will continue to reject thee and all thy works, for I (have) dedicated myself to the living God and to His Son"—*credidi Deo uiuo et Filio eius*: his *De Symbolo*, §14 [Burn edn., our ref. 17 above, p. 52]). To say to the Devil, "I'm not afraid of you, old chap: fifteen years ago I believed in God and Christ" would make little sense!

Indeed the historical fact seems to be that in Latin *credo* in the baptismal rite did duty for both συνταασσομαι [*syntassomai*] (above, our ref. 5) and πιστευω [*pisteuō*] in Greek. The overt symmetry of Greek ἀποταξις / συνταξις [*apotaxis/syntaxis*], ἀποταγη / συνταγη [*apotegē/syntagē*], etc., was not preserved in Latin. For the negative pole in these pairs, as we have seen, *renuntio* was standard ("to reject, to renounce"), and remained central. Occasionally, as positive counterpart to that negative performative, is found *convertor* and perhaps *adscribo*. More frequently, however, the two concepts συνταασσομαι and πιστευω seem to have converged in Latin into one, and standardly the direct and explicit contrast is between *renuntio* on the one hand and *credo* on the other. (Echoes of this survived perhaps in later positions that faith is an adherence or adhesion [*adhaesio*]?)

An illustration of this direct contrast, and simultaneously of the clearly performative quality of *credo*, is the commentary on Romans 13:12 ("Let us put off, therefore, the works of darkness, and put on the armour of light") proffered by the fifth-century Quodvulteus of Carthage. (St. Paul's words are ἀποθωμεθα [*apothōmetha*] and ἐνδυσωμεθα [*endysōmetha*]; the Vulgate here reads *abiciamus . . . et induamur*, but an earlier Old Latin version is being used in this case). "What", Quodvulteus asks, "is 'Put off the works of darkness' other than 'Renounce the Devil, his pomps, and his angels'? And what is 'Put on the amour of light' other than 'Range yourselves on the side of, dedicate yourselves to, pledge your allegiance to, God the Father Almighty'?" (*Quid est deponere opera tenebrarum, nisi renuntiare diabolo, pompis et angelis eius? Et quid est "induite uos arma lucis", nisi: Credite in deum patrem omnipotentem?*). "To believe", in the modern sense, would be quite inapt here.

Another instance, where *credo* implicitly but more or less manifestly presupposes not merely belief but knowledge of God's existence and proceeds from there to denote not that, but a pledging of oneself (in this instance, a being pledged, by proxy) to His service, is St. Augustine's comment on infant baptism, where the parents of the child are to reply on its behalf (to take the vow on its behalf) that yes, the child is hereby pledged (pledges itself) to God, even though at that age the standard presupposition and tacit prerequisite of knowledge in its mind about God do not, of course, but exceptionally, obtain. At that age, he says in so many words, the child does not even know whether there be a God or not, and nonetheless the sponsors aver: "He makes the pledge". (*interrogamus enim eos, a quibus offeruntur, et dicimus: Credit in deum? de illa aetate, quae, utrum sit deus, ignorat; respondent: Credit.*—St. Augustine's letter to Bishop Boniface, 7. Full ref. below.)

Again, the phrase *credere remissionem peccatorum* is clarified when treated in relation to infant baptism. Exorcism of a child would not be reasonable, St. Augustine says, if the child were not held "in the family of the Devil"; its renouncing the Devil would not be so, if it had nothing of the Devil in it; and its *credere* the remission of sins would not, if no sin were attributable to it. Now there is no reason why a sinless person should not believe in the remission of sins, should not believe that they are remitted. This passage demonstrates both that "the remission of sins", or forgiveness, is not propositional, and that *credo* does not mean "to believe". Rather, it is a matter, evidently, of contracting oneself into, or otherwise placing oneself in a position of, an operative acquittal. (*quid in illo agit exorcismus meus, si in familia diaboli non tenetur? . . . quomodo ergo dicturus erat eum renuntiare diabolo, cuius in eo nihil esset? quomodo conuerti ad deum, a quo non esset auersus? credere inter cetera in remissionem peccatorum, quae illi nulla tribueretur?*—St. Augustine, *De Peccatorum Meritis et Remissione*, 1:34/63). Other texts, similarly, for adults indicate that in being baptized one attains the forgiveness, or remission, of sins. It is not a matter of holding or even of arriving at a view intellectually that sins are forgiven as a generic proposition, but rather of having one's own sins forgiven existentially as an historical fact at that moment and by that act. One is baptized into the remission of one's sins.

References: for *convertor*, I have in mind the usage of St. Augustine, in, for instance, his reference to baptism in *Contra Litteras Petiliani*, 3:8/9 as well as the passage quoted above about remission of sins. In such cases his Latin remarks seem to preserve echoes of a three-fold formula like the Greek? For the former text I have used the edition of M. Petschenig (Corpus Scriptorum Ecclesiasticorum Latinorum, vol. 52, 1909, pp. 170-171), as reproduced in *Oeuvres de Saint Augustin*, 30:4ème série, *Traités anti-donatistes*, vol. 3: *trad. de* G. Finaert, *introd. et notes par* B. Quinot, [Paris]: Desclée de Brouwer, 1967 (Bibliothèque augustinienne), p. 606 (French trans., p. 607). For the other: *De Peccatorum Meritis et Remissione et de baptismo paruulorum ad Marcellinum libri tres . . .*, recc. Carolus F. Urba et Iosephus Zycha, *Sancti Aureli Augustini Opera*, sect. VIII, pars I (Corpus Scriptorum Ecclesiasticorum Latinorum, vol. 60), Vindobonae: F. Tempsky, and Lipsiae: G. Freytag, 1913, pp. 63-64. For both this, and for checking the original of the Petschenig, I have consulted the photomechanical re-issues, New York and London: Johnson Reprint, 1962 and 1963 respectively.

For Quodvultdeus, *Contra Iudaeos, Paganos et Arrianos*, 1:11, in R. Braun, ed., *Opera Quoduultdeo Carthaginiensi Episcopo Tributa*, Turnholti: Brepols, 1976 (Corpus Christianorum, series Latina, vol. 60), p. 228. The Boniface reference on St. Augustine and child baptism is *S. Aureli Augustini Hipponiensis Episcopi Epistulae*, rec. Al. Goldbacher, Vindobonae: Tempsky (the first two *partes* also Pragae: Tempsky), and Lipsiae: Freytag, 5 voll., 1895-1923 (Corpus Scriptorum Ecclesiasticorum Latinorum, voll. 34, 44, 57, 58), pars 2 (1898), p. 528, lines 19-21.

With regard to the Niceta passage, we may perhaps observe that the only translation that I have seen—which, in the usual fashion, renders *credo* by "believe"—simply takes no notice of the fact that here the verb occurs in a past tense. *Niceta of Remesiana: Writings . . .*, Gerald G. Walsh, trans., in Roy Joseph Deferrari, ed., *The Fathers of the Church: a new translation*, vol. 7, New York: Fathers of the Church, Inc., 1949, p. 53. (Admittedly, a present perfect could be argued for; but even so, the usage is sufficiently unusual that it would have to be not merely defended, but explained.)

33 Only in our day, however: it was not always so. There was a time when it was not a mistranslation to render *credo* into English as "believe", but it has become so, since the latter word has changed its meaning in English. See our next chapter, below.

34 We are speaking here of believing as an explicit concept: self-conscious, verbalized, the object of attention. As we endeavoured to clarify in the Islamic case above, this is not the same thing as belief as a name for the pervasive intellectual background of those things to which attention is consciously given, the tacit presuppositions of whatever is being articulated, the world-view in terms of which everything is perceived. Thus when we said above that the verb *credo* did not in those centuries mean "to believe", and developed this a little in reference 32 just above, our point was not that those who used this verb did not believe (also while using it), but that they did not use this term to conceptualize their believing. In this present note we shall comment a little on the presuppositional matter, and shall then indicate that when the early Christians did articulate or self-consciously affirm their vision of the world as distinct from others', they employed other terms than *credo* (and than πιστευω [*pisteuo*]) to designate what was going on in their minds.

The reasons for *credo*'s having come to be thought of as meaning "I believe" in modern times are extremely complex: some of them are examined in our next chapter, and more in my *Belief and History*. In addition, one such reason is that in it, as a term, no doubt beliefs were implied, were presupposed. (And the implication, the presupposition, become the more important the more a modern student of the texts does not share them, or is in explicit or tacit uncertainty about them, or is aware that his readers may be.) Yet this is true of all words; and one must learn to move beyond it. No one can say anything without implying and presupposing a whole range of beliefs. The meaning of every sentence, every word, that any man, woman, or child utters involves a whole world-view. (A Platonist perceives a "table", let alone a "sunset", differently from an Aristotelian, and both perceive them differently from a Taoist. A sensitive ear will hear a difference in the meaning of the word "table" on the lips of the three.) The historian of religion, of all people, would be exceptionally stupid if he or she did not take each world-view seriously. Nonetheless, every word has as well its specific meaning; and cannot be understood without heed given to this. One cannot renounce the Devil without believing in him. *"Credo" in early Christian literature means "I believe" no more (and no less) than does "renuntio".*

If one reads, for instance, chapter 43 of the *Apostolic Constitutions*, to take one example somewhat at random, where the priest who performs the baptism "blesses and glorifies the Lord God . . . giving thanks that He has sent His son to be enhumanized for us that He might save us . . . " and says to God " 'Look down from Heaven and sacralize this water, give grace and power, so that he who is being baptized . . . may be crucified with (Christ) and may die with Him . . . and may rise again into adopted sonship . . . ' " and so on, it is altogether transparent that the writers, the priest, the baptizand, and the congregation (and for many centuries the readers and users of the text) all believed a great many things that Sir John Ayer, to take also that example at random from our own day, does not. These beliefs are utterly presupposed on the part of all of them—so utterly, that there is in the text no mention of anyone's believing them.

This "taking for granted", however, although operative in the Church intramurally and especially in its most sacred and central moments such as in the sacraments, nonetheless could not and did not always obtain. There were disputes, or at least consciousness of difference of ideas, between the Christian movement and the surrounding world (subsequently, also within the Church); and there was instruction in Church doctrine for new converts or inquirers. The phrase *regula fidei* has in recent scholarship been increasingly stressed as designating the norms of the latter, as has been also a need to distinguish between it and the creeds. For example, to take a recent Roman Catholic writer: "a distinction between creed and *regula fidei* . . . has been gradually brought to the state of being an established conclusion of research . . . beyond all doubt, so that it can be taken for granted . . . "—Crehan, *Baptism* . . . [our ref. 12 above], p. 135. Other scholars discriminate between the baptismal creeds proper and "declaratory creeds": an Anglican writes, "declaratory creeds of the ordinary type had no place in the baptismal ritual of the period. If in the fourth century and thereafter their role was, as we saw, secondary, prior to the fourth century they had no role at all"—Kelly, *Creeds* (our ref. 12 above), p. 48; compare his p. 95: "nothing has come to light . . . ". We noted this writer's mentioning "certain reservations" about his otherwise firm statement that "the true and original use of creeds" was "in the context of baptismal initiation" (our ref. 27 above); these reservations, he goes on to develop, have to do precisely with what he calls "declaratory creeds", rather than baptismal, although I myself feel that further clarification would be helpful (or is requisite) along the lines of our further distinction here between belief and faith, to which he is not sensitive. He does say, in his "Conclusions" on this aspect of his study: "Admittedly great stress is laid on orthodox belief by many of the writers we have consulted, and they are all convinced that there is one, universally accepted system of dogma, or rule of faith, in the Catholic Church. But this is never unambiguously connected, even by theologians like St. Irenaeus and Tertullian, with any set form of words" (his p. 95). Again, in his other study, in the course of a discussion on doctrinal norms in the early Church, he remarks: "The truth is that, although the idea was present in embryo, no single term had been earmarked to denote . . . the authoritative handing down of doctrine, or the doctrine so handed down" —Kelly, *Doctrines* (above, our ref. 27), p. 35.

Of the things believed, most never did get expressed in formulae; and several, only gradually. The most salient example of these latter is that in the earliest period baptism was in many instances in the name of Christ only; modern scholars are at pains to indicate that this does not at all signify that those Christians did not believe in God, but rather that such belief was taken for granted, the early converts being Jews. (By the same argument, a [new] commitment to God was superfluous also for a devout [*sic*], committed [*sic*] Jew becoming Christian.) "If, therefore, at any given time one article is absent from the baptismal creed, this does not mean that the Church at that time had ceased to believe, or did not yet believe, in that article, but that it was not set forward prominently . . . "—Crehan, p. 135. (In the twentieth century, the leading New Testament scholar Rudolf Bultmann has been busy setting forth an array of early Christian beliefs, many of which classically never got formulated, and objectivizing them; he tends to call them "myth", and speaks of demythologizing, as if the twentieth-century West's world-view were of some different order. [Cf. above, our chap. 3, ref. 41.]).

Secondly, we may turn to the words by which the Christian movement did express to itself and to outsiders its awareness of its holding to be true some matters that others did not so hold, did not "believe", did not share as conceptualizations. A careful study of this matter could prove rewarding; I have not made it. On going, however, quickly through the first section of the Hahns' volume (above, our ref. 29) of the collected documents and passages —that is, the section (pp. 1-21) entitled *Regula fidei* (as distinct from their second section [pp. 22-159], entitled *Die Taufsymbole*)—one may note what words and phrases appear. There turns out to be a variety of these, of differentiable levels: ranging from some such as καθ' ἡμας (p. 5), *apud nos* (p. 9), "according to us", through a class of terms like (παρα)λαμβανω (both,

p. 6), *trado* (pp. 7, 11), for what we "have received", "what has been handed down" to us, etc., to notions like *praedico* (pp. 9, 11, 12), *annuntio* (p. 9), "proclaim, announce", and finally to *οἶδα, ἐπιγιγνωσκω* (both, p. 5), *nosco* (pp. 7 *bis*, 9, 17), we "know". The first of these groups, which is the most casual and seems also statistically the smallest, is the only one that might in some fashion be equated with modern believing. The second group, specifying what has been transmitted (down through the Christian movement—from the Apostles, etc.) would include such terms as *κατεχω* (p. 6), "holding fast" (what has been received), and probably *διδασκαλια* (p. 14), "teaching". The third group is much employed: the noun *κηρυγμα*, of course, and also the verbs (*προ*)*κηρυσσω* (pp. 1, 4, 13, etc.), *ἀποδεικνυμι* (pp. 4, 5 *bis*), we "show forth", we "make known". The fourth group is particularly interesting; in addition to the repeated "we know", one should include here also the frequent use of words for "truth". What moderns usually call the *regula fidei* appears sometimes so or as *κανων της πιστεως* (p. 1, fn.) but also as *κανων της ἀληθειας* and *regula veritatis* (pp. 6, 7; cf. p. 1, fn.). Cf. the use of the adverb *ἀληθως* (p. 1 passim), "truly". Our categories also occur mixed, as one might expect: "the truth that has been proclaimed"—*ἡ . . . κηρυσσομενη ἀληθεια* (p. 1, fn.); "we find it to be proclaimed"—*εὑρομεν προκηρυσσομενον* (p. 4); "we truly know . . . [the "know" is repeated three times] and we say just what we were taught"—*οἰδαμεν ἀληθως . . . οἰδαμεν . . . οἰδαμεν . . . . Και ταυτα λεγομεν ἁ ἐμαθομεν* (pp. 5-6); and so on. On this question more work waits to be done: my presentation here does not pretend, of course, to be more than highly preliminary and indicative. It does suggest that the early Christian movement, as well as operating within a vision that it had seen, could on occasion articulate that vision in contradistinction from that of those who had not seen it, while proclaiming the splendours in life available to those who joined; but it suggests also that by and large they spoke in terms of something that they had discovered, and of something of which the truth was an occasion for joyous proclamation more than for reflective argument or self-conscious analysis.

I also get the impression, and suggest in my renderings above, although this would have to be considered with a wider range of data than I have examined here, that on the whole when speaking of its ideas the Church tended to use the first person plural, whereas the existential performatives *πιστευω* and *credo* are normally used in the first person singular.

References: *The Apostolic Constitutions*, Funk edn. (our ref. 29 above), pp. 448, 450. Hahn, *Symbole*, our ref. 29 above.

35 We have sufficiently set forth Christian baptismal accounts to make clear, I trust, the kind of service that it was and what it was "about": something other than believing in a particular way. We have also remarked on how the early Christians themselves perceived what they were doing, noting their use of military-oath metaphors, of words like "promise", "vow", "engagement", "pact", and the like. To this sort of exposition one could go on adding: for instance, Justin Martyr in writing his reasoned apologetics presenting to the non-Christian world a careful statement of what Christians were

up to, begins his description of baptism with the words, "In what manner we dedicated ourselves to God . . . I shall now explain": his words are Ὃν τρόπον δὲ καὶ ἀνεθήκαμεν ἑαυτοὺς τῷ θεῷ . . . ἐξηγησόμεθα, and this phrasing must surely be taken quite seriously as a clear indication of how he perceives the ceremony —as an act of formal self-commitment or consecration; he does not at all suggest that even for an interested outsider baptism would come across as a formal declaration of what it is that Christians believe. (*Apologia* 1:61, opening clause).

Rather than multiply examples of this kind of thing, we may instead elaborate, just a little, two subordinate points, on the ideational dimension of the rite.

First: while there is little mention, throughout the instructional sessions, the preparatory homilies, the post-baptismal reception periods, and the like, of things that an intending or new Christian should believe, yet there are here and there presentations (not so many as one might have expected) of or references to teachings; things that, one might say, he or she should *know* —but not that he or she "should" know, even, so much as things that it becomes his or her privilege to know. Yet even these matters, one may observe, in some eras and areas preceded, and in others followed, the ceremony: it is not they with which the ceremony itself was concerned. They are not what baptism itself was about.

On the "privilege" matter, we may note that in several cases the convert must not disclose these to outsiders; not even, once he or she is baptized, must the initiate disclose them to catechumens who have begun the process of becoming Christian(s) but have not yet taken the plunge.

One instance of such instruction's following the ceremony is Cyril himself. The opening lecture of the *Mystagogae* (1:1) eloquently declares to the group that, now that they have been baptized, the moment has come for full instruction in order that they mäy know (*sic*) . . . : τῶν ἐντελεστέρων . . . μαθημάτων . . . ἵνα εἰδῆτε. In North Africa, contrariwise: there it was a custom for Christians to remain in the catechumen state for many years, often postponing the baptism ceremony virtually until just before death, although they were recognized and recognized themselves as within the Church community, were ceremonially marked and named as Christians, and partook of some sacraments. It would collide with virtually all the evidence available to suppose that such persons did not *believe* the Christian message (or that their eventual baptismal act was a sign of their coming to do so).

Moreover, the teaching that was at issue in all these instructional matters (Latin, *doctrina*; Greek διδαχη, διδαχαι, διδασκαλια [*didachē*, *didachai*, *didaskalia*]) was at least as much moral and practical as it was theoretical teaching. (One vivid illustration of this is the influential early text entitled the *Didache*, quite preponderently moralist and procedural. Cf. also the later *Didascalia*. On the historical change of the meaning of the term *doctrina*, cf. our ref. 38 below.)

In Antioch, the questioning of the candidate for baptism in order to ascertain whether he have the qualifications for "citizenship" in the "new and great city" of the Church, involved also a sponsor's testifying on the candidate's behalf as to his worthiness to be enrolled; and the questioning was "about his mode of life" and "what the catechumen has done" (not: what he has believed, or believes), although it is carefully pointed out that the sponsor (called "godfather") "does not make himself responsible . . . in connection with future sins, as each one of us answers for his own sins before God", but attests only as to the candidate's behaviour (*sic*) up to this point. It is evident that the actual questioning here is moralist—even though it be also evident that, as ever, an ideational substratum tacitly pervades this entire text. (Theodore, *Ad Baptizandos* 2:2, Homily 12, §14-15). Moreover, this presentation goes on to portray with almost melodramatic power the notion that the actual pronouncing of the *credo* (or in this instance πιστευω [*pisteuō*]: *[wa-]mhaymen [']nā'*) comes after "the judgment and fight with the Demon . . . are at an end; and when by God's decision the Tyrant has submitted and yielded . . . [and] you are completely free from any disturbance from him": that is, when the candidate has, by divine grace, now the extraordinary moral power to make the act of solemn engagement that he now makes. Once again, belief (a world-view) is patently implicit; but it is not what baptism is about.

Secondly, there were indeed some quite intellectualist questions having to do with the rite of baptism itself, even though these were neither decisive nor stressed. They were such theoretical issues as the legitimacy of so simple a substance as water for so solemn a rite; whether faith without baptism suffices, and what is the significance of baptism by John (for Christ Himself; perhaps also for the Twelve), or (for contemporaries) by heretics; and so on. These are in our sense doctrinal questions to which, for instance, Tertullian's treatise *De Baptismo* is addressed. One may say that in this sense, about early Christian baptism some belief questions were explicit. They played no part in the ceremony itself, however; and in any case this leaves intact our thesis that the central Christian belief questions—and they were indeed central, we do not deny—were for the baptismal sacrament implicit, rather.

References for the above: For Justin Martyr, I have used A. W. F. Blunt, ed., *The Apologies of Justin Martyr*, Cambridge (England): [Cambridge] University Press, 1911 (A. J. Mason, gen. ed., Cambridge Patristic Texts), where this passage is p. 90 (in the Athens edn. [our ref. 29 above], p. 194). For Cyril: Piédagnel (our ref. 4 above), pp. [82]-84 (-85). For North Africa, see "The Making of a Catechumen", in the Africa section (chap. 6) of Whitaker, *Documents* (our ref. 12 above), pp. 90-92. A good bibliography on the history of the Christian catechumenate in general is available in Thomas Ohm, *Das Katechumenat in den katholischen Missionen*, Münster: Aschendorff, 1959, p. 8, fn. 1 (this work itself hardly deals otherwise with the early centuries). For the *Didache*, an easily accessible and convenient edition (Greek text [after Harris] and English translation) is that of Kirsopp Lake, ed., *The Apostolic Fathers*, vol. 1, London: Heinemann, and Cambridge, Mass.: Harvard University Press, [1912], 1970, pp. [303]-333. The important recent scholarly study, with re-edition of the text, is Jean-Paul Audet, *La*

Didachè: instructions des Apôtres, Paris: Lecoffre (J. Gabalda et cie.), 1958 (Études bibliques). (On the meaning of the title, originally in the plural, see Audet, pp. 91-103, 116-120, and [247]-254; chiefly, however, the eloquent testimony to the moralist connotation of the title is the text itself. This is so, dramatically, from the very opening sentence [Lake, p. 308; Audet, p. (226)] and for the first part generally [the "Two Ways"]; yet also later in the work's more manifestly Christian-and-ritualist sections, it continues as more a manual of discipline, of behavioural instruction, and is still not doctrinal in the post-Enlightenment sense of that word.) For the *Didascalia Apostolorum*, the Funk edn. (above, our ref. 29); see also s.v. in F. L. Cross and E. A. Livingstone, edd., *The Oxford Dictionary of the Christian Church*, 2nd edn., London &c: Oxford University Press, 1974. For Theodore of Mopsuestia, I have given here the Mingana trans. (our ref. 5 above), pp. 24, 25, 33. For Tertullian, I have used the Evans edn. of the *De Baptismo* (above, our ref. 16).

36 Throughout this section it has been sufficiently set forth, I trust, what the creeds were "about": something other than believing. Here, however, we consider one final passage illuminating for the meaning for Christians of the verb πιστευω [*pisteuō*]. It has already been remarked (above, our ref. 31) that this Greek term differed from the Latin *credo* in harbouring a more intellectualist component, even if that component be still subordinate to the notion of self-dedication and *s'engager*. I do not find the word *credo* in the early centuries in Church usage naming (as distinct from implying or presupposing) a theoretical activity of the mind. Some might recognize or concede that its use as the first word in the Creeds indeed named primarily rather a practical or moral movement, but would yet contend that a theological asseveration was consciously included. I am suggesting that this came to be in part the case in subsequent centuries (as we explore in our next section, below); but meanwhile I acknowledge that something of this was already more true for the Greek term than, so far as I can see, for the Latin.

Illustrative of what that intellectualist component consisted of, and what it did not, and therefore of what the Creeds were felt to be about, is, I suggest, the following sentence of Origen: οἱον ὁ πιστευων τι ἑστιν ἡ δικαιοσυνη οὐκ ἀν ἀδικησαι, και δια το τεθεωρηκεναι ἡτις ἐστιν ἡ σοφια, πεπιστευκως εἰς την σοφιαν οὐκ ἀν τι μωρον λεγοι ἠ πραττοι, ἐπει ὁ πιστευσας τῳ ἐν ἀρχῃ προς τον θεον λογῳ ἐν τῳ κατανενοηκεναι αὐτον οὐδεν ἀλογως ποιησαι. This occurs in his commentary (19:23/6) on the Gospel of John, in exegesis of John 8:24, where Christ is being presented as affirming "Unless you have faith (πιστευσητε [*pisteusēte*]) that I am, you will die in your sins". Origen has been speaking of having faith that Jesus is the Christ (το . . . πιστευειν ὁτι Ἰησους ἐστιν ὁ χριστος), of having faith in Christ (πιστευειν τῳ χριστῳ [*pisteuein tō*i *christō*i]), and of faith absolutely (πιστις, ὁ πιστευων [*pistis, ho pisteuōn*])—noun and verb occurring ten times in this section; then comes the above sentence. It has been translated as follows: "Just as he who has believed what justice is could do no wrong, and he who has perceived what wisdom is could neither do nor say foolish things, so whoever believes in the word that was in the beginning with God, in contemplating him, will do nothing irrational".

To begin with, the first clause so rendered makes no sense at all. History at large is conspicuously disfigured with instances of those who have believed what justice is—believed that it is *x* or *y* or *z*—and have done much wrong; and each of us is familiar enough with the same phenomenon in our own and our neighbours' lives. This sentence of Origen's is a telling illustration, surely, of the thesis (developed in my *Belief and History*, chap. 3) that at a minimum πιστευειν [*pisteuein*] means to discern, to recognize, to perceive the truth: intellectually to grasp aright what its object objectively is. (This is precisely what "to believe" nowadays takes pains *not* to mean.) "He who *rightly discerns* what justice is can do no wrong" is a possible translation of this text. Even this is, however, minimal: as the second and presumably parallel example that Origen here adduces makes clear, our verb goes beyond and adds something decisive to a theoretical recognition of the truth. He who has perceived (perhaps more lovingly: has contemplated) what wisdom is, and then has *dedicated himself to* that wisdom, cannot speak or act unwisely. What else can the Greek mean?

To have beliefs about wisdom is no guarantee of wise talk or wise behaviour, Origen must have known as well as we do. True insight into, plus fidelity towards, a virtue ensures a virtuous life.

Returning now to our first clause, may we not say that we are presented then with three possible interpretations. "He who has faith in justice cannot act unjustly" means either (i) he who has truly recognized what justice is cannot prove unjust; or (ii) he who has truly recognized what justice is, and has dedicated himself to living accordingly, cannot; or (iii)—like (ii) but omitting (i) rather than including it: he who dedicates himself to what justice (truly) is cannot act unjustly. If one take this clause alone, all three are logically possible. In the second of Origen's three clauses here taken alone the first of these three possibilities collapses (because of the other verb), and we are left with the second and third; considering the infinitive τεθεωρηκεναι [*tetheōrēkenai*] and the tense of the perfect participle πεπιστευκως [*pepisteukōs*], the third perhaps is the more likely. Taking the total context, then, my own considered preference is perhaps for the second interpretation even in the first clause, but I would not argue against the third (and indeed would choose the third for the second clause: our verb then having sometimes the second, sometimes the third, of our three meanings, in quick succession).

The remainder of this particular passage is also compelling.

Πιστευω never for Christians means "to believe" in the sense of having a belief, however firmly held. It either signifies recognizing a truth (like the Islamic *shahādah* that we cited: above, our chap. 3, pp. 42f.—"I bear witness to the truth that . . . ", with the truth in question being along with its truthfulness presupposed), or else, with this recognizing also denoted or else implicit, it signifies appropriating that truth to oneself, undertaking to order one's life accordingly, consecrating one's total person to the truth that one's intellect has descried (been enabled to descry). Of these two, only the demons do the former alone (James 2:19); and tremble. In the early Christian Creeds, *credo*, I suggest, denoted the latter; πιστευω denoted it plus sometimes the former as perhaps an additional component, of awareness, more or less consciously added.

Reference: A. E. Brooke, ed., *The Commentary of Origen on S. John's Gospel: the text revised, with a critical introduction and indices*, Cambridge [England]: [Cambridge] University Press, 2 voll., 1896, vol. 2, p. 32 (cf. pp. 31-33). (In the Erwin Preuschen edn., Leipzig, 1903 [*Origines Werke*, 4te Band], p. 325 [324-326].)

37 On the concept that faith has something called an "object", see above, our chap. 4, ref. 41.

38 Of course the transition was complicated: a great many factors were at work. The influence of Greek thought, and especially of the Greek attitude to thinking, was one matter of significance—even if it now seem somewhat over-simplified for a highly influential Hibbert Lecturer at the turn of the century to speak one-sidedly of "the transition by which, under the influence of contemporary Greek thought, the word Faith came to be transferred from simple trust in God to mean the acceptance of a series of propositions, and these propositions, propositions in abstract metaphysics"—in a lecture on "The Incorporation of Christian Ideas, as Modified by Greek, into a Body of Doctrine". One must note, even, that as we have remarked, the word "doctrine" originally meant "teaching" and included, even emphasized, moral and practical teaching, and had much to do with the will, the affections, and behaviour; the shift by which this word "doctrine" has come to mean theoretical teaching, and specifically formulated propositions, is itself part of the process that we are considering. This process has been completed, however, much more recently than one might suppose: I have discovered, for instance, that still in the eighteenth century John Wesley discriminates decisively between "doctrine" and "opinion", meaning by the latter what we to-day would call propositional beliefs, and by the former non-propositionalized teaching, largely moral. (Cf. below, our chap. 6, ref. 69.)

Another element in the early process was that the Creed and other liturgical formulae and rites shifted from being a ceremony for the admission of proselytes to being a test for Christians. A recent authority (Dix) writes: "The . . . original usage [of the creed] was at baptism. . . . The Council of Nicaea in A.D. 325 carried the use of the creed . . . further. It was no longer to be only a test of belief for those entering the church from outside . . . the creed was to be made a test for those already within the church. . . . And since the old formulae, however well they might serve to distinguish a pagan or a jew from a christian, were too imprecise to distinguish an Arian from an orthodox christian, the Council drew up a new creed".

References: Edwin Hatch, [*The Influence of Greek Ideas and Usages upon the Christian Church*, A. M. Fairbairn, ed., London and Edinburgh: Williams and Norgate, 1890 (The Hibbert Lectures, 1888)]; *The Influence of Greek Ideas on Christianity*, New York: Harper & Row—Harper Torchbooks, 1957, p. 310. Dom Gregory Dix, *The Shape of the Liturgy*, Westminster: Dacre Press, [1945], 1949, pp. 485-486.

39 Although to-day the formalization of the practice in Catholic ceremonial

renewal is without official sanction, Crehan notes: "The practice of asking the congregation at the close of a Mission to renew their baptismal vows . . . may be due to a survival in the *sensus fidelium* of this contractual view of baptism" (Crehan, *Baptism* [our ref. 12 above], p. 110 fn.). Similarly, in the Anglican Church the practice of Confirmation has been (in most versions of the Prayer Book since 1662) explicitly linked with "the reaffirmation of Baptismal Vows". Confirmation, after a long and complicated history, has become a ceremony in which the Christian takes on him- or herself the pledges made on his or her behalf by others at infancy, formally accepting one's baptismal oath of loyalty as one's own. In the most recent wording, the question and answer emerge as follows (with no reference to belief):

> BISHOP Do you reaffirm your renunciation of evil and your commitment to Jesus Christ?
>
> CANDIDATE I do, and with God's grace I will follow him as my Savior and Lord. (p. 417: see full reference at end of this note)

Indeed, in Baptism itself the latest proposal in phrasing substitutes explicit performatives for the earlier, and now anachronistic, "believe". After the three questions about renunciation (and their answers, "I renounce them"), the formula runs as follows:

> *Question* Do you turn to Jesus Christ and accept him as your Savior?
> *Answer* I do.
> *Question* Do you put your whole trust in his grace and love?
> *Answer* I do.
> *Question* Do you promise to follow and obey him as your Lord?
> *Answer* I do. (pp. 304-305)

Once again, doctrine is here presupposed, not mentioned. (This is a truer translation of classical baptismal services than has been seen in English for long.) The traditional verb "believe", however, does creep back in again in the subsequent congregational response to the celebrant's invitation to those "who witness these vows [*sic*]": "Let us join with those who are committing themselves [*sic*] to Christ and renew our own baptismal covenant [*sic*]" (p. 305). For "The Baptismal Covenant", as it is called (p. 306), thereupon recited includes the Apostles' Creed (p. 306, retaining "believe"), followed by further promises and pledges (pp. 306-307). I predict that before long (perhaps in the next revision?) the word "believe" will be superseded here also, and in fact will be dropped from all ceremonies and formulae of the English-speaking Church, as it has been dropped here from the actual Baptism ceremony.

Reference: *The Draft Proposed Book of Common Prayer and Administration of the Sacraments and Other Rites and Ceremonies of the Church, according to the use of the Protestant Episcopal Church in the United States of America otherwise known as The Episcopal Church; Together With The Psalter or Psalms of David*, New York: Church Hymnal Corporation, 1976.

40 See, most provocatively, Georges Dumézil, *L'Idéologie tripartie des indo-européens*, Bruxelles: Latomus—Revue d'Etudes Latines (Collection Latomus, vol. 31), 1958.

41 The West has been fairly consistent historically in discriminating three components in human personality; but not in identifying which three they be. Ever since the Greeks, and what Bruno Snell is represented as calling their "Discovery of the Mind" (that phrasing is for our particular purposes hardly sophisticated [indeed, he himself took pains to annotate the subtler German original]; in world-history terms one might say, their conceptualizing of reason) there has been persistent agreement on the rational intellect as one ingredient in the threefold complex. (In modern times, no doubt, the concept of rationality has dwindled in Western consciousness, of late drastically: losing for many its original metaphysical dimension [the foundation of its human significance], and for most its mediaeval coverage of both intellect and will, becoming equated with the gradually shrinking former only—until to-day it for many evaporates, and with Gilbert Ryle and others we have in effect a proposal—however un-self-conscious historically—that "the concept of mind" be now dropped.) The other two of a triad, however, have been diversely specified. The Semitic stress on will (which, it has been argued, was not a concept in classical Greek thought) was imported into Western civilization by the Church. The tendency to think in terms of intellect, will, and feeling is modern: the gradual coming into prominence of a "feeling" concept can be observed through the Enlightenment and the Romantic Movement.

The three elements of the human *psyche* were, for Plato, reason, pluck, and desire (*το λογιστικον, το θυμοειδες, το ἐπιθυμητικον* [*to logistikon, to thymoeides, to epithymētikon*]). For St. Augustine, various sets of three-in-one's were mentioned (examples are *esse, nosse, uelle*; *mens, notitia, amor*), the most important being *memoria*, intellect (*intellectus* or *intelligentia*), and will (*voluntas*)—the unexpected *memoria* here we might perhaps almost be tempted to translate as "self-consciousness". (To the development of individual self-consciousness in the West St. Augustine's contribution was decisive especially through his *Confessiones*, his memory objectified and publicly rendered. With this *memoria* as the historical dimension of temperament—with biographical self-awareness as a basic component of personality, in Western modes of thinking—it is interesting to compare and to contrast Sanskrit *vāsanā*, the temperament and qualities inherited by a person through *karma* from his or her previous, unremembered, lives. [Cf. above, our chap. 4, ref. 82.])

References:

Bruno Snell, *Die Entdeckung des Geistes: Studien zur Entstehung des europäischen Denkens bei den Griechen*, Hamburg: Claassen & Goverts, [1946], 1948. T. G. Rosenmeyer, trans., *The Discovery of the Mind: the Greek origins of European thought* [Oxford: Blackwell, and Cambridge (Massachusetts): Harvard University Press, 1953], New York: Harper & Row—Harper Torchbooks, 1960. For his reservations about the title, see pp. 8, 9; Eng. trans., pp. viii-ix, where also *das Geist* is rendered rather as "intellect".

Gilbert Ryle, *The Concept of Mind*, London etc.: Hutchinson's University Library, 1949.

On the concept of feeling, see the carefully annotated articles by Ursula Franke et al. s.v. *Gefühl* in Joachim Ritter, ed., *Historisches Wörterbuch der Philosophie*, Basel/Stuttgart: Schwabe, Band 3, 1974, coll. 82ff.

Plato, *Republic*, Book 4, 434d to 444a, and elsewhere. I have used Ioannes Burnet, ed., *Platonis Res Publica*, Oxonii: Clarendoniano, n.d. [sc. 1902?] (Scriptorum Classicorum Bibliotheca Oxoniensis).

St. Augustine: *Confessiones*, 13:12/11; *De Trinitate*, 9:4/4, 5/8, etc.; *De Trinitate*, Books 10-15 passim. I have used the following ednn.: *Sancti Aureli Augustini Confessionum libri tredecim*, ed. Pius Knöll, Vindobonae, Pragae: Tempsky/Lipsiae: Freytag [1896], New York and London: Johnson reprint, 1962, p. 353. Sancti Aurelii Augustini, *De Trinitate libri XV*, edd. W. J. Mountain, Fr. Glorie, Turnholti: Brepols, 2 voll., 1968 (Corpus Christianorum, series Latina, vol. 50—Augustini Opera, pars 16), pp. 297-535. In some older editions the triads *mens*, *notitia*, *amor* and *memoria*, *intelligentia*, *voluntas* are entered as titles of Books 9, 10 of the *De Trinitate* respectively; e.g., the Benedictine edn. as reproduced in the Bibliothèque augustinienne series, *Oeuvres de Saint Augustin*, P. Agaësse et al., edd. et tradd., [Paris]: Desclée de Brouwer, vol. 16, 1955, pp. 72, 114. The literature is immense on St. Augustine's conception of the *imago Dei* in man, and on its influence. For a striking four-page "Table des triades", see Olivier du Roy, *L'Intelligence de la foi en la Trinité selon Saint Augustin: genèse de sa théologie trinitaire jusqu'en 391*, Paris: Études augustiniennes, 1966, pp. [537]-540.

42 "Faith . . . is in the will": *fidem, quae in voluntate est*—St. Augustine, *De Praedestinatione Sanctorum*, 5/10. This and the other statements about to be adduced occur in the midst of his vigorous anti-Pelagian argumentation. Pelagius interpreted faith as an act of man's free will; Augustine differed subtly on the question of freedom, but not on the question of will. In reply to his opponents' stand that not all who hear the truth spoken, respond to it in committed allegiance, some rather choosing (willing) to be loyal, others choosing not to be, he asks rhetorically: Who will not recognize that fact? Who deny it? "*Multi audiunt verbum veritatis: sed alii credunt, alii contradicunt. Volunt ergo isti credere, nolunt autem illi.*" *Quis hoc ignoret? quis hoc neget?* (6/11). As he has just affirmed, however: "It is not that having faith or not having faith is not a matter of decision of the human will; but in those who have been chosen, the will is priorly made ready by the Lord"—*non quia credere vel non credere non est in arbitrio voluntatis humanae, sed in electis praeparatur voluntas a Domino* (5/10).

The three quotations here adduced are from *Oeuvres de Saint Augustin, 3ème série: La grâce—Aux moines d'Adrumète et de Provence: De Gratia . . . De Praedestinatione Sanctorum* . . . [etc.], texte de l'édition bénédictine, introduction, traduction et notes par Jean Chéné . . . et Jacques Pintard, [Paris]: Desclée de Brouwer, 1962 (Bibliothèque augustinienne, 24), pp. 496, 496-498, 496 respectively.

In the second quotation, note that *contradico* in standard Latin does not mean "not to believe" a proposition, but rather "to oppose, to take a stand against" a proposal. See, e.g., *Oxford Latin Dictionary*, Oxford: Clarendon Press, 1968- , in process, s.v., fascicule 2, 1969, p. 434.

One may note our reff. 32 above and 58 below for a few further illustrations of Augustine's position, but I by no means pretend to proffering here a balanced study of his views on faith. Those views would, however, presumably corroborate more readily even than Aquinas, whose position we do consider a little more extensively, the theses of this present work.

43 One example from among many: *ad actum fidei requiritur actus voluntatis et actus intellectus*—"Requisite to the act of faith is [both] an act of the will and an act of the intellect": *Summa Th.*, 2:2:4:5 (Caramello, II:31). Cf. 2:2:5:4 (II:38). More flatly: . . . *cum credere sit voluntarium*—ibid., 2:2:1:6 (II:9); etc. I notice a tendency to preserve the will part more in *credere* than in *fides*, with *actus fidei* following the former. Cf. *fides . . . est quodammodo ex voluntate credentis—De Veritate*, 14:3, ad 11 (Spiazzi, p. 287). He is not unaware that for St. Augustine, faith was located in the will—*Dicit enim Augustinus . . . quod fides in credentium voluntate consistit: Summa Th.*, 2:2:4:2 (listed among the first objections that he must answer); cf., with differing word order, 2:2:5:2 (id.) (II:28, 36). He could not, of course, have the historical awareness available to us, nor self-consciously see himself, as we may see him, as innovatively involved in a long-range development: the role of the will in faith inherited from earlier centuries is still present in his thought, but the process of a shift to the intellect is crystallized in him. For him, the will remains no doubt still an essential component: *illud quod est ex parte voluntatis . . . est . . . essentiale fidei* (*De Veritate*, 14:3, ad 10 [Spiazzi, p. 287]). Nonetheless—and he seems to have been the first in the history of Christian theology to do this—he explicitly located faith (as potentially distinct, however, from the act of faith) in the intellect, as its "subject": *Summa Th.*, 2:2:4:2, entitled *Utrum fides sit in intellectu sicut in subiecto* (Caramello, II:28-29).

Reference specifications: *S. Thomae Aquinatis . . . Quaestiones Disputatae*, vol. 1: *De Veritate*, ed. Raymund[us] Spiazzi, Taurini, Romae: Marietti, 1964. For the *Summa Theologiae*, see above, our chap. 1 ref. 13.

The text specifies that Thomas's reference to Augustine is from "*De Praed. Sanct.*" (cf. just above, our ref. 42). The Caramello edition of the *Summa* (II: 28, 36) and some other modern editors, following the Leonine text, print the words in italics, as if a direct quotation. I take it to be indirect discourse, rather, not being able to find this actual phrasing in the passages designated in that Augustine work, chap. 5 (according to Caramello, II:36, it is 5/10), nor in the Migne reference given (44:968). As a paraphrase, however, rather than a quotation, the statement is certainly valid (cf. just above, our ref. 42).

For the novelty of Thomas's position, see Roger Aubert, *Le problème de l'acte de foi: données traditionnelles et résultats des controverses récentes*, Louvain: Nauwelaerts, and Paris: Béatrice-Nauwelaerts, [1945], 4ème édn., 1969, p. 53, fn. 22: "le premier dans l'histoire de la théologie, il attribue pour sujet à la vertu de foi l'intellect spéculatif".

44 At least, in his scholarly writing—which is how we here consider him, and of course how he has been primarily known and received through all subsequent centuries. We leave aside all question as to whether as a person he lived a life of faith less intellectualistic than that set forth in his voluminous scholastic written output: how far Thomas the monk differed from or supplemented Thomas the teacher. We leave aside also both Thomas the composer of prayers (in this role he has also been influential), and Thomas the poet. (Of those who are familiar with *Panis angelicus* as sung to the music of, for instance, César Franck, many are unaware that the poem was composed, evidently, by Thomas as part of one of his hymns for the new feast Corpus Christi introduced into Church life by Pope Urban IV in 1264, who is said to have requested Thomas to compile the Mass and Office for it. The authenticity of the attribution of authorship for the whole is not unquestioned, but is accepted by the most recent and careful scholar Weisheipl; Eschmann regards it as "beyond discussion" [p. 424] that Thomas composed the liturgy [item #76 in his catalogue] but leaves in doubt whether the present text of the whole may be original or a revised version.)

We leave aside also Thomas the mystic. On this and his "disavowal" at the end of his life of his intellectualist writings, see below, our ref. 63.

References: James A. Weisheipl, *Friar Thomas d'Aquino: his life, thought, and work*, Garden City, New York: Doubleday, 1974, p. 400; cf. pp. 176-184. I. T. Eschmann, "A Catalogue of St. Thomas's Works: Bibliographical Notes", added as an appendix to the English translation of the fifth edition of Gilson's *Le Thomisme*: Etienne Gilson, *The Christian Philosophy of St. Thomas Aquinas*, trans. L. K. Shook, [New York: Random House, 1956], London: Gollancz, 1957, pp. 381-439.

45 Bernard was more of a saint than an intellectual. Although himself erudite, a brilliant stylist, and certainly acutely intelligent, and with many scholarly tomes to his credit, yet he was not one of those who feel that man's true destiny is fulfilled in knowing. He took seriously St. Paul's dictum, "Knowledge puffeth up, but love edifieth" (I Corinthians 8:1; in the Vulgate, as he often quoted, *scientia inflat; caritas vero aedificat*). Typical is his observation that those who desire knowledge may do so out of idle curiosity or the vanity of wishing to be known or for pecuniary profit or prestige, but that only those who desire to know for others' welfare or their own edification avoid the abuse of knowledge. (Sermo 36, from his *Sermones super Cantica Canticorum*, in S. Bernardi, *Opera*, J. Leclercq et al., edd., Romae: Editiones Cistercienses, 1957- [in process], vol. 2, pp. [3]-8; this passage is from pp. 5-6.)

For one delightful passage in which this acute thinker and mystic discriminates between faith and belief (*fides* and *opinio*), see his Tractatus *De Consideratione*, 5:3:6 (*Opera*, vol. 3, pp. 470-471). On this passage cf. further below, our ref. 51.

With *scientia* he contrasted *sapientia.* I have translated the former as "knowing, knowledge"; the latter is regularly rendered "wisdom", but for St. Bernard it, and the corresponding verb *sapere*, preserve a good deal of their original base of *sapor*, "taste". The term conceptualized what was for him very much an experiential matter. It is interesting to compare the Muslim thinker Ghazzālī's term *dhawq*—also "taste", in Arabic—which he contrasts with (mere) *'ilm*, knowledge. Interesting, further, would be a general essay on the use historically of the metaphor of seeing for man's knowing of God, as distinct from that of tasting or of feeling. Modern English has tended to reserve this last metaphor for the emotions.

46 *Itinerarium mentis in Deum*. Written in 1259. I have used the edn. of the Fathers of the Bonaventura College (*auctoritate* Bernadini), *Doctoris Seraphici S. Bonaventurae . . . Opera Omnia*, Ad Claras Aquas (*Quaracchi*): Ex Typographia Collegii S. Bonaventurae, 10 voll., 1882-1902, 5: [293]-316. A recent English translation constitutes the first item in *The Works of Bonaventure, Cardinal, Seraphic Doctor, and Saint, translated from the Latin by* José de Vinck, Paterson, New Jersey: St. Anthony Guild Press, 4 voll., 1960-1966, 1:1-58: "The Journey of the Mind to God".

47 The title of the seventh, concluding, chapter of the *Itinerarium* is (in the translation of de Vinck just cited), "On mental and mystical ravishment in which repose is given to the soul that rises toward God in ecstatical love". The original reads: *De excessu mentali et mystico, in quo requies datur intellectui, affectu totaliter in Deum per excessum transeunte*. He speaks of "pass[ing] over to God" (*in Deum transiit*: why not translate "into God"?) in "a rapture of contemplation" (*per contemplationis excessum*: rather "through leaving contemplation behind"?), in which passing over, if it is to be perfect, all intellectual activities must be given up (*in hoc autem transitu, si sit perfectus, oportet quod relinquantur omnes intellectuales operationes*). References in the editions mentioned in our preceding ref. 46 just above: Latin, 5:312, English, 1:55-57.

Bonaventura's position on the nature of faith is touched upon throughout his writings, of course, but is formalized chiefly in his commentary on the Sentences of Peter Lombard, on the 23rd distinction (*De Fide . . .*). (In *Opera Omnia*, the Quaracchi edn. cit. [above, our ref. 46], 3:469-506.) Cf. also the subsequent two distt. (ibid., pp. 506-553). For further discussion of these passages, and generally of his position on faith, especially in its relation to knowledge, see below, our ref. 71.

48 We have remarked above (our ref. 44) that we "leave aside" here the non-intellectualist matters of St. Thomas's life. Nonetheless, it is not uninteresting to reflect on the fact that the ideas that a man has—and expresses, so that it may become they that primarily or exclusively affect others and are communicated to later centuries—may or must themselves be in significant part the outcome of his whole personality and not merely of his mind. What a person sees, notices, attends to, and follows up intellectually, is a function of his will and heart (and historical situation) as well as of his mind. This is the more true, the more total his intellectual integrity. Since the intellectual integrity of his readers is often less than of a writer—and conspicuously so, in the case of a great thinker in the realm that is our concern here—this dimension of what went into his thought may become less emphasized, or

even noticed. Also, of course, as is central to the argument of this book, the historical situations of the world's great religious thinkers (including the religious community in which they lived and the world-view with which they worked) have differed from each other and from ours. It is the glory of human intellectuality that we can communicate and understand—and preserve each our intellectual integrity—across such differences.

49 A modern may be hard put to it to realize to what length Thomas (and other classical and mediaeval intellectuals) carried this. For him, for example, not only is man's chief business to know, but also things in the material universe (what we in recent times call "objects") are real (*vera*) insofar as they correspond to ideas in the mind of God: are "true" according to the knowledge of God. That is, unlike the position of most thinkers to-day, for him truth precedes being (except in the case of God Himself, for whom they co-incide).

50 He was, of course, by no means uninterested also in the ethical; yet he subordinates it finally to the speculative. Unlike the modern, pragmatically oriented who think of the truth as conducing to practice, and even as defined by it, he regarded good works as rendering man better able to know. By good works, man's knowledge of God is perfected: *de actibus humanis . . . agit secundum quod per eos ordinatur homo ad perfectam Dei cognitionem, in qua aeterna beatitudo consistit.* Just preceding this statement is the important affirmation, *licet in scientiis philosophicis alia sit speculativa et alia practica, sacra tamen doctrina comprehendit sub se utramque. . . . Magis tamen est speculativa quam practica.*

These quotations are from *Summa Th.*, 1:1:4 (Caramello 1:4).

51 In the modern world, the secular intellectual Edward Shils speaks of "the transcendent value of science" (in addition to and in many ways prior to its utilitarian value). "Scientists are sustained", he observes sociologically, by "the faith that truth is valuable and that cognitive activity of the scientific sort is an intrinsic good", and asks "whether it is conceivable" that this faith, both among scientists themselves and in the society that economically and otherwise supports them, might wane, to the point where "what is already discovered might be retained" but the pursuit of truth not yet discovered might no longer be operative. Edward Shils, "Faith, Utility, and the Legitimacy of Science" in *Daedalus: Journal of the American Academy of Arts and Sciences*, Summer 1974, pp. 11, 4, 4, 12, 13.

Going back a few centuries, this matter in the case of the English philosopher John Locke is discussed in my *Belief and History*, pp. 83-84. St. Bernard of Clairvaux, to take another example, from the century before Aquinas, also illustrates the theme explicitly. In, for instance, the same passage that we cited above (our ref. 45) in which this thinker comments on the difference between faith and belief (*fides* and *opinio*), he considers also the relation between faith and apprehension, understanding (*intellectus*). Faith is not belief, he says, since the latter is holding to be true what one does not know to be false; about belief there is or can be uncertainty. Faith has no such ambiguity: otherwise, it would not be faith, but merely belief. How then, he asks, does faith differ from apprehension, awareness? It is no less certain than this latter, and yet involves a shrouded quality (*habet tamen involucrum*) as apprehension does not. It has to do with truth not yet discovered (*necdum propalatae veritatis*). *About what one has apprehended there are no further questions to be asked.* (This, for Bernard, is what the term *intellectus* denotes.) Faith, accordingly, has to do with willing, and is an anticipatory apprehension, a foretaste or "sipping" of truth yet to be fully grasped. Faith is that by which we know what it is that we wish to know (*Nil autem malumus scire, quam quae fide iam scimus*).

Faith, then (here I am paraphrasing; the rest is translation) is the will to know the truth and the somewhat dim apprehension that it is there to be known, awaiting us.

The Bernard passage reads in full: *Possumus singula haec ita diffinire: fides est voluntaria quaedam et certa prelibatio necdum propalatae veritatis; intellectus est rei cuiuscumque invisibilis certa et manifesta notitia; opinio est quasi pro vero habere aliquid, quod falsum esse nescias. Ergo, ut dixi, fides ambiguum non habet, aut, si habet, fides non est, sed opinio. Quid igitur distat ab intellectu? Nempe quod, etsi non habet incertum non magis quam intellectus, habet tamen involucrum, quod non intellectus. Denique quod intellexisti, non est de eo quod ultra quaeras; aut, si est, non intellexisti. Nil autem malumus scire, quam quae fide iam scimus. Nil supererit ad beatitudinem, cum, quae iam certa sunt nobis, erunt aeque et nuda.*—Bernard, *De Consideratione*, 5:3:6 (Leclercq edn., our ref. 45 above, vol. 3, p. 471).

52 The role of the will in determining belief has been seen as a bugbear by moderns who interpret Thomas's *credere* as signifying belief—and rightly so. The idea of willing to believe (sc. what is uncertain) is so horrendous to intellectuals that one may allow oneself to be surprised that so eminently intellectual a thinker as Thomas could be imagined to have held and to have advocated such an untenable position. Deliberately to believe something uncertain constitutes rather his idea of heresy, as well it might. The problem arises from the misunderstanding of *credere* as meaning "to believe" in the modern sense. If it be recognized as "believing" in the original sense (see our next chapter, below), of "beloving", "holding dear", "placing one's heart on", "pledging allegiance to", then the misunderstanding is at once dispelled. More accurate: it does not arise. Thomas wrote: *credere* [*est*] *actus intellectus assentientis vero ex imperio voluntatis* (*Summa Th.*, 2:2:4:5, response [Caramello, 11:31]). This means that a pledging of one's allegiance to the truth is an act of the intellect done under the sway of the will. Surely in saying that, he is right, is he not? (If, that is, one is to use the concepts "intellect" and "will".) (On the meaning of *assentio*, see further below, our ref. 58.) Faith is the will to know the truth, we have seen Bernard implying (our ref. 51 just above); this is Thomas's implication here too.

Part of the modern problem, of course, lies in the fact that Thomas tends to be read in the light of the subsequent history of ideas and of language, rather than in the light of the history that preceded him. He had inherited—as we have observed in our preceding section, on baptism—a meaning of *credo* primarily involving the will (one's giving one's loyalty to goodness); and he was involved in the transition of intellectualizing it: a giving of one's loyalty to truth. He would have been scandalized, however, at any interpretation involving loyalty to what one merely considered the truth, loyalty to belief. This became prevalent only many centuries later.

Many moderns read Thomas, and others like him, as if they were defining faith as agreement with what he (they) regarded as true. This is not what he is saying here. For one thing, *assentio* does not mean intellectual agreement. Secondly, and equally of central importance (this point will be taken up again in our concluding chapter, below): faith is defined here as an attitude to what is true (not to what he thought to be true). There is no reason why a Muslim, a Hindu, an atheistic Buddhist, a secular humanist, should not agree with Thomas's definition of faith that we have just quoted.

It is my impression that modern philosophers have devoted little attention to the question as to how it is that we know (*sic*) that there is more to the world, and indeed to any part of it, than is yet known; and how do we know (*sic*) that that knowledge is worth having. It may be that as modern academics are increasingly faced with undergraduate students not imbued with a will to know, they may come to speculate once again on the relation between that will and knowledge.

Thomas's averring of *credere* to be an act of the intellect under the command of the will, often taken as virtually a definition, is found in slightly varying forms at several places in addition to the one just quoted: e.g., *Summa Th.*, 2:2:2:9, response (Caramello, 11:23) and 2:2:4:2 ad 1 (11:29) etc.

53 That Thomas had in mind something strikingly similar to the pursuit of a truth not yet apprehended, is made explicit more than once. For example, in the *Summa Contra Gentiles* he writes: "Since, therefore, human beings through divine providence, are oriented to a higher good than human frailty is capable of knowing through experience in the present life—as will be investigated in the sequel—it was fitting that their mind be called forth towards something higher than our reason can attain at present, so that it might learn to aspire to something and earnestly to move towards something, that surpasses the entire condition of present life" (1:5/29—Pera edn., vol. 2, p. 7). Another example: "Faith that is a virtue makes a person's mind adhere to the truth as such (literally: the truth that consists in God's knowing), in a transcending of the truth of one's own apprehension"—*De veritate*, 14:8, response (Spiazzi edn., p. 295).

These are as good ways as any, surely, of stating our point about the intellectual being devoted to truth as such, and the mystery that the human mind can be loyal not to the truth that it knows but to the truth that transcends what it knows.

All intellectuals know (*sic*) that there is more truth than is humanly known. Might one not regard it as a defining characteristic of either the intellectual or the scientist, to know that the real world transcends our knowledge of it? As I have elsewhere remarked, a logic that makes no room for human beings' knowing more than they know may serve perhaps for the construction of machines, but is empirically irrelevant to the intellectual processes of human beings.

Edition used for this: *Summa: S. Thomae Aquinatis doctoris angelici Liber de Veritate Catholicae Fidei contra errores Infidelium, qui dicitur Summa Contra Gentiles*, edd. Cesla[us] Pera, D. Petr[us] Marc et al., Augustae Taurinorum: Marietti, 3 voll., 1961-1967. (The title-pages of voll. 2 and 3, which were published first, read *seu* rather than *qui dicitur* [vol. 1] before the subtitle, a point of some significance for our ref. 106 below; they read also Taurini, Romae rather than Augustae Taurinorum.)

54 These two sentences interpret very generally what I see as Thomas's position; but perhaps might be referred particularly to, for instance, *Summa Th.* 2:2:4:5 (Caramello, II:31-32): *Utrum fides sit virtus.* Cf. also 2:2:5:2, esp. ad 2, ad 3 (II:37). On the convergence of truth and goodness, see also *Summa Th.* 1:16:4 (I:95-96). For the meaning of *assensio*, see below, our ref. 58.

55 *Summa Th.*, 2:2:4:5 (II:31-32). In making this distinction Thomas was following Peter Lombard.

56 Although he held (felt? supposed? knew? recognized?) that truth and goodness finally converge (he used the term "God" to name that convergence), yet human beings, he was aware—and devils!—may take a more short-range position and know truth, may even pursue it, for immediate purposes of their own: may use it even perhaps to deceive, and in any case for proximate selfish advantage. No matter how knowledgeable, or how acutely intelligent, such a person might be, some of us to-day would not call that person an intellectual. Unlike some of us, Thomas was willing to attribute to persons not of goodwill —and to devils—a certain, but quite unvirtuous, kind of faith. For Thomas on the New Testament passage (James 2:19) on the devils' relation to faith and truth, see his *Summa Th.* 2:2:5:2 (Caramello, II:36-37); for my own historical interpretation, see my *Belief and History*, pp. 73-80, and also below, p. 102 here. I do not wish to underestimate the importance of goodwill in general, including one's love of one's neighbour and of God, for Thomas's idea of *fides formata.* In the remainder of the paragraph in our text, however, I develop the moral dimension in his concept of faith only insofar as it pertains to the point under discussion: namely, his position as an intellectual. That faith should or must involve love (or, by Protestants as distinct from Roman Catholics, is conceived as in some way involving it) is a thesis that has received more attention in general than in the specific matter that here engages us: namely, faith as a relation or attitude of the human being to truth. Faith is that (God-given?) quality by which some of us *love* the truth. In the love of truth, the relation between intellect and will, or among intellect, will, and feeling, deserves more exploration than it nowadays customarily receives.

On Thomas on loving that truth of which one is yet in pursuit, and to which one pledges one's loyalty, many a passage might be cited: explicitly, for example, *Cum enim homo habet promptam voluntatem ad credendum, diligit veritatem creditam*—*Summa Th.*, 2:2:2:10 (II:24).

57 Above, our chapter 4, ref. 59.

58 Behind the Latin *assensio* and *assensus* lies in part (especially through

Cicero) the Stoic συγκαταθεσις [*synkatathesis*] concept, designating our human capacity (rather mysterious, once one ponders it) to move beyond our awareness of our perceptions to an awareness (even: an activating awareness) of the world perceived. It denominates our victory over—our being saved from—solipsism. As a technical philosophic concept the Stoic term had had sometimes to do more with the reality of the real, and less perhaps with its goodness, than did Christian (or Islamic, or Hindu) usage. Modern humanity seems endangered by a kind of corporate solipsism at the spiritual and moral, if as yet only partially at the empirical, level. (It thinks of "values" as human evaluatings, having become unable to recognize an external realm of value of which human evaluation is the less or more accurate apprehension. For growing doubt even at the empirical level, see below, our chap. 7, ref. 6.)

It is also worth recalling, in less sophisticated fashion, that the words *assentio*, *assensio*, *assensus* come from, and presumably bring with them something of, *sentio*, *sensus*, and the realm of feeling. In modern English the term "assent" has in large measure ceased to imply the carrying of one's sentiment along with one's mind. It represents much less than it once did, or than did the Latin for these mediaeval writers, that movement beyond the recognition of the truth of an idea to an apprehension of the reality of that which the idea represents, on the one hand; and that movement of integrity, on the other hand, whereby the whole person follows through, with heart and will, what the mind has recognized as valid.

St. Augustine's characterization of faith in these terms is found in his *De Praedestinatione Sanctorum* 2/5 (Chéné-Pintard edn., [our ref. 42 above], p. 472): *ipsum credere, nihil aliud est, quam cum assensione cogitare*. This remark was much canvassed in subsequent centuries. Thomas's discussion of this "definition" constitutes his *Summa Th.*, 2:2:2:1 (Caramello 11:15-16: *Utrum credere sit cum assensione cogitare*). Augustine uses the verb and noun *assent-* throughout his discussions elsewhere also, as do other mediaevals. I am not aware of a good historical word-study.

The use of this term as the name for the human move to translate moral theory into practice is nicely illustrated by a remark of Seneca. One acts, says he, insofar as one be rational, when one "has experienced an impulse, and then *adsensio* has confirmed that impulse. Let me say what *adsensio* is. I ought to walk; but I do walk, only after I have said this to myself and have given approbation to this judgement of mine"—*Omne rationale animal nihil agit nisi primum specie alicuius rei inritatum est, deinde impetum cepit, deinde adsensio confirmavit hunc impetum. Quid sit adsensio dicam. Oportet me ambulare: tunc demum ambulo cum hoc mihi dixi et adprobavi hanc opinionem meam; oportet me sedere: tunc demum sedeo: L. Annaei Senecae ad Lucilium Epistulae Morales*, ed. L. D. Reynolds, Oxonii: Clarendoniano, 2 voll., [1965], 1969 (Scriptorum Classicorum Bibliotheca Oxoniensis), 113 (= 19:4):18, vol. 2, p. 476. Cf. also *A. Gellii Noctes Atticae*, ed. P. K. Marshall, Oxonii: Clarendoniano, 2 voll., 1968 (Scriptorum Classicorum Bibliotheca Oxoniensis), 19:1:18-20, vol. 2, p. 562.

Similarly in pre-modern English. Of the five meanings, arranged historically, in the Oxford English Dictionary s.v. "Assent", the first is "The concurrence of the will, compliance with a desire". This is annotated as "archaic". Rather similar are the next two; while only the last is given as "Agreement with a statement, an abstract proposition, or a proposal that does not concern oneself; mental acceptance or approval", with the parenthetic annotation that this is "the ordinary modern use" ("modern" in this case referring to the end of the nineteenth century: this volume was published in 1888).

The first meaning of *assensio* and *assensus* proffered by the recent *Oxford Latin Dictionary*, Oxford: Clarendon Press, 1968- , in process, fascicule 1, 1968, s.vv., is "approval, approbation, applause".

Cf. further below, our ref. 90.

59 Since the Latin words *verus*, *veritas* refer to what in modern parlance is designated by "the real" as well as "the true", I have allowed myself the liberty of on occasion introducing both modern concepts into my translations/paraphrases. Cf. Thomas's own discussion in his treatise devoted explicitly to this matter, *De Veritate* (our ref. 43 above), as well as, more succinctly, his *quaestio* devoted to it, with the same title, in his *Summa Th.*: namely, 1:16 (Caramello 1:93-99). Of the former work the title is usually in modern times translated rather one-sidedly as "On Truth"; e.g., St. Thomas Aquinas, *Truth*, James V. McGlynn, trans., Chicago: Henry Regnery, 3 voll., 1952-1954. Why not *Reality*?

Many moderns are unaware of the drastic extent to which the concept "truth" has become shrunken and denatured in modern thought, to the point where some would even restrict it to a realm constituted by statements (so that an interest in truth is watered down to merely an interest in true sentences). Insofar as any of my readers may be victims of this dominant tendency (and perhaps even as an indication of the extent to which also I unwittingly am?) I have perhaps betrayed my own principles in speaking of faith as a human relation to or attitude to truth, rather than as a human relation to or attitude to reality. Thomas as an intellectual was defining faith as a committed loyalty to, and love of, reality as such. Faith is a God-given capacity resolutely to know reality, to love it, and to live always in terms of it. (This differs from various modern predilections such as to live in terms of one's own preferences, or to satisfy one's "needs", or the like.)

60 "I have no desire to insist upon my views. If I have stated anything wrongly, I leave it all to be corrected"—*nec sum pertinax in sensu meo; set si quid male dixi, totum relinquo correctioni. . . .* The words are St. Thomas's, spoken shortly before he died, as reported by Bartholomaeus of Capua as a witness at the first canonization inquiry, Naples, 1319. *Processus Canonizationis S. Thomae Aquinatis*, M.-H. Laurent, ed. §80; originally published as a supplement in *Revue thomiste*, Saint-Maximin; reprinted in D. Prümmer, ed., *Fontes Vitae S. Thomae Aquinatis: notis historicis et criticis illustrati*, Tolosae: apud Ed. Privat, Bibliopolam [n.d.; sc. ca. 1935?], p. 379. The correcting he envisages being effected, of course, by the community of which he was a member: the Roman Church.

61 With "explicit belief" here (sc. in propositions, which we discuss below)

I do not equate Thomas's concept of *explicite credere* (for instance in his *Summa Th.* 2:2:2:7 and 8 [Caramello, II:20-22]), a concept that might be elaborated at some length. One may note in passing that he makes this concept compatible even with *fides . . . occulta* (2:2:2:8 *ad* 2 [II:22]), and, in any case, his "nevertheless" paragraph (*Si qui tamen . . .*) that concludes article 7 here (II:22) is significant.

More important for our purposes is his consideration of the question of the "articles" of faith (*articuli fidei*, 2:2:1:6-9 [II:8-13]) and especially that of *enuntiabilia*, discussed below.

62 Or: perhaps intellectually right. He was not so arrogant as to suppose that his views were always or necessarily correct, the views of those who disagreed with him wrong. Cf. our note 60 just above.

63 "*Omnia que scripsi videntur mihi palee*"; a little later, "*Omnia que scripsi videntur michi palee respectu eorum que vidi et revelata sunt michi*". Once again, these statements by Thomas are quoted in the deposition of Bartholomew at the Naples proceedings (above, our ref. 60), as in Prümmer, *Fontes*, p. 377. William of Tocco and Bernard Gui, each in his equally contemporary life of their friend the friar, report rather that the word used was *modicum* (we might translate "mediocre"): *talia sunt mihi revelata, quod ea quae scripsi et docui, modica mihi videntur.* (Guillelmus de Tocco, *De Hystoria Beati Thome de Aquino*, 47; Bernardus Guidonis, *Legenda Sancti Thome de Aquino . . . de ortu, vita et obitu ac gestis ejus*, 27—in the latter case the concluding words are *modica michi respective videntur*; both as in Prümmer, *Fontes*, pp. 120, 193 respectively.)

This whole incident, however, is sufficiently problematic as to lend itself none too readily to serving as a basis on which to construct any important interpretation. It would hardly be persuasive to any not already persuaded of whatever inferences might be drawn from it. For it came, at the very end of his life, when Thomas was evidently ill. (The best presentation of the incident is perhaps that in Weisheipl, *Friar Thomas* [our ref. 44 above], pp. 320-323.) I have not been able, despite considerable effort, to find the study of the mystic aspect of Thomas's personality that is referred to by Gilson in a somewhat inadequate footnote: Étienne Gilson, *Le Thomisme: introduction à la philosophie de Saint Thomas d'Aquin*, 5e édn., Paris: Vrin, 1944 (Étienne Gilson, dir., Études de philosophie médiévale, 1), p. 8, fn. 2. I find only moderately helpful Conrad Pepler, *The Basis of the Mysticism of St Thomas*, [London]: Blackfriars, 1953.

A point about which there could perhaps be no dispute, is that set forth in the sentences leading up to the quotation mentioned in our previous note (above, our ref. 60): namely, that primary for Thomas was his direct love of truth/reality, sacramentalized for him in the figure of Christ; subsidiary thereto was his intellectual construction and explicit attempt to delineate in words that truth, that reality, which transcends all words. He clearly recognized throughout his life that truth, reality, though apprehensible by man here below, is so only in part, that it transcends all thought; even if the recognition became still clearer, more vivid, as he approached death. He was also throughout his life aware (unlike some moderns) that truth and reality are not passive in relation to man, with human understanding of them a totally human, one-sided achievement: rather, the relation of the human mind and person to truth/reality is a function primarily of that truth, that reality, and only secondarily and in response is it a human doing.

64 *fidem diffinit* [Abaelardus] *aestimationem. Quasi cuique in ea sentire et loqui quae libeat liceat; aut pendeant sub incerto in vagis ac variis opinionibus nostrae Fidei sacramenta, et non magis certa veritate subsistant*—Bernard of Clairvaux, in his long letter (No. 190) to Pope Innocent II, known as his *Tractatus de Erroribus Abaelardi*, or as *Contra quaedam capitula errorum Abaelardi*: chap. 4 (para. 9). In *Sancti Bernardi . . . Opera Genuina*, Parisiis et Vesontione: Gauthier, 2 voll., 1835, 1:158 and 2:48-63 (this passage: 2:56), and reprinted thence (reading *definit* for *diffinit*) in J.-P. Migne, ed., *Patrologiae Latinae*, vol. 182, Paris, 1862, col. 1061 (Joannes Mabillon, ed.). In the Cistercian edition of his *Opera* (above, our ref. 45), this letter has not yet been published.

Modern scholars are aware that Abelard was misunderstood in this matter. See, especially, Jean Cottiaux, "La conception de la théologie chez Abélard", *Revue d'histoire ecclésiastique*, 28:[247]-295, [533]-551, [788]-828 (1932). Cf. M. D. Chenu, *La Parole de Dieu*: 1, *La Foi dans l'intelligence*, Paris: Éditions du Cerf, 1964, pp. 82-83.

For him, no less than for his critics such as St. Bernard, as for Augustine and the others, the object of faith, although not manifest, is nonetheless real. Faith is a relation to non-corporal matters, he says, and is (like *intelligere*) distinguished from *cognitio* (much as *savoir* is in our day from *connaître*) in that the latter is for him a relation to the same matters, explicitly, but one that involves an experiencing of their very presence (while faith, he says, explicitly, is a dedicating of oneself to pursuing them as a goal). *Scientia*, on the other hand, differs from *fides* (as it does also from *intelligere*) in that its object is matters of immediate empirical sense perception, even though no more real.

He quotes the scripture on "knowing" (*cognoscere*) God and Christ's manifesting Himself to those who love Him, and goes on: *Sed profecto aliud est intelligere seu credere, aliud cognoscere seu manifestare. Fides quippe dicitur existimatio non apparentium, cognitio vero ipsarum rerum* [*sic*] *experientia per ipsam earum praesentiam.* At another place: *Est quippe fides existimatio rerum non apparentium, hoc est sensibus corporis non subjacentium; spes vero, exspectatio aliquod commodum adipiscendi, quando videlicet quis credit se aliquod bonum assecuturum esse.*

References: *Petri Abaelardi Introductio ad Theologiam*, 2:3 and 1:1. I have used the edition in J.-P. Migne, ed., *Petri Abaelardi . . . Opera Omnia* which is *Patrologiae Latinae*, Turnholti: Brepols, vol. 178, 1855, coll. 1051 D and 981 C respectively. The statement *Scientia est de apparentibus, existimatio de non apparentibus* is quoted without reference and attributed to Abelard, in Chenu, *Parole*, p. 81; I have not found it in the original, and am left a trifle unsure with regard to it.

65 *fides de qua Philosophus loquitur . . . Sed fides de qua loquimur*—*Summa Th.*, 2:2:4:5, ad 2 (Caramello, II:31).

66 It is not altogether clear to me whether the choice of *fides* in Latin to translate classical Greek πιστις [*pistis*], otherwise a rather questionable rendering, was a result of (or to what extent was but another instance, rather, of the same historical development as) the choice of the former term by the Latin-speaking Church and the latter by the Greek-speaking Church for verbalizing the new Christian concept of faith. In the latter case this appropriated the same choice already made by Hellenizing Jews—the Septuagint, Philo, etc.—for rendering the Hebrew האמין [heᵉmîn]. Boethius (cf. our ref. 67, just below), the first great Latin translator of Aristotle, was of course a Christian. For further discussion on the relation between πιστις and *fides* (and *credo*) see above, our ref. 31.

67 *fides opinio vehemens*, Aristotle (*Topica*, 4:5—126b 18) is represented as saying in the translation by Boethius that was current in the mediaeval West: Manlii Severini Boetii, *Opera Omnia*, tom. 2, in J.-P. Migne, ed., *Patrologiae . . . Latinae*, Paris: apud Garnier Fratres, vol. 64, 1891, col. 950. The original reads: ἡ πιστις ὑποληψις σφοδρα—Aristotelis *Topica et Sophistici Elenchi*, rec. W. D. Ross, Oxonii: Clarendoniano, 1958 (Scriptorum Classicorum Bibliotheca Oxoniensis), p. 77. That this term as used by Aristotle signified for Thomas not faith but belief—that is, what "belief" means for modern speakers of English—Thomas further makes clear in firmly distinguishing his own concept (the Christian concept generally) of *fides* from it, by indicating that the Aristotelian word applies to a position that might be wrong (*cui potest subesse falsum*: *Summa Th.*, 2:2:4:5, ad 2, the conclusion of the first sentence cited in our ref. 65 just above).

More fully, the Boethius translation given above reads: *videtur enim stupor admiratio esse superabundans, et fides opinio vehemens*; the point being made by the passage is explicitly that *fides* is a member of the genus *opinio*. An alternative wording, from a recently discovered twelfth-century manuscript, *fides opinatio certa*, is given (p. 228) (and the Boethius reading above is confirmed [reading *superhabundans*], p. 80) in the recent works of Laurentius Minio-Paluello, ed., *Aristoteles Latinus, V, 1-3, Topica: Translatio Boethii, Fragmentum Recensionis Alterius, et Translatio Anonyma*, Leiden: Brill, 1969 (Union Académique Internationale, Corpus Philosophorum Medii Aevi, L. Minio-Paluello, ed., V, 1-3). Thomas's contemporary and fellow Dominican William of Moerbeke, who did a number of fresh translations of Aristotle, partly at Thomas's request and for his use, appears not to have made a rendering of the *Topica*.

68 Discussing *fides* as *substantia rerum sperandum* (Hebrews 11:1), Thomas says that faith, as theological virtue, is different from belief, for which the word *fides* is also used in common parlance: *fides* as commonly understood—"insofar as we use the verb *credo* in speaking of our attitude to what we believe exceptionally strongly"—*distinguitur a fide communiter accepta, secundum quam credere dicimur id quod vehementer opinamur*—Aquinas, *De Veritate*, 14:2 (Spiazzi edn. cit. [above, our ref. 43], p. 284). In some ways similar,

and in some ways different, a version of this point is found in his discussion of the same matter in his *Summa Th.*, 2:2:4:1, where the virtue faith is differentiated from belief, or perhaps from trust, as *fides* is commonly taken to signify, insofar as this latter is not oriented to the goal of (final) beatitude: *distinguitur virtus fidei a fide communiter sumpta, quae non ordinatur ad beatitudinem speratam* (Caramello edn., 11:27).

Another instance where he alludes in passing to the clear difference in his own understanding between belief and religious faith, even where the same word might be used, is in his commentary (3:23:2:3) on the *Sententiae* of Peter Lombard—*loquitur de fide quae est opinio . . . , non autem de fide infusa*: *S. Thomae Aquinatis . . . Scriptum Super Sententiis Magistri Petri Lombardi*, ed. Maria Fabianus Moos, Parisiis: Lethielleux, 1956, 3 tomes in 2 voll.; vol. 2, p. 729, para. 159. Cf. also below, our ref. 76.

69 *fides est media inter scientiam et opinionem—Summa Th.*, 2:2:1:2 (Caramello, 11:4). (Cf. our ref. 71 below.) Again: *differunt secundum perfectum et imperfectum opinio, fides et scientia*—ibid., 2:1:67:3 (1:295). The latter passage, however, explicitly states that this holds only *ex parte subiecti*, while if the matter be considered in terms, for instance, of what is known, as distinct from the person knowing, then this ranking no longer holds. On this, see further just below, our ref. 72. The other passage is presently supplemented with still others with more elaborate and exact discriminations in "belief": see below, our ref. 76.

70 Above, our chapter 3, pp. 41-49, with reff. 20-26 and ref. 32; and especially my articles "A Human View of Truth" and "Faith as *Taṣdīq*" (above, our chapter 3, ref. 34).

71 On the relation in Bonaventura's thought between *fides* and *scientia*, see his commentary on Peter Lombard's *Sententiae*, particularly on Book 3, Distinction 23, "De Fide . . .", and especially art. 1, quaest. 4: *Utrum fides sit certior quam scientia*. (*S. Bonaventurae Commentaria in quatuor libros Sententiarum Magistri Petri Lombardi*. In the Quaracchi edn. cit. [above, our ref. 46] of the *Opera Omnia*, this is vol. 3, pp. 480-483.) See also his remarks there on Dist. 24, art. 2 (Quaracchi, vol. 3, pp. 517-524) for a comparison of *fides* and *cognitio*. In the former passage he explicitly deals with Hugh of St. Victor's making faith intermediary in a series between *opinio* and *scientia*; he says that no doubt the knowledge of God that will be the sure and open vision of Him in the next world will be supreme, but faith surpasses mundane sorts of knowledge. In the latter passage, note especially the *Conclusio* that, so far as that *scientia* is concerned to which reasoning leads us, it and faith may come together in such a way that *fides sit principale et scientia subserviens* (p. 522).

More generally: for Bonaventura, *cognitio* is, as befits a person of his temperament and outlook, a somewhat more favoured term than *scientia*; and the *cognitio* and the *scientia* of God elicit more of his attention than do the human sorts. All knowledge is from God (Quaracchi, vol. 6, p. 205; cf. vol. 6, p. 76); but human knowledge might be called rather *similitudo scientiae* than actually *scientia* (vol. 6, p. 162). Like Bernard (cf. above, our ref. 45), by whom he was influenced, he is basically more interested however in *sapientia* than in either *scientia* or even *cognitio*. Note his statement, *Quidquid scimus, hoc est per participationem sapientiae increatae* (vol. 9, p. 38). On the other hand, from time to time he again, like Bernard, quotes 1 Corinthians 8:1 on *scientia* as "puffing up" us human beings, derogatorily; he is disdainful of knowledge that is not accompanied by good works (vol. 6, p. 428, §21; vol. 8, p. 132, §2).

72 Moderns who make do without a concept of perfect knowledge, eschatologiless, can easily misinterpret this, and the position that *fides* is less than *scientia*; particularly so if they read it as confirming their own preconviction that faith "has less cognitive value" than does science. The statement cited in our text as it stands requires that one recognize that "science", as well as "faith", has different meanings in mediaeval and modern ideologies. This is apart from the fact that in any case the position was held by Thomas only with reservations. Explicitly, for him, faith is less perfect than *scientia* considered from the point of view of the subject; but is nobler (*nobilior*) than (human) *scientia* (here on earth) considered in terms of its object, which is ultimate truth/reality: *fides est nobilior quam scientia, ex parte obiecti: quia eius obiectum est veritas prima—Summa Th.*, 2:1:67:3 ad 1 (Caramello, 1:296 of the second sequence of pagination). Cf. *ex parte subiecti* in our ref. 69 just above, which this passage almost immediately follows. In this regard the love of a higher truth is superior to the attainment of a lower.

Similarly, he explicitly states that *fides* is not in a series with *opinio* and *scientia*, intermediate between them, in this: that they two are not virtues, while faith is—*De Veritate*, 14:3, ad 5 (Spiazzi edn. [above, our ref. 43], p. 287).

73 Standardly. Similarly, at the opening of his major discussion on faith, he refers to it as a cognitive disposition (*cognoscitivus habitus*)—*Summa Th.*, 2:2:1:1 (Caramello, II:4); unfaith he calls a *defectus cognitionis*—2:2:2:2, ad 3 (II:16-17); and so on.

Elsewhere he says, more cautiously, *fides cognitio quaedam est—Summa Th.*, 1:12:13, ad 3 (Caramello, 1:62 of the first sequence of pagination). Again, more dynamically, he speaks of *cognitio fidei* as in process *ab imperfectis ad perfectum*—ibid., 2:2:1:7, ad 3 (Caramello II:10).

74 For example: *fideles habent . . . notitiam—Summa Th.*, 2:2:1:5, ad 1 (Caramello, II:7). R. Bernard translates this *une claire connaissance*. Saint Thomas d'Aquin, *Somme théologique*: *la foi*, traduction française par R. Bernard, Paris, Tournai, Rome: Desclée (Société Saint Jean l'Évangéliste), 1940 (Éditions de la Revue des jeunes), vol. 1, p. 35. At another place, while it is a *cognitio*, nonetheless it is a *cognitio . . . non perfecta per manifestam visionem —Summa Th.*, 2:2:2:1 (Caramello, II:16).

He speaks also of faith as a "perceiving". For example, *invisibilia Dei . . . percipit fides*—ibid., 2:2:2:3, ad 3 (II:18). More exactly: faith perceives these matters more, and more loftily, than does natural reason.

75 Sir Karl Popper, even, illustrates the drift of modern ideology away from the personal by writing of *Objective Knowledge* (in contradistinction from Michael Polanyi's championing, in his Gifford Lectures, of natural

science as *Personal Knowledge*). Herein not merely does Popper understand as "objective" the object of knowledge, but knowledge itself is so conceptualized, and is thus divorced from any knower.

Popper holds that knowledge exists in, for instance, the British Museum, rather than in people's heads. It would be possible to contend that on this matter he is wrong. For if biological warfare obliterated human life on earth, or some other disaster all life, but left the British Museum or Widener Library and their contents standing, there would be no knowledge on our planet (even if the means of re-attaining knowledge remained for some future race of intelligents).

Faith has to do with the human relation to truth. (So does knowledge.) Modern objectivization is in danger of going so far as to suggest that there is no such relation. Popper, however, is himself not not a person. Nor is he a person without faith; for he is striving to arrive at the truth, and he knows that it is there, even though he himself miss it (as we all do in varying degrees, and as Thomas recognized). He also knows (but how?) that it is worth pursuing.

Accordingly (in accord, also, with our own interpretations set forth in our concluding chapter below) it would be preferable, rather than holding this new form of objectivization to be simply wrong, to regard it as an approximation to the truth. In some ways it is a disappointingly distant one, certainly. For instance, it adds to the doleful depersonalization of modern thought, already extreme enough, and helps one to understand the world that the natural sciences investigate much more than it helps to understand human beings, or science as their achievement; and it fails to understand the function of symbols and their role in human life (even the symbolism of language, even scientific language). Yet in some ways it must be seen also as a major improvement over certain alternative views of objectivization, in that it transcends the facile binary polarity of subjective/objective by portraying a "third world" beyond the subjective and the empirical-material, and sees a special relation between this "third world" and humanity. (It fails, however, to transcend that polarity insofar as he calls his third world "objective" primarily in the sense that he sees it as not subjective.) The "third world" is for Popper a human construct. He compares birds' nests as constructs, which comparison seems to imply that curious misunderstanding of symbols and signs just mentioned. Most tellingly, however, he speaks not only of truth but regularly of "approximation to the truth" (e.g., pp. 55 bis, 265; ". . . to truth", 55, 103, 265 bis, 334, 335 bis; cf. "nearer to the truth", pp. 44, 52, 148; "search for truth", pp. 44 bis, 54, 126). This, if taken seriously, would indicate that (for all his and his circle's resolute rejection of any such thing) he is implicitly aware of a fourth reality, which transcends us (he does know that we transcend ourselves: pp. 146ff.) and by which his third world (as well as his second?) is judged.

See Michael Polanyi, *Personal Knowledge: towards a post-critical philosophy*, London: Routledge & Kegan Paul [and Chicago: University of Chicago Press], 1958, [1962]; New York: Harper & Row—Harper Torchbooks

1964. Karl R. Popper, *Objective Knowledge: an evolutionary approach*, Oxford: Clarendon Press, 1972.

76 Usually he uses the words *opinio* and *opinor* incidentally, casually. Occasionally, however, he explicates his understanding of them, in a way that makes visible to a modern reader that they denoted in his mind what "belief", "believe" do in ours. See, for instance, *Summa Th.*, 2:2:1:4 (Caramello, ii:6) and 2:2:2:1 (ii:16).

77 *prout cadit sub fide, non potest esse falsum*—see our ref. 80 below. Cf. also his distinguishing the Christian conception of what faith is (of what *fides* means) from Aristotle's, in that the latter uses the term in reference to something that could be false—above, our ref. 67.

78 For example: *Et si quidem hoc fit* [sc., *assensum intellectus*] *cum dubitatione et formidine alterius partis, erit opinio; si autem fit cum certitudine absque tali formidine, erit fides.—Summa Th.*, 2:2:1:4 (Caramello, ii:6).

79 Cf. above, our reff. 67, 68.

80 Faith is a commitment to the truth as such: a love of it, a pledging of one's loyalty and adherence to it. It is, therefore, of a different order from wondering whether, or deciding that, any given thesis be true or false. In principle, it differs from all intellectual activities that have to do with the true/false alternative: *distinguitur iste actus qui est credere ab omnibus actibus intellectus qui sunt circa verum vel falsum—Summa Th.*, 2:2:2:1 (Caramello, ii:16).

Similarly, in an earlier article the argument is that in connection with any virtue, such as justice or temperance as well as faith, a particular belief that a person may hold may be false, but the virtue itself cannot be. Faith is not the belief, but is a movement towards a truth not yet attained. Therefore

> *ei* [sc. *fidei*] *non potest subesse falsum.*
> . . . *fidei non potest subesse aliquod falsum.*
> . . . *prout cadit sub fide, non potest esse falsum*
> —*Summa Th.*, 2:2:1:3 (Caramello, 11:5-6).

81 *Summa Th.*, 2:2:2:2 (Caramello, ii:16-17).

82 *Summa Th.*, 2:2:2:2 (Caramello, ii:16). The clause occurs in the third objection, so that the words are in a sense not strictly Thomas's but are put by him in the mouth of those from whom he proceeds to dissent. Nonetheless, he dissents not from this part of the position, but from the inferences that its proponents would draw from it. It is teasing to reflect on whether Thomas is being casual or subtly acute when, in his reply to this third objection, he first substitutes *credere Deum* for *credere Deum esse* as the wording for what is being considered (even though the point that he is making is that this *does not* obtain here in its faith aspect: *credere Deum non . . . sub ea ratione qua ponitur actus fidei*), and then adds a phrase that could be taken as predicative of *esse: Non . . . credunt Deum esse sub his conditionibus quas fides determinat*, shifting the meaning significantly—and in this case, quite deliberately.

83 The Fathers of the English Dominican Province early this century

translated both this and *credere Deum* as "to believe in a God". The Order has since changed its mind, and now renders it "belief in God", with a footnote saying, "Certainly the older English translations that keep 'to believe in God' for *credere in Deum* only at the cost of translating *credere Deum* as 'believe in *a* God' are far off the mark".

The "Summa Theologica" of St. Thomas Aquinas, literally translated by Fathers of the English Dominican Province, London: Washbourne, Publishers to the Holy See, 18 voll., 1911-1922 (rev. edn., London: Burnes Oates & Washbourne, Publishers to the Holy See, 22 voll., [1921?]-[1925?]), vol. 9 (1916; rev. edn., [1928?]), pp. 32-33.

St. Thomas Aquinas, *Summa Theologiae: Latin text and English translation, Introductions, notes, appendices and glossaries*, Thomas Gilby, gen. ed., Blackfriars—London: Eyre & Spottiswoode, and New York: McGraw-Hill, 60 voll., 1964-1976, vol. 31 (T. C. O'Brien [ed. and trans.], 1974), pp. 65-69, with 65n.

84 For Thomas, although that God exists is not self-evident to mankind (*Summa Th.*, 1:2:1 [Caramello, 1:10-11 of the first sequence of pagination]). yet it is certainly true (1:2 [1:10-13]), it is known (he uses the words *cognoscere, notum, scibile*, etc.—1:2:2 [1:11-12]), it can be demonstrated (1:2:2 [1:11-12]), it can be proven (1:2:3 [1:12]). Accordingly, it is not an article of faith. *Deum esse, et alia huiusmodi quae per rationem naturalem nota possunt esse de Deo, . . . non sunt articuli fidei, sed praeambula ad articulos*—1:2:2 (1:11).

85 This is so for somewhat the same reasons, but *a fortiori*, one might logically hold, perhaps. Yet it is well nigh ludicrous to image Thomas or any scholastic theologian discussing such an unthinkable thesis. The very phrase *articuli opionis* would be laughably, or poignantly, absurd—especially as something religiously significant.

86 *credere Deum esse convenit etiam infidelibus*—*Summa Th.*, 2:2:2:2 (Caramello, II:16). Cf. our ref. 82 above. The relation between *fides* and *credere*, although close, is not one of identity (cf. above, our reff. 31, 66); and it is not fully clear to me to what extent *credere* here implies not only recognizing intellectually a truth but, further, some acknowledging of it, accepting it, appropriating it to oneself, if not actually committing oneself to it and living in terms of it. Even the devils, after all, tremble! (James 2:19; cf. below, our ref. 158.) And the persons without faith (*infideles* who *credunt Deum esse*) that Aquinas had heard of and had in mind were primarily, one may suppose, heretics, Jews, and Muslims—whose recognition of God's existence was not inert, not a merely theoretical view. The insouciant faithless were not a conspicuous group in mediaeval society. Probably "acknowledge", at least, would be a more accurate translation than "recognize", here. Certainly "believe" will not do; it is simply a mistranslation.

Similarly, I suggest, the then recent distinction between *fides quae creditur* and *fides qua creditur*, which Thomas accepted, is not adequately communicated to us if the former be interpreted as "the belief that is believed". At one level, it is indeed the case that the word *fides* (also "belief" in mediaeval English: "to repeat one's belief") was used by some at the time as designating the "statement of faith" (modern "creed") to or through which one pledged one's allegiance (the Church pledged its allegiance), in which one's (the Church's) faith was expressed. Yet that was superficial, or anyway secondary, derivative; serious thinkers went well beyond it, to the truth/reality that the statement expressed. I would render the words, rather, as—minimally—"faith that is recognized" (sc. as faith; that is seen to be worth aspiring to), while not abandoning my sense that the focus of Thomas's interest was, rather, *veritas quae creditur*. One notes, anyway, that *fides* here as a term is used to designate that to which human beings are related, in addition to its two more usual references, to the relation itself, and to the human side of the relation. Only the last of these is named in the verb *credo*.

87 Unless it be lifeless or unformed. *Fides autem informis non est virtus—Summa Th.*, 2:2:4:5 (Caramello, II:31).

88 That faith is a virtue—*Summa Th.*, 2:2:4:5, the entire article (entitled, *Utrum fides sit virtus*). (Caramello, II:31-32.) Cf. *De Veritate*, 14:3 (article with the same title; Spiazzi edn. [above, our ref. 43], pp. 285-287).

89 That faith is not, as some might have expected, to be reckoned as one of the intellectual virtues—*Summa Th.*, 2:1:62:2 (Caramello, I:273-274 of the second Sequence). Cf. *De Veritate*, 14:3, ad 9 (Spiazzi [above, our ref. 43], p. 287). We may note in passing that neither is belief an intellectual virtue; but this is for altogether different, and quite modern, reasons. Neither belief, or for that matter even knowledge (*scientia*) is a virtue at all—since the mind (*ratio*) is involved but not the will. *De Veritate*, 14:3, ad 5 (Spiazzi, p. 287). Thomas would presumably have been scandalized at anyone's believing something wilfully, as are his modern readers who hear him as speak ing of belief when he talks about faith: the idea would be as irrationa him as it is to them, and a vice rather than a virtue.

90 *fides est habitus mentis, qua inchoatur vita aeterna in nobis, fa* *in-* *tellectum assentire non apparentibus—Summa Th.*, 2:2:4:1 (Caram II:27; the passage is given in this edition in italics). Given the facts that primary meaning of *assensio* was "applause", and the philosophic meanin "acting in terms of" one's ideas, realizing the validity of one's pe both senses of "realize", my interpretation here of *assentire* i malist, as it were; in order not to overstate my argument. I rather e that a more accurate translation would add to "to recognize", d to rejoice in, and to respond positively to", the non-empirical real our life and world. As we saw with *āstikya* and *buddhi* in the Hin (above, our chapter 4), faith is the capacity to say "Yes!" to trans—to reality which we recognize as greater than we have yet seen.

91 To the object of faith he devotes t question in his treatment *De Fide*; and to its being ultimate tr ultimate reality; or, for the modern world, truth-and-reality) its (*Utrum obiectum fidei sit veritas prima*): *Summa Th.*, 2:2:1 llo, II:3-4). That God is truth (*Utrum Deus sit veritas*): ibid., -97 of the first sequence). That He is *veritas prima*: ibid., en *pondeo* paragraph—*non solum in*

ipso sit veritas, sed . . . ipse sit ipsa summa et prima veritas (Caramello, 1:96).

In affirming that the "object" of faith is *prima veritas*, he went on to elaborate this, as we also shall presently do, by distinguishing between the formal and the material objects. In the latter case, the affirmation holds "in a certain fashion"—*quodammodo*: 2:2:1:1 (II:4); proximately, however, the matter bears elaboration. Cf. below, at our reff. 118 and especially at 119.

92 Passim. For example, the question *De Obiecto Fidei* in all its ten articles—*Summa Th.*, 2:2:1 passim (Caramello, II:3-15).

93 These two sentences of ours constitute a vast understatement, especially the first. The second renders a direct affirmation of his own: *per fidem non apprehendimus veritatem primam sicut in se est*—*Summa Th.*, 2:2:1:2, ad 3 (II:5). Regarding the first, one does well constantly to bear in mind Thomas's vivid sense that truth/reality/God transcends us, and especially goes far beyond anything that our intellects can grasp. *Nam divina substantia omnem formam quam intellectus noster attingit, sua immensitate excedit: et sic ipsam apprehendere non possumus cognoscendo quid est*—*Summa Contra Gentiles*, 1:14 (paragraph 117 *a*; Pera edn. [above, our ref. 53], vol. II, p. 22). Again: "The final limit of human awareness of God is that one know that one knows nothing of God, inasmuch as one knows that what God is surpasses all that we know about God"—*De Potentia*, 7:5, ad 14. (Full ref. below.) Thus Thomas resorts, emphatically, to the *via negativa*, or as he calls it, the *via remotionis* (the title of chapter 14 of book 1 of the *Summa Contra Gentiles* (Pera, vol. II, pp. 22-23); cf. chapp. 14-27 passim (Pera, vol. II, pp. 22-39, passim). The only progress in this knowledge is a more and more elaborate negation: *Tantoque eius notitiae magis appropinquamus, quanto* [illegible]*ra per intellectum nostrum ab eo poterimus removere*—ibid., 1:14 (para 1[illegible] Pera, vol. II, p. 22). Again: "We know God truly only when we recogniz[illegible]t He is above all that is possible for human beings to think about God"[illegible] *enim solum Deum vere cognoscimus quando ipsum esse credimus su*[illegible] *omne id quod de Deo cogitari ab homine possibile est*: ibid., 1:5 (para. 30[illegible] vol. II, p. 7). It may be that *credimus* here would be better translated [illegible]ognize and to act accordingly"? It is logically impossible to take it as [illegible]g "believe" after the *cognoscimus* that precedes it.

For the *De* [illegible] I have used the edition of Paul[us] M. Pession, in S. Thomae Aquin[illegible] *Quaestiones Disputatae*, vol. 2, *De Potentia*, . . . [&c], P. Bazzi et al., edd., Romae: Marietti [1953], 9th rev. edn., pp. 1-276. The passage cited is [illegible] p. 200.

94 In general, Thom[illegible] firm in restricting his use of the term "see" to the mind's relation to [illegible]ly and accurately knows. Neither faith nor belief can be of things seen[illegible] *nec opinio potest esse de visis*: *Summa Th.*, 2:2:1:4 (Caramello, II:6[illegible]wledge (*cognitio*) of faith differs, he says, from that other kind of [illegible] that I have called "knowing and understanding", and that he cal[illegible] (more fully, *cognitio quae est scientia*) in that the former is wan[illegible]ng"—*fides cognitio quaedam est. . . . Sed . . . determinatio . . . non* [illegible]*isione credentis. . . . Et sic, inquantum deest visio, deficit a ratione c*[illegible]*e est in scientia: Summa*

Th., 1:12:13, ad 3 (1:62). (It is amusing to note that in modern English what he called faith we tend sometimes to call "vision"—especially of artists, statesmen, intellectuals, and the like: a capacity to perceive and to respond to the not yet apprehended, or to live by or to be loyal to what is only dimly perceived—and that contrariwise we have come to use the word "science" sometimes for a mundane form of knowledge that may lack just this quality.) On occasion he relaxes this a little, however; especially in terms of what he calls *lumen fidei*. In this "light of faith" those of us who dedicate ourselves to the pursuit of something worthwhile, to the discovery of some truth not yet known, to living in terms of goals yet to be attained, see, as strict empiricists who claim to live only in terms of the immediate and the tangible presumably fail to see, that there is more to life than meets the eye. Thus, for example, *lumen fidei facit videre ea quae creduntur—Summa Th.*, 2:2:1:4, ad 3 (11:7). Moreover, he avers that one sees (*sic*) that that transcendent truth or those transcendent realities to which one gives one's loyalty, are worth being loyal to, are worth pursuing—*non enim crederet nisi videret ea esse credenda*: ibid., ad 2 (11:6). In this fashion, at least, if not otherwise, *sunt visa ab eo qui credit* (loc. cit.; Caramello, 11:6—in my copy reading *ab eo qui credi*, evidently a misprint). Again, for persons of faith, *per lumen fidei videntur esse credenda* —2:2:1:5, ad 1 (11:7).

95 This is so, for him, in relation to every truth. "We construct propositions for no other purpose than that through them we may have knowledge concerning things. This is so in scientific knowledge; similarly also in faith"—*non enim formamus enuntiabilia nisi ut per ea de rebus cognitionem habeamus, sicut in scientia, ita et in fide: Summa Th.*, 2:2:1:2, ad 2 (Caramello, 11:5). This is an extraordinarily important principle (not least, for a comparativist: we shall return to it in our concluding chapter). Any failure to appreciate it quite vitiates any attempted understanding of Thomas's views on faith. Truth/reality lies for him (ibid.; see also his *De Veritate*, passim, esp. 1:2-3 [Spiazzi (above, our ref. 43), pp. 4-6]) in the mind of the knower, as well as in the thing known (in the former case in a peculiarly human form of propositional complex); he never made the egregious modern mistake of imagining that it lies in the propositions themselves disengaged from persons. It has been his ill-luck that during the era of his greatest popularity and influence (roughly from the middle of the nineteenth to the middle of the twentieth century), his position tended to be interpreted preponderantly in Aristotelian terms ("the synthesizer of the Bible and Aristotle"); only more recently has it come to be recognized that his thought is, on the Greek side, deeply rooted as well in that of Plato and Plotinus. This was the case notably through Augustine, whom he quotes as much as (more than?) Aristotle; also through Dionysius the pseudo-Areopagite, on whom he wrote a commentary. The Christian understandings that he inherited, and that he re-worked in the light of the new Aristotelian views, were already a synthesis of Biblical and (Neo-)Platonic. This, apart from the fact that Aristotle himself was less impersonalist in this matter than he is sometimes made out to be by recent objectivistic thought.

96 *Summa Th.*, 2:2:1:1 and 2:2:1:2 (Caramello, II:3-5). These articles include the following statement, of crucial import and in our realm one of the most reverberating of all that he has penned: *Actus autem credentis non terminatur ad enuntiabile, sed ad rem*—"The person's act of faith does not have its terminus in the proposition, but in the reality": 2:2:1:2, ad 2 (II:5). This is immediately followed by the remark—here explanatory and subordinate but in its own way almost equally fundamental—that we cited in our previous note (our ref. 95 just above): *non enim formamus. . . .* The former statement should be read along with a vivid recalling of his sense of truth's (God's) transcending the intellect's grasp, mentioned in our ref. 93 above.

97 *ea quibus fides assentit . . . sub assensu fidei non cadunt nisi secundum quod habent aliquem ordinem ad Deum . . . nihil cadit sub fide nisi in ordine ad Deum . . . cadunt sub fide inquantum per haec ordinamur ad Deum*—*Summa Th.*, 2:2:1:1 (Caramello, II:4).

98 "The sin of infidelity consists in the active renunciation of faith. . . . The infidelity of heretics is such a renunciation occurring in a situation where the truth is altogether obvious"—*Cum enim peccatum infidelitatis consistat in renitendo fidei, hoc potest contingere dupliciter. Quia aut . . . Aut renititur fidei Christianae . . . in ipsa manifestatione veritatis, et sic est infidelitas haereticorum: Summa Th.*, 2:2:10:5 (Caramello, II:56).

This applies specifically to heresy. With regard to the alternative sort of infidelity, that of those who have not yet taken on faith—which in Thomas's eyes is less serious, though still a sin—his position differs somewhat from the Islamic, and from that set forth in the statement in our text. For as we have here been discussing throughout, and as we remarked above in our Islamic discussion (above, our chapter 3, ref. 29), faith in Christian understanding involves not something *mubīn* (perspicuous) but mystery. It involves giving allegiance to truth not yet fully known. If one were to include a discussion of this, some modification in the wording of the statement in our text would be in order, to take account of some of the complications. Fundamentally, however, since faith was for Thomas in principle a dedicating of oneself to the truth as such, not to particular truth, in the end his position here is not starkly different—though his views were, of course, distorted by the fact that he knew next to nothing about the non-Christian world.

We deal with this larger matter somewhat, later on in this section.

99 *Summa Th.*, 2:2:5:3 (Caramello, II:37). Cf. 2:2:5:4, ad 1 (II:38).

100 *si enim non pertinaciter, iam non est haereticus, sed solum errans*—*Summa Th.*, 2:2:5:3 (II:37).

101 *non habet habitum fidei neque formatae neque informis*—*Summa Th.*, 2:2:5:3 (Caramello, II:37; this edition has the passage in emphatic type). Cf. 2:2:5:4, ad 1 (II:38).

102 *fidem non habet de aliis articulis, sed opinionem quandam*—*Summa Th.*, 2:2:5:3 (II:38).

103 See our ref. 100 just above. Cf. also *quem* [sc., *habitum fidei*] *tamen*

habet ille qui non explicite omnia credit, sed paratus est omnia credere— Summa Th., 2:2:5:4, ad 1 (II:38).

104 Of this vexed and subtle question, on one aspect of the dynamic interplay at one stage in its intricate and continuing development, the thirteenth-century syncretic movement called Ryōbu Shintō—to take an entrancing yet somewhat random example—it would be illuminating to have St. Thomas's observations, and to see how he would interpret the data in terms of his system of ideas. If he were living in our world, it seems highly unlikely that he would fail to be interested.

105 As one instance of the kind of book that a modern theologian may well find it engaging to read, and fascinating to ponder, see for example, Toshihiko Izutsu, *A Comparative Study of the Key Philosophical Concepts in Sufism and Taoism—Ibn 'Arabî and Lao-tzŭ, Chuang-tzŭ*, Tokyo: The Keio Institute of Cultural and Linguistic Studies, 3 parts in 2 voll., 1966-1967 (Keio Studies in the Humanities and Social Relations, voll. 7, 10). As the title indicates, this particular work is a study of ideas—of beliefs, some might say—not of faith: it includes no consideration of the significance of the ideas for those who adopted them, the meaning in and for a life lived in terms of them. The author does, in passing, note that the conceptualizations were historically generated out of something humanly special, were the product of what we might call faith (in such remarks as: "Ibn 'Arabî's philosophy is . . . an extraordinary world-view because it is a product of an extraordinary experience of an extraordinary man"—1:14). And while the work does not explicitly concern itself with the quality of living that those ideas would in turn inculcate (or have historically inculcated) in others, nevertheless that issue is raised by implication, one might contend, in the concept of "the perfect man" in the two systems. In any case, a modern Christian theologian with any knowledge of the faith of the two communities, or with any imagination, would recognize swiftly a relevance of such a study to his own. Among mediaevals, admittedly, a St. Bernard or a St. Bonaventura would perhaps be more entranced by this than a St. Thomas; more to the latter's taste, one may suppose—or to a modern of his type—would be a comparative study of Sunnī (as distinct from Ṣūfī) ideas with Confucian (as distinct from Taoist); and of the faith that each crystallized.

106 It is for, I should guess, most readers a mistranslation to render the title of his *De veritate catholicae fidei* as "On the Truth of the Catholic Faith"—although this is how it appears in, for instance, the recent and hardly unauthoritative version, St. Thomas Aquinas, *On the Truth of the Catholic Faith: Summa Contra Gentiles, translated, with an introduction and notes, by* Anton C. Pegis [Book I], James F. Anderson [Book II], Vernon J. Bourke [Book III], Charles J. O'Neil [Book IV], Garden City, New York: Doubleday (Image Books), 5 voll., 1955-1957. Such readers are likely to understand "the" Catholic faith (and with capital "C", e.g., Pegis, vol. 1, p. 62) as distinguished from the Jewish faith, the Islamic faith, nowadays the Protestant faith, and so on. Such a conceptualization of *catholica fides* is the work of

modern minds, and is far from how the matter appeared to the author (and to his readers for some centuries), for whom faith was one and "universal".

At the very least, the point may be put in the following way. For St. Thomas, the form of faith professed by Christians in the Church was the only form known to him, and was felt to be identical—co-extensive—with faith universally; therefore a modern may recognize that for its author this title verbalized *both* what we to-day would call "universal faith" *and* what we today might specify as the faith of the Roman Catholic Church. Inasmuch as these two no longer totally co-incide, are no longer viewed as co-extensive, therefore a modern translator is faced with a choice between them, if he is unable to come up with some device that will somehow express the convergence. By his choice, he indicates which of the two is in his view the more important, and of which he is willing to let go if pressed. (The decision is actually so made, probably unconsciously. Strictly, it should be made rather in terms of which the translator judges that St. Thomas would view as the more important of the two.) To me it would seem obvious that the universal or generic truth of that about which he was talking was for St. Thomas logically prior to the particular; his interest in what we might call the Roman Catholic faith was derivative from his view that this was in fact faith as such, generically. Indeed this was why he wrote the book—*contra errores infidelium*: against the fallacies of those "who are without faith". He was definitely not writing "on the truth of the Catholic faith against the errors of other forms of faith" (or ". . . other faiths")!

For the Latin phrasing of the title I have used the Pera edition (above, our ref. 53). In any case, apart from his title, Thomas says quite explicitly in his opening paragraphs what his intention in writing this work is: namely (not to prove that a particular faith, or a particular form of faith, or even faith generically, is true; but rather) to make manifest the truth (or: the reality) that such faith proclaims. He says this in so many words: *propositum nostrae intentionis est veritatem quam* FIDES CATHOLICA *profitetur . . . manifestare*—1:2 (sc., Liber I, cap. ii; Pera edn., vol II, p. 3, §9). Thus the "truth of faith" (*veritas fidei* in the title) is not its validity; but rather, the reality about which it speaks. (This reality is God; as is confirmed in that in the remainder of this sentence he goes on to state that it is indeed his duty, in the words of Hilary, " 'that my every word and sense may speak of Him' "—*debere me* Deo *conscius sum, ut* eum *omnis sermo meus et sensus loquatur*—ibid.) That is, the "of" here is in the sense not, as the grammarians say, of a subjective genitive but of a possessive: it is not that the faith is true, but that the object of faith is truth. This, of course, is in line with his general position: that the object of faith is *prima veritas*. (Thus, we might say that the title could well be translated: "On the reality of that to which faith is oriented". Even if, more apologetically, *de Veritate* here were to mean "on the genuineness of . . .", then the full title even so would indicate that the book is on the genuineness of what faith universally is all about. Some would perhaps regard it as not too far-fetched to say that this present book of ours is on that same subject?)

Thomas does use the phrase *Christiana religio* twice in this work; but again this does not mean "the Christian religion" but is here rather of the order of "piety in Christ". He is explicit, in his opening chapter, that *religio* he understands as "piety"—*religioni . . . quae etiam pietas nominatur*: 1:1 (Pera edn., vol. II, §7, p. 3). On *fides christiana*, cf. below, at our ref. 108. On the meaning of "Christian" in such phrases, cf. also that ref.

The nickname *Summa Contra Gentiles* is found in none of the manuscripts. Once concocted, however, it gained currency relatively quickly, and occurs "in all early catalogues". See Weisheipl, *Friar Thomas* (above, our ref. 44), p. 359. Ceslaus Pera, in the course of his elaborate introduction to the work, calls it "more convenient, no doubt, but less appropriate"—*commodius, certe, minus apte creditur*—vol. 1, §442, p. 539. Cf. also the General Introduction (unsigned; perhaps by Pegis?) in Pegis et al., transs., *On the Truth of the Catholic Faith*, 1:17.

107 Similarly (as we have seen in our chapter 3 above), moderns, whether outsiders or Muslims, misunderstand mediaeval Islamic articulations and definitions as expositions of Islamic faith. They were not that, and are misconstrued insofar as they have been manoeuvred into becoming that. They were, and can serve us (us all) as, mediaeval Islamic apprehensions and characterizations of human faith—of cosmic faith.

108 St. Thomas does indeed use the phrase *fides christiana* in his writings. In my *Belief and History* (above, our chapter 1, ref. 4), I made the following statement: "In Catholic thought, it is my impression that throughout the Middle Ages the dominant custom was for the concept *fides* to be used without specification" (p. 125, at note 30). Through the sumptuous new computer-based concordance it is now possible to specify this more precisely. In the Thomas corpus the ratio of *fides* alone to *fides christiana* (or *christiana fides*) is 132 to 1.

In this and in other ways it becomes apparent that the thesis of this present study, and its fundamental interest in faith as the generic relation between man and God, with a concern then for faith in its specifically Christian form derivative from or illustrative of or conducive towards that, are arguably closer to classical Christian (and for that matter, to classical Muslim or other) orientations than are many modern positions superficially or ostensibly more orthodox.

(The neologism "Islamic faith" not only does not occur in traditional Muslim writing; further, it is impossible to translate it as such into Arabic. [One might resort to paraphrase: an anthology of Muslim passages on faith that I have had in mind to edit, I have thought of entitling perhaps *al-īmān 'inda al-muslimīn*.])

For the meaning of *fides christiana*, cf. just below, our ref. 109.

The statistical calculation above is based upon figures in *Index Thomisticus: Sancti Thomae Aquinatis Operum Omnium Indices et Concordantiae in quibus verborum omnium et singulorum formae et lemmata cum suis frequentiis et contextibus variis modis referuntur quaeque auspice Paulo VI Summo Pontifice consociata plurium opera atque electronico IBM automato usus digessit*, Robertus Busa, Stuttgart-Bad Cannstatt: Frommann-Holzboog, 23 voll., 1974-1975. *Fides* (entry 32701, part 2, vol. 9, pp. 354-442) is given 8,569 times; *christianus* plus *fides* and *vice versa* are entries 16237-a and -b (part 2, vol. 4, p. 76, pp. 76-77), where they appear 7 plus 58 times.

109 On the shift over the centuries of the adjective "Christian" from meaning "pertaining to Christ" towards meaning "pertaining to Christians" (and similarly of, for instance, the adjective "Muslim" from meaning "committing oneself to God" to meaning "pertaining to Muslims"), and its significance, see my *Questions of Religious Truth*, New York: Scribner's, and London: Gollancz, 1967, chap. 4, "Christian—Noun, or Adjective?".

For most moderns, accordingly, it would be more accurate, or at the very least less ambiguous, to render mediaeval *fides christiana* as something like "faith in Christ" or ". . . through Christ". In modern English, "Christian faith" might not distort Thomas's concept verbalized in this form, for some readers; for others it easily might. With the definite article—"the Christian faith"—it almost certainly would, for most.

Similar considerations apply to *religio christiana*; cf. our ref. 106 above. This last is a phrase that he uses rarely: a mere 37 times throughout his whole writing (*Index Thomisticus* [above, our ref. 108], part 2, vol. 4, p. 77, entry 16237-c: note that items 00035-36 diverge). *Christiana doctrina* occurs even less often: 11 times in all (ibid., part 2, vol. 7, pp. 933-934). He was interested rather in *sacra doctrina* (the opening *quaestio* of *Summa Th.*, 1:1 [Caramello, 1:2-9]): he did not yet know, but we to-day do, that this has Islamic, Buddhist, and other sub-divisions as well as the sub-division that we call Christian.

On "religion", "Christian religion", "the Christian religion", see my *Meaning and End . . .* (above, our chap. 1 here, ref. 10), its chap. 2, "'Religion' in the West"; and cf. chap. 3 there, §vi, on "Christianity" as a concept.

The process with which one is here involved is the gradual loss in the modern world of a transcendent meaning for terms and concepts, accompanied then also by the purely mundane intellectual error of reading these terms of earlier centuries as if they had been denuded of their transcendent reference even then.

It would, of course, be grotesque to suggest that Christ is of anything but major, indeed monumental, importance for Thomas. (Even so, he uses the concept markedly less than the concept "God"; and I find this fact important, especially in contrast to the "unitarianism of the Son" among modern Protestants.) Nevertheless, the *adjective* "Christian" is not among his most common words (a total of 469 occurrences).

110 See his article *Utrum fides sit una*, in *Summa Th.*, 2:2:4:6 (Caramello, II:32). This is elaborated in our ref. 111, just below.

111 In his article on this matter (our ref. 110, just above) he quotes Ephesians 4:5 (*Unus dominus, una fides*), and then against those who object that faith is various he writes as follows:

"If 'faith' be taken as referring to the human quality, a habit (disposition), it can be considered in two ways. One way is from the side of its object, and in that case faith is one: for the formal object of faith is primordial reality (or: ultimate truth), by cleaving to which we give our allegiance to whatever things are comprised under faith. The other way is from the side of the subject; and in this case faith becomes diversified, in accordance with what pertains to those diverse subjects. Yet it is evident that faith, just like any other human disposition (habit), gets its generic quality in relation to the formal reckoning of its object, whereas it is individuated in relation to its subject. Therefore, if faith be taken as that quality by which we give allegiance, in that case faith is generically one, differing numerically among diverse people.

"If, on the other hand, faith be taken as referring to that to which allegiance is given, in that case also faith is one. For that to which allegiance is given by all people is the same. This is so, even though the items of allegiance, to which all in common give allegiance, be diverse, nonetheless, these all reduce to one.

"Accordingly, the position over against the first objection [namely, that faith has to do both with transcendent realities and with various mundane things, and therefore must be differentiated] is that the mundane matters that are set forth in faith have to do with the object of faith only insofar as they relate to a transcendent reality, which is primordial truth, as stated above. Therefore faith is one, concerning both mundane and transcendent things. It is, however, otherwise with wisdom and discursive knowledge; these consider mundane and transcendent matters severally, according to the particular qualities of each.

"Over against the second objection [namely, that confessional formulations of faith differ], the position is that that difference . . . arises not from any diversity in that to which allegiance is given, but from the diverse position of those who give their allegiance to the one thing to which allegiance is given. . . ."

In modern language: people's symbols differ but they are objects of faith only insofar as they relate those people to what is symbolized; and that is the same for all.

The Latin reads: *Sed contra est quod Apostolus dicit. . . .*

Respondeo dicendum quod fides, si sumatur pro habitu, dupliciter potest considerari. Uno modo, ex parte obiecti. Et sic est una fides: obiectum enim formale fidei est veritas prima, cui inhaerendo credimus quaecumque sub fide continentur. Alio modo, ex parte subiecti. Et sic fides diversificatur secundum quod est diversorum. Manifestum est autem quod fides, sicut et quilibet alius habitus, ex formali ratione obiecti habet speciem, sed ex subiecto individuatur. Et ideo, si fides sumatur pro habitu quo credimus, sic fides est una specie, et differens numero in diversis—Si vero sumatur pro eo quod creditur, sic etiam est una fides. Quia idem est quod ab omnibus creditur: et si sint diversa credibilia quae communiter omnes credunt, tamen omnia reducuntur ad unum.

Ad primum ergo dicendum quod temporalia quae in fide proponuntur non pertinent ad obiectum fidei nisi in ordine ad aliquod aeternum, quod est veritas prima, sicut supra dictum est. Et ideo fides una est de temporali-

bus et aeternis. Secus autem est de sapientia et scientia, quae considerant temporalia et aeterna secundum proprias rationes utrorumque.

Ad secundum dicendum quod illa differentia praeteriti et futuri non contingit ex aliqua diversitate rei creditae: sed ex diversa habitudine credentium ad unam rem creditam, ut etiam supra habitum est.—Summa Th., 2:2:4:6 (Caramello, II:32).

112 Above, our chap. 1, ref. 13, p. 180, regarding Thomas. Given his reservations on the diversity subjectively, however, perhaps the difference between his position and my own is in the end minimal.

113 *Summa Th.*, 2:2:1:6-10 (Caramello, II:8-15).

114 *in nullo alio differunt nisi quod in uno plenius explicantur quae in alio continentur implicite—Summa Th.*, 2:2:1:9, ad 2 (II:13). Another example: *quaedam explicite cognita sunt a posterioribus quae a prioribus non cognoscebantur explicite*—2:2:1:7 (II:10).

115 *Summa Th.*, 2:2:1:3 (II:5-6), especially objection 3 and his reply thereto. This is considered further below, in our text three paragraphs hence and at our ref. 117, where the Latin is cited of which our sentence in the text here may pass as a paraphrase.

116 This matter, and variant versions of the same point, are discussed in his *De Veritate*, 14:12 (Spiazzi [our ref. 43 above], p. 304), and in *Summa Th.*, 2:1:103:4 (Caramello, I:497 in the second sequence of pagination). The special case canvassed in *Summa Th.*, 2:2:1:3 (II:5-6) is considered further just below, our ref. 117.

117 A modern comparativist, surveying the variegated religious history of our race, might be tempted to report—or a modern theologian, pondering the past of his own tradition, to aver—that belief is human and an historical construct, while the faith of which it is the inadequate expression is divine and eternal and true. More exactly: it can happen that persons of faith may hold beliefs that as products of human imagination are false, but the faith involved in them is true (otherwise it is not faith). It is arresting to find that Thomas said it first: *Possibile est enim hominem fidelem ex coniectura humana falsum aliquid aestimare. Sed quod ex fide falsum aestimet, hoc est impossibile—Summa Th.*, 2:2:1:3, ad 3 (II:6).

118 This is re-iterated throughout. That it is the "starting point and foundation" for him is apparent from this fact and in that it is set forth as the first article of the first question of his treatment of faith in his *Summa Th.* (2:2:1-16 [Caramello, II:3-83]); cf. above, our ref. 91 and just below, our ref. 119.

119 *in fide, si consideremus formalem rationem obiecti, nihil est aliud quam veritas prima. . . . Si vero consideremus materialiter ea quibus fides assentit, non solum est ipse Deus, sed etiam multa alia. Quae tamen sub assensu fidei non cadunt nisi secundum quod habent aliquem ordinem ad Deum. . . . Et ideo etiam ex hac parte obiectum fidei est quodammodo veritas prima, inquantum nihil cadit sub fide nisi in ordine ad Deum. . . .*

Ad primum ergo dicendum quod ea quae pertinent ad humanitatem Christi et ad sacramenta Ecclesiae vel ad quascumque creaturas cadunt sub fide inquantum per haec ordinamur ad Deum. Et eis etiam assentimus propter divinam veritatem.

Et similiter dicendum est ad secundum, de omnibus illis quae in sacra Scriptura traduntur.

Ad tertium dicendum quod etiam caritas diligit proximum propter Deum; et sic obiectum eius proprie est ipse Deus, ut infra [sc. 2:2:25:1 (Caramello, II:129-130)] *dicetur—Summa Th.*, 2:2:1:1 (II:4).

I find it noteworthy that *ordinamur* in the argument *ad 1* here is in the first person: it is not simply that the objects of faith are oriented to God but, as we have said in the sentence in our text, that through them persons are so oriented. This is a foundation principle for the comparativist understanding of any religious tradition other than one's own (or of one's own tradition at an historical period other than the present). I also find it noteworthy that the argument *ad 2* here, regarding scripture, applies equally—although Thomas did not know this—to, for instance, the Qur'ān; and is in fact virtually the argument that I myself used a decade ago (before I had read Aquinas) in my Taylor Lecture at Yale Divinity School, "Is the Qur'an the Word of God?" (my *Questions of Religious Truth* [our ref. 109 above], chap. 2; cf. also that work's chap. 3, "Can Religions Be True or False?"). That the Bible is, and that the Qur'ān is not, divine revelation were two among Thomas's presuppositions ["beliefs"]; there is no reason, however, why an intelligent modern Muslim, or anyone else who might dissent less or more seriously from Thomas on either or both of those two views, should not nevertheless appreciate, even learn from, even agree with, Thomas's analysis of what faith is, as he has here set it forth.

In addition to this passage, see also Thomas's subsequent discussions in which he specifies that human faith is faith not in God simply but (a) in God Himself, and (b) in God's dealings with man, for man's salvation.

Implicit in God's *esse* are all those things in which transcendently our beatitude consists; and implicit in His providence are all those things that are historically made available to us as our route towards beatitude. The various articles of the creeds, says Thomas in his discussion of variety among these, are contained within one or other of these two basic principles. Faith therefore involves (a) those matters the vision of which will constitute our blessedness in life on high and (b) those by which we are led to that.

. . . omnes articuli implicite continentur in aliquibus primis credibilibus, scilicet ut credatur Deus esse et providentiam habere circa hominum salutem. . . . In esse enim divino includuntur omnia quae credimus in Deo aeternaliter existere, in quibus nostra beatitudo consistit: in fide autem providentiae includuntur omnia quae temporaliter a Deo dispensantur ad hominum salutem, quae sunt via in beatitudinem—Summa Th., 2:2:1:7 (II:10). Again: *illa per se pertinent ad fidem quorum visione in vita aeterna perfruemur, et per quae ducemur in vitam aeternam—Summa Th.*, 2:2:1:8 (II:11).

Once again, there is here set forth a foundation principle for the comparative historian of religion. An understanding of faith across the centuries and across the world requires first an appreciation of the relation that that faith represents, for those persons whose it is, to a transcendent truth in and around them, yet not merely that but secondly an appreciation also of their relation in that faith to—or better: through—the specific and concrete realities of their particular religious traditions, by which the first is mediated. In the modern world, our awareness of the diversity, both in time and in space, of this latter matter is so much fuller than was Thomas's that we are hesitant to be as unreserved as was he in his asseveration that faith everywhere and at all times is one; it is a pity, nonetheless, if we let go of that perception for no better reason than that our awareness of the former point may be less vivid than was his.

120 On sacraments and scripture, cf. the first passage quoted in the preceding note (our ref. 119), just above (2:2:1:1, ad 1 and ad 2 [11:4]). On ritual and ceremony (though, stark intellectual that he was, he tended to regard these as at a somewhat different level; note the *quaedam*): *omnes caeremoniae sunt quaedam protestationes fidei, in qua consistit interior Dei cultus. Sic autem fidem interiorem potest homo protestari factis, sicut et verbis —Summa Th.*, 2:1:103:4 (1:497).

In the latter argument here Thomas is, curiously, less lenient of diversity than he is elsewhere regarding "belief". Contrariwise, most modern Christians are but little discomforted by diversity of ritual and ceremonial expression of what they may yet regard as "the same faith". It may be that Thomas's attention had been less drawn to differences in this sphere, even historically.

121 Cf. our reff. 112-117, above.

122 *Conc[ilium] Vaticanum I . . . Sessio III . . . : Constitutio dogmatica "Dei Filius"* . . . ; Cap. 3. *De fide.* §1, and . . . *Canones* 1, 2. As cited in Henricus Denzinger, ed. ([rev. by] Adolfus Schönmetzer), *Enchiridion Symbolorum* . . . , editio xxxiii, Barcinone, Friburgi Brisgoviae, Romae, Neo-Eboraci: Herder, 1965, p. 589, para. 1789/3008, p. 593, paras. 1810, 1811/3031, 3032.

123 The problem of the "cogency" is major. Even though one understand what faith is said to be, or is, nonetheless it is not easy to have it. It does not follow "naturally" from a recognition of how things are, as this Vatican document stresses, as Islamic theology agrees, as Hindus and Jews know, and so on. One cannot simply choose to have faith, many acute analyses throughout history around the world have held. Even the modern West is not unaware that its "lack of faith" is a sickness, without a remedy's being thereby automatic, or even accessible. This problem is taken up again in our concluding chapter below; yet the topic of this book is what faith is, and especially, is not: a mere prolegomenon to the question (new, in the light of modern comparative knowledge; but no more simple for that) as to how (either historically, or metaphysically) persons become faithful.

124 The non-orthodox were more nearly aware of the distinction between the two; but were slapped down for their pains. The influential German theologian Georg Hermes (1775-1831), as one example, discriminated between *der Glaube* and *der wirksame Glaube*, in a fashion that approximates to our distinction between "belief" and "faith". The approximation is not

close, however; his discrimination may be seen as marking an historical phase on the way towards that modern divergence. The former of the two, *der Glaube*, is for him rather "knowledge" (*Erkenntniss*). It is a recognition of truths (or, of realities: *Wahrheiten* [*Wirklichkeiten*]—3:469). This was his primary interest: throughout most of his life and most of his writing when he said *Glaube* he meant something intellectual, and its theoretical validity was the problem that centrally engaged him. Although for him it is more than what we would call "belief", yet in the end he makes quite clear that it is less than what we would call "faith". On one occasion (3:469) at the end of his life he characterizes the distinction that he has made as one between *der Vernunftglaube* and *der Herzensglaube.* The former he calls also *Erkenntnissglaube* (3:472 bis), and referring to it speaks further of *des bloss philosophischen oder Erkenntnissglaubens* (3:473—the word "mere" [*bloss*] occurs also at 3:469). This, he asserts, is not enough (*nicht genug*—3:469). Indeed, it is a dead belief or dead awareness (*ein todter Glaube*—3:471). Effective faith, on the other hand, which alone is salvific (*Heilshandlung*—3:469), is not this merely intellectual judgement or recognition of truths, but is rather a giving of oneself to them (*Hingebung* 3:469), involving a free choice of the will; it is correlative with the virtues of Hope and Love.

Although I myself have not gone into the matter closely, it is my impression that it would make a decidedly rewarding study to examine in historical perspective the position set forth by Hermes and the rejection of it by opponents, especially the papal commission that presently condemned his work (1835). They would seem to provide an illuminating illustration of a given moment in the transition of *glauben* from its traditional Christian meaning (having to do with faith) to its post-Enlightenment meaning (having to do with belief), with Hermes representing more of the latter, the official denunciation representing more of the former, and the misunderstanding between the two sides representing a significant, and perhaps even crucial, phase in the growing modern confusion, on this issue, of the Church and Western society. The support for Hermes in Germany, and the widespread disquiet with the Vatican's action, are noteworthy.

Although they definitely represent his thought, there is perhaps a slight problem about his use of the two terms *Vernunftglaube* and *Herzensglaube* (roughly, English "belief" and "faith"). The former he took no doubt from Kant; it is not clear to me whether he got the latter from the German-speaking Protestant Pietist movement. In any case, the terms do not seem to occur in his major publication: Georg Hermes, *Einleitung in die christkatholische Theologie*, Münster: Coppenrath, 2 voll. [1819-1829], 2te Aufl., 1831-1834. They are developed rather in his subsequent and incomplete work posthumously published as edited by one of his disciples: Georg Hermes, *Christkatholische Dogmatik*, ed. J. H. Achterfeldt, Münster: Coppenrath, 3 voll., 1834 (3:469). It is from this latter work that all quotations here given have been taken, and to which our page references refer.

125 Harent, "Préparation rationnelle de la foi; le fidéisme", being §vi, coll. 171-237, of his Foi (our ref. 127 below).

126 Harent, Foi (our ref. 127, just below), esp. coll. 189-190. This view was formalized official Church doctrine: for example, quaint though it seem to-day, Vatican I had anathematized anyone who might hold that a knowledge of God is not possible in the natural light of human reason—Denzinger, *Enchiridion* (our ref. 122 above), p. 593, para. 1806/3026. In general, although the irritability and other peculiarities of his style are his own, Harent is, as we have indicated, setting forth established Church positions of his time, interpreted in ways then widespread; it is these facts that make his presentations significant for us.

Because of his firm conviction of the reasonableness and the lucidity of the "preambles" of faith, he evinces disdain, curiously (given his propensity for *foi-croyance*; cf. below, at our ref. 130; cf. also our ref. 132), for what we might call mere religious "belief" (as distinct from knowledge), as the intellectual theses of religious persons who hold or profess to hold any basic ideas that cannot be positively known and rationally demonstrated. "To believe", in this sense (the dominant modern sense of the term), is in his eyes not merely wrong but pitiful.

127 In *Dictionnaire de théologie catholique, contenant l'exposé des doctrines de la théologie catholique, leurs preuves et leur histoire*, commencé sous la direction de A. Vacant, continué sous celle de E. Mangenot [et] de É. Amann, avec le concours d'un grand nombre de collaborateurs, Paris: Letouzey et Ané, 15 voll., 1903-1950. (The work appeared in fascicules, from 1899. What is sometimes designated a 16th volume, entitled *Tables générales*, began to appear in fascicules in 1951 and was completed with fascicule 18, dated 1972.) The article in question is S. Harent, Foi, tome 6 (1920): coll. 55-514.

128 Although I have not made an exact count, my impression is that his ratio of *foi chrétienne* to *foi* would perhaps not be quite so low as was Thomas's (above, our ref. 108), for he does speak of the former from time to time (some examples: coll. 100 bis, 119). This is to be expected, given the century in which he is writing. Nonetheless, the burden of his presentation, and especially in its expository as distinct from its polemical parts, has to do with *la foi* as such. (Note the article's title.)

129 Harent, often; e.g., coll. 164, 177-178, 232, 348-349.

130 Some examples: *la foi . . . est la croyance* (Harent, Foi, col. 79); *le sens de* foi-croyance *est le sens normal et prédominant* (75); *la foi est . . . une croyance* (84). Note, curiously, *notre* [sic] *conception de la foi-croyance* (77); cf. *foi dogmatique* (78, cf. 79). Indeed, in the earlier part of his presentation he is at pains to stress this conception and to denounce alternatives (e.g., coll. 72-84, passim). Elsewhere also in passing he uses on more than one occasion the word *croyance* for *foi* rather un-self-consciously. Further, he attacks (coll. 129ff.) those who take too seriously St. Thomas's position (*Summa Th.*, 2:2:1:2, ad 2; cf. above, our ref. 96) that propositions, in faith, are a means to an end, that end being God (*prima veritas*) Himself, and who therefore hold that propositions are not the object of faith.

There is ambiguity, however, also here, both in his use of the historically evolving and multivalent term *croyance*, and in what he says about it. It is difficult to read the early parts of his article, such as those just adduced, without feeling that he there had in mind a conception of *croyance* as having a proposition as object (explicitly so, coll. 129-130), and that at least in this sense he is saying here that faith is belief. (By many he would surely have been so read, even in 1930.) Nonetheless: (a) elsewhere he affirms that by *croyance* he does *not* mean this (our ref. 132 below); and (b) once he has passed beyond castigating those with whom he disagrees and is setting forth his own (the Church's) position (in effect, once he has moved, from arguing against "modernists" and "liberals", to propound rather the traditional teaching of the Church), he himself stresses (coll. 376ff.) that God Himself is, without any intermediary (*immédiatement*, col. 377), the formal object of faith, both as motive and as supreme material object, and he insists that of its several material objects all the others are subordinate to the principal object, God. ". . . *toutes les vérités que Dieu a révélées . . . sont pour elle* [sc. *pour la foi*] l'objet matériel. *Mais ces vérités révélées ne sont pas toutes sur la même ligne, pour ainsi dire. . . . Au sommet, l'objet principal de la révélation, Dieu; le reste, objet purement matériel, n'a été révélé qu'à cause de lui, afin de le mieux connaître. . . . Aussi, . . . l'objet que nous croyons avant tout, c'est Dieu*" (col. 378).

131 Harent, Croyance, in *Dictionnaire de théologie catholique*, (above, our ref. 127), tome 3, coll. 2364-2396. My edition of this volume, the *3ème tirage*, is dated 1923, but the article was presumably published before the 1920 article, Foi, above.

132 Our choice of the English word "beliefs" here is problematic, perhaps. It is offered as a translation of *croyance* only tentatively, but confidently as a descriptive term for material actually covered in the article in question. As remarked above (our ref. 130), he does not in his article Foi clarify what he means when, in the early sections there, he calls *foi* a *croyance*; though he gives the impression there, later withdrawn, that he intends belief. Here, however, in the article Croyance, while substantially he discusses non-Christian beliefs under this heading, yet formally it emerges that by it he again does not mean "belief" in the standard modern sense. What he says there is that in theological usage the word does not mean *croyance* in most of the current French senses of that "ambiguous" (col. 2364) term, nor in several of the senses set forth s.v. in the *Vocabulaire de la Société française de philosophie* (coll. 2367-2368). "Conviction" would be a minimal English rendering (with operationalist connotations of "convicted" as well as of "convinced"). (Cf. col. 2365, lines 13-14.) It is evident that he is primarily influenced by the Christian sense of *credere*. Yet in fact he extends his usage (beyond *foi*, partly consciously [col. 2367]), as we observe in the remainder of this paragraph in our text, to cover other comparable convictions held loyally without either intellectual or moral reservations. *Croyance* in the secular modern sense of belief he dismisses as "altogether improper" and uninteresting to boot (col. 2364; cf. 2365, lines 4-6).

The axiom (for him, we may and must call it that) with which we end this paragraph in our text, that it is impossible for God to be mistaken or to mislead, he quotes (his column 189 of the FOI article, with slightly variant word-order) from the encyclical *Qui pluribus* of Pius IX of 1846.

In the Christian case, for him (cf. above, our ref. 126), one would perhaps have to conclude that *croyance* signifies "recognition".

133 Of this seminal thinker the first major work has continued basic and influential: Maurice Blondel, *L'Action* [Paris: Alcan, 1893] Paris: Presses universitaires de France, 1950, 1973; this has not been superseded by the revised two-volume version [Paris: Alcan, 1936-1937] Paris: Presses universitaires de France [1937-1949] 1949-1963. Much else of his substantial writing is also relevant: not least, *La Pensée*, Paris: Félix Alcan, 2 voll., 1934; Presses universitaires de France, 2 voll., 1948-1954. For a sympathetic study, with bibliography, of this thinker's role in the development of our problem, see Aubert, *L'Acte de foi* (above, our ref. 43), pp. 277-294 et passim (see s.v. in index).

134 By his view of faith virtually the whole of Karl Rahner's prolific output is, of course, informed, although he has written relatively little directly on the matter. His position is concisely suggested, however, in the readily accessible preparatory section that he has contributed to the entry FAITH (the bulk of that entry is by another hand) in the encyclopaedia *Sacramentum Mundi* which he and a group under his direction have recently edited.

The absurdity into which the persistence of the verb "believe" as a modern rendering for the concept of having faith (German *glauben*) has fallen, is well demonstrated in the very opening paragraph of this presentation. In this, in the German original the verb *glauben* occurs four times, the adjectival noun *Gläubiger* once, and the noun *der Glaube* eight times. In the English this last is consistently rendered as "faith" (so also the title and sub-title of the article); but the former two appear misleadingly and unfortunately as "believe"—the verb three times with a parenthetical indication (also in the original) to specify that this term does not mean what one might expect (and indeed, in the context, the standard meaning makes sheer nonsense of the material). The fourth time, however, such clarifying reservations are not explicit—but in this case the verb (both in the original and in the translation) is proffered within quotation marks (in English: "What the person . . . 'believes' "). This signals the negative point that the word does not have its normal meaning, but otherwise leaves the dilemma unresolved.

It makes sense, doubly so in the light of our present study, to say, as does this paragraph, "faith may always be assumed to be present" in all human beings, including those, a Christian theologian may well discern, who have never heard of Christian positions (cf. our concluding chapter, below); or to aver that anyone "obedient to the dictates of his conscience", therein and to that extent is justified by faith; yet surely it strains the English language in the twentieth century to call the former "a believer" (even "potentially") who is "already in possession of what he is to believe", and to say that the latter "believes"—even if one adds, as is here done, "in the theological sense". Rahner's thought is lucid, and his points good; but modern German serves him poorly to express them, and in English, where *glauben* is rendered quite anachronistically, the position emerges in a form that is quite inept.

Karl Rahner, "Way to Faith", being §1 of the entry FAITH in *Sacramentum Mundi: an Encyclopedia of Theology*, New York: Herder and Herder, and London: Burns & Oates, 6 voll., 1968-1970. All quotations here are from 2:310 (I have used the 4th imp., 1969). The German original is from *Sacramentum Mundi: Theologisches Lexikon für die Praxis . . .* , Freiburg, Basel, Wien: Herder, 4 Bde., 1967-1969. In the German, this essay has the format of an independent entry, s.v. GLAUBENSZUGANG, 2:414-420, following the main article GLAUBE (coll. 390-413) with its various sub-sections, whereas in English it constitutes rather the first part of the main article and precedes therefore the other sub-sections. The piece is reprinted in the abridged one-volume edition: Karl Rahner, ed., *Encyclopedia of Theology: The Concise* Sacramentum Mundi, New York: Seabury, 1975 (our quotations: p. 496).

One may note, further, the relatively minor item of this author mentioned above, our chap. 1, ref. 13 (*Faith Today*). Moreover, on the comparativist issues that concern us most nearly, the following articles are not irrelevant: "Weltgeschichte und Heilsgeschichte" and "Das Christentum und die nichtchristlichen Religionen", in Karl Rahner, *Schriften zur Theologie*, Band 5, Einsiedeln, Zürich, Köln: Benziger, 1962, pp. 115-135, 136-158.

135 Jean Mouroux, *Je crois en toi: structure personnelle de la foi*, Paris: Éditions de la Revue des jeunes (Collection Foi Vivante), 1949. This reprints with a slight addition the author's article "Structure 'personnelle' de la foi", from *Recherches de science religieuse*, 29: [59]-107 (1939). The book has appeared also in the following editions: 2nd edn., Paris, Éditions du Cerf (Collection Foi Vivante), 1954; with the significantly modified subtitle, *la rencontre avec le Dieu vivant*, ibid., [1965], 1968; English version (of the 2nd edn.), *I Believe: the personal structure of faith*, trans. by Michael Turner, [London, 1959] New York: Sheed & Ward, 1959. This presentation of faith as an interpersonal quality claims to be authentically traditional, true to scholastic teaching; and I would take the liberty of opining that in this matter Mouroux is more right than was, for instance, Harent, whose defence of Thomist form left room for so little Thomist substance. One must note, however, that Mouroux's power and warmth owe much also to other strands in the Christian tradition in addition to the scholastic—especially, St. John of the Cross. (One of the strengths of this presentation is that a reader of the work need not agree before he or she starts with the author's ideas, to see the point of what he is saying.)

Note that he avers that it has in our day become (*sic*) trite to speak of faith as a personal encounter. *Il est devenu banal de parler aujourd'hui de la foi comme d'une rencontre personnelle avec Dieu, et nous nous en réjouissons* (1968, p. 121). Again: *la foi est une relation* inter-personnelle (1968, p. 121); *. . . en son essence la foi sera la réponse de la personne humaine au Dieu personnel et donc* la rencontre de deux personnes (1968, p. [45]).

136 A careful survey of developments over the preceding half-century or so

(and an outline of earlier history) is provided in the impressive doctoral thesis of Roger Aubert (above, our ref. 43).

137 Eugène Joly, *Qu'est-ce que croire?* Paris: Arthème Fayard, 1956 (*Encyclopédie du catholique au XXème siècle*, Henri Daniel-Rops, ed., vol. 6—1ère partie, *Je sais, je crois*). Eugène Joly, *What is Faith?* trans. from the French by Illtyd Trethowan, New York: Hawthorne [1958], 5th printing, 1960 (*Twentieth Century Encyclopedia of Catholicism*, vol. 6, section 1: *Knowledge and Faith*). As is evident, the French is original; since I am citing this not, however, as indicative of the author's personal views but as an item from the encyclopaedia, which was published in the two languages, I allow myself for illustrative and historical purposes to give quotations in the official English, with the French text cited also in the notes. Whether I should myself have chosen the English words "belief", "believe" wherever Trethowan has done, would constitute a separate problem; and there are other points where a careful comparison of the two texts is subtly illuminating. Yet the role of the work in English has been with these terms as here presented, and it is this with which we are here concerned. (The issue is similar with Rahner and *Sacramentum Mundi* as above, our ref. 134.)

The two chapters mentioned are 4 (pp. 44-47 in the English) and 5 (pp. 48-52). In French: chap. IV: *La foi est un engagement* (pp. 37-39); chap. V: *La foi est une rencontre* (pp. 40-44).

138 p. 110. *La foi est une rencontre du Dieu vivant, une ouverture au Dieu vivant*—p. [109].

139 p. 110. *La rencontre entre Dieu et chaque personne est un mystère qui ne peut être classé dans aucune catégorie*—p. [109].

140 p. 117. *La foi, comme l'amour, est un être vivant*—p. 115.

141 pp. 108-109. *La foi, c'est l'ouverture à l'inquiétude et au désir. La foi, c'est la disponibilité pour le départ et le dépassement. La foi, c'est la quête de ce Dieu*—p. 108. I might juxtapose here (although I am not sure how Joly would respond to this: favourably, I think) a suggested paraphrase of St. Augustine's comparable comment fifteen centuries ago: "Just as no one of you dare say, 'I have arrived' (at justice, in this case), similarly no one dare say, 'I have not set forth on the journey towards it; I have not undertaken to pursue it' "—*Sicut nemo uestrum audet dicere: Iustus sum; sic nemo audet dicere: Fidelis non sum*—Enarratio 2 in Psalmum 32, Sermo 1, §4. D. Eligius Dekkers et Iohannes Fraipont, edd., Sancti Aurelii Augustini, *Enarrationes in Psalmos I-L*, Turnholti: Brepols, 1956 (Corpus Christianorum, series Latina, vol. 38—Augustini Opera, pars 10:1), p. 249.

142 p. 131. . . . *son contenu intellectuel*—p. 127.

143 Viewing faith as a relation to something greater than oneself, I find myself disquieted with talk of faith's "content" since the content of anything is normally smaller than the container. The phrase seems an innovation (from the time of Hegel, perhaps: *Glaubensinhalt*). I know of no careful study of its history; for a preliminary note on its use in German, Swedish, French, and English, see my *Belief and History* (above, our chap. 1 here, ref. 4), p. 95 and note 44, pp. 127-130.

144 p. 131. *la croyance . . . est le contenu* [*de la foi*]—p. 127.

145 p. 131. *l'Église enseignante . . . nous apprend infailliblement la croyance*—p. 127.

146 p. 131. *inséparable*—p. 127.

147 p. 131. *une formulation humaine inadéquate, contingente, perpétuellement réformable*—p. 127.

147a p. 132. *la présence de Jésus-Christ dans l'Eucharistie*—p. 128.

148 "God has revealed all that it was necessary for us to know *about* him and about his plans for the world"—pp. 131-132 (emphasis mine). The French here is less compromising: *Dieu nous a révélé tout ce qu'il était nécessaire que nous connaissions de Lui et de ses desseins sur le monde*—p. 127.

149 Hebrews 11:6. The passage is Joly, pp. 108-109, in the English. " '*Sans la foi il est impossible de plaire à Dieu.* Pour aller à Dieu il faut croire qu'Il existe et qu'Il récompense ceux qui le cherchent' "—p. 107 (the second sentence here is in italics in the original French).

150 This completes the quotation given at our ref. 141 above. Again the French is less provocative than the English: . . . *la quête de ce Dieu dont on devine qu'Il existe*—p. 108.

151 We are deliberately by-passing an interpretation of "believing", in faith, which, it might be contended, deserves more attention than I find myself able to give it. It might rank as a third proposed resolution of the issue, for modern times. It is the view that "to believe" means to accept a proposition as true on the authority of another person. We have mentioned this above in passing two or three times as a thesis that has indeed seemed to play a certain role in Roman Catholic thought during the course of the nineteenth and early twentieth centuries. I have never quite succeeded, however, in persuading myself that it deserves to be taken very seriously. I was interested to find that Harent, also, dismisses this view. (See his article CROYANCE [our ref. 131, above], coll. 2366-2367.) Part of my problem with it has been that although several seem, curiously, to aver (to have been taught?) that this is what the term means, at least in theological references if not elsewhere, nonetheless I am not sure that I have ever met anyone either in person or on the printed page who actually used the words so—at least, not consistently or even frequently. It is sometimes difficult to get very far beyond the feeling that the suggestion has been primarily an apologetic ploy. It was perhaps widely taught in Catholic education for a time. In favour of the plausibility of this particular interpretation of "belief" are first, that it preserves (even when the object has become a proposition) the interpersonal dimension, and the sense of trust (as in "I trust that . . ."; yet "I believe that he will come" and "I trust that he will come" are nowadays not interchangeable); and second, that supporting precedents can be found, and have in fact been regularly cited, all the way back to St. Augustine, as well as from St. Thomas and later. (Harent rebuts the Thomist argument.) On inquiry it would appear that these instances in the past were, however, rather incidental, and on the whole were traditionally used if at all as illustrations of the fact that our knowledge transcends our individual experience, rather than as essential elements ingredient to the concept of believing itself. In any case,

given the radical shift in the meaning of English "belief", adumbrated in our next chapter, there is a major difference between on the one hand arguing that we become persons of faith (or of hope, or of love) by living among persons of faith (hope, love), or even contending that most people in fact get their beliefs from their fellows, and on the other hand holding that "to believe" *means* to adopt one's neighbour's propositions. In any case, the divergence of faith from all this is illumined for me by the following consideration. One might trust the Church and therefore believe all its teachings, and the Church has taught that there is a devil, with docile members of the Church having been expected then to believe in a devil; yet the phrase *credo diabolo* has never been and could not be used. One may believe in the devil, and even may do so because one trusts another's word; yet it would be wrong to have faith in the devil, on these or on any other grounds, the Church well knows.

Faith is not, and I do not believe that anyone has ever seriously thought that it was, simply believing what other people tell you.

152 "The Bible: Belief as non-Scriptural", being chap. III of my *Belief and History*. In passing, note also here, our ref. 59, chap. 6, below.

153 Luke 18:8.

154 This is re-iterated: Matthew 6:30 / 8:26 / 14:31 / 16:8; Luke 12:28.

155 I Corinthians 13:13.

156 This passage is studied more fully in the other work (our ref. 152 above).

157 ὅτι εἷς ἐστιν ὁ θεος is, among the several variant readings for the text of this verse, the one most recently in tentative favour. Cf. the third (1975) with the second (1968) edition of Kurt Aland et al., *The Greek New Testament*, New York, London, Edinburgh, Amsterdam, Stuttgart: United Bible Societies.

158 και τα δαιμονια πιστευουσιν και φρισσουσιν.

159 As I personally happened to do, one delightful spring day in 1968.

160 Irenaeus, *Adversus Haereses*, 4:6:5. The remark comes in the course of an argument in which the author is rejecting the position of Valentinus and other "pseudo-Gnostics" that God is unknown. Far from there being a question of our "believing" in God, or believing anything about Him, God has revealed Himself so that we *know* Him (he uses the words ειδεναι [*eidenai*] and γινωσκεσθαι [*ginōskesthai*] in Greek, which appear as *scire* and *cognoscere* in the Latin version, each several times repeated in 4:6:4). The judgement against those who do *not* respond in faith is, he says, just; for they *see* (the terms are ὁρωμενος [*horōmenos*] . . . ἰδοντας [*idontas*], *videretur* . . . *viderunt*) and yet *non* . . . *crediderunt* (μη . . . πιστευσαντας [*mē pisteusantas*], 4:6:5). It would be absurd to translate *credo* here by "believe". What the word does mean, rather, Irenaeus himself takes time off to specify: *credere autem ei est facere ejus voluntatem*—πιστευειν δε αὐτῳ ποιειν αὐτου το θελημα (ibid.).

The work was written in Greek, but survived in full and was influential only in Latin; of the original only fragments are available, but they happen to include this passage in full. For the text in both languages, I have used the edition of F. Sagnard, et al., edd., Irénée de Lyon, *Contre les hérésies*, édition critique, Paris: Éditions du Cerf (Sources chrétiennes, H. de Lubac, C. Mondésert et al., dirr., nos. 100, 152, 153, etc.), 1952- (in process); libre 4 (1965), Adelin Rousseau et al., edd., tome 2, pp. 446-449.

161 To be faithful to Christ, for this fifth-century author, is to be faithful to God. And in answer to his own question, what (generically) is faith, he says that in his view it is a loyal giving of the heart, is a being loyal, is a loyal observing of commands. *Quid est igitur credulitas vel fides? Opinor, fideliter hominem Christo credere, id est fidelem deo esse, hoc est fideliter dei mandata servare.* He comes back in his next chapter to this assertion that faith is pledging allegiance and the observing of commands: *fides [est] credere, . . . mandata servare.* More fully: *cum, ut diximus, hoc sit hominis Christiani fides, fideliter Christum credere, et hoc sit . . . Christi mandata servare. . . .* —Salvianus, *De Gubernatione Dei*, 3:2/7 and 4:1/1. I have used the edn. of Carolus Halm, *Salviani Presbyteri Massiliensis Libri qui supersunt*, Berolini: apud Weidmannos, 1877 (Monumenta Germaniae Historica, 1:1), pp. 25, 35. (In the Pauly CSEL edn., pp. 44, 63.) For an English rendering, see Eva M. Sanford, trans.: *On the Government of God: a treatise . . . indited by Salvian, Presbyter of Marseilles . . .* , [New York: Columbia University Press, 1930] New York: Octagon, 1966, pp. 80, 98.

162 *De Praedestinatione Sanctorum*, 2:5. In the 1962 edn. (above, our ref. 42), p. 472.

163 Sermo 43:9, in Cyrillus Lambot, ed., Sancti Aurelii Augustini, *Sermones de Vetere Testamento*, Turnholti: Brepols, 1961 (Corpus Christianorum, series Latina, vol. 41—Augustini Opera, pars 11:1), p. 512.

164 Anselm, *Proslogion*, 1; the penultimate sentence. In the Schmitt edn. (above, our chap. 1, ref. 1), p. 100. Once again, it is quite absurd to translate *credo* here by "believing", once the context be taken into account. The remark culminates a longish argument in which nothing makes any sense at all unless the fact be recognized—it is fully plain—that the author presumes the reality of God, and takes for granted that his readers will do so also; it is a matter of recognizing God rather than consciously "believing" in Him. And then at the climax of the quite impassioned disquisition he exclaims that he wishes "to understand, to some degree, Thy truth, to which my heart is loyal and which it loves. For it is not", he concludes, "that I seek to understand in order that I may pledge my allegiance; rather, I pledge my allegiance in order that I may understand": *desidero aliquatenus intelligere veritatem tuam, quam credit et amat cor meum. Neque enim quaero intelligere ut credam, sed credo ut intelligam.* (Note, in passing, the parallelism of *credit* and *amat.* Note also that the object of the verb *credo* here is *veritatem*, which is a logically impossible object of the first person of the modern verb "to believe". Indeed it is *veritatem tuam*, which makes the usual translation—especially for the minds of those who make fun of the statement—all the more grotesque.)

165 Even the maxim *credo quia absurdum*, which no one quite knows who first said, nor in what context, and which is without authority, becomes historically intelligible (even if still not persuasive) if taken as signifying:

"I take on total commitment, because it goes beyond mere theoretical apprehension". Christians are not absurd who say, for instance in response to the criticism that Trinitarian doctrines are obscure, "I could not worship a God whom I could understand". (Cf. a modern presentation of the same point in an ex-husband's observation to his estranged wife's confession of bewilderment, in a modern popular London and New York drama: "I couldn't believe in a god so simple I could understand him"—James Callifer, in Graham Greene, *The Potting Shed, A Play in Three Acts*, New York: Viking, 1957, p. 115.)

166 This expression, attributed to St. Augustine, was current in the Middle Ages as a statement of that thinker's position, and stands until to-day as his "well known formulation" (*la fameuse formule d'Augustin*—Chenu [above, our ref. 64], pp. 80f., quoting it). I have not, however, despite sustained search, succeeded in locating an exact source; I should be grateful if any reader can help me. If it should turn out that the actual wording is not original but is a later echo of, for instance, the received title of his treatise *De fide rerum quae non videntur*, it may nonetheless serve us here as a characterization that for centuries in the Church carried weight, an illuminating indication of how faith was persistently understood—in addition to its being an at least reasonably accurate representation of Augustine's own thought (except perhaps for the term "virtue"? I am not sufficiently familiar with the exact history of concepts here to know whether to wonder if this word here not be a trifle anachronistic).

An alternative translation of the expression quoted in our text might be: "Faith is the capacity to give one's allegiance to the intangibles"—and of the book-title, "On living in loyalty to non-material realities".

Actually, even the title of the treatise here mentioned is a whit problematic; the manuscripts seem to justify rather the form given in the most recent critical edition: *Liber de fide rerum inuisibilium*. The more traditional wording is defended, however, by McDonald in her fairly recent critical edition; and in any case it occurs in the opening sentence. See the text of M. P. J. van den Hout, ed., Sancti Aurelii Augustini, *De Fide* . . . &c, Turnholti: Brepols, 1969 (Corpus Christianorum, series Latina, vol. 46—Augustini Opera, pars 13:2), pp. [xxxiii]-[lxiv], [1]-19, esp. p. [1] (see also pp. lxi-lxii); and Sister Mary Francis McDonald, *Saint Augustine's De Fide Rerum Quae Non Videntur: a critical text and translation with introduction and commentary—a dissertation* . . . , Washington, D.C.: Catholic University of America Press, 1950 (Catholic University of America Patristic Studies, vol. 84), esp. p. 116.

Apart from the book-title and its opening sentence, another possible quasi-source perhaps underlying the alleged definition occurs in St. Augustine's commentary on Luke 17:5, although here it serves rather as a subordinate qualifying clause: . . . *hanc fidem* . . . *qua creduntur ea quae non videntur*—*Quaestionum Evangeliorum libri duo*, in Sancti Aurelii Augustini . . . *Opera Omnia*, tom. 3 (pars 2), Paris, 1841 (J.-P. Migne, ed., Patrologiae . . . series [Latina], tom. 35), col. 1352.

167 Being rather scientific in my outlook and contending that the argument of this present study is rational and in principle aspires to be inductively persuasive, I am interested in experimental procedures that may serve to corroborate or to refute its conclusions. Those enamoured of verifiability and falsifiability in the philosophic/theological realm might, accordingly, be interested in the following proposal. Certainly in my scholarly studies of the history of Islamic, and more recently of Hindu and other, ideas I have always endeavoured to check empirically any hypotheses that I might form and any interpretations that I might proffer; not only by studying with careful sensitivity whatever evidence generates the hypotheses in the first place and seems to confirm it, but also by extrapolating to other data to see whether the thesis illuminates or is refuted by quite disparate material. In the course of such endeavours, also I have learned much. In the present case it has occurred to me that there is perhaps an interesting and illuminating way to check my contention that *credo* normally in classical and mediaeval usage meant something other than "believe" in the modern sense (cf. our next chapter, below). This would be to investigate whether its traditional counterpart *dubito* similarly meant something other than "to doubt" in its modern sense also (meant something correlative with the proposed interpretation of *credo*). I have not myself made this investigation, and I commend the idea to others interested (for example, to doctoral students who might think of taking it up for possible dissertation work). My prediction, based on superficial noting of a few cases but not in this instance on a systematic and sustained inquiry, is that it will turn out that normally *dubito* in relevant contexts in Christian writing in Latin meant not an entertaining of intellectual doubts but an existential *vacillation* before practical self-involvement. *Dubito* as a Latin term comes from *duo*, "two", and signifies fundamentally the condition of "being in two minds" about an action, the inability to make up one's mind to act, a wavering. The representation that occurs to me is the picture of a person standing on the edge of a diving board on the shore of a northern lake on a sunlit but frosty morning, wondering whether to plunge in or not: aware that once in the water, the freshness will be invigorating and the experience of swimming delightful, yet hesitant nonetheless to jump. In such a situation, *dubito* designates the condition of the person who fluctuates undecided, while *credo* names the act of taking the plunge.

(It would be possible, one may suppose, to translate the former's ambivalence into intellectualistic terms, and one might picture the person as weighing up the theoretical cogency of, on the one hand, his or her memory of previous mornings' dips when the subsequent pleasure of diving and swimming proved well worth the price of that momentary shock of cold water, or the trustworthiness of fellows' shouts of joy who are already in, against the calculable possibility that *this* morning the temperature may be a whit colder, his or her desire to swim a trifle less genuine, or whatever. It is only in the nineteenth and twentieth centuries, that—as with the "no parking" sign of our Islamics chapter, above—the situation has changed to the point where an altogether different problem is conceived, and there is a significant intellectual question as to whether the lake is really there, or is but a mirage in the morning sunshine.)

I shall, of course, be extremely interested if anyone tries this experiment and proves my hypothesis about *dubito* usage wrong.

Chapter 6

1 The term was used not only literally, of hand-wrought products, as with the housewife's turning milk into butter. It also occurred figuratively: for example, in Pope's 1726 translation of the Odyssey. The original of this last at one point reads ἀνδρας, ἐπην δη γειveαι αὐτος (20:202). Here humankind is said to be generated by—we might go so far as to paraphrase, "is created at the hands of", "is the handiwork of"—God. Pope rendered it as: "thy manufacture, man". Almost a century earlier, the Puritan divine and pamphleteer Nathaniel Ward had had his colonial shoemaker ask rhetorically of the King: "Doth it become you . . . to . . . take up the Manufacture of cutting your Subjects throats . . . ?".

Alexander Pope, *The Odyssey of Homer*, Maynard Mack et al., edd., London: Methuen, and New Haven: Yale University Press (John Butt, gen. ed., The Twickenham Edition of the Poems of Alexander Pope, 11 voll., 1961-1969; voll. 9, 10), 10:245. For the Greek text, I have used the edition of P. von der Mühll, ed., *Homeri Odyssea*, Basilae: Helbing & Lichtenhahn, 1946, p. 379. Nathaniel Ward, *The Simple Cobler of Aggawam in America* [1647], P. M. Zall, ed., Lincoln: University of Nebraska Press, 1969, pp. 50-51.

2 Nehemiah 13:26. In the King James Authorized Version: ". . . Solomon king of Israel . . . was beloved of his God . . . ; nevertheless even him did outlandish women cause to sin". Revised Standard Version: ". . . foreign women". Hebrew: הנשים הנכריות.

3 Line 80 of the original version. Alfred Tennyson, *Poems* [London: E. Moxon, 2 voll., 1842] Boston: William D. Ticknor, 2 voll., 1842, 2:7. In the later longer version (as "The Passing of Arthur") constituting the conclusion of his expanded *Idylls of the King*, London: Strahan, 1870, p. 393.

4 The latter forms were more prevalent in early centuries; later the *-i-* forms prevailed. See A. Walde, *Lateinisches etymologisches Wörterbuch*, 3. Aufl. von J. B. Hofmann, Heidelberg: Carl Winter's Universitätsbuchhandlung, 2 voll., 1938-1954 (H. Hirt und W. Streitberg, H. Güntert, edd., Indogermanische Bibliothek: Erste Abteilung, II. Reihe, Erster Band), 1:793-794. A. Ernout et A. Meillet, *Dictionnaire étymologique de la langue latine: histoire des mots*, 4ème édn., Paris: Klincksieck, [1959], 1967, p. 367. L. R. Palmer, *The Latin Language*, London: Faber and Faber, [1954], 1968, p. 216, taking notice of the chronological shift only in Latin, and in no other languages, would seem to make only the *-u-* grade original there.

5 See, for instance, John R. Clark Hall, *A Concise Anglo-Saxon Dictionary* [1894], 4th edn., with a supplement by Herbert D. Meritt, Cambridge: [Cambridge] University Press, [1960], 1966, pp. 215-216, 222, s. vv. *lēof* (*gelēof*),

lufu. Cf. *lēoflic*, *luflic*. Cf. also (*ge-*) *lufian*, p. 222, and (*ge-*) *līefan*, p. 218.

6 The most convenient and authoritative survey of these is found in Julius Pokorny, *Indogermanisches etymologisches Wörterbuch*, Bern und München: Francke, 2 Bde., 1959-1969, 2:683-684.

7 In addition to the standard Sanskrit dictionaries, s.v., see also Manfred Mayrhofer, *Kurzgefasstes etymologisches Wörterbuch des Altindischen . . .* , Heidelberg: Carl Winter Universitätsverlag, 1956- (in process), 3:107-108.

8 See s.v. *ilẹven v. (2)* in Hans Kurath, Sherman M. Kuhn, John Reidy, edd., *Middle English Dictionary*, Ann Arbor: University of Michigan Press, 1952- (in process), Part I.1 (1968), pp. 63-64. Cf. also s.v. *ilēve n. (2)*, ibid., p. 62, and our ref. 5 above.

9 For the etymology, see our ref. 12 below. "*Grundebedeutung von glauben 'gutheissen'* "—Friedrich Kluge, *Etymologisches Wörterbuch der deutschen Sprache*, 6th edn., Strassburg: Trübner, 1899, s.v. *Glaube* (p. 147). Cf. further our ref. 13 below.

10 I know of no historical study of the development of this meaning, or the transition from it gradually to the more modern. The matter is complicated in that *glauben* in our day means both "to have faith" and "to believe". The bifurcation, historically, in English between "belief" and "faith", the gradual divergence between "believing" and "having faith", and the gradual convergence in many people's minds between believing (*opinio*) and faith, have had their counterparts also in German; but the historical process there has been impeded and has been simplified, both in involuted ways, by the fact that while in English two different verbalizations have been at work, in German there has been but one. Curious is that the only other work in English, so far as I am aware, with a title like *Faith and Belief* is an English translation of a German work bearing the simpler title *Über den Glauben*. The translators explain the English version as follows: "The German word *Glaube* may mean 'belief' or 'faith.' In this translation we have usually rendered it by 'belief'; but the reader should bear the other possibility in mind if any phrases strike him as slightly strange. In quotations from Thomas Aquinas *fides* has been translated by 'belief' instead of the more customary 'faith,' for the sake of consistency with the German text." This constitutes "Translators' Note", p. [2] in Josef Pieper, *Belief and Faith: a philosophical tract*, trans. Richard and Clara Winston, New York: Random House (Pantheon Books), 1963. Cf. Josef Pieper, *Über den Glauben: ein philosophischer Traktat*, München: Kösel, 1962.

11 Already in the early nineteenth century it was somewhat precious in poetry: "Beloving and beloved she grew, a happy child"—Robert Southey, *A Tale of Paraguay* [London, 1825], 2:10 (line 90—Maurice H. Fitzgerald, ed., *Poems of Robert Southey*, London: Oxford University Press, 1909, p. 669). In the seventeenth century, on the other hand, it appears to have been fairly straightforward. "[T]hose persons cannot but be accounted hard hearted, barbarous, fierce and sauage, who beloue not them of whom they are loued"—Thomas Wright, *The Passions of the Minde in Generall* [London, 1601, 1604, . . . 1630], Thomas O. Sloan, ed., Urbana: University of Illinois Press,

1971, p. 212. (The passage evidently appeared in the 1604, if not the 1601, edition, but the Illinois version, to which alone I have had access, is a fascimile of the 1630 text.) Again, "if Beautie were a String of Silke, I would weare it about my Necke for a certaine Testimonie that I beloue it much" is offered as English counterpart to ". . . *ie l'affectionne fort*" in John Wodroephe, *The Spared Houres of a Souldier in His Travels, or The True Marrowe of the French Tongue . . . —Les Heures de relasche d'un soldat, voyageant . . .*, Dort: Nicolas Vincentz, pour George Waters, 1623, p. 322.

12 Of these two words, it may be noted that the former involves an emphasis more on the notion of loving, the latter (cf. *geloben*) more on that of pledging, commitment; this parallels the corresponding pair *lieben* and *glauben*. In the latter, a thinking highly of, loving, is presupposed, while allegiance is stressed.

It is curious that, in the matter of the vowel gradation, it was the reverse pattern of connotations that developed in the English pair "believe" and "belove".

For the etymology, see our ref. 13, just below.

13 For the etymologies of all these terms, see Friedrich Kluge, *Etymologisches Wörterbuch der deutschen Sprache*, 20. Auflage bearbeitet von Walther Mitzka, Berlin: Walter de Gruyter, 1967, s.vv.; esp., s.v. *Lob*.

14 Henry B. Wheatley, ed., *Merlin, or The Early History of King Arthur: a prose romance (about 1450-1460 A.D.)*, London: Kegan Paul, Trench, Trübner, 2 voll., 1899, 1:50.

15

> I [God] told ye [angels] then he [Satan]
>   should prevail and speed
> On his bad Errand, Man should be seduc't
> And flatter'd out of all, believing lies
> Against his Maker; no Decree of mine
> Concurring to necessitate his Fall,
> Or touch with lightest moment of impulse
> His free Will, to her own inclining left
> In even scale. But fall'n he is, and now
> What rests, but that the mortal Sentence pass
> On his transgression. . . .
>
> —Milton, *Paradise Lost*,
> 1667 edn., 10:40-49.

I have used the edition of H. C. Beeching, *The Poetical Works of John Milton*, London: Oxford University Press, [1900?], 1928, pp. 382-383. Notice the word "Will", and the manifestly moral quality of the whole matter. "Believing" here was an "act" (cf. line 1 of this book 10 in the poem), a wilful "transgression" (line 49).

It is a pallid, almost vacuous interpretation that would see the almost histrionically dramatic choice of Adam and Eve as a propositional error of the intellect. (The analogy of the reverberating decision that Milton here presents is more closely with that equally fateful option that we saw being enacted in reverse fashion in early Christian baptism, above. Here man is seen as originally choosing wrongly, on the cosmic scene; there he redeems the sorry consequences by turning his back on wrong and grandly opting for glory.)

16 "Sermon . . . compyled & sayd in the Cathedrall chyrche of saynt Poule Within the cyte of London by the ryght reuerende fader in god Iohn bysshop of Rochester, the body beynge present of the moost famouse prynce kynge Henry the .vij. the .x. day of Maye the yere of our lorde god .M.CCCCC.ix. . . . Enprynted at London . . . by Wynkyn de Worde" [1509-1510], as reprinted in John E. B. Mayor, ed., *The English Works of John Fisher*, (1459-1535), London: Trübner, for The Early English Text Society, Part 1, 1876, pp. 268-288.

17 Fisher, "Sermon" (our ref. 16, just above), p. 271, lines 13, 19.

18 p. 271, lines 16-17.

19 p. 273, lines 27-28.

20 p. 273, line 29.

21 Mayor (our ref. 16 above). His running gloss is printed in the margin, opposite the passages to which it refers.

22 Careful inquiry seems to unearth the point that some religious persons to-day practise a kind of private or closed-circuit speech by having in their minds when they use the term "believe" (especially, "I believe") religiously a meaning different from that that they themselves use in other contexts and different also from what they communicate to their hearers in *these* contexts. I personally have been rather astonished to discover this among various of my friends on whom I have tested this out (also with *je crois* in French). That this astonishment is in the end "superficial" is worked out further in our concluding chapter below. Cf. also above, our chap. 5, ref. 151.

23 From among many. Another similar example, from diverse manuscripts of certain mediaeval poems, is set forth and discussed in my *Belief and History* (our chap. 1 above, ref. 4), pp. 41-42, and note 6, p. 106.

24 Sir Frederic Madden, ed.; London: Society of Antiquaries of London, 3 voll., 1847.

25 Madden, in his Preface to the work just cited, vol. 1, p. xxxiv.

26 Line 2856; vol. 1, p. 121.

27 Line 4340: vol. 1, p. 185.

28 Lines 13941, 13942, 13945; vol. 2, pp. 158-159.

29 The juxtaposition of "lief" and "loath" was sufficiently standard that the Oxford English Dictionary gives it a special entry s.v. lief: "3. Antithetically to *loath*, in senses 1 and 2. Also *absol*[*utely*], esp[ecially] in *for lief or loath*. *Obs*[*olete*] exc[ept] *arch*[*aic*]".

30 Line 13943; vol. 2, p. 159.

31 Line 13944; vol. 2, p. 159. The editor questions whether *cristre* be a slip for *criste*.

32 It is *the* earliest recorded in the Oxford English Dictionary, s.v., which follows Morris (cf. our ref. 33 just below) in dating this homily to ca. 1175. Modern scholarship is inclined to see it as a half-century later. I have checked

the Kurath-Kuhn-Reidy *Middle English Dictionary* (above, our ref. 8; s.v. *bilēve*, Part B.3, 1958, pp. 853-854) for possible antecedents; there the earlier date is assigned to another homily cited as using our word in much the same sense, while this present passage is the chronologically next instance given and is attributed to 1225. (A couple of other texts, using "belief" as correlative of "love" [*luue, luueð*] are also dated as 1225, with an alternative date of 1200 mentioned as possible though less likely.)

33 *Old English Homilies and Homiletic Treatises . . . of the Twelfth and Thirteenth Centuries; edited from Mss. in the British Museum, Lambeth, and Bodleian Libraries; with Introduction, Translation, and Notes, by* Richard Morris, First series, London: Trübner, for the Early English Text Society, 1868, p. 101. The text reads: *cristene men ne sculen heore bileafe bisettan on þere weordliche eahte*. The Morris translation (p. 100) reads: "Christian men should not put their trust in temporal possessions".

34 The next five words following on the clause that we have just cited, concluding the sentence, are: *ac on heore god ane* (p. 101). More accurately, then: "but on their God alone".

35 *þe ȝitsere þe biset his iþonc on his ehte: he bið þes deofles bern* (p. 101).

36 As we saw St. Thomas doing a century later: cf. above our chap. 5, ref. 81.

37 Another homily, on the Creed, published in the same Morris collection already mentioned (above, our ref. 33), pp. 72-77. The text reads: *Credo deo. Ih ileue gode. þ*et *oðer is: Credo* deum. *ich ileue þet god is. þos twa þing doð alle heðene men.. ah þ*et [*þridde*] *ne leueð nan: bute þe gode* cristene .*M*òn. and *þe godfurhte* and *þe lefulle* qui credit in deum—p. 75.

38 These two clauses (preceded by *þe* and joined by "and") follow immediately on what we have just quoted above, our ref. 37. In the margin the modern editor annotates "luuene" with the query "?leuene".

39 For an example of a contrast between giving one's allegiance to Christ and giving one's allegiance to the Devil, verbalized in each case by the root *leve*, by a poet who clearly himself "believes" in both God and the Devil in one of the modern senses of the term, see lines 671-676 of the late mediaeval verse romance *Roland and Vernagu* in Sidney J. H. Herrtage, ed., *The Taill of Rauf Coilyear; . . . with the fragments of Roland and Vernagu, and Otuel*, London: Trübner, for the Early English Text Society, 1882 (The English Charlemagne Romances, Part VI), p. 55.

Again, for an example of the use of our verb in close conjunction with words for loyalty, pledging one's troth, and the like, see the late fifteenth-century verse "tale" of Rauf Coilyear, lines 943-944, ibid., p. 32. And so on, almost endlessly.

40 A vivid instance of such passages is the opening part of Passus 10 in the B version. Illustrative are lines 32-37, 51-57, 66-70, 184 (Skeat, vol. 1, pp. 286-290, 298). That the poet does not pull his punches is well brought out in such a modern rendering as Wells's: "If these clerics . . . take Christ for their topic . . . / So these men drivel from the dias that the deity is known

to them, / And gnaw God with their gorge when their gut labors" (his lines 54-60, p. 113).

For additional passages of a similar sort, cf. lines 428-433 (Skeat, vol. 1, p. 320; Wells, lines 452-458, pp. 126-127); lines 450-451 (Skeat, vol. 1, p. 322; Wells, lines 475-476, p. 127); line 442 (Skeat, vol. 1, p. 322; Wells, line 466, p. 127).

The Vision of William Concerning Piers the Plowman: in three parallel texts, together with Richard the Redeless, by William Langland (about 1362-1399 A.D.), edited from numerous manuscripts with preface, notes, and a glossary by . . . Walter W. Skeat, Oxford: Clarendon Press, 2 voll., 1886. William Langland, *The Vision of Piers Plowman: Newly Rendered into Modern English by* Henry W. Wells [London and New York: Sheed & Ward, 1935], New York: Greenwood, 1968.

41 "Litel loueth he that lorde"—Passus 10 B 62 (Skeat, vol. 1, p. 288).

42 The original reads:

> *Aren none rather yrauysshed · fro the rizte byleue*
> *Than ar this cunnynge clerkes · that conne many bokes*

(10 B 456-457; Skeat, vol. 1, p. 322). Henry Wells's usually excellent translation limps here:

> None are so readily ravished from the right doctrine
> As these cunning clerks who construe many volumes

(Wells, *Piers Plowman* [our ref. 40 above], p. 128; his lines 482-483). Williams, on the other hand, sees, and lets her readers see, the point of the passage, by translating "from the true faith"—Margaret Williams, full ref. below, p. 183, line 456; though I would find "from true faith" a more authentic rendering.

Again in the following line, Wells says of "plowmen and peasants and poor common labourers" that they are the most "sober in doctrine" (for *sadder of bileue*—line 457). A few lines further on, however, he is himself pushed into translating the same term (here spelled *byleue*) as "faith" rather than "doctrine", in that the simple folk, "Shoemakers and shepherds and such simple peasants" who "were imperfect . . . in knowing" and even in "living", nonetheless, he says, "Go into the bliss of paradise for their pure faith" (Wells, lines 486, 490, 490, 489, p. 128; original of this last, *for her pure byleue*: 10 B 463 [Skeat edn., vol. 1, p. 324]). Salvation is not by belief, he is saying, and not by works, but by faith.

Piers the Plowman, by William Langland, translated and with an introduction by Margaret Williams, New York: Random House, n.d. [sc. 1973? copyright 1971].

43 *Pierce the Ploughmans Crede (about 1394 A.D.), transcribed . . . edited . . . collated . . .* by Walter W. Skeat, London: Trübner, for The Early English Text Society, 1867.

44 Lines 791, 793, 795 (in the Skeat edn. [our ref. 43 just above], p. 30).

45 Line 799 (Skeat edn., p. 30).

46 Including *leue þou þe trewþe*—line 827 (Skeat edn., p. 31). With this compare the King James Authorized Version translation in 1611 of II Thessalonians 2:13, discussed below at our p. 119; although "trewthe" may preserve more of "troth", "trustworthiness" here in the mediaeval poem than in that early-seventeenth-century usage. The first four meanings of "truth" in the Oxford English Dictionary are as follows:

> 1. The character of being, or disposition to be, true to a person, principle, cause, etc.; faithfulness, fidelity, loyalty, constancy, steadfast allegiance; 2. One's faith or loyalty as pledged in a promise or agreement; a solemn engagement or promise, a covenant; 3. a. Faith, trust, confidence. b. Belief; a formula of belief, a creed; 4. Disposition to speak or act truly or without deceit; truthfulness, veracity, sincerity; formerly sometimes in wider sense: Honesty, uprightness, righteousness, virtue, integrity.

47 It ends also with a disclaimer by Piers that he is but a lowly person (*But, for y am a lewed man*—line 845 [Skeat's edn., p. 31]): peradventure he might be mistaken in some of his theoretical points, and if so he asks God's mercy and His help for all to live lives of fidelity and good works.

48 The editor of the first printed edition (1553) of this poem felt that by that time his readers might need to be alerted to the fact that "leue" is "beleue". See his glossary at the end, s.v. ([*Pierce the Ploughmans Crede*, London: Reynold Wolfe, 1553.] I have used the version in the Skeat edn., pp. xviii-xix.)

49 Examples: Skeat, in the margin of his edition, p. 30; Wright, in the glossary to his, (2:) 598. (Thomas Wright, ed., *The Vision and Creed of Piers Ploughman*, London [1842], 2nd rev. edn., London: [John Russell Smith, 2 voll., 1856] Reeves and Turner [Library of Old Authors], 2 voll., 1883. In this edn., the passage in question is found as lines 1577ff. at [2:] 497ff.)

50 *þis is þe holy beleue*—line 802 (Skeat edn., p. 30).

51 From Wycliffe, Sermon VIII: "þe eiȝtþe Sonedai Gospel aftir Trinite", in Thomas Arnold, ed., *Select English Works of John Wyclif*, Oxford: Clarendon Press, 3 voll., 1869-1871, 1:19-21.

52 "*And* it sufficib [*sufficiþ?*] not to seie, Lord, Lord, *but it nediþ to lyve wele to a mannes lyves ende*"; "*. . . preestis . . . mut* [glossary: "*must*"] *seie wele in herte and wele in mouþe and lyve wele, for ellis a man shal not be saved*"—p. 21.

53 Oxford English Dictionary, s.v. "Believe", vol. 1 (1888), p. 783, col. 2, section 6, under the date 1380. (Italics mine.) Subsequent scholarship is dubious on the attribution.

54 So the King James Authorized Version. In Greek, the word in question is ἀπειθης [*apeithēs*].

55 *The Holy Bible, containing the Old and New Testaments,. with the Apocryphal Books, in the Earliest English Versions, made from the Latin Vulgate by John Wycliffe and his Followers*, Josiah Forshall and Sir Frederic Madden, edd., Oxford: [Oxford] University Press, 4 voll., 1850, 4:585.

56 This matter is studied in an unpublished paper of my former student William C. McCahill, Jr., submitted to a Harvard seminar of mine in 1972-1973: "*Feith* and *Bileue*: a study of the words in a Middle English Bible", in which the renderings in the two Wyclif versions of the Latin words *fides* and *credere* from the Vulgate are investigated.

57 Oxford English Dictionary, s.v. "Belief", 1888. The final sentence here quoted is illustrated by reference to a quotation, given later on in the body of the article, to Wordsworth's lines: "Of one in whom persuasion and belief/Had ripened into faith", from his long poem "The Excursion" (first published 1814). The poem is reprinted as vol. 5 in William Knight, ed., *The Poetical Works of William Wordsworth*, Edinburgh: William Paterson, 11 voll., 1882-1889. The lines in question are Book IV, lines 1302-1303, and are found on p. 197 of this edn.

58 πιστευω [*pisteuō*], along with the noun πιστις [*pistis*].

59 In the Hebrew Bible (the "Old Testament"), the verb אמן [*āman*]—base for the largely post-Biblical Hebrew term for (Jewish) "faith", אמונה [^{e}*mûnāh*]—occurs a great number of times. Christian scholars have often remarked that the Christian concept "faith" is primarily a New Testament one, Greek-based. One might also remark that a Jewish concept "faith" was developed at roughly the same late chronological period. In the "Old Testament", the Jewish Bible, a noun "faith" as counterpart to the verb is hardly found. The standard Hebrew noun that corresponds to this verb is in the Biblical text אמת [*'^{e}meth*]. The 1611 English translators of the Bible used the word "believe" 44 times in their version of the Old Testament, the word "faith" as such only twice there, although "faithfulness", "faithful", and the like are found 53 times. (In all but one instance these render forms of the root *'-m-n*, but in a ratio of five times out of six this verb is rendered by other English terms.) In their New Testament English the figures are, "believe" 253 times (282 counting related forms, such as "unbeliever"), and "faith" 244 times (298 counting related forms).

On the preponderance of the verb over either of the nouns in Biblical Hebrew, cf. our remark on this Semitic phenomenon in our ref. 60 just below, on the comparable Qur'ān situation. In the modern world, however, both Jews and many Muslims have come to share the Western propensity to think largely through nominal concepts.

I have made these calculations from Robert Young, *Analytical Concordance to the Bible . . .*, 22nd American edition, Grand Rapids, Mich.: Eerdmans [1970], 1973, and from other sources.

We do not here otherwise investigate the Hebrew Bible, for its faith/belief relation. Such an investigation would, of course, consider also other roots besides אמן—for example, בטח - ירא - ידע.

On the meaning of πιστ- in the New Testament I have, of course, consulted the careful study of Rudolph Bultmann and Artur Weiser, in Gerhard Kittel, Gerhard Friedrich, et al., edd., *Theologisches Wörterbuch zum Neuen Testament*, Stuttgart: Kohlhammer, 10 voll., 1933- (in process), 6:174-230. I have also examined James Barr, *The Semantics of Biblical Language*, London, etc.: Oxford University Press, 1961, esp. chap. 7, " 'Faith' and 'Truth' . . . ", pp. [161]-205. These studies present much that corroborates, and virtually nothing that contradicts, the theses of our present inquiry (or that of my companion volume, *Belief and History*); they were written, however, without reflection on the problem that here engages us, and were translated without that reflection or on the change of meaning of the words "believe" and especially "belief".

The German article has appeared in English translation in two differing versions. (i) Rudolf Bultmann and Artur Weiser, *Faith*, Dorothea M. Barton, trans., P. R. Ackroyd, ed., London: Adam & Charles Black, 1961 (Bible Key Words from Gerhard Kittel's *Theologisches Wörterbuch* . . .). (ii) *Theological Dictionary of the New Testament*, Gerhard Kittel, Gerhard Friedrich, et al., edd., Geoffrey W. Bromiley, ed. and trans., Grand Rapids, Mich., and London: Eerdmans, 10 vols., 1964-1976, 6:174-228.

60 *āmana*, along with *īmān*. In the Qur'ān, the verb is strikingly more common than is the noun. The former occurs, I calculate, 537 times, and next to *Allāh* is one of the most common concepts in the scripture; the noun considerably less than one-tenth that often. In subsequent Arabic literature, especially theology, this ratio becomes less drastically one-sided. Moreover, the noun is in formation and in Qur'ān usage a verbal noun. As is appropriate for a Semitic language, and a Semitic orientation to life and the world, the conception of faith is here more verbal than nominal. Although in this present study I am posing "faith" as a concept of universal applicability, this fails to transcend the nominalist bias of the Indo-European languages. "To be a person of faith", or even "to live, or to act, in faith", would be a more fundamental category of thought for both the Jewish and the Islamic traditions, classically. I have perhaps been unduly inhibited by the quality of the English language from developing this dimension of human faith adequately in my own thinking and especially in this book. In my *Meaning and End of Religion* (above, our chap. 1 here, ref. 10) I argued that the use of a noun concept "religion" has been in danger of being seriously misleading, yet allowed the adjective "religious" to stand; so here it might be that my thesis of faith as a human quality could best be conceptualized in a language (such as Japanese?) in which adjectives are basic rather than being normally derivative from, and subsidiary to, nouns.

(In the Arabic Qur'ān the word *mu'min*, "person of faith", "faithful", is an adjective/adjectival-noun/participle that is derivative from, and subsidiary to, the verb *āmana*. It occurs an additional 230 times.)

I have used the 'Abd al-Bāqī concordance (above, our chap. 3 here, ref. 8).

61 The King's speech, more fully:

> My honour's at the stake, which to defeat,
> I must produce my power. Here, take her hand,
> Proud, scornful boy, unworthy this good gift. . . .
> . . . Check thy contempt;
> Obey our will which travails in thy good;

Believe not thy disdain, but presently
Do thine own fortunes that obedient right
Which both thy duty owes and our power claims;
Or I will throw thee from my care for ever
Into the staggers and the careless lapse
Of youth and ignorance; both my revenge and hate
Loosing upon thee in the name of justice,
Without all terms of pity. Speak. Thine answer.

Bertram. Pardon, my gracious lord; for I submit . . .
(2:3:149-167)

It may be noted that parallel to "believe not thy disdain" is, two lines earlier, "Check thy contempt" (hold your contempt in check, do not give it free rein). Contrasted is "Obey our will" in the line immediately preceding, and ". . . obedient right . . . " in the following one: that is, act in accordance with not your own feelings (of disparagement) but our royal command. (The King has ordered the Count to marry Helena; he has objected, protesting that he despises her unaristocratic station.) The King does not dispute the facts, but is telling Bertram to act in terms of allegiance to the throne, not to his own views. His subject's "I submit" at the end here is along the same line.

Other comparable instances of Shakespeare's use of "believe" in the sense of "set one's heart" are considered in my *Belief and History* (above, our chap. 1, ref. 4), p. 62 and ref. 53, p. 114.

For the text of *All's Well that Ends Well* above, I have followed that of G. K. Hunter (revising that of W. O. Brigstocke, 1904) in The Arden Edition of the Works of William Shakespeare, London: Methuen, [1959], 1967, pp. 58-59.

62 This matter also is considered at more length in my *Belief and History*; cf. our ref. 61 just above.

63 Figures here are calculated from the presentations in Marvin Spevack, *A Complete and Systematic Concordance to the Works of Shakespeare*, Hildesheim: Georg Olms, 6 voll., 1968-1970, 4:464 and 968-970.

64 "The Modern History of 'Believing': the drift away from faith", being chap. 11 of my *Belief and History* (cf. our reff. 61, 62 above).

65 "I-Thou" was launched as an explicit conceptualization in modern Western culture by Martin Buber, who incidentally has played a much larger role in the history of recent Christian thought than of recent Jewish, and who produced one of the rare comparative studies of faith, in his pioneering work on its "Two Types". He perceived clearly and felt deeply the distinction between faith as interpersonal and as propositional, and set it forth commandingly in that essay. Although he was not unaware that it over-simplifies to correlate the distinction glibly with that between Jewish and Christian, nonetheless the fact that the thinking of the Christian community had in his day gone further down the slippery slope from the one to the other led him to make his presentation in less historical terms than those that we proffer

here. His interpretation did not, and could not yet, recognize the gradual transitions that have been taking place and to which we here, and in my *Belief and History*, are able to call attention. He did recognize the propositional "type" as foreign to Jesus, but under-estimated how slowly and how exteriorly the Church has taken it up.

Martin Buber, *Ich und Du* [Leipzig: Insel, 1923], and *Zwei Glaubensweisen* [Zürich: Manesse, 1950], as reprinted in his *Werke*, 3 voll., München: Kösel, and Heidelberg: Lambert Schneider, 1962-1964, 1:[77]-160 (and 161-170), [651]-782, respectively. Of the former, two English translations have appeared: *I and Thou*, Ronald Gregor Smith, trans. [Edinburgh: T. & T. Clark, 1937], 2nd edn., New York: Scribner's, 1958; and *I and Thou: a new translation with a prologue "I and You" and notes by* Walter Kaufmann, New York: Scribner's, 1970. The other work has appeared in English as *Two Types of Faith*, Norman P. Goldhawk, trans., London: Routledge & Kegan Paul, and New York: Macmillan, 1951. A paperback edition (New York: Harper & Row—Harper Torchbooks/Cloister Library, 1961) bears on the cover also the sub-title: *A study of the interpenetration of Judaism and Christianity.*

66 In Shakespeare's writing, "believe" is one of his most common verbs (about 300 occurrences), and yet in the form "believes" it is one of his least (this form appears only four times in all). In general this verb's third-person usages (including past tense, participle agreeing with a subject other than "me", "you", etc.) constitute less than one-tenth of the total; and constitute notably less than one-fifth of first-person occurrences. My calculations are based on Spevack (above, our ref. 63; cf. also my *Belief and History*, p. 52, and its reff. 10, 40, of chap. II, pp. 107, 111).

67 Although our term was launched into Western civilization as a mighty concept primarily in the first person singular (*credo*), the residual affinities of the first person plural also are not quite negligible. Of believing as a human activity, it would be a rewarding exercise to investigate a differential analysis pertaining to those who have conceived it as something that "we" human beings do, on the one hand, and those, on the other, who have considered the beliefs of, in effect, "those other people over there". The point is raised a little, particularly with regard to Hume, in my *Belief and History* (pp. 52-53, 111). At the end of the nineteenth century, the chapter on Belief in William James, *The Principles of Psychology*, was—quite un-self-consciously—cast in terms of the fact, and the problem signified in it, that we (*sic*; sc. we human beings) believe something. An instance: "Under what circumstances do we think things real?". Further, when he gave examples, he moved quite naturally to the first person singular ("When I believe that some prehistoric savage . . .").

In the twentieth century, on the other hand, this sort of orientation waned. Major issues are involved in all this, to which we shall be returning.

"Belief" is a sub-title of the important chap. XXI, "The Perception of Reality" in William James, *The Principles of Psychology*, New York: Henry Holt, 2 voll., 1890, 2:283-324. The quotations that we have given here are from 2:287 (original in italics) and 320 respectively.

68 Cf. above, our chap. 3, pp. 48-49.

69 This judgement is not merely impressionistic, although for the modern day it is strongly that; but can be documented for various centuries including our own. In the eighteenth, for example, I have noticed that John Wesley in the course of his writing uses the English verb "to believe" sometimes in its traditional Christian sense of being in, or coming into, a faith-relation to, and sometimes in the modern sense, of holding an opinion, whereas so far as nouns are concerned he seems to evince no such inconsistency. The noun that in his mind naturally goes along with the verb whenever it is used in the former sense is "faith", and in the latter, "belief" (or, "opinion"). For one example of the verb's ambiguity, from among many, cf. successive pages in the anthology of Albert C. Outler, ed., *John Wesley*, New York: Oxford University Press, 1964 (John Dillenberger et al., edd., Library of Protestant Thought), pp. 95-96-97. (It is also an observable fact that in the former instances of the use of "believe", directly parallel verbs tend to be such as "to love", "to walk", "to know", while in the latter they are "to be persuaded", "to think", "it appears to me that", and so on.) I have begun to collect a number of passages from Wesley's *Works* (London: Thomas Cordeux, 16, voll., 1810-1820) and later editions of his Sermons, etc., for a study of his use of the terms "faith", "doctrine", "belief", "opinion", etc., and counterpart verbs, but am hopeful that someone else, rather, may take up such an investigation. I have done enough to suggest that an inquiry along these lines would indeed be rewardingly illustrative.

For the nineteenth century, it is noteworthy that while Christians consistently spoke of "salvation by faith", the only instance that I have ever found of the phrase "salvation by belief", rather, is in the title of a critic ridiculing the idea. Dwight Hinckley Olmstead, *The Protestant Faith; or, Salvation by Belief* [New York, 1874, 1885] New York and London: Putnam's, The Knickerbocker Press, 3rd edn., 1897.

70 If not precedents, yet there were phenomena in mediaeval India somewhat comparable to this as to various other modern Western religious developments. The differences also, however, are significant. Cf. just below, our ref. 71.

71 In the light of our Qur'ān chapter above, and also in the light of Christian history, it may seem at first blush odd to call this situation "novel". As we have remarked, doctrines, ideational patterns, concepts, have throughout human history served, just as have rites, legal patterns, images, music, and many other mundane things, as channels or transcendent reality and as forms for faith. What was new here, and what it has been the task of this chapter (and the concomitant second chapter of my *Belief and History*) to attempt to help to clarify, is that these ideas began to take in the nineteenth-century West the new form of self-conscious and almost deliberate "beliefs" in the unprecedented meaning of that evolving term (in the unprecedented situation of the West's evolving civilization).

Our remark above (our chap. 3, at ref. 31) that classical and mediaeval Muslims were hardly conscious of believing anything, is to be collated with this. Classical and mediaeval Hindu civilization was in a pluralist situation formally somewhat comparable culturally to ours; and Hindu understanding of knowledge and of human ideation has been significantly different from Western. From such understanding the West may have something yet to learn, as it struggles to forge ahead beyond its classical "knowing" and its modern "believing". (Cf. above, our chap. 4 at reff. 2, 10; and our concluding chap. below.)

Of course, many Christians in the nineteenth-century West (for instance, my parents) were believers still in the old sense, not in the new; but increasingly, many were not. For fewer and fewer of the intellectual leaders of the Church was it possible to hold the traditional positions except as beliefs.

72 [Samuel Langhorne Clemens] *Mark Twain's Notebook, prepared for publication with comments by* Albert Bigelow Paine, New York and London: Harpers, 1935, p. 237: "There are those who scoff at the schoolboy, calling him frivolous and shallow. Yet it was a schoolboy who said: 'Faith is believing what you know ain't so.' "

73 For an illuminating and provocative survey of recent literature by Christian thinkers on faith without belief, without intellectual "content", see M. Colin Grant, "Faith and Belief", *Iliff Review*, 34/2:21-27 (1977).

74 "Perhaps the best way to characterize Quine's world view is to say that . . . there is fundamentally only one kind of entity in the world, and that kind is the kind studied by natural scientists—physical objects; and, second, that there is only one kind of knowledge in the world, and it is the kind that natural scientists have"—Richard Schuldenfrei, "Quine in Perspective", *The Journal of Philosophy*, 69/1 (January 13, 1972):5.

Chapter 7

1 Does the *jīvanmukta* in India constitute an exception? This Hindu concept, of the person who in this lifetime here on earth attains full apprehension of, by, in, ultimate truth/reality, is an important ingredient in a total coherent interpretation of human life. It has served as a concept that in Western thought would be called "eschatological" (a term whose form presupposes Semitic-Christian views of history); and at that level it elicits, and repays, serious recognition. The issue for us here is whether in addition it conceptualizes observationally actual cases of historical human beings, and interprets empirical data to which non-Hindus also need to give explanatory heed. I am not sufficiently familiar with usage of the concept and with its material, and have not wrestled sufficiently with the problems that arise, to know whether they (and the phenomena of mystic rapture elsewhere) involve realities that would in the end force a revision of the conceptual scheme with which I am operating. It is evident that I think not, else I should not allow my text to stand, even with this caveat. Yet is serves as a useful reminder that every interpretation of historical data is still particularist in the sense of growing out of a prior metaphysical view, or being integrated into a new

but still particular one. Certainly my own view is that ultimate truth-and-reality transcend(s) every human relation with it—a view that is more continuous with the Western scientific, the Islamic, and some other Hindu, positions than with this one. The problem may, however, be circumvented simply by not using the concept "faith" for those persons seen as superseding the finite. Compare, for instance, the discussion by St. Thomas Aquinas that Christ did not have faith, it being the one virtue that may not be attributed to Him.

Another potential exception of which note might comparably be taken is the theological asseveration of some groups that others' faith may be genuine but is partial, whereas ("the"?) Christian faith (or, in another view, [the] Islamic faith) is true faith, is perfect, is final, is unlimited. This is widely held or implied by a number of present-day Christian theologians; yet relatively few have thought the thesis through carefully, and self-consciously defended it. (One who has is H. H. Farmer). I am contending here that the actual faith of any specific Christian—whether an Aulén, a Bernard, a Calvin, . . . a Zinzendorf—is specific, personal, finite. I contend, further, that to postulate, as would some, in addition to these specific Christian instances of faith, a generic Christian faith, is a limited version of a postulated generic faith globally.

My faith is limited, historically specific; the faith of Christians is ideally perfect, as such thinkers know, however imperfect actually; yet so is the faith of all men, as these thinkers have tended perhaps not to know or not to reckon with. The issue here is whether there be, at any ontological level of reality, a Christian faith that is both timeless (rather than historically limited) and distinct (e.g., from Islamic or Buddhist faith). Of those thinkers mentioned, all four have differed among themselves (in historically particularized ways) in their conceptions of faith; but Bernard, Calvin, and Zinzendorf agree on this, that they did not think that there was such a reality. The notion of a distinctive type of faith, one among others, that is specifically Christian is a nineteenth- and twentieth-century innovation. The earlier view in Christian thought, we may recall, was that faith was generically one, but that it occurred outside the visible Church only spasmodically and then as an individual matter, God bestowing it not through and in terms of the religious tradition as in the case of Christians but apart from it, even despite it. Cf. above, our chap. 5, ref. 108, and my forthcoming "Towards a Theology of Comparative Religion".

On *jīvanmukti* the leading treatise from the Hindu side is that by the fourteenth-century commentator Sāyaṇa, (above, our chap. 4 here, at ref. 21, etc.), written, after he had withdrawn from public office and worldly life, under the name Vidyāraṇya. I have seen the following edition: *Śrīmad Vidyāraṇyakṛto Jīvanmuktivivekaḥ*, Vāsudeva Śāstri Paṇaśīkara, ed., Mahādeva Cimaṇājī Āpaṭe, publ., Pune: Ānandāśramamudraṇālaya, Śaka 1811/A.D. 1890 (Ānandāśramasaṃskṛtagranthāvaliḥ, 20). For an English translation: Manilal N. Dvivedi, trans., *The Jivanmukti-Viveka; or the Path to Liberation in this Life, by Swâmi Śri Vidyâraṇyasarswati*, [Bombay]: Tookaram Tatya, for the Theosophical Publication Fund, 1897. (I have unfortunately been unable to locate a copy of the more recent edition, of the Sanskrit text with accompanying English translation, [Subrahmaṇya Śāstri and Śrīnivāsa Ayyaṅgar, Adyar: Theosophical Publishing House, 1935].) From the side of modern Western scholarship, see three articles by Joachim Friedrich Sprockhoff: "Die Vorbereitung der Vorstellung von der Erlösung bei Lebzeiten in den Upaniṣads", "Die Idee der Jīvanmukti in den späten Upaniṣads", and "Der Weg zur Erlösung bei Lebzeiten, ihr Wesen und ihr Wert, nach dem Jīvanmuktiviveka des Vidyāraṇya", all in *Wiener Zeitschrift für die Kunde Süd*[- *und Ost*]*asiens und Archiv für indische Philosophie*, 6:151-178 (1962), 7:190-208 (1963), 8:224-262 (1964), and 14:[131]-159 (1970).

The question *Utrum in Christo fuerit fides* constitutes Thomas Aquinas, *Summa Th.*, 3:7:3 (Caramello edn. [above, our chap. 1 here, ref. 13], III:48).

Herbert H. Farmer, *Revelation and Religion: studies in the theological interpretation of religious types*, London: Nisbet, 1954.

2 George P. Elliott, "Yakov's Ordeal", book review of *The Fixer* by Bernard Malamud, in *The New York Times* [Sunday] *Book Review*, September 4, 1966, p. 1.

3 After this thesis had been developed, I was delighted and encouraged to find a comparable thesis set forth in terms not of faith but of culture by the brilliant social anthropologist Clifford Geertz, in a paper contending that human nature is not a given to which the various cultures of the world have been added on, or even out of which they have been educed, but rather that a basic ingredient of human nature is the capacity, and indeed the necessity, to live in terms of one or another such culture. See Clifford Geertz, "The Impact of the Concept of Culture on the Concept of Man", in John R. Platt, ed., *New Views of the Nature of Man*, Chicago & London: University of Chicago Press, 1965, pp. 93-118.

4 If Christian readers feel that this wording is too humanistic or too mystical, they may be reminded of the orthodox dictum, that in Christ God "became human in order that we might become divine". They and Muslims might however, prefer a variant wording in our text: ". . . towards becoming what God wishes that we be". Yet that Christian dictum stands:

αὐτος γαρ ἐνηνθρωπησεν, ἱνα ἡμεις θεοποιηθωμεν—Athanasius, *De Incarnatione*, 54. Rather than the usual translation ". . . become divine", as above, for the concluding verb here, one might argue for ". . . might become God"; or, over against modern anthropocentric insensitivity to what is involved in this miracle, insist on ". . . be made" rather than "become". Cf. also the same concept in Irenaeus, *Contra Haereticos*, Liber 5, Praefatio, concluding sentence, and Origen, *Contra Celsum*, 3:28, also the concluding sentence.

Editions used: Robert W. Thomson, ed. and trans., Athanasius, *Contra Gentes and De Incarnatione*, Oxford: Clarendon, 1971 (Henry Chadwick, gen. ed., Oxford Early Christian Texts: Athanasius), p. 268 (§54, lines 11-12). Adelin Rousseau et al., edd., Irénée de Lyon, *Contre les hérésies*, Paris: Éditions du Cerf, 1952- (in process) (Sources chrétiennes, H. de Lubac, C. Mondésert, et al., dirr., nos. 100, 152, 153 etc.), livre v, tome 2, 1969, p. 14, lines 36-39 (Latin), p. 15, lines 37-40 (Greek). Marcel Borret, ed., Origène: *Contre Celse* (above, our chap. 5, ref. 29), tome 2, p. 68, lines 46-51.

5 My *Belief and History* (above, our chap. 1 here, ref. 4).

6 In an otherwise admirable essay, remarkably sensitive and both formally and substantially open to transcendence, even at a conceptual level, two modern social scientists have popularized the unfortunate phrase "the social construction of reality". By this they intend that perceptions of reality and conceptualizations of it are human constructs generated and made prevalent by corporate groups in varying ways. This is a thesis fundamental to my own argument in this present study, and one of which it is in our day intellectually naive not to see the validity and to feel the force. Nonetheless, by speaking of the social construction "of reality", when they mean that of the perception of reality, they fall victim to and enhance the modern incapacity to recognize (*sic*) that reality precedes and transcends our apprehension of it. Unwittingly, they to this extent further rather than heal the divisions among human beings, and among societies (to say nothing of furthering the disintegration within human beings and within societies). If interpretations of reality differ among groups not because each is but an approximation to or abstraction from reality itself, where are we? Can we never improve our apprehension; or never be insane? And if reality does not transcend our perception of it, what is our awareness of transcendence an awareness of?

Peter L. Berger and Thomas Luckmann, *The Social Construction of Reality: a treatise in the sociology of knowledge*, New York: Doubleday [1966], Anchor Books, 1967.

I have chosen these writers to illustrate my point not because they are particularly poor in this positivistic error, but on the contrary, to suggest that even the most open and humane among "scientific" thinkers in modern Western culture are in danger of this kind of unwitting surrender.

For a consideration of this matter in the natural sciences, see for example Michael Polanyi, "Science and Reality", *British Journal for the Philosophy of Science*, 18:177-196 (1967). The opening two sentences read: "The purpose of this essay is to re-introduce a conception which, having served for two millennia as a guide to the understanding of nature, has been repudiated by the [*sic*] modern interpretation of science. I am speaking of the conception of reality" (p. 177).

7 Some, indeed, would go on to say even that science also is a myth: a powerful myth; a myth capturing much truth; a myth enabling man to live, in significant though limited part, in true relation to reality. It would be, then, a myth both like and unlike other great myths in human history.

8 It may seem entrancing to speculate as to whether these two objectives are correlated each with one of the hemispheres of the human brain (or: knowing with the left, understanding with a balanced interplay between the two).

9 On this concept see Wilfred Cantwell Smith, "Objectivity and the Humane Sciences: a new proposal" in *Transactions of the Royal Society of Cana-*

da, 1974: Fourth Series, vol. 12, Ottawa, Royal Society of Canada, 1975, pp. [81]-102; reprinted in Claude Fortier et al., *Symposium on the Frontiers and Limitations of Knowledge/Colloque sur les frontières et limites du savoir*, Ottawa: Royal Society of Canada, 1975, pp. [81]-102, and in abridged form in Willard G. Oxtoby, ed., *Religious Diversity*, New York: Harper & Row, 1976, pp. [158]-180.

10 The heliostatic and (almost) heliocentric propositions of Copernicus (to make his calculations come out right, he placed the sun at a little distance from the centre) are neither meaningless, nor true. Yet we may surely see that neither are they simply false; and especially, we may recognize that they were not simply false when first made.

Indeed, historically and otherwise, even the proposition that the earth is flat is itself not flatly false. It is (has been) an approximation to the truth. The surface's curvature approximates to a straight line more closely than most approximations to the truth with which we live our lives or think our thoughts, and the flatness idea serves well for a great multitude still of practical and contemplative purposes (—though these do not include flying the Atlantic nor contemplating the earth from a space-ship). Copernicus's idea is a closer approximation. That the sun hastens around our galaxy while the latter retreats swiftly from its neighbours, is still closer. That all scientific, and religious, statements have been and are, both in practice and in principle, expressions of historical approximations to truth attained by human persons, many of them valid, none of them absolute or final, is an interpretation consonant with theses developed later in our present argument.

The analogy between scientific and religious statements (or "beliefs"), in this matter, is not as distant as has usually been imagined.

Note: the above observations are my own, made before I had read Thomas S. Kuhn, *The Structure of Scientific Revolutions*, Chicago, London: University of Chicago Press [1962], 1970 (International Encyclopedia of Unified Science: voll. 1 and 2—Foundations of the Unity of Science, vol. 2, no. 2). Nonetheless, it is interesting to compare my interpretations of the facts with Kuhn's view that the historical succession of scientific statements, mutually incompatible, indicates that there is no truth (his pp. 170-173). My view, derived from a study of the comparative history of religion but equally applicable to the history of science, is that a variety of statements, made within differing world-views (Kuhn's "paradigms") may be logically incompatible with each other (when considered simultaneously) and yet that this does not rule out, and indeed suggests rather, that each is an approximation to an in principle always transcendent truth. This view allows for the observed historical progress in science (a progress not quite matched in the history of religion).

11 The perceptive anthropologist Rodney Needham, for instance (above, our chap. 3, ref. 3), although not making the distinction explicitly in these terms, in effect might almost be said to discriminate as to meaningfulness between (other persons') first-person statements ("I believe . . . "), which he says that he can understand (p. 192) or, if theological, can at least accept (p. 191), and third-person ones ("they believe . . ." this and that). That these

latter are normally illegitimate and finally meaningless, it is the general purport of his book to contend.

12 Some modern theorists have distinguished between statements and propositions. The former are always in the words of some particular language, and can therefore readily be shown to be inescapably culture-specific, their meaning historical. Indeed, for many the concept of proposition, in contradistinction from this, is calculated expressly to escape from relativism and historicity, from personalism. The work of comparativist historians, however, means that moderns know too much to be taken in by this aspiration to have propositions true (or, false) absolutely. The postulating of metaphysical entities of this sort hardly suffices for escaping human finitude. One may dub as proposition what a statement in English and an equivalent statement in French have in common; yet that equivalence is a function of the fact—historical, contingent—that speakers of English and of French share, to this extent at least, a common world-view. Nonetheless, that world-view, like all world-views, is in its turn historical, transient. It is not the case that all languages, or all eras, are such that a proposition can be expressed equally in any of them. Statements are constructs in words expressing concepts; every proposition exists (has existed) in one or another conceptual system. Its validity, and indeed its meaning, therefore have their locus within that system which has existed on earth at certain times and places, not at others. I should hold, more accurately: they have their locus in the historical persons and groups of persons whose minds and hearts have participated in, or who have understood, that particular system. Propositions, therefore, may transcend the limitations in time and space of certain languages (to some degree); but they do not escape time and space altogether, to lay hold upon timeless or absolute truth. (They may enable persons to do so, in part.) It is the task of modern thinkers who know and understand the history of thought, to construct new concepts able to express in propositions of wider generality the previously incommensurate statements and propositions of until now disparate systems. Specifically but by no means only, this is a task in the religious realm, a task to which the comparative historian of religion, as well as the several theologians (as well as philosophers who are alert) must contribute. When it is attained, however, the resulting conceptualizations will not in their turn be timeless and absolute, will not themselves escape from being culture-specific. Their virtue, rather, will reside simply in their being appropriate to modern times. They will be specific to the new world culture into which we are flounderingly moving. Propositions are always relative. Truth is not relative, because the truth itself is not propositional. It is always a human achievement, finite, specific, and partial, to translate the truth about anything into propositional terms. (The translation soon or eventually clamours to be superseded).

13 Cf. above, our chap. 5, ref. 60.

14 It is worth pondering whether to this definition should (or need) be added, "or one's society, or one's age". The matter is of potentially large import. The locus of truth is persons, I have contended (not propositions).

The role of individuals in apprehending new truth, or in newly articulating old, is often solitary. Yet to a significant degree also, truth is apprehended in community. This is important in several ways, among which verification, for example, is but one. One's neighbour is important to the knowing process, as to all human processes.

15 There are two matters here. One is the conceptualizations ("beliefs") that any person of faith ought to have, of the universe generally. The other is the conceptualization specifically of faith that any intellectual ought to have. In the case of an intellectual who is himself or herself a person of faith and is, further, intelligent enough and modern enough to rise to self-consciousness, the two matters are integrated, and finally converge.

We are taking for granted, of course, that any intelligent conceptualization of anything ought to be internally coherent, on the one hand, and on the other hand, consonant with the known data, and illuminative of these. We are taking for granted also, again of course, that an intellectual's conceptualizations on all matters (his or her own life—and death, and intellectuality—included, as well as the external universe and its various parts, and human history) will move towards coherence with each other and consonance with what is known.

(Involved here, then, is the faith of an intellectual, as well as the intellectualization of faith.)

INDEX

Library of Congress Cataloging in Publication Data

Smith, Wilfred Cantwell, 1916-
Faith and belief.

Includes bibliographical references and index.
1. Faith—Comparative studies. I. Title.
BL626.3.S58 234'.2 78-63601
ISBN 0-691-07232-9